D0944865

George W. Goethals and the Army

George W. Goethals and the Army

Change and Continuity in the Gilded Age and Progressive Era

Rory McGovern

University Press of Kansas

© 2019 by the University Press of Kansas
All rights reserved

A portion of this book appeared originally as "The School
of Experience: George W. Goethals and the U.S. Army,
1876–1907" in *Journal of Military History* 81, no. 2 (April
2017): 395–424.

Published by the University Press of Kansas (Lawrence,
Kansas 66045), which was organized by the Kansas Board
of Regents and is operated and funded by Emporia State
University, Fort Hays State University, Kansas State
University, Pittsburg State University, the University of
Kansas, and Wichita State University.

Library of Congress Cataloging-in-Publication Data

Names: McGovern, Rory, author.
Title: George W. Goethals and the Army : change and
    continuity in the Gilded Age and Progressive Era /
    Rory McGovern.
Description: Lawrence, Kansas : University Press of Kansas,
    [2019] | Includes bibliographical references and index.
Identifiers: LCCN 2018058627
    ISBN 9780700627707 (cloth : alk. paper)
    ISBN 9780700627714 (ebook)
Subjects: LCSH: Goethals, George W. (George Washington),
    1858–1928. | Generals—United States—Biography. |
    United States. Army—History—20th century. | United
    States. Army—History—19th century. | United States.
    Army. Corps of Engineers—History—19th century. |
    United States. Army. Corps of Engineers—History—
    20th century. | Panama Canal (Panama)—Design and
    construction. | World War, 1914–1918—Transportation—
    United States.
Classification: LCC E181.G59 M35 2019 | DDC 355.0092
    [B]—dc23
LC record available at https://lccn.loc.gov/2018058627.

British Library Cataloguing-in-Publication Data is available.

Printed in the United States of America

10 9 8 7 6 5 4 3 2 1

The paper used in this publication is recycled and contains
30 percent postconsumer waste. It is acid free and meets the
minimum requirements of the American National Standard
for Permanence of Paper for Printed Library Materials
Z39.48–1992.

For Jillian

Contents

Illustrations

Acknowledgments

Writing history is a team sport, and I have had the privilege of playing with all-stars. This book has been six years in the making. In that time, dozens of people contributed in various ways to its development and the ideas it presents. I am extremely grateful to all of those who had a hand in shaping it. Their time and effort have made this a far better product than it otherwise would have been.

I would not have been able to write *George W. Goethals and the Army* without the patient guidance and mentorship of my advisor at the University of North Carolina, Joe Glatthaar. From day one of graduate school, he pushed me to think more deeply and write more clearly, expanding my horizons as both a historian and a US Army officer. He was routinely there to give me encouragement or a good strong nudge when it was most needed, consistently with his usual good cheer.

The rest of the faculty and staff in UNC's Department of History were equally essential to the development of this project. They are excellent role models for any aspiring historian, and I am deeply in their debt. I am especially grateful for Wayne Lee, whose scholarly versatility should be a model for us all; and for Benjamin Waterhouse, John Chasteen, and Mike Morgan, whose close reading and insightful comments and criticism have been invaluable. I must also thank Joy Mann Jones, who is the real backbone of the department and is the unsung hero in every successful graduate student's experience.

Likewise, I cannot turn away from UNC without a special thanks to friends and colleagues. Through discussions in and out of the classroom and the many helpful suggestions about ideas I wrestled with throughout the process, they have shaped this work from beginning to end. They were also excellent company during much-needed breaks from work and provided the talent for what is unquestionably the best pub trivia team I have ever joined. In particular, I am especially thankful for the help, criticism, encouragement, and friendship of Erika Huckestein, Lars Stiglich, Ansev Demirhan, Neil Floetke, Kirsten Cooper, Lorn Hillaker Beth Hasseler, Caroline Nilsen, Mary Walters, Brian Fennessy, Allison Somogyi, Jessica Auer, Corey Ellithorpe, and Shannon James.

I am lucky to have attended UNC and gone on to a subsequent assignment in the Department of History at the US Military Academy with John "Rocky" Rhodes and Brian Drohan. Both have given generously of their time and considerable talents to offer much-needed advice and criticism throughout the writing process. They have been more helpful than they know, and I look forward to future collaborations with them.

At West Point, I enjoyed an unparalleled environment to continue my development as both an officer and historian. Ty Seidule, Gail Yoshitani, Greg Daddis, and Sean Sculley created a climate within the department at large and the American History Division that provided all the motivation and mentorship any historian could ask for. Sam Watson, Jen Kiesling, Rob McDonald, Greta Bucher, and David Frey each went out of their way to provide valuable guidance and assistance at various stages of the process. Sam Watson in particular gave generously of his time in reviewing an early draft of this book. I also benefited from many insightful conversations about ideas related to this project with colleagues among the rotational faculty, and I would like to thank in particular Andy Forney, Greg Hope, Amanda Boczar, Danny Sjursen, Nick Sambaluk, Mark Askew, Kyle Hatzinger, Ben Griffin, Logan Collins, Rich Hutton, Nick Browning, Tony Salinas, and Lauren Pearlman.

From the West Point crowd, Ben Brands deserves special thanks. I cannot count the number of hours we spent in each other's living rooms or around our backyard fire pits talking about professionalism and officer development in the late nineteenth and early twentieth centuries. I am deeply grateful for his ideas, encouragement, and critiques; and also his willingness to exchange both sources and scotch as we each pursued our own distinct but related projects. Readers will do well to keep an eye out for his work when it is published.

Similarly, I am profoundly indebted to J. P. Clark, an exceptionally talented officer and scholar who is the model of what a good mentor should be. I cannot quite imagine my professional life having taken the form it has without his guidance and mentorship. He steered me toward graduate school, an assignment to West Point, and my current career field in the army. He has helped me overcome several obstacles that have arisen over the course of researching and writing about Goethals and has routinely proven to be one of the ablest and most effective readers and critics of the various forms this project has taken.

Beyond friends and colleagues already mentioned, there are many others to thank. Audrey Noonan and Chris Pisano generously opened their basement and provided excellent company during a months-long research trip. The Omar Bradley Research Fellowship, through the US Army Center of Military History, twice provided funds to finance lengthy research trips that were vital to this work. I would also be remiss if I did not acknowledge and thank the accessible and helpful staffs at the various archives I visited, especially Suzanne Christoff and her team at the US Military Academy Special Collections and Archives, Tim Nenninger and his team at the National Archives, and the stalwarts of the Library of Congress Manuscript Division.

Similarly, I am thankful for the support of those whose efforts came in the final stages. Michael Neiberg and Jackie Whitt of the US Army War College provided good advice and excellent examples of scholarship. David Woodward provided a close reading and valuable comments on the manuscript that improved the final product. Tom Rider produced three beautiful maps. I am also extremely grateful for Joyce Harrison, Kelly Chrisman Jacques, and the rest of the editorial staff at the University Press of Kansas, who have encouraged and shepherded *George W. Goethals and the Army* along since our first meeting, and also for Elaine Durham Otto, who painstakingly copyedited the final manuscript. It has been a real pleasure to work with such professionals.

I owe my final and most important thanks to my family. For various reasons and in many contexts, I learned resilience and persistence from my mother, Elizabeth, and my brother, Ryan, and cannot imagine having completed this project without their examples. My mother was also my earliest and longest-serving writing teacher, never letting me leave for school in the morning with a weak conclusion. I hope this book measures up.

My daughter, Shannon, arrived when this book was at an early stage.

She has kept me laughing and playing ever since and has helped give me a new perspective on life that can only aid any biographer whose subject was also a parent. I am also thankful for my son, Connor, whose imminent arrival when the manuscript was due did more to keep me on time and on target than any contract or editor's admonitions ever could.

Finally, I cannot thank my wife, Jillian, enough. George Goethals came home from work with me six years ago and became the house-guest who refused to leave. He went so far as to accompany us to three homes on two continents in the intervening years. Through it all, Jillian has been ever supportive and encouraging, and she has been my best sounding board, travel buddy, editor, and occasional therapist. She enlivens and enriches everything—this book and so much more. And it is to her that this book is dedicated.

Germany
October 17, 2018

Prologue

June 12, 1912, brought pleasant weather to the lower Hudson valley, allowing West Point's graduation ceremony to be held outdoors. Overlooking the Hudson River at the north end of a grassy plain that served as the cadets' drill ground, the official party—consisting of the superintendent, the graduation speaker, and a handful of alumni and aged veterans of the Civil War—gathered around the main stage. At ten o'clock sharp, the band struck up a martial tune and the corps of cadets marched with crisp precision from their barracks toward the official party. Ninety-six graduating members of the class of 1912 took their seats in front of the stage while cadets from the classes of 1913–1915 stood in formation, ready to cheer as their friends made the transition from cadet to lieutenant.[1]

After a laudatory introduction from the superintendent, Col. George W. Goethals took the stage. He was nervous, having harbored a hatred of public speaking since his teenage years, and he was acutely aware that this was only the second time that West Point had invited an officer below the rank of brigadier general to serve as graduation speaker. Looking out at a multigenerational audience that included officers who long before had helped defeat the Confederacy and cadets who would soon help lead a gradually modernizing army, he may have felt reassured about his decision to focus his remarks on how to succeed as a military officer during times of change and uncertainty. "The duties and problems which confront the army officer in recent years are more numerous, more varied, and complex than in former days," he began. The key to success, Goethals explained, was to have the strength of character to be fully dedicated to any assigned mission, to recognize there was much left to learn, and to accept practical experience as the best possible tutor. After all, he reminded the assembled cadets, the program of instruction and training at West Point had provided them not with the full extent of all knowledge and abilities required to succeed but with "the foundations of a structure yet to be raised."[2]

Goethals derived these themes from his own career. As a quiet and unaccomplished teenager, he had reported for duty at West Point as a new cadet in 1876. At that time, the army was organized for and accustomed to its traditional role of guarding the coast and policing the frontier. Moreover, the army Goethals entered lacked formalized and robust systems of training and education to prepare its rising leaders for high command and modern warfare. Neither young Cadet Goethals nor the army he entered was equipped for the challenges that lay ahead.[3] When invited to speak at West Point in 1912, however, Goethals was two years away from opening the Panama Canal to commercial traffic and six years away from successfully leading the War Department's efforts to build and sustain an army of nearly four million soldiers during the First World War. Retiring in 1919 at the end of an accomplished and celebrated career, Goethals was a changed officer departing a changed institution. This book examines how the institution evolved in the late nineteenth and early twentieth centuries by tracing Goethals's experiences within it.

Many scholars have considered this question before, but few have approached an essentially institutional problem from an individual perspective. Goethals spent most of his life serving in the army, wearing the uniform from the end of Reconstruction to the conclusion of the First World War. Over the course of that career, he experienced the entire trajectory of army reform during the Gilded Age and Progressive Era. A detailed examination of that experience offers the chance to reexamine from a new angle the well-traversed ground of the army's transformation from a force dedicated to defending the coast and policing the frontier to a modern army with a global reach, able to support a rising power's increasingly global goals.

Goethals's career reveals that the army's culture was at odds with both the spirit of military reform and the specific program of reforms implemented by Secretary of War Elihu Root and supported by a cadre of likeminded officers in the wake of the war with Spain in 1898. The Root reforms were structural in nature and were intended to mold an army capable of meeting the demands of the twentieth century by creating formal systems of military education, rationalizing the command structure, and establishing the General Staff Corps—a new entity responsible for developing war and mobilization plans well in advance of any crisis and coordinating the execution of those plans as crises arose.[4] Successful officers of Goethals's generation, however, had advanced despite the absence of formal and rigorous systems of training and education, and they believed that their successes validated the unsystematic process of experiential learning that the army had long relied upon to develop its officers. This influenced an institutional culture that extolled the virtues of self-development and self-education, which in turn produced officers who hesitated to adapt in the absence of crisis and valued more highly the ability to improvise than the ability to plan deliberately. Although such officers tolerated the minority of committed reformers in their midst and even accepted some of their ideas, they never truly embraced either the form or the spirit of reform, tending instead to bend new concepts and structures to serve old and comfortably familiar concepts and habits.

Goethals's experience demonstrates clearly that the gulf between the army's structural reforms and its institutional culture generated internal resistance to and diluted the effect of the Root reforms. The full potential of those reforms remained unrealized until the Second World War, with the ascension of a new generation that embraced the ideas and values at the heart of the reforms, thus completing a long and slow evolution in the army's institutional culture. Among the more prominent officers of this younger generation were Dwight D. Eisenhower and Omar N. Bradley—who, as members of West Point's class of 1915, happened to be among the cadets in formation listening to Goethals's address on that sunny June morning in 1912. Prior to their generation's rise to preeminence within the army, the Root reforms constituted not the completion of military reform but "the foundations of a structure yet to be raised."

The long cultural evolution that is at the heart of this narrative of army reform cannot be considered independently of the myriad changes that American society experienced in the late nineteenth and early twentieth centuries. Practitioners of "new" military history have done much valuable work in the past several decades demonstrating that armies generally reflect the societies they serve.[5] Their scholarship shows, however, that this truism does not necessarily mean that the pace of change within the army consistently matches the pace of change within society. In the late nineteenth and early twentieth centuries, the United States Army failed to keep pace with the shifting values, standards, and norms related to training and education within American society. At the same time, the army kept abreast of changes to managerial and organizational theory and practice that emerged during the managerial revolution that was a hallmark of the Gilded Age and Progressive Era. Falling behind in one key area provided the army with the means to resist reform, while keeping pace in another key area provided the impetus to complete reform. Ultimately, the army's interactions with and responses to broader social change had an indelible impact on the institution itself. Understanding institutional reform in the army in this way offers valuable insights into the dynamics of change and reform in any national institution, military or civil.

Military reform in the late nineteenth and early twentieth centuries was the product of evolving concepts of professionalism and a redefinition of the role and purpose of the army. These, in turn, were heavily influenced by the closing of the frontier, changing views of the nation's proper role in the world, progressivism, and the managerial revolution. Any examination of reform and institutional culture in the army around the turn of the century must account for these trends and their impact upon institutional culture and military reform.

Since the Census Bureau declared the frontier to be closed in 1890, scholars have struggled to define and explain its effect on the United States. The traditional view holds that the frontier was a westward-moving place and a process that encouraged the development of democracy, spurred individualism, and fostered egalitarianism.[6] More recently, however, scholars have challenged that interpretation, fraught as it is with racial and nationalistic bias. One such revision accepts that the frontier was both a place and a process, but emphasizes the effects that the experience of the frontier had on various cultures and subcultures in North America.[7] This book approaches the frontier and its effects on the army from that perspective. The frontier was both a place and a process that continued to affect the army's institutional culture long after it ceased defining such a large part of the army's mission and reason for being.

As the United States consolidated its control over the continent, it became considerably more active on the world stage. Many scholars have concluded that an active and imperialist US foreign policy in the late nineteenth and early twentieth centuries was the product of political, economic, and social ideologies that collectively produced both a rationale and a broad base of support for expansionist policies. Such policies drove American interventions in Latin America and Asia from the war with Spain in 1898 onward.[8] They also shaped Woodrow Wilson's approach to foreign policy during his presidency from 1913 to 1921, conditioning him and the American people to believe that the United States could and should create and lead a new world order. This, in turn, decisively influenced both policy and public opinion on American involvement in the First World War.[9]

Some scholars have taken this rather imperialist outlook and ascribed it as the driving motive for military reform.[10] Others take a different view. While denying that reform was intended solely for imperial expansion, they implicitly connect a more active foreign policy with early twentieth-century military reform by pointing to perceived threats from European powers and a rising Japan as principal motivations and inspirations for reform.[11] Both of these interpretations fall somewhat short. While the latter more accurately describes the principal motive for those advocating reform, it fails to address the causes for the army's ultimate but extremely tardy embrace of reform prior to the Second World War. In the end, it was the army's experiences abroad—especially its more problematic experiences—that did more to shape reform by altering the institutional consensus on what reforms were desirable, feasible, and acceptable.

Looking beyond the army, the reformist spirit of the Progressive Era also played a major role in shaping military reform. Responding largely to the consequences of urbanization and industrialization, progressive reform swept the United States beginning in the 1890s. Scholars have struggled to provide a coherent interpretation of the Progressive Era, debating whether progressivism was a unitary movement or a conglomeration of related movements. Recent scholarship has shown that progressivism was either a singular, middle-class movement that advanced upon multiple and sometimes contradictory fronts, or it was a loose collection of movements that drew strength from diverse and sometimes antagonistic bases of support.[12] The variable trends and impulses of progressivism offer important context to how the Progressive Era officer corps could boldly advocate for and accept some aspects of reform while simultaneously and conservatively resisting other aspects. It explains why those historians who have pointed to progressivism as the causal factor for military reform have come to vastly different conclusions about the military reformers' desired ends.[13] Most important for this study, it helps explain how a national institution could, paradoxically, foster an institutional culture at odds with reformist structures that it imposed upon itself.

Related to the reformist impulse of the time, the so-called managerial revolution of the late nineteenth and early twentieth centuries dramatically influenced both the army's culture and its evolving structures. The managerial revolution was a hallmark of the Gilded Age and Progressive Era, at least partially embraced by progressives and traditionalists alike. The concept of the managerial revolution has been promulgated by historians whose work interprets it as the general point of transition between a time when local and informal groups were central to American life and a new age in which such groups were supplanted by much larger, formal, and bureaucratically structured organizations. According to this interpretation, efforts to systematically bureaucratize political, economic, and entrepreneurial systems of management constituted a logical adaptation in response to the problems of mass industrialization and urbanization.[14]

In the process, the principle of "scientific management" of people and resources became widely popular. Taking hold first in businesses and factories, it was applied with increasing regularity to problems in most other spheres of American life. "Scientific management" informed the military's approach to reform and shaped the new institutional structures it created. Perhaps more important, the transmission of new managerial theories—at first from railroads to other large corporations, and then from the corporations to American society—more broadly marks the point at which the United States began to accept modern notions of professional expertise and specialization based on rigorous training and education. By the end of the nineteenth century, this new concept of professionalism had spread to many other American occupations, including medicine, law, education, journalism, and social work.[15]

Shifting from a concept of professionalism based on personal identification and self-study to one based on expertise and specialization grounded in formal training and education, American views on the value and purpose of education underwent a profound change. For most of the nineteenth century, American society generally accepted that education should be widely accessible and intended not only to disseminate knowledge but also to produce upstanding and moral citizens. With a booming industrial economy late in the century, that view of education came under attack on several fronts. An unlikely alliance of interest groups advocated for reform in American education. Whereas traditionalists continued to believe that the moral effect and mental discipline derived from education was more important and lasting than the knowledge imparted by education, reformers came to value the transmission of knowledge itself for its own sake.[16]

Scholars continue to debate the root cause of education reform in this period, pointing to businesses interested in producing not only managers conversant in the latest theories of scientific management but also efficient, vocationally trained workers; progressives who advocated for reform as a means of improving the condition of the lower class; and progressives who viewed education reform as a means of "Americanizing" newly arrived immigrants.[17] Regardless of its origins, educational reform in this period introduced within American society new curricula, systems of pedagogy, and a general sense that education could be simultaneously practical and intellectually rigorous. In this respect, society outpaced the army, whose views on education remained stubbornly traditional, despite the efforts of some reformers. Falling behind in this respect profoundly affected the course of military reform.

The closing of the frontier and the concurrent loss of the army's frontier mission, the development of new concepts of the proper role of the United States in the world, the emergence of progressivism, the managerial revolution, and advances in the practice and theory of education influenced both the army's institutional culture and the course of military reform in the late nineteenth and early twentieth centuries. Many then and since have characterized military reform as a process of professionalization—but "professionalization" is a problematic term riven with conditional assumptions and biases that change over time.

Historians have long debated when, how, and why the army became a legitimate, autonomous profession. The traditional interpretation that long dominated the field holds that it was not a profession until reforms in the early twentieth century established a general staff capable of crafting and coordinating war plans and created a formally institutionalized system of training and education to produce competent, well-trained officers capable of leading at the most senior levels of the army. Adherents of this school of thought have referred to the last decades of the nineteenth century as a "Military Renaissance" in which a small body of far-sighted reformers emerged to professionalize the institution. According to this interpretation, the army began to move out of its dark ages with individual initiatives that collectively helped set conditions for transformational reforms during Elihu Root's tenure as secretary of war from 1899 to 1904.[18]

Many have found this interpretation unconvincing. A competing school of thought places the origins of military professionalism earlier in the nineteenth century. This interpretation holds that the late nineteenth-century military "renaissance" was not the origin of the American military profession but the rebirth and reapplication of older ideas of how to make the army and its officers more expert in the theory and practice of warfare—ideas that had become more broadly acceptable to a society better conditioned by progressivism to accept occupational specialization and professional autonomy, and conscious enough of its status as a rising global power to embrace a larger and more powerful army. Further, this interpretation holds that the Root reforms were incomplete and that their only unqualified success was the establishment of an effective institutional system of military education for its officers.[19]

More recently, historians have carried the challenge to the military renaissance thesis even further. Some push beyond the assertion that the Root reforms were incomplete and question whether they had any real impact on military thought and practice, rightly calling attention to the human element of institutional reform. Patterns of thought and behavior that have existed long enough to become habit do not change as quickly or as easily as organizational and institutional structures, which can be created, destroyed, or altered in only the amount of time it takes to write and sign the necessary orders.[20] Others focus on American military professionalism prior to the Civil War, suggesting that adherents of the military renaissance thesis have missed the earlier formation of a distinct American military profession because they have unfairly analyzed past degrees of professionalism according to modern standards.[21]

As one historian has written, "Like most complex human phenomena, professionalism is a shifting, relative, constructed phenomenon, not an unconditional or permanent one."[22] This position is strongly supported by those who have identified forms of military professionalism rooted in personal identity and self-study as early as the late eighteenth century that parallel similarly framed and similarly dated forms of professionalism identified by sociologists who have studied the development of civilian professions within American society.[23] Their scholarship persuasively demonstrates that professionalism is a highly contingent social and cultural construction subject to change according to shifts in social attitudes and cultural values.[24]

Because professionalism is a social and cultural construction that—like society and culture themselves—is subject to generational adjustment, it is impossible to understand professional reform in the army during the late nineteenth and early twentieth centuries without understanding how military officers thought about professionalism, professional competence, and reform. Such perceptions were at the bedrock of the army's institutional culture. This work examines the relationship between army reform and institutional culture through the lens of one officer's career, which spanned nearly the entire period of reform.

George W. Goethals was a lieutenant and a captain during the post-Reconstruction years of debate about reform and the future of the army. He was a major when the most significant reforms were created, and he helped with their implementation. As a major general during the First World War, he directed a significant part of the army's rapid adaptation to resolve crises in the mobilization effort caused largely by years of internal resistance to reform. Following Goethals's career and analyzing reform from his perspective builds upon past efforts to shift the focus away from the intent behind reform and toward the reality of reform, which was determined far more by the interaction of society with the army's institutional structures and culture than by the hopes and plans of any one reformer or collection of reformers.[25]

Because a close study of a representative individual can shed considerable light on the social and cultural dynamics of a larger group, a biography of Goethals serves as a vehicle for examining the broader problem of the relationship between reform and the army's institutional culture.[26] His experiences, military thought, managerial philosophy, notions of professionalism, and attitudes about training and development are applicable on both individual and collective levels. And where Goethals's experiences and attitudes can be applied on the collective level, they frame the army's institutional culture and reveal his generation's relative ambivalence about reform.

Institutional culture is defined as the "habitual practices, default programs, hidden assumptions, and unreflected cognitive frames" that constitute a "repertoire . . . of habits, skills, and styles." It informs decisions and behavior of and within an organization established for political or social purposes, and it is the guiding feature of this analysis of army reform during the late nineteenth and early twentieth centuries. It is influenced by the broader culture of the society that the institution serves and is transmittable within the institution from generation to generation through socialization, indoctrination, teaching, imitation, actions, and symbols.[27] While institutional culture is subject to evolution over time, the pace of change tends to be relatively slow because cultural change necessarily involves questioning and adjusting established habits and traditions, a process which invites resistance in any institution, especially military institutions that are guided to a significant degree by habit and tradition.[28]

Through Goethals, this book examines the army's institutional culture from the perspective of a generation of officers who entered the army between 1870 and 1890 and whose careers spanned the late nineteenth century until the close of the First World War. This generation bridged the gap between the old army, organized to function as a frontier constabulary and coastal defense force, and the modern army, organized for expeditionary warfare. Yet the transition from old to new did not happen in a vacuum. The generation that built the bridge between the old army and the new did so with familiar tools and materials. Those who implemented the new reforms did so in terms of old concepts that they still believed to be sound and were generally consistent with the prevailing institutional culture. This profoundly affected the course of reform. These officers were, for the most part, the captains and majors who manned the first General Staff and graduated with the earliest classes of the Army War College. In effect, they were the engineers who built the machines of reform after receiving the necessary plans and directives from their superiors.[29]

These officers continued to shape the course of reform as they advanced to higher positions within the army's hierarchy. The captains and majors of the early 1900s eventually became the generals of 1917–1918 who were responsible for charting the course of both the war effort and the still-evolving army. The attitudes that these officers developed earlier in their careers informed their decisions as generals. At the end of this narrative, then, this generally midlevel analysis becomes a view from the top. Because it recognizes the natural feedback loop within institutions that produce their own leaders, this hybrid approach is particularly well suited for studying change over a long period of time within an institution like the army that promotes its leaders from within.

Biography lends itself to this type of analysis, and George W. Goethals is a fairly representative officer of his generation. Having entered the army before most of the major reform initiatives were enacted, and having left it immediately after the First World War, he experienced the entire trajectory of military reform during the Gilded Age and Progressive Era. He interacted extensively with both sides of the ideological and bureaucratic divide over the merits of reform: the General Staff and the traditional administrative bureaus within the War Department.[30] He held assignments in two of the traditional bureaus and the first General Staff, and was also assigned to the Army War College at its inception. Of most significance, he never had a readily discernible ideological agenda. Prior to World War I, he had been neither an advocate for nor an opponent of reform. Goethals therefore represents the uncommitted center of his generation of officers, providing an opportunity to examine the interactions of institutional culture and military reform from a perspective largely untainted by ideological burdens. This is a quality noticeably lacking in works that analyze reform from the perspectives of leading reformers and in works that take the opposite approach and rely above all on the perspectives of leading antireformist partisans.[31]

Because he was an engineer, some will object to the notion that Goethals can be considered a representative officer of his generation. Compared with the rest of the army, the Corps of Engineers was a relatively small and highly technical branch. The frequent interactions with civilians that were part and parcel of its civil engineering projects had a real potential to produce a subculture of engineer officers isolated from the army's broader institutional culture. At first glance, some of Goethals's experiences seem to reinforce this view. When the class of 1880 graduated from West Point, Goethals was one of only two who were assigned to the Corps of Engineers.[32] Later in life, he would complain that throughout his career, some non-engineer colleagues believed that he "was not considered as belonging to the army, being then dubbed a 'mud digger.'"[33] But one should neither jump to conclusions based on a cursory reading of numbers nor allow intraservice parochialism to obscure the larger picture.

It is true that the Corps of Engineers was smaller and more technical than branches of the line—infantry, cavalry, and artillery. But for Goethals and his fellow engineers, much like their colleagues in the line, small amounts of training and a more significant interplay of skill, personal connections, and chance defined their career trajectories. In fact, the only major difference in this regard was that line officers were subject to even less formal training and interaction with institutional systems than were engineer officers, who received so little formal training that they considered it to be a thoroughly insignificant part of their lives. Despite the more technical nature of engineering, institutional systems and structures affected the careers of engineers and line officers to comparable degrees.[34]

Furthermore, the civil aspects of the mission of the Corps of Engineers did not isolate its officers from the mainstream army's institutional culture. Engineers like Goethals still weighed in on the army's professional debates and reforms of the day, mixed well with their colleagues from the line both at war and when assigned to continental departments during peacetime, and they were integrated into both the General Staff and the newly institutionalized military education system after the Root reforms were implemented in 1903. This preserved not only their personal identity as army officers but also their acceptance within the larger community of army officers. As one of his friends remembered about Goethals's relationship with his West Point classmates, of whom the vast majority were not engineer officers, "Throughout his life he was their leader and the center about which the members of the class gathered whenever they held a reunion."[35]

After a lifetime of service as an artillery officer, division and corps commander, and army chief of staff, Maj. Gen. Charles P. Summerall put it most succinctly when he said, "General Goethals was one of the great army figures of our day."[36]

Goethals's contemporaries certainly did not disqualify him as a representative officer of his generation simply because he was an engineer. Neither should we. A thorough examination of the course of Goethals's life and career reveals broadly applicable lessons that clarify the long, often tortured course of military reform by bringing to the forefront the underexamined relationship between institutional culture and institutional reform.

George W. Goethals
and the Army

1

Education

George W. Goethals was the middle child of John and Marie Baron Goethals. Belgian by birth, John had immigrated to Brooklyn from Amsterdam in 1848. Marie arrived three years later. Although she had also come by way of Amsterdam, they had not met prior to her arrival in New York. The two married and settled into a house on State Street in Brooklyn, with John having found secure employment as a carpenter in a well-established shop across the East River on Ninth Street in New York. In 1856, John and Marie earned full American citizenship and welcomed their first child, a boy named John after his father. George was born two years later on June 29, 1858. Annie was born in 1860, completing the recently established Brooklyn branch of the Goethals family.[1]

Goethals led an unexceptional childhood. He grew up in a working-class neighborhood with his older brother as his closest playmate. He was somewhat introverted, a trait that he never quite outgrew. He tended to follow his older brother's lead in their youthful adventures around Brooklyn, displaying a keen fascination with the local volunteer fire company and with the soldiers encamped at nearby City Park and Fort Greene during the Civil War. These soldiers passed at least some of their idle time by arming the Goethals children with sticks and drilling them. There is no evidence that John Goethals served in the military during the war, which had little impact on the lives of the Goethals family.[2]

As Goethals approached school age, the form and function of education in the United States was on the precipice of major changes. The singular goal of producing good and productive citizens had long been at the foundation of American educational thought. Horace

Mann, whose views dominated American education for much of the nineteenth century, argued that the true purpose of education was to provide students with the means and general awareness they needed to fulfill civic obligations as adults. He argued that the specific facts of any given lesson would be lost over time, but the value of education lay in imbuing students with mental and physical discipline, and secondarily in the general promotion of literacy and basic arithmetic abilities. This philosophy found nearly universal acceptance in a society that believed providing a child with the means to become a well-functioning adult allowed that child to lead a reasonably successful life.[3] This traditional view framed Goethals's early education.

Along with his brother, Goethals began his education in the fall of 1864 at a public school near their home in Brooklyn. He was studious enough to satisfy his parents, but frequently demonstrated a penchant for mischief. Because they were kept after school so often, George and John cut holes in the fence surrounding the schoolyard so they could slip away during the noontime recess to eat meals at home on days they had misbehaved in the morning and already knew they would be punished and forced to stay late after school. At times the punishment would be corporal, but this did not keep the Goethals boys from acting out. "We had a theory in those days that a short hair in the palm of the hand would keep the strap from hurting," recalled John. "The great difficulty was to keep the hair in place."[4]

In 1868, the Goethals family moved across the river to a home on East Fourth Street near what is now Manhattan's East Village so the elder John Goethals could be closer to work and avoid the inconvenience and occasional hazards of a daily commute by ferry. George was enrolled in Public School No. 15 to continue his education, placed one grade behind his brother due to his age. At that school, Goethals matured into a more serious student. He caught the attention of Nathan P. Beers, the school's headmaster. Seeing promise in George, Beers advanced him ahead a full year, back into the same class as John, and kept a close eye on his progress.[5]

George did not begin to take his studies seriously out of any newly discovered love of learning. Instead, it had much to do with ambition. According to his brother, "At that time, George had an idea that he wanted to be a lawyer, and he studied hard."[6] Marie Goethals had always worked to stoke ambition in her sons and their friends. A boyhood friend recalled with reverence more than a half-century later that Marie took as much interest in his goals as those of her sons, urging him, whenever she saw him, to work hard and keep pursuing his dream of attending the US Naval Academy.[7]

Marie's efforts began to bear fruit as her children matured. Both George and John did well enough in school to place lofty goals within reach. Though driven, however, George lacked focus. Toward the end of grammar school, he abandoned his legal ambitions and began to imagine becoming a doctor, but it was not to be. John also had designs on the medical profession, and the family could only afford to support one son's medical training.[8] After graduating in 1872 at the age of fourteen, Goethals spent his summer working as a cashier and bookkeeper in a fruit and vegetable market before matriculating with the entering class at the City College of New York. At the time, City College was free for male residents of the city who had attended a municipal public school for at least twelve months and could pass the college's entrance examination.[9]

Goethals applied for admission to City College and took its entrance examination in June 1872. A shy fourteen-year-old, he was nervous enough as he prepared to be examined and judged that he allowed the registrar to record his name as George Washington Goethals without objection or correction, if he had even noticed it at all. He had actually been christened George William, but Washington stuck with him for the rest of his life and into posterity. Goethals may not have been aware of the error until he arrived at West Point, but as he later explained, after the army knew him as George Washington Goethals, he had "never seen fit to have the records of the War Department changed, as it requires an unnecessary amount of red tape."[10]

Goethals's performance on the entrance examination was thoroughly unexceptional. He fared well enough to be admitted, but not well enough to stand out in any significant way. He received a marginally acceptable score in English grammar; average scores in writing, arithmetic, US history, and algebra; and high scores in spelling, reading, and geography.[11] He had a strong intellect, as Nathan Beers had previously recognized, but he was not naturally gifted. Goethals would have to work hard to achieve any greatness inside or outside the classroom. Ambition had led him to become more studious during his time in grammar school, yet his ambition had not been sufficiently consistent or focused to become true motivation and allow him to reach his full potential. City College would provide some of that necessary motivation.

American education was fertile ground for reform by the time Goethals entered City College. In the years following the Civil War, alternatives to Horace Mann's theories became increasingly popular. More and more, American society perceived an intrinsic value in knowledge itself. Educators began to argue that the true purpose of school was not to build character and shape good citizens, but to impart knowledge. As society gradually embraced the notion that there was a practical value to education, innovation and reform transformed the field, especially in colleges and professional training.[12]

The late nineteenth century was nothing short of revolutionary for higher education. In a nation remade and redefined by the Civil War, American society embraced a view of education that was less rigid and purely theoretical and more democratic, egalitarian, scientific, technical, practical, and open to new pedagogical techniques. New colleges and new leadership at older institutions emerged, each with a distinct interpretation of what was wrong with American higher education. Deeply rooted trends and traditions in American higher education faced challenges from many quarters, including its woeful neglect of women, overly rigid curricula, strict focus on character development rather than scholarship, dependence upon rote memorization and recitation, and relative inaccessibility for average people.

While no one institution claimed to have solutions for every perceived problem, American higher education became a laboratory unto itself, defined in the late nineteenth and early twentieth centuries by bold innovation and experimentation. Land-grant colleges and free or inexpensive urban institutions like City College democratized higher education, offering unprecedented opportunities to children of workers, artisans, and farmers. New universities introduced collaborative seminars, developed curricula that combined theoretical scholarship with practical training, and gave students more leeway to pursue their own academic interests through the introduction and refinement of elective systems. Most institutions of higher learning looked resolutely forward, fully embracing and often leading innovation and change. As one university president declared, "In this day of unparalleled activity in college life, the institution which is not steadily advancing is certainly falling behind." At the time that Goethals enrolled, City College was a vibrant institution that had embraced some, though not all, of these reforms.[13]

In a more vibrant intellectual environment, Goethals's scholarly abilities improved somewhat, but his goals continued to fluctuate. While consistently above average, his academic performance varied as his ambitions changed. Early in his time at City College, Goethals gave serious consideration to a career as a naval officer and directed his efforts toward preparing for admission to the US Naval Academy. As long as he had a well-defined goal to fuel his ambition, he performed remarkably well in his studies. He finished his first year ranked thirty-first out of a class of 158, and then ranked eleventh out of a class of 104 at the end of his second year.[14] After receiving word from the secretary of the navy that there would be no vacancies for midshipmen from his district, Goethals redirected his ambitions toward going into business. On at least two occasions, he was prepared to drop out of City College to pursue potential business opportunities, but ultimately yielded to his father's wishes that he continue his studies. Goethals's academic performance suffered because of his ambivalent commitment to completing his education. He finished his third year ranked twenty-fourth out of a class of seventy-five.[15]

Although he certainly showed potential, Goethals's collegiate career through 1875 was unremarkable, a fact that his City College classmates noticed and commented upon many years later. One classmate remembered Goethals only as a "quiet, reserved, almost shy boy" who "was one of the group that tried for a high stand."[16] Another described him as "rather quiet and reserved, undemonstrative, and not a brilliant or exceptional student; just one among many."[17] More tellingly, a third classmate declared, "My recollections of George W. Goethals at the College include nothing salient" and that "he was an average student, just one of us, without any special distinction."[18]

Early in the winter in 1875, however, Democratic congressman Samuel Sullivan "Sunset" Cox announced that his Sixth New York Congressional District had an unexpected vacancy at West Point after the academy found its previous nominee academically deficient. The news piqued Goethals's interest. As the son of an immigrant carpenter, however, he had no strong political connections to help him secure the nomination. He sought advice from his grammar school principal, Nathan Beers, who was not only happy to help but also in an excellent position to do so.[19]

In 1875, New York City was a highly functioning testament to the maxim that all politics are local. Beers had strong connections with one of his school's trustees, a man by the name of Miehling, and a coroner named Henry Waltman, who together constituted the most significant political power in Cox's district. Beers pressured Miehling, who in turn took Goethals's case to Waltman. Here Goethals's army career almost failed to launch, as the coroner had already promised the nomination to his own nephew. That young man, however, was the only child of parents who were aghast at the idea of their son in the army. They persuaded him to decline the nomination, prompting Beers and Miehling to resume lobbying on Goethals's behalf. Waltman relented and sent word to the congressman that he had decided that Goethals should have the nomination. Congressman Cox then waived his usual competitive examination process and nominated Goethals on April 17, 1876.[20] Wasting no time, Goethals reported to West Point and was one of seventy-three cadets to pass the medical and academic examinations required for admission, although another four would be added to the rolls later in the summer. He and his classmates were immediately processed and sent to begin military training at their first annual summer encampment at West Point.[21]

Transferring from City College to West Point in 1876, Goethals was actually moving against the grain of progress in American higher education. The army had failed to keep pace with the changing perceptions and practices of education in American society, holding fast to an increasingly outdated view that ascribed a purely moral value to education. As the gateway to a career as an army officer, West Point's most significant military function was to introduce cadets to the military profession. Life at the academy immersed Goethals and likeminded cadets in military culture and imbued them with a sense of purpose and a deep personal identification with the army.[22] Theoretically, such commitment would take the form of self-study, which the army perceived to be the measure of an officer's level of professionalism. Originally an unwritten rule inherited from eighteenth-century norms, the army codified this general conception of professionalism in the 1890s

Although this may look more like tactical training, these West Point cadets photographed in 1889 were merely marching to dinner. Routines like this also took place while Goethals attended and were meant to introduce cadets to life in the military and the army's culture, which most late nineteenth-century officers considered to be West Point's primary purpose. (Library of Congress, Prints and Photographs Division, LC-USZ62-62092)

by instituting a system of annual efficiency reports that required each officer to submit a summary of any extracurricular reading or other efforts to improve his professional knowledge and expertise throughout the course of the year.[23]

When Goethals arrived, then, West Point was by its own volition a stagnant institution of higher education mired in the comfortable anachronisms of an earlier time. While other American colleges and universities implemented significant changes—including the transition to the elective system, expansion and diversification of curricula, and adoption of more inclusive and engaging forms of pedagogy—West Point remained committed to a highly technical curriculum focused primarily on mathematics and science, and it conducted instruction through rote recitation, frequent grading, and competitive daily ranking of cadets' academic performance. This stubborn adherence to tradition was a deliberate policy. The leadership of West Point and the army alike believed that theirs was the best method to condition cadets' minds to analyze and solve military problems and that the academic system that produced Generals Grant, Lee, Jackson, and Sherman required no adjustments. Essentially, West Point's curriculum was designed to develop the mental and physical discipline that officers believed to have fostered martial excellence in the past and would continue to do so in the future.[24]

As it was intended, life at the academy introduced Goethals to the army and inspired within him a deeply held identification with and commitment to it. But there was an ugly side to this process of socialization to the military profession. Hazing new cadets had been a practice at West Point since at least the 1830s, when it had maintained a generally benign and harmless character that was limited, for the most part, to a cadet's first summer encampment prior to the Civil War. The postwar years brought a general decline in discipline among the corps of cadets because officers assigned to West Point seldom enforced regulations that seemed trivial in light of their wartime experiences. The consecutive assignments of two weak and ineffective academy superintendents between 1864 and 1871 only exacerbated this trend. Hazing grew to encompass the entire fourth-class (freshman, or "plebe") year and ranged in severity from periodic public humiliation to significant physical violence. Despite the efforts of more active and energetic superintendents, such hazing continued through Goethals's cadet years and beyond, until a 1901 congressional investigation in the wake of a cadet's death in 1900 produced legislation barring the worst forms of hazing.[25]

The immediacy of the sharp change from a civilian to a military existence and the hazing that accompanied it made the transition a harsh experience for cadets. Although Goethals faced the same strains and difficulties as the rest of his classmates, he adjusted well to life at the academy. The competitive environment at West Point and the clear end of a commission as an army officer finally provided Goethals with a well-defined goal on which he could focus his energies. He emerged from his summer training in a frame of mind that allowed him to excel in the classroom.

The introduction to the military profession that West Point pro-

BEARING THE REMAINS TO THE CEMETERY.
THE FUNERAL OF GENERAL CUSTER AT WEST POINT.—[From Sketches by Theo. *

Goethals and other cadets were immersed in military life and culture from their earliest days in the service. This engraving, originally published in the October 27, 1877, edition of Harper's Weekly, *depicts George Armstrong Custer's funeral at West Point after his remains were recovered from the Little Bighorn battlefield. As a young cadet not yet halfway through his second year at West Point, Goethals participated in the funeral procession. (Library of Congress, Prints and Photographs Division, LC-USZ62-71379)*

vided led Goethals to identify so deeply with the army that it moved him to channel his ambitions toward rising to the top of his class. This was no easy feat—West Point deliberately fostered an intensely competitive environment. Accordingly, he put all of his energies into his studies. When "lights out" was sounded at ten o'clock each night, Goethals would lie prone on the floor while his roommates draped a large blanket over him, taking care to weigh it down along the edges with books at regular intervals, so he could continue to study by the undetected light of a kerosene lamp well into the night.[26] According to his older brother, when their father wrote Goethals to express his concerns about too much study at the expense of sleep, Goethals replied "that he would not be satisfied to merely plod through his studies, that he was there for work and he was going to do all in his power to come out at the head of his class."[27] He very nearly achieved that goal. He was rated second in his class at the end of every academic year. At the end of his first-class (senior, or "firstie") year, he was still rated second overall and was the top cadet in civil and military engineering after achieving a perfect score in that department.[28]

Goethals also thrived outside the classroom at West Point. Although he remained somewhat introverted and clung to a long-held fear of public speaking that he would never escape, he began to feel more confident and socially at ease in relationships with his fellow cadets on an individual basis.[29] As he became more comfortable, he became very popular. Gustav Fiebeger, a graduate of West Point's class of 1879 and one of the few close friends that Goethals carried throughout his entire adult life, recalled Goethals's popularity in an obituary written for West Point alumni shortly after his famed friend's death in 1928. "With a winning personality," Fiebeger explained, "he was dignified, yet friendly, modest, but self-confident, honorable and upright, cheerful in disposition, quick at repartee and somewhat sarcastic in a pleasant way, military in carriage and neat in dress, never coarse in language or thought."[30] Well-liked within the corps of cadets, many of whom referred to him playfully as "Goat," the class of 1880 elected Goethals to be their president and selected him to design their class ring. According to Fiebeger, Goethals's relationship with his classmates was such that "throughout his life he was their leader and the center about which the members of the class gathered whenever they held a reunion."[31]

Ultimately, while West Point had inspired Goethals to excel in and out of the classroom because it thoroughly imbued him with a strong sense of purpose and belonging, its academic impact on him was far less substantial. Goethals always recalled his time at West Point fondly, but he did not value it as an educational experience. More than three decades after he had stood in their place, he told the graduating class of 1912 that West Point provided cadets not with the knowledge and abilities required to succeed as officers but with "the foundations of a structure yet to be raised" and that their real education would be introduced gradually through practical experience.[32] He derived that narrative from his own career, which he interpreted as proof that edu-

A young Goethals not long after his admission to West Point. (Library of Congress, Prints and Photographs Division, LC-USZ62-137647)

Goethals as a first-class cadet in 1880. Part of the transformative effect West Point had on Goethals can be seen when comparing this photograph to the previous one. (1880 Class Album, Special Collections, US Military Academy Library)

cation sets one onto a path, but thereafter, the path has much more of an effect upon the traveler than he has on the path.

Goethals came to this conclusion in spite of the fact that his first assignment as a commissioned officer was at another educational institution. His academic success allowed him to become one of only two members of the class of 1880 to be commissioned as a second lieutenant in the Corps of Engineers.[33] After a brief stay at West Point to serve as an astronomy instructor, Goethals departed for Long Island when the next Engineer School of Application class began in the fall of 1880.

Postgraduate professional education was not uncommon in American society in the late nineteenth century. It became more popular because of both the increasingly widespread belief in the intrinsic and practical value of education and the emerging consensus that occupational specialization in the modern industrial age required formal training and education. When Johns Hopkins University established individual schools for selected professions in 1876, other universities soon followed suit. At first, universities and colleges themselves established curricula for specialized training in the professions their graduates would enter. Gradually, however, nationally centralized professional organizations began to exert more authority in validating and recognizing universities' professional schools and programs as legitimate. In the late nineteenth and early twentieth centuries, professional associations such as the American Medical Association and the American Bar Association emerged and began to assert considerable authority in reforming and standardizing professional education and training within the fields of business, medicine, law, social work, education, journalism, engineering, and forestry, among others.

In general, the notion that training and education had a legitimate and necessary role in occupational and professional specialization was becoming much more popular in American society in the late nineteenth century, and its popularity only continued to grow in the decades to come. The experience of the Civil War, the expansion and diversification of the economy, and the growth of enormous corporations revealed that the modern industrial age was defined by problems and issues of previously unimaginable complexity, size, and scope. A society of generalists could no longer thrive under such conditions. American society therefore began to embrace specialization in most walks of life. Whether one was to be a lawyer or a factory worker, Americans generally came to recognize and acknowledge that some amount of formal training and education was necessary to qualify a person for a specific occupational group and life as a productive member of society. [34]

This produced a rapidly growing consensus that education provided critical opportunities for occupational or professional success. Accordingly, another aspect of the transformation of higher education in the United States in the late nineteenth century was the development of robust programs of specialized vocational and professional education. The army, however, failed to keep pace with the society it served in this particular area, remaining wedded to increasingly antiquated philosophies and methods of occupational and professional training and education despite the best efforts of reformers who rightly argued that the military profession demanded similar forms and institutions of specialized postgraduate training and education.

Education and training played only a minor role in an army officer's career in the late nineteenth century, featuring prominently only during the first few years in the careers of Goethals's generation of officers. They expected this early training to provide an introduction to the military profession and, in the case of specialized branches of the army, a base of technical knowledge. Thereafter, officers expected practical experience to serve as their tutor. They continued to see little need for more rigorous education or institutionalized training systems. [35]

To an extent, the army acknowledged some need for specialized training for officers to be introduced to the various branches of the army they joined upon commissioning. Recognizing that West Point did not produce expert practitioners of all its arms, the army generally entrusted lieutenants' technical training to the units to which they first reported after graduation. It experimented with schools of application—formal schools with standardized curricula to provide branch-specific training to newly commissioned lieutenants—for infantry, cavalry, and artillery in the 1820s, and again for artillery from 1857 to 1861. These measures were limited and temporary due to a lack of interest, resources, funding, and, in at least one case, the outbreak of the Civil War. Within three years of the war's end, the army's technical branches—the Corps of Engineers, the Signal Corps, and the artillery—each opened schools of application. These evolved gradually in form and concept, but with the exception of the artillery school, they remained incomplete experiments that continued to be refined throughout the 1880s and 1890s and were not fully trusted within the institution itself for quite some time.[36]

This acknowledgment of the need for postgraduate military education was not confined to the technical branches. Despite continued confidence in the systems and processes that produced the Civil War generation, some in the army's high command began to accept that recent and ongoing changes in tactics, military organization, and technology called for a better trained officer corps. Ironically, while many officers pointed to the Civil War to justify their resistance to reform, some of the leading proponents of new experiments in postgraduate military education had served as Union generals. It was William T. Sherman, then serving as commanding general of the army, who ordered the establishment of the School of Application for Infantry and Cavalry at Ft. Leavenworth, Kansas, in 1881. The school's purpose was to train junior officers in small-unit tactics. Its target audience consisted primarily of the most junior officers of the line, second lieutenants. Instruction and curriculum in the early years were haphazard, but by 1889 the school had developed a practical program that prepared young officers for small-unit leadership within the context of the army's frontier mission. Despite its progress, however, regimental officers demonstrated a marked reluctance to send officers to the school, especially those whom they believed showed early talent and potential.[37]

Goethals experienced a similarly unfinished and haphazard curriculum at the Engineer School of Application from 1880 to 1882. After graduation, he made the short trip from West Point to Willets Point, New York, a somewhat sprawling post on a peninsula extending into the Long Island Sound in northern Queens County. Henry L. Abbot, a Civil War veteran with a distinguished record, had designed the school "with a view to meet the actual needs of young officers resulting from the fact that while admirably trained in the rudiments of their profession," they still had "much to learn about the use and care of delicate surveying, astronomical, and other instruments in constant use by the Corps of Engineers."[38]

From such humble beginnings, Abbot continued to modify the course until 1885, when it had expanded to a two-and-a-half-year curriculum and earned official sanction from the War Department. At the time Goethals attended, however, the school was slightly less than two years in length and still maturing. In addition to familiarization with specialized engineering equipment, Goethals studied survey procedures, military reconnaissance, astronomy (Willets Point had a state-of-the-art observatory that discovered a comet in June 1881), meteorology, field fortifications, military photography, harbor mining, and coastal defense.[39]

While undoubtedly more helpful to Goethals than sending him straight from West Point to his first assignment, precious little of the material was immediately relevant to a junior engineer officer. Not much of the course beyond the familiarization with engineering equipment and the instruction in survey and reconnaissance was actually applicable in Goethals's duties during his first two decades of service. Fortunately for those who came later, the curriculum that the War Department approved in 1885 included more practical instruction in civil and military engineering.[40] But these changes came too late to benefit Goethals, whose experiences at Willets Point had no lasting or meaningful impact on him. His surviving correspondence contains not a single reference to or recollection of his time at the Engineer School of Application. Its total absence reveals much about his perception of its value.

Elsewhere in the army, improvements to postgraduate military education were negligible, limited, or slow to materialize. Under the leadership of visionary reformers Arthur L. Wagner and Eben Swift, the program of instruction at Ft. Leavenworth expanded in the late 1880s and 1890s to include more advanced tactics, strategy, logistics, war games, and a standard orders process. Although Wagner and Swift implemented significant reforms, the near-term result was an awkward situation in which a relatively advanced curriculum was thrust upon a student body littered with the army's most junior officers. Older regimental commanders looked upon the Leavenworth schools with jaundiced eyes and continued to send only their seemingly expendable lieutenants whose absence from their units would not be sorely missed. As George C. Marshall, who with a mere four years of service reported to Ft. Leavenworth in 1906, later recalled, "The opposition to any studious preparation of the older officers was very decided." The Leavenworth schools did not truly mature until the 1910s, and they failed to gain wider acceptance within the army until after World War I.[41]

As Wagner's and Swift's efforts suggest, the failure of the officer corps to grasp the possibilities of more robust training and education was not due to a lack of effort within certain parts of the officer corps. Sherman was not the only officer from the Civil War generation who recognized the need for a more structured system of military education. His erstwhile wartime subordinate John B. Schofield shared that view. In the early 1890s, then serving as commanding general, Schofield attempted to implement officers' lyceums at each post. But Schofield's efforts were, to their detriment, based on the waning interpretation that professionalism was defined by personal identification and self-study rather than training and education. Schofield's plan called for officers to select a military topic that interested them and produce essays on it on an annual basis. That was the extent of Schofield's guidance on the matter, and many commanders interpreted Schofield's lack of emphasis on the lyceum to be an indication of how much effort they should put into it. Unsurprisingly, then, Schofield's lyceum program produced little that was useful in the short amount of time that it existed.

Vague and hardly enforceable pronouncements of policy like Schofield's lyceum program stood little chance of inspiring a fundamental shift in the army's institutional culture, which was characterized, in part, by a distinct and persistent strand of anti-intellectualism. This severely limited the development of effective systems of military training and education within the army. Tellingly, Goethals's time at Willets Point in his first two years out of West Point was actually the last formal training he received in nearly four decades of service.[42]

In the end, formal training and education shaped Goethals's career only to a very slight extent. He would learn his trade outside the classroom. Like many of his peers, Goethals experienced military education during a time when systems of military education were either stagnant or still under development, reinforcing a view that formal education had no significant place in the military. That attitude was strong and lasting. Despite his later experiences with the realities of modern industrialized warfare in the First World War, Goethals clung to this view. Speaking to a journalist early in his retirement, Goethals argued that "the best man . . . learns in the only school that is worth anything—experience." He explained, "No system of training will carry an incapable or unfaithful man to success. . . . The world today is a practical one, and it demands results."[43]

Armies typically reflect the societies they serve, but on this point, the army lagged behind society. As American educational institutions and professions established specialized institutions of higher and post-graduate education and shaped a new conception of professionalism, the army's officer corps remained steadfastly anti-intellectual, implicitly endorsing outdated notions that equated professionalism with personal identification and self-study. This was the single most important factor that delayed the ultimate fulfillment of military reform until the interwar years.

Anti-intellectualism was partly a choice. The army consciously idolized the Civil War generation and resisted most attempts to alter the methods and systems that produced it. It smacks of irony, then, to consider that some of those most closely associated with various late nineteenth-century proposals for military reform—including Emory Upton, William T. Sherman, and John M. Schofield—had been Civil War generals. Despite attempts at reform, cultural predilections that had become ingrained within the very fabric of the institution over the course of a century proved too difficult to break.

At the same time, the army's anti-intellectualism was also partly the result of circumstances not entirely within its control. Throughout much of the late nineteenth century, the army could not embrace a new conception of professionalism based on specialized training and education—and an educational system appropriate for that conception—because of its small size and its disposition on the frontier. It could not adopt the educational philosophies and methods proposed by civil and military reformers until well after its mission and disposition, and the institution itself, ceased to be defined by its experience of the frontier.

2

The School of Experience

Nineteenth-century Americans perceived their western frontier in terms of both place and process. As a place, they considered it to be land that they were entitled to possess. Many also saw it as an outlet for a national population that increased by at least 25 percent each decade.[1] Perhaps more important, many Americans believed that expansion to the Pacific Ocean was a divinely ordained process that strengthened the nation by spreading democracy and Christianity, improving civic-mindedness, and encouraging a rugged sense of individualism and self-reliance.[2] Spurred by a complex and interactive milieu of motivations, Americans worked individually and collectively throughout the nineteenth century to acquire and control the American West, both physically and demographically. George W. Goethals saw that goal realized during his lifetime. In 1870, approximately 2 million Americans lived west of the Missouri River. By 1900, that number had increased to more than 10 million, and Americans generally considered their frontier to be a thing of the past.[3] Far from a relic of recent history, however, the frontier experience maintained its overwhelming influence upon the army well into the early twentieth century. The frontier was an all-consuming and deeply habit-forming place and process that indelibly shaped the army's institutional culture.[4]

In November 1882, fresh out of the Engineer School of Application at Willets Point, New York, Goethals reported for duty on the staff of the Department of the Columbia, eager to play a small role in the army's expansive and complex frontier mission.[5] Ambling into conflict with those whose lands the United States presumed to expand onto and across, the army waged dozens of campaigns against Native Americans from the Atlantic to the Pacific from the Revolution to the late nineteenth century.[6] But fighting did not define the army's frontier mission. In fact, most soldiers spent far more of their careers dedicated to myriad other tasks supporting American expansion. The army was regularly called upon to protect railroads, assist settlers traveling overland, deliver federal mail, conduct explorations and geographical surveys, and build the roads and canals that facilitated trade and communication throughout the expanding United States. Still, its principal role was to serve as a frontier constabulary force, operating in turns both against rogue settlers operating outside the bounds of established law and policy and—more frequently and forcefully—against Native Americans.[7]

The army's size did not match its expansive mission as the federal government's "most visible agent" of expansion.[8] At the conclusion of the Civil War, it was more than 1 million soldiers strong. Only four years later, however, just under 37,000 soldiers remained in the ranks. Those soldiers were widely dispersed among 255 posts scattered throughout the western frontier and along the Atlantic and Gulf Coasts. The army continued to trim its ranks, fluctuating between a high of 28,565 and a low of 24,140 soldiers from the day Goethals entered West Point in 1876 until the eve of the war with Spain in 1898. But the army was not able to persuade Congress—whose members were as committed to maintaining federal installations in their home districts and states as they are today, and for many of the same reasons—to allow it to close a proportional number of posts. While it succeeded in closing some posts and consolidating some units at larger installations in the late 1880s, the army remained widely dispersed and was forced to rely upon small-unit operations to execute its expansive continental mission. In 1889, 27,759 soldiers garrisoned just under 140 posts, the largest of which was home to only 700 soldiers. Dispersed as it was, the army's ability to systematically educate and train its officers was severely limited.[9]

In light of its disposition, a passive approach to officer development was both natural and necessary. As long as the army's frontier mission and disposition remained unchanged, more robust systems of training and education were neither feasible nor advisable. Mature systems of military education and officer development could not take hold in an environment in which junior officers were decisively engaged in the day-to-day operations of an army that functioned largely at the small-unit level. Junior officers frequently commanded units at small frontier outposts, unable to put aside the steady pace of their many and varied duties. Perhaps understandably, the army proved reluctant to move those who performed their duties exceptionally well. Rather than attend further schooling, promising junior officers were assigned to more pressing mission requirements by superior officers who were equally beleaguered by the breadth of their mission and the comparative paucity of their resources. The army could do little else but hope that the experiences officers gained in the course of the execution of their duties would teach them all that was necessary to succeed at higher ranks.[10]

Goethals's first such experiences were in the Department of the Columbia, which encompassed all of Oregon, Washington Territory, and the district of Alaska, as well as most of Idaho Territory. Since August 1881, Brig. Gen. Nelson A. Miles commanded the department. This was a promising connection for Goethals. Famous for his campaigns in the Indian Wars, Miles would become the commanding general of the army by the end of the century.[11] Goethals was also fortunate to be assigned to a functioning frontier department, gaining uncommon exposure to life with line units and officers outside the Corps of Engineers. In 1883, only ten out of 103 officers in the Corps of Engineers performed duties in commands that included tactical line units.[12] At the same time, this undoubtedly proved to be a challenging assignment for a young lieutenant with no experience outside of West Point and the Engineer School of Application. As the only engineer officer assigned to the command, he was by default the senior engineer in the department, and Miles expected him to be the resident expert on all engineering matters. Caught in the awkward tension between his commander's expectations for expertise and the army's expectations that he would learn gradually through experience, Goethals had only a limited base of theoretical knowledge to rely upon and no mentor to guide him.

Furthermore, the young lieutenant soon found that it was a mixed blessing to serve on the staff of the ever petulant and irascible Nelson Miles. "Always fearful of conspiracies," his biographer rightly notes, "Miles divided the world into two clearly distinguishable factions: those wise enough to agree with him and those mean-spirited enough to allow their jealousies to affect their judgment."[13] Surviving service under a commander with an infamously quick temper and legendary ability to bear grudges would be a tall order for any officer. For a new lieutenant finding his way in the army without the benefit of a mentor, it would prove to be an impossible task.

Things started well enough. Miles, who was on leave in Boston and Washington for the first six months of Goethals's assignment to Vancouver Barracks, had placed regional development to support the expansion of railroads and settlements at the top of his department's priorities.[14] A considerable amount of land within the Department of the Columbia had not yet been adequately explored and mapped. As the department's engineer, Goethals spent much of his time doing just that, particularly in the northern reaches of the Washington and Idaho Territories. He spent the bulk of his assignment to Vancouver Barracks in the field conducting reconnaissance missions, leading exploration parties, and laying out wagon roads, railroads, and telegraph lines.[15]

Driven by the same work ethic he demonstrated at West Point, Goethals was completely dedicated to his work. His energetic efforts drew the notice of all who observed him, even at the highest levels. Notably, Miles ordered Goethals to reconnoiter and plan the route for part of General Sherman's tour of the Pacific Northwest in the summer of 1883. He deeply impressed Sherman, who reported to Secretary of War Robert T. Lincoln that Goethals was "a most intelligent young Engineer officer." Sherman noted that Goethals had conducted a reconnaissance of the party's route prior to its arrival and had "submitted to me . . . his report with sketches, which I found most valuable and accurate, so that I resolved to adhere strictly to his advice though it differed somewhat from my own preference based on the best information at Washington."[16] Sherman was so impressed that he told Miles that Goethals was "one of the most promising men in the Army," and he forwarded the maps Goethals prepared to Lincoln so they could be copied and used in the various War Department offices in Washington.[17] Miles expressed his own confidence in Goethals by ordering him to escort Sherman's party for two weeks in August 1883 before diverting him to assist a cavalry detachment attempting to locate a pass through the Cascade Mountains.[18]

While most of Goethals's duties at Vancouver Barracks involved reconnaissance and mapmaking, he also gained limited experience in civil and military engineering. He selected sites and built new buildings on post, established a new post cemetery, and constructed roads throughout the department.[19] In October 1883 the Spokane River washed out the only bridge that could be used to bring much needed supplies to Fort Spokane, home of the Second Infantry Regiment. Miles hurried Goethals to the site to consult with the regimental commander and replace the bridge as quickly as possible. This comparatively simple task made a profound impression on Goethals. Relatively unschooled and completely inexperienced in building bridges more intricate than a pontoon bridge, and in the unfortunate position of still being the most knowledgeable engineer present, Goethals set to work. He learned how to build a bridge on the job. As he later recalled, "It might not have been hard for a bridge engineer," who "would have known exactly what to do." Goethals, however, was painfully aware of his own ignorance. "I had to find out as we went along," he explained years later. In order to complete the work, he "had to read books all night and give orders all day." Despite these difficulties, Goethals succeeded. "We built the bridge," he boasted, "and on time."[20]

This relatively simple mission left a major impression on Goethals. Years later, after his work on the Panama Canal had gained him celebrity status, enterprising reporters would seek interviews with the famed engineer to produce articles that would appeal to an interested national audience. Hoping to explore the challenges associated with building the Panama Canal, the journalist Samuel Crowther may have been a little frustrated when Goethals spoke at length about that small bridge across the Spokane, insisting that it was "the hardest task I ever had." Crowther was incredulous. The man across from him had quite literally moved mountains, and here he sat waxing poetically about a small, thoroughly unremarkable, and short-lived bridge constructed almost four decades earlier and torn down shortly thereafter. That was the achievement of a novice, not a master. When pressed on that point, Goethals explained with characteristic curtness, "I never had built a bridge, and I did not know much about bridge building."[21]

Such was the state of officer development at the time. The army was not an institution that actively developed its leaders. Rather, it was an institution that could identify the need to build a bridge and send an officer utterly lacking expertise and experience to build it, either completely unaware of the officer's lack of qualifications or confident that he would eventually figure it out.

Entering his second year of duty at Vancouver Barracks glowing with satisfaction from both his work and the praise it brought him, Goethals was unaware that he would soon experience his almost inevitable fall from Nelson Miles's fleeting grace. Since assuming command of the Department of the Columbia, Miles had developed a keen interest in Alaska, unsuccessfully badgering both the War Department and Congress for funds to organize an expedition to explore its interior. Miles eventually took matters into his own hands. Conjuring up fictive "frequent reports of disturbances of the peace between the whites and Indians in Alaska," he dispatched a small expedition up the Yukon River led by his aide-de-camp, Lt. Frederick Schwatka. Although it revealed little that was not already known about the region, Schwatka's subsequent reports reanimated public interest in Alaska and encouraged Miles to dispatch additional expeditions.[22]

Possibly because of his impressive performance reconnoitering for Sherman's tour, Miles approached Goethals in early 1884 about leading one such expedition. Goethals declined the assignment. He had recently become engaged to Effie Rodman, the daughter of a prosperous whaler from New Bedford, Massachusetts, and the long-visiting sister of a fellow lieutenant at Vancouver Barracks. Lucky to have found and successfully wooed an eligible young lady in a remote and barren social setting, Goethals was eager to marry and had no interest in interrupting those plans. Miles was enraged. Always fearful of conspiracies and quick to assume ill-intent, it did not take much for the general to permanently banish someone from his trusted inner circle—and after refusing the Alaska mission, Goethals was most definitely on the outside. Miles hastily sent a letter to the adjutant general requesting Goethals's relief. The request was promptly forwarded for consideration to the chief of engineers, who decided to transfer Goethals to an engineering district in Cincinnati commanded by Lt. Col. William E. Merrill. The adjutant general issued the necessary orders, and Goethals departed Vancouver Barracks in September 1884.[23]

Service in the Department of the Columbia provided Goethals with
the first practical experiences of his career. He learned much about
working with troops of the line, reconnaissance, and mapmaking—
all skills that would prove useful later in his career during the war
with Spain in 1898. At the same time, while serving on Miles's staff,
Goethals was an inexperienced officer in the unenviable position of
being the sole expert on all things related to engineering in his department. While he proved on more than one occasion to be capable of
learning on the job and performing his duties well, he suffered from
a lack of training and the absence of a more experienced engineer officer to serve as his mentor. By 1884, Goethals had been an engineer
for four years. In that time, he had gained no practical experience in
constructing and maintaining coastal fortifications or planning and
directing river and harbor improvements, missions to which the Corps
of Engineers assigned the majority of its officers in the late nineteenth
century.[24]

In all likelihood, Goethals was blissfully unaware of just how significant this gap in his development was. The army's habit of entrusting
young officers to develop themselves was problematic precisely because
those officers were quite understandably ignorant about what they did
not know. But by a sheer stroke of luck—angering Miles to such an
extent that the general requested his relief at the precise moment a
duty position for an engineer lieutenant was opening in Cincinnati—
Goethals fell under the tutelage of a titan in the field. This forced the
young lieutenant to grapple with his lack of experience and placed him
in the orbit of an exceptional mentor who took innovative measures to
remedy his new subordinate's professional inadequacies.

Early in his new assignment with the Army Corps of Engineers First
Cincinnati District, Goethals conducted the preliminary investigation
for a potential river improvement project near New Albany Harbor,
Indiana. He dutifully examined the river and its commercial traffic
and spoke at length with local landowners. Goethals reported, "When
the river is high enough to cover the bottom lands, it is stated that the
force of the current sweeps over these lands from the mouth of Falling
Run to Middle Creek, and it is anticipated that in time the soil will
be entirely cut away, and the channel will then run in this direction
instead of crossing into the Kentucky shore, as it does now."[25] As Mer-

rill, chief of the First Cincinnati District, prepared to forward a copy to the chief of engineers in Washington, DC, he drafted a letter to include as an addendum to Goethals's report. "It has been suggested," he began, "that there is a probability of the river changing its channel, and making a cut-off through Middle Creek." Dismissing the notion, Merrill wrote, "I cannot see the slightest likelihood of such a change, as the route by way of Middle Creek is as long as the present channel, and there is therefore every inducement for the river to continue through the present open door rather than to batter down the side wall to make a new channel, neither shorter nor straighter than that in which it now flows." His inexperienced subordinate had much to learn about rivers and river improvements.[26]

The First Cincinnati District was an excellent place to learn. Its responsibilities included river improvements along the Ohio River and several of its tributaries. Projects on the Ohio demanded the vast majority of the district's time and resources, to such an extent that the chief of engineers created the Second Cincinnati District in 1880 to take responsibility for several tributaries of the Ohio and relieve some of Merrill's burden. Since 1824, improving the Ohio River to make it more accessible for commercial shipping had consumed the efforts of engineers assigned to Cincinnati. Even at normal water stages, navigating the river was a difficult and treacherous proposition. At lower stages, large swaths of it were simply impassable.[27]

Before the Civil War, Cincinnati-based engineers aimed to maintain a channel in the river at least thirty inches deep, which would allow easy passage for most types of commonly used shallow-draft steamers. They dredged channels in some sections of the river and constructed wing dams along river embankments in other parts, attempting to increase the depth of the river by concentrating its flow and restricting its width. They also spent much time and effort removing snags in the river caused by the buildup of rocks, trees, and other debris after storms and floods. Their work allowed commerce to flow relatively freely, except during winter months when ice flows threatened commercial shipping, especially on the uppermost reaches of the river and its northern tributaries.[28]

After the Civil War, the Army Corps of Engineers was much more heavily engaged on the Ohio River. In addition to managing improvement efforts, army engineers received orders to operate and maintain the Louisville and Portland Canal in Kentucky after Congress purchased it from private owners. Complicating matters, however, new technology and shipping techniques gradually rendered old approaches to river improvements obsolete. By 1870, the heyday of shallow-draft steamboats had passed. With more powerful steam engines, shipping companies could move goods and commodities in greater bulk and far more efficiently by using tugboats to push or pull several interconnected barges. Problematically, though, the tugs and barges carried a deeper draft than the steamboats of old. River commerce now demanded a consistent channel depth of six feet—more than the dredging and wing dams upon which army engineers had previously relied could provide.[29]

In June 1870, Merrill took charge of what eventually became the First Cincinnati District. He had graduated at the top of West Point's class of 1859 and served with some distinction in the Civil War. Assigned after the war to the Mississippi River Commission, Merrill soon gained a reputation as both a leading expert on the construction of large railroad bridges over inland waterways and a soldier with an aptitude for solving complex problems in nontraditional ways. That aptitude and the need to deepen the channel along the upper Ohio River to six feet inspired his designs for the Davis Island Lock and Dam—the most radical and significant engineering project on the Ohio River in the late nineteenth century. When Goethals reported for duty, Merrill's project was only a year away from completion.[30]

The Davis Island Lock and Dam was necessary because the city of Pittsburgh was a hostage of climate and geography. Although its position at the confluence of the Allegheny, Monongahela, and Ohio Rivers imbued it with vast commercial potential and attracted industrialists to the area, water levels around Pittsburgh dropped sharply during dry weather, often to a depth of mere inches, bringing all shipping and river trade to a standstill. Such dry spells usually lasted for several months, causing seasonal economic downturns that extended downriver to Cincinnati, Louisville, and other burgeoning towns where industries and communities depended upon coal shipments from Pittsburgh.[31]

The situation in 1871 was particularly extreme. The Ohio River became prohibitively shallow in May and did not rise again until the following winter. Coal and goods earmarked for points downriver lin-

gered idly in Pittsburgh's once bustling warehouses. Moreover, there
was no longer a navigable water route to ship the coal mined from
the Monongahela River valley, which fueled Pittsburgh's factories and
plants in the industrial district on the northern side of the city. To
keep them operational, coal had to be transported from the landings
along the Monongahela in convoys of mule-drawn wagons through
the heart of downtown Pittsburgh, causing traffic jams and significant
damage to city streets not designed to withstand such heavy loads.
Reacting to what had become an intolerable situation, Pittsburgh's industrial and business leaders, with the active support of businesses and
communities downriver, petitioned the Corps of Engineers to develop
at Pittsburgh a permanently navigable harbor on the Ohio River.[32]

Merrill had already been considering ways to canalize the Ohio in
order to deepen its channel to six feet. He had come to believe that
a system of locks and dams was the appropriate solution. When the
petition to develop a harbor at Pittsburgh reached his desk, Merrill
proposed the construction of an entire system of locks and dams along
the Ohio River, beginning with a first set five miles downriver from
Pittsburgh, near Davis Island. His plan, however, drew strong objections from Pittsburgh's coal shippers.[33]

Utterly confused as to why coal shippers would oppose a measure
that would make shipping easier, Merrill accompanied a coal barge
on a trip downriver to investigate what they found objectionable. He
learned that locks are especially problematic for boats guiding a substantial number of barges. A boat with several barges connected by a
complex system of chains and cables would have to pause in front of
a lock, "break tow" to get all barges through, and pause again on the
far side of a lock to reassemble their barges. As coal fleets' use of the
river was already restricted to high water stages that usually lasted for
only three days, forcing the fleet to break tow and pass through a lock
one at a time would mean that only one-third of Pittsburgh's coal fleet
could be used during any given high water stage.[34]

Understanding this, Merrill determined that in order to meet the
needs of all parties concerned, he would have to develop a lock-and-
dam system with two defining characteristics. First, the locks needed to
have larger dimensions than any others then existing in order to allow
solitary ships and smaller tow-and-barge systems through at any given
time. Second, the locks would have to be complemented by novel,

not-yet-designed movable dams that could be raised in order to build a navigable harbor upriver from the dam at low water stages and lowered to allow large coal shipments to pass through without "breaking tow" during high water stages. Nothing of the sort had ever been attempted in the United States, so Merrill searched abroad for inspiration, triggering an unprecedented exchange of hydraulic technology between the United States and Europe.[35]

Poring over European models, Chanoine dams then in use on the Seine River caught Merrill's attention. In the Chanoine design, French engineers employed a series of rectangular wooden or metal panels, known as "wickets," placed side by side. In the lowered position, the wickets lay parallel with the river bottom, resting flat on top of a dam foundation with metal supports and mechanical apparatuses that, when activated, elevated the wickets upward at steep angles to reach the raised position. In the raised position, the force of the water pushing downriver against the face of the wickets locked the supports into place in the dam foundation, thus forming an effective dam. Merrill planned a system in which a Chanoine dam would connect on one side of the river with a lock, which he designed to be 110 feet wide and 600 feet long.[36]

Initially, he limited construction to one lock and dam at Davis Island. Although his plan called for several, Merrill understood that the design it was radical and needed to be proven before it could be replicated. According to Merrill, the purpose of the Davis Island project was not only to improve the harbor at Pittsburgh but also "to demonstrate the only way of radically improving the navigation of the Ohio River." Merrill "hoped and expected" that his work would be "so successful as to lead to a demand for others like it," but he thought it "best not to press the matter until the pioneer dam . . . fully demonstrated its usefulness."[37]

Merrill managed many other projects in addition to the Davis Island Lock and Dam, and he certainly could not handle the full breadth of his mission alone. Like other engineer district chiefs, his staff included civilian assistants and one engineer lieutenant. The lieutenants who rotated in and out of his office came to look up to him as an almost fatherly figure as he demonstrated genuine interest in their development as engineers and officers.[38] Merrill's approach to officer development was based on a clear recognition that the lieutenants in his charge did not follow a standardized career path and had distinct bases of knowledge built upon equally distinct prior experiences. Accordingly, he tailored his approach to each officer's level of experience.

Prior to Goethals's arrival, Lt. Frederick A. Mahan was Merrill's assistant. Mahan had worked under Merrill on the Ohio since 1872. He was also the son of Dennis Hart Mahan, who had served as the chair of West Point's Department of Civil and Military Engineering from 1832 until his death in 1871 and had written the texts that the academy continued to use in its engineering classes. Given such a pedigree, he arrived with an uncommon breadth of theoretical knowledge and practical experience. Merrill developed Mahan by challenging him with incrementally increasing levels of responsibility. He first had Mahan assist him in studying foreign concepts of movable dams, and then brought Mahan into the planning process for the Davis Island project. As the plans continued to be refined, Merrill placed his talented subordinate in charge of several smaller dam construction and channel improvement projects elsewhere along the Ohio River. With Mahan succeeding in every mission assigned to him, Merrill decided that he was ready for a major project.[39]

In 1875 Merrill persuaded the chief of engineers to extend Mahan's assignment at Cincinnati so that he could assign the lieutenant as the engineer directly in charge of construction at Davis Island. From 1878 to 1884, Mahan oversaw construction at Davis Island, responsible for not only the execution of Merrill's plans but also the hiring and management of a civilian staff and labor force. Merrill saw to the rest of his district, loosely supervised Mahan, and maintained personal control of higher-level organizational systems and logistics supporting the Davis Island project.[40]

In 1884, after twelve years of service in the same assignment, Mahan earned a promotion to captain and transferred out of the First Cincinnati District. Goethals replaced him in September of that year after the long journey from Vancouver Barracks. A cursory review of his new subordinate's background revealed to Merrill that Goethals did not have the requisite knowledge or experience to manage the Davis Island construction site as Mahan had done. Instead, Merrill made arrangements for one of his civilian assistants to take charge of the work. He had other plans to remedy his new lieutenant's lack of experience.

Wanting to make a good first impression, Goethals reported for duty in an immaculately clean dress uniform. Merrill looked him over and curtly informed Goethals that if he wished to continue to wear that uniform, he could remain in the office for clerical duties; but if he wanted to learn how to be an engineer, he would thereafter report in clothes more suitable for hard work in the field. Merrill was as much a product of the school of experience as Goethals would become, and he was an avid proponent of the benefits of experiential learning. Accordingly, he created an intricately controlled and calculated program of practical instruction to immerse Goethals in the art and science of inland river engineering.[41]

Frequently wearing overalls on duty, Goethals became a student in Merrill's improvised academy of river improvements. Some of his education involved conducting preliminary examinations for potential new projects within the district, from which he could learn how to discern which projects were both necessary and feasible. Most of his other training took place within and among civilian work crews. He started at the very bottom and worked his way up as he mastered the various tasks on each crew, serving first as a rodman on hydrographic surveys, then as the chief of a surveying party, then as the foreman of a concrete team, and finally as the chief of construction for a small project. Goethals's assignments took him not only through the various aspects of the Davis Island Lock and Dam project as it neared completion but also to myriad other construction, repair, and dredging projects along the Ohio and some of its tributaries from Pennsylvania to Kentucky.[42]

Merrill and his engineers completed the Davis Island Lock and Dam in the late summer of 1885 and then subjected it to two months of tests before finally opening it for public use in early October. The Ohio River Commission and Pittsburgh Chamber of Commerce planned a grand opening and dedication ceremony for the occasion, and asked Merrill for a list of officers who contributed to the effort and deserved invitations to the ceremony. Merrill included Goethals on the list, but Goethals was unable to attend, having reported for duty at West Point in August 1885 to serve as an instructor in the Department of Civil and Military Engineering.[43]

There, Goethals was responsible for teaching engineering theory and concepts related to the design and construction of fortifications and basic military structures to cadets in their final year at the academy.[44]

Officers' assignments to academic departments at West Point in the late nineteenth century typically began with a request from the department's professor. As vacancies or the need for additional instructors arose, department heads submitted lists of "qualified" officers directly to the War Department, at which point the appropriate bureau chief made the final selection. Heads of West Point's academic departments determined a given officer's level of qualification based on his performance as a cadet, and their lists of requested officers typically consisted of their best students from four or five years earlier.[45]

Because Goethals was still known at the academy for achieving a perfect score and finishing first in the Department of Civil and Military Engineering for the class of 1880, the department head placed Goethals at the top of a list of five preferred candidates that he included with a request for two officers to report to West Point in the summer of 1885. Although the chief of engineers endorsed the request, he based the decision less on Goethals's previous academic record than on the fact that he considered Goethals to be a nonessential member of Merrill's district. Thus Goethals received his next significant developmental opportunity not because of any perceived need or concern for his development but because of a perception that he was expendable and could move without inconveniencing Merrill's work. After all, unlike Mahan before him, Goethals had not taken over any substantial projects in the Cincinnati District.[46]

Serving as an instructor in the Department of Civil and Military Engineering was an opportunity for Goethals to enhance his knowledge of engineering theory and practice. The established methods of pedagogy at West Point had not changed since Goethals had been a cadet, continuing to rely on rote memorization and daily classroom recitation. While this may not have been the best way to teach cadets, it certainly forced instructors to have a firm command of all assigned texts. In order to fulfill his duties as an instructor, Goethals had to spend many hours studying and committing concepts to memory.[47] This could have been a pointless exercise, as Goethals's perfect score in the department in 1880 indicated that he had already memorized the assigned text from front to back. However, West Point had begun to revise its outdated engineering texts in 1882 in order to incorporate technological and procedural advances and innovations in an updated engineering curriculum. By the time Goethals joined the faculty in

1885, the department was using new texts that reflected the most up-to-date knowledge in the engineering community. By studying to fulfill his responsibilities as an instructor, Goethals necessarily absorbed the latest concepts in his field, setting conditions for his continued rise within the Corps of Engineers.[48]

This was an exceptionally uncommon opportunity. At the end of Goethals's first year on the faculty, the chief of engineers reported that only 5 out of 108 officers in the Corps of Engineers were assigned to West Point, where the normal course of their duties would keep them abreast of the latest developments in their field. In this instance, Goethals benefited from the army's inability to standardize procedures to ensure the relevance and quality of the experiences to which officers were exposed in their various assignments, and from which officers were expected to learn their trade.[49]

Still, Goethals's career nearly became mired in obscurity after he left West Point in 1889. The Corps of Engineers assigned him to a sleepy, secondary engineering district in Cincinnati that was adjacent to Merrill's, giving him responsibility for minor improvements along tributaries of the Ohio River in order to allow Merrill's district to work almost exclusively on more significant projects.[50] He did not have time to settle in before he received new orders.

Another engineer lieutenant, Graham D. Fitch, had received orders to transfer from Milwaukee to the Nashville District in order to assist Lt. Col. John W. Barlow's efforts to improve the Tennessee and Cumberland Rivers. Prior to arriving in Nashville, however, Fitch grew so ill that his ability to continue serving in the army was in doubt. The chief of engineers ordered him to Washington to be evaluated by a medical board. Viewing the projects in the Nashville District as critically important, the chief of engineers then searched for a lieutenant to fill the vacancy. Because he had just arrived and did not have time to become essential to any projects near Cincinnati, he received orders to report to Barlow in Nashville.[51] For Goethals, this was another stroke of incredible luck. Work on the Tennessee River would challenge Goethals more than anything in his career to date and provided opportunities that proved to be important stepping-stones to the Panama Canal.

Inhabitants of the Tennessee River valley developed a strong interest in the commercial potential of their river when steamboats began

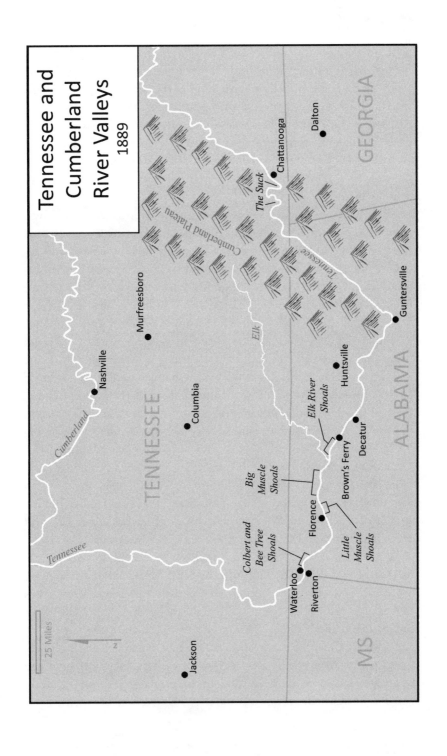

Tennessee and
Cumberland
River Valleys
1889

GEORGIA

Dalton

Chattanooga

The Suck

Cumberland Plateau

Tennessee

Elk

Guntersville

Murfreesboro

Nashville

Cumberland

Columbia

TENNESSEE

Huntsville

Elk River
Shoals

ALABAMA

Decatur

Brown's Ferry

Big
Muscle
Shoals

Florence

Tennessee

Little
Muscle
Shoals

Colbert and
Bee Tree
Shoals

Waterloo

Riverton

MS

Jackson

25 Miles

N

plying the Mississippi and Ohio Rivers after the steamboat *Enterprise* made the first journey of its kind on that route in 1815. But there were significant hazards impeding navigation of the Tennessee, particularly in its middle section between southern Tennessee and northwestern Alabama. The sharp bends below Chattanooga, Tennessee, known in the nineteenth century as "the Suck," were particularly dangerous even for experienced hands. The real problem, though, lay nearly two hundred miles downriver from Chattanooga, at northern Alabama's Muscle Shoals.[52]

The Muscle Shoals region contained four hazards. Moving downriver from east to west, a boat would first encounter an area of wide shallows at the Elk River Shoals just after passing Brown's Ferry. After negotiating the shallows, the boat would next come upon Big Muscle Shoals, a fifteen-mile stretch of rapids and cascades in which the river fell a total of eighty-five feet. The channel here was narrow where it existed at all. Big Muscle Shoals had formed because of the presence of flinty rocks deposited on top of and among the limestone and sandstone that makes up so much of the Tennessee's riverbed. With the river unable to cut a channel through these unyielding rocks, this area around Muscle Shoals became a wide, shallow basin full of cascades, reefs, and river islands. It was so wide, in fact, that a fifty-foot rise in the river at Chattanooga would only produce a five-foot rise at Big Muscle Shoals. Three miles downriver from Big Muscle Shoals lay Little Muscle Shoals. This was a four-mile, slightly less extreme version of its larger cousin. The town of Florence, Alabama, lay one mile further downriver, just above Colbert and Bee Tree Shoals, an eight-mile stretch of shallows and shoals made up of sand, broken gravel, and rocks in which the river fell another twenty feet in elevation.[53]

While Colbert and Bee Tree Shoals could not be ignored, Little Muscle Shoals, Big Muscle Shoals, and Elk River Shoals were more significant problems. Together, they constituted thirty-seven miles of nearly continuous hazards, with Big Muscle Shoals and Elk River Shoals being an absolute obstruction to navigation of the river at all times except during periods of extremely high water. According to engineers who surveyed the area in 1867, there was "no channel at low water in this part of the river," and "in many places a person can walk across the river without wetting his feet." They reported that "the lightest flatboat cannot descend the shoals without being assisted in many places on rollers."[54]

To commercial interests, then, Muscle Shoals divided the Tennessee River into two separate rivers. A major trade imbalance developed between them. Steamboats could ply the waters between Paducah, Kentucky, and Florence, Alabama, with relative ease, but communities upriver from Florence could only ship goods downriver two or three months out of the year when conditions were good enough to allow flatboats to traverse the shoals. Otherwise, these communities had to rely on small keelboats. Business owners in Knoxville tried to entice steamers to run the gauntlet at high water stages in the 1820s and 1830s, but the journey was more risky than profitable. On average, only one steamer made the attempt per year.[55]

The only viable solution to problems posed by the Muscle Shoals hazards appeared to be a lateral canal around the lengthy belt of obstacles. The state of Alabama accepted the challenge and managed the first attempt to build such a canal. Its plans were ambitious and proved to be far too expensive. Frustrated engineers were forced to scale back their plans and work only at Big Muscle Shoals. There they built a canal just over fourteen miles long, sixty feet wide, and six feet deep, with seventeen locks to mitigate the descent of the river. Although the canal's design and construction were sound, the decision to limit all improvement efforts to Big Muscle Shoals doomed the project to insignificance and oblivion. The canal opened in 1836 and was nearly useless, unreachable on either end except during periods of peak water levels because engineers had taken no complementary measures to facilitate navigation through the Elk River Shoals above the canal or Little Muscle Shoals below the canal, which fell into disuse and disrepair after 1838.[56]

Advocacy for river improvement projects at Muscle Shoals increased significantly after the Civil War. Government officials and local communities alike argued that completely opening the Tennessee River for commercial navigation from its head to its mouth was an excellent way to stimulate the region's economy and hasten its recovery from the war.[57] The Muscle Shoals area remained impassable for large vessels, and although communities on the upper Tennessee built their own steamboats for local trade, they remained unable to ship goods downriver to Paducah and beyond. This frustrated the rapidly developing commercial-industrial sector in Chattanooga, where businesses saw a viable river route as both a much-needed commercial boon and a means of checking the rising power and prices of the railroads. Responding to advocates for renewed Tennessee River improvements in 1871, the Corps of Engineers established a new district at Chattanooga under Maj. Walter McFarland. It charged the district with ensuring open navigation of the full river for at least nine months per year.[58]

After careful study, McFarland developed a plan that called for restoring and expanding the first canal at Big Muscle Shoals, then addressing the problems at Elk River Shoals and Little Muscle Shoals in order to facilitate access to the main canal. At Elk River Shoals, McFarland intended to build a short, two-lock canal and blast a channel through the reef that separated the foot of that canal from the head of Big Muscle Shoals. At Big Muscle Shoals, he planned to expand, widen, and strengthen the old canal; consolidate its seventeen-lock system into nine locks; dam the creeks and ravines that emptied into the canal; and carry the canal over the mouth of Shoal Creek by constructing an aqueduct ninety feet long and sixty feet wide. At Little Muscle Shoals, McFarland believed that the channel could be deepened and the rapid current managed through dredging and the construction of wing dams along the embankments of the river. Ready to proceed, the renewed work at Muscle Shoals hit its first delay when the building that doubled as McFarland's house and headquarters—in which the only copies of the canal plans were kept—burned to the ground on January 13, 1874.[59]

Work finally began in 1875 under contracted labor. However, it soon became mired in significant delays resulting from problems with contractors, disease in the laborers' camps, and a dearth of appropriations. In 1876, McFarland was reassigned to duty along the Canadian border and replaced by Maj. William R. King, who led the project for a decade, making important enhancements and corrections to the effort. But despite King's efforts, construction at Muscle Shoals fell farther behind schedule. Funding was a perennial problem that caused engineers to cut back on their labor force, further slowing the effort. Nor did it help when work paused after the notorious Jesse James gang intercepted and robbed the district's paymaster as he made his way from a bank in Florence to the engineer camp at Big Muscle Shoals on March 11, 1881. Enraged engineers and laborers formed a posse and pursued the robbers until losing their trail on the banks of the Cumberland River, effectively putting off any canal work whatsoever until they returned from the pursuit. Haltingly and ploddingly, the work dragged on.[60]

Barlow assumed control of the district in 1886, just as the Corps of Engineers expanded the district's scope of responsibility northward to include improvements on the Cumberland River as well as the Tennessee River.[61] Drawn to the most recent addition to the district's enlarged mission, Barlow devoted more of his time and energy to the Cumberland than to the Tennessee. He envisioned improving navigation on the Cumberland by constructing a system of thirty locks and dams similar to Merrill's planned system on the Ohio. As work began in 1888 a short distance upriver from Nashville on the first lock and dam in the system, Barlow moved his district headquarters from Chattanooga to Nashville. When citizens of Chattanooga held a mass meeting to protest the planned move, Barlow insisted that the work on Muscle Shoals was almost complete and that he was therefore needed more in Nashville where the Cumberland project was in its infancy and required more attention. Against this backdrop, George Goethals reported for duty to Barlow at his Nashville headquarters in October 1889.[62]

Barlow's reports leave little evidence indicating how he employed or interacted with Goethals. In Goethals's efficiency report for 1890, Barlow demonstrated a favorable opinion of his new subordinate, describing him as "energetic, industrious, prompt, & efficient in performance of duty," as well as "a true gentleman, an accomplished engineer, and a thorough army officer." But this report also hints at a detached lack of familiarity, as the only specific details that appear within his other comments were copied precisely from the individual report that Goethals had to produce summarizing his professional reading and study outside of the normal scope of his duties.[63] Furthermore, Barlow's reports on the district's operations leave little evidence that he had any military or civilian subordinates at all. Presumably, then, Barlow was either extraordinarily active, taking a direct, hands-on approach to managing work on the Tennessee and Cumberland Rivers and delegating little to his subordinates—or he was unhesitant to assume full credit for everything that happened in the district without acknowledging those in local control of the division's many projects.[64]

Available evidence suggests that Barlow attempted to shoulder an impossibly heavy load on his own. As the pace of construction on the Cumberland increased, he began to lose control and awareness of work on the Muscle Shoals. Describing progress made on the canals at Muscle and Elk River Shoals between July 1, 1889, and June 30, 1890, Barlow reported that "the eleven locks were completed and are in working order." Later, in the appendix attached to this report, Barlow indicated that as of June 30, none of the nine locks at Big Muscle Shoals nor either of the two locks at Elk River Shoals were operable because all of the locks were still missing the machinery needed to operate their gates and valves. Furthermore, tests of the locks had revealed that major structural problems plagued the canal. He revealed some of these setbacks to a local newspaper in January 1890, which reported that "a system of hydraulic engines will have to be put in at each lock, to facilitate their working as they are under to[o] high a pressure to be worked readily by hand."[65]

While Barlow's reports to his superiors about Muscle Shoals were inconsistent, the information he gave to the communities affected by the project was misleading at best. As early as the summer of 1889, the people of Florence anticipated the imminent opening of the canal. This community viewed itself as a rising commercial center and looked to the opening of the canal as the key to its future power and prosperity. The issues of the *Florence Herald* reveal much about the town's relationship with Barlow and his answers to the town's inquiries about the canal. In June 1889, the paper reported on an upcoming ceremony for the grand opening of the canal. In August, an article proclaimed, "It is confidently assured that the Tennessee River will be opened for through navigation on September 1" and that "only a little finishing up remains to be done." The following spring, the editors were "reliably informed that work on the canal is nearing completion." And in May 1890, they "learned that the Muscle Shoals canal would be ready to open in June, if no mishap occurred."[66]

By 1890, work at Muscle Shoals had been in progress for fifteen years, and the communities along the Tennessee River, particularly those around and upriver from the shoals, were growing increasingly restless. In June, one member of Florence's Chamber of Commerce complained to his congressman that "Barlow told me 18 months ago that he thought the canal would be opened July 1, 1889, but for some reason the work has dragged along from year to year in the most unreasonable manner."[67] In March, an enterprising reporter from the *Chattanooga Times* pressed the matter with Barlow, who replied with a monumental nonanswer. According the *Florence Herald*, Barlow "said in effect that if the water didn't go any higher and if the masonry stood the present test and if it didn't take too long to make the repairs now necessary, it was probable that in the course of four weeks he might be able to say something."[68]

Florence, however, had grown quite tired of Barlow's equivocations. The *Herald* fired a broadside at Barlow in its July 9, 1890, issue. The editors lamented that work on the canal had "dragged its slow length for more than a generation," noting that "a formal opening has been promised year after year, the patience of those most vitally interested has been exemplary, and still we have no more than promises." Demanding a resolution to the problem, the editors declared that "the time has gone by, however, for promises to be satisfactory" because "the growing interests along the Tennessee have, within the last few years, grown too great and strong to be fed on such airy meat."[69]

The community's frustration matched that of Brig. Gen. Thomas Casey, then serving as the army's chief of engineers. Since the fall of 1889, Casey had been steadily increasing pressure on Barlow to explain the delays and articulate an appropriate plan of action so "a final presentation of the matter can be made, and the commercial interests of that section of the country know for a certainty what it can depend upon in the future."[70] Tired of the delays and concerned about opening the river before an anticipated increase in railroad fares in the fall, Casey considered drastic options to resolve the problem.

Hearing rumors of his possible relief, Barlow wrote to Alabama's powerful Joseph Wheeler, an ex-Confederate general and sitting congressman from northern Alabama, asking if the rumors were true. "If such a project is on foot," he complained, "it must have originated, I think, from the pressure brought to bear on the Washington authorities to have the canal opened at an early day." Indignantly, he wrote, "To relieve me just now would to my mind imply censure and I don't think I deserve it" because "it would be like depriving an officer of command near the close of the battle, on the eve of victory or defeat."[71] Seeking to save his position, Barlow turned to his lieutenant. Several days after venting to Wheeler, Barlow wrote to General Casey, "I have the honor to report that 1st Lieut. Geo. W. Goethals, Corps of Engineers, has been assigned—subject to the approval of the chief of engineers—to the local charge of the work of improving the Tennessee River, between Decatur, Ala. and Waterloo, Ala." Continuing, he explained that "the necessity for his services in local charge of this work" had become "more urgent than the temporary duty to which he was assigned at Nashville, Tenn."[72]

Willing to wait and see how this new arrangement would work out, Casey agreed to the request and allowed Barlow to remain in charge of the Nashville district. At the time, Goethals was already in the area leading a survey of Little Muscle Shoals. Barlow ordered him to finish the survey, then "establish an office, and take station temporarily at Florence" in order to complete and open the Muscle Shoals Canal in time to allow passage through the canal prior to a scheduled hearing on railroad rates in Chattanooga that fall. Goethals complied and assumed local control of the Muscle Shoals Canal on August 11, 1890.[73]

He soon discovered the full extent of the canal's structural problems. Sections of its walls and embankments failed to retain water when the canal was filled to maximum capacity. The problem was most extreme below the highest lock in the system, where water passed freely through the embankment and threatened the structural integrity of the canal's retaining walls. The necessary repair work had been under way for some time prior to his arrival in Florence, but Goethals found that it was not being carried on with an appropriate sense of urgency. He put new energy into the effort by organizing two shifts for round-the-clock work to accelerate repairs and taking personal charge of the night shift.[74]

By October, the repairs were mostly complete, and tests validated the structural integrity of the canal. Having learned from Barlow's mistakes the importance of fostering open and cordial relations with the interested public, Goethals invited several journalists and residents of Florence to tour the canal and observe preparations to open it for navigation. To much local acclaim, Goethals and his crew of engineers and laborers filled the entire length of the canal system from the Elk River Shoals to Big Muscle Shoals on November 8, 1890, and formally

This advertisement is indicative of how central the river trade was to late nineteenth-century communities along the Tennessee River. It is no coincidence that this image so explicitly connects the river and its steamships to a local industrial exposition as the Muscle Shoals Canal was about to open. (Library of Congress, Prints and Photographs Division, LC-DIG-ppmsca-42007)

opened the system for commercial navigation two days later. The same day, the steamer *R. T. Cole* crossed the canal with a shipment of grain bound for Chattanooga. It arrived before the hearing on railroad rates, to the delight of communities and businesses along the middle Tennessee River.[75]

The army rewarded Goethals for his success. He took and passed the examination for promotion to captain, although he would have to wait until January 1892 to be promoted.[76] More important, the chief of engineers gave Goethals command of his own district. On March 18, 1891, the Corps of Engineers created an independent engineering district at Florence, responsible for maintaining and operating the Muscle Shoals Canal and for managing all improvements on the Tennessee River between Chattanooga and Colbert Shoals. Acknowledging his successful completion of the Muscle Shoals Canal, the chief of engineers placed Goethals in charge of the district.[77]

This was Goethals's first independent command. When he originally arrived in Florence to assume local control over work on the Muscle Shoals in August 1890, he was still a subordinate of Barlow's and a part of the Nashville District. Having always been subordinate to a nearby commander, Goethals's previous duties had been limited to the realm of technical engineering problems. Now he faced significantly more complex problems of organizational leadership, including force structure, administration, logistics, and advocacy. The experience taught him much, providing practical instruction on similar problems he would face later in his career in Panama and in Washington during World War I. In this way, Goethals's duties in Florence closely aligned with the army's preferred experiential method of officer development, working in this case exactly as intended.[78]

By placing Goethals in charge of the Florence District, the chief of engineers took a significant risk. Although he had graduated from West Point and accepted his commission nearly eleven years earlier, and although he had already proven his abilities and potential for continued success, Goethals was still a lieutenant with a relatively limited base of experience. Of forty-nine engineering districts dedicated to river and harbor improvements in 1891, only sixteen were commanded by officers below the rank of major. And only two of these, including the newly created Florence district, were commanded by lieutenants. By giving a district to Goethals, Casey not only demonstrated confidence in his abilities but also presented him with opportunities that al-most none of his peers shared. Even in 1892, after Goethals had been promoted to captain and the Corps of Engineers had consolidated some of its districts, only fifteen out of forty-five districts dedicated to river and harbor improvements were commanded by officers below the rank of major.[79]

The Florence District, defined by four major project clusters, pre-sented plenty of challenges and opportunities for Goethals to learn and grow, both as an engineer and as an organizational leader. Close to Chattanooga—encompassing a stretch of river from the area known as "the Suck" down to Guntersville, Alabama—Goethals managed work to clear natural obstructions from the river and improve the channel by blasting and dredging its shallows. At Elk River and Big Muscle Shoals, his engineers and laborers busily operated, improved, and maintained the canal system. At Lower Muscle Shoals, where a planned canal failed to attract the necessary budget appropriations, Goethals's crews limited their efforts to improving the depth of the channel by dredg-ing the riverbed and constructing wing dams along the river embank-ments. Farther downriver, Goethals and his engineers drafted plans and began working on a canal through Colbert and Bee Tree Shoals.[80]

Simultaneously managing multiple projects across more than 250 miles of river provided an excellent practical lesson in organizational leadership. From Barlow's negative example in 1889 and 1890, Goeth-als learned that a district engineer could not become personally in-volved in all of the minute details in one project without losing sight of the rest of the district's work. An effective leader must be able to identify the critical points that require personal involvement and at-tention and willingly delegate direct responsibility for other points—with clear guidance and general supervision—to trusted subordinates. When Goethals first arrived in Florence in August 1890, he was ex-tremely involved in minute details, going so far as to oversee the night shift personally. This was entirely appropriate at the time because the project was at a point of crisis and he had been sent specifically to see the Muscle Shoals Canal through to a rapid completion.

But he could not sustain that approach as a district engineer. Like Major King at Muscle Shoals from 1876 to 1886, Goethals subdivided his district. He organized his divisions around each of the district's four project clusters and placed one of his civilian assistants in charge of each division, effectively making one subordinate in charge of each of his principal lines of effort. This approach also sparked one of the more meaningful professional and personal relationships in Goethals's life. Sydney B. Williamson was a civilian engineer who had joined the Florence District at the behest of his brother, another engineer who served as Goethals's division chief responsible for improvements between Elk River Shoals and Chattanooga in 1891.

After Williamson proved his worth on a survey upriver, Goethals brought him into the district headquarters to help create plans for the canal at Colbert and Bee Tree Shoals. On the job, Williamson was never happier than when his supervisors allowed him to "do the work in my own way except as to the regulations and general policies of the Engineer Department." He thoroughly enjoyed working for and with Goethals. In turn, Goethals developed great faith in Williamson, entrusting him with the district's most difficult technical problems. Thus began one of Goethals's few lifelong friendships and closest professional relationship. Williamson would serve as his trusted deputy in every major engineering assignment he held in the future. More important, this organizational structure allowed Goethals to manage the entire district more effectively and gave him the flexibility to focus his personal attention on points of friction as they arose.[81]

Managing the Florence District also exposed Goethals to problems of logistics and personnel administration—problems to which he had only limited exposure in past assignments. He led a permanent workforce of approximately seventy people dedicated to operating and maintaining the canals at Elk River Shoals and Muscle Shoals. The workforce fluctuated periodically when certain projects demanded hired labor rather than contracted labor. Goethals was responsible not only for planning and executing the projects within his district but also for paying salaries; acquiring and maintaining tools, boats, machines, and a small railroad; feeding, housing, and looking after the health of the workforce; and projecting and managing an annual budget. Although proficiency in administration and logistics is an essential element of high command, most army officers in the nineteenth century received no training whatsoever in these areas. Those who became talented or at least passably proficient administrators and logisticians learned through practical experience. In Goethals's case, administering and supplying the Florence District was the sole foundational experience that taught him concepts, techniques, and procedures that he would use against much larger administrative and logistical problems while leading the construction of the Panama Canal and while serving as the War Department's chief logistician during World War I.[82]

Finally, this independent command provided Goethals an invaluable opportunity to refine his technical knowledge and project management abilities to levels that ultimately shifted the boundaries of what was then considered possible. Although managing the daily maintenance and operation of the canals and channel improvement projects occupied the bulk of the district's time and resources, the most significant project planned and implemented in the Florence District between 1891 and 1894 was the canal around Colbert and Bee Tree Shoals, the last notable hazards for river navigation in northern Alabama. The Colbert and Bee Tree Shoals constituted a nearly continuous eight-mile low-water hazard that was the district's natural next project after the Muscle Shoals Canal opened. Anticipating this, Goethals ordered surveys of the area to be completed in August and September 1890, and he developed a plan for a canal seven feet deep and eight miles long.[83]

The canal required a system of locks at its lower end near Riverton, Alabama, to mitigate the twenty-foot fall in the river from the head of the Colbert Shoals to the foot of the Bee Tree Shoals. Common wisdom of the time called for a flight of two locks. Goethals believed it could be accomplished through a single lock with an unprecedented twenty-five-foot lift. In consultation with his trusted assistant Williamson, Goethals developed a plan and pitched it to skeptical superiors in Washington. They doubted that such a lock—nearly double the lift of the highest locks then existing in the United States—could be built. In 1892, a centralized board of more conservative officers forced revisions to the plan, calling for two locks separated by a mile-long pool, with respective lifts of twelve and thirteen feet each. Undeterred, Goethals continued to advocate for his plan for a single lock. By 1893, he had managed to persuade the chief of engineers to approve the single-lock plan over the continued objection of the original board. Construction began that summer.[84]

The effort did not go smoothly, but it ultimately succeeded. Excavation of the lock site was extremely troublesome because it was mired in quicksand that seemed to have a knack for breaking expensive equipment. Construction fell further behind when the contractor hired to build the lock walked off the job. Goethals then eschewed the contracting system and placed Williamson in charge of construction. Together, their design and successful construction of the Riverton Lock at the foot of the canal around Colbert and Bee Tree Shoals established the precedent for the mega-locks they would design and build in Panama twenty years later.[85]

Goethals did not stay in Florence long enough to see the completion of the canal and its innovative high-lift lock. By opening the Muscle Shoals Canal, successfully managing an independent district for more than three years, then designing and doggedly advocating for the Riverton Lock, Goethals had caught the attention of the chief of engineers, Brig. Gen. Thomas L. Casey. When an officer on his staff in Washington died unexpectedly in September 1894, Casey selected Goethals to fill the vacancy. In early October 1894, Goethals received orders that the Nashville District would reabsorb his Florence District and that he was to report to Washington immediately for duty on Casey's small staff of three engineer officers.[86]

Thus closed an important chapter in Goethals's career. His assignments with the Department of the Columbia and the First Cincinnati District from 1882 to 1885 and then with both the Nashville District and the Florence District from 1889 to 1894 were his most significant developmental experiences in the army. While West Point imbued Goethals with a sense of purpose and a deep identification with the army, and the Engineer School of Application improved his abilities as an engineer, Goethals learned how to be an innovative engineer and an effective officer through practical experience during these assignments. In combination, they provided enough opportunities to allow Goethals to make a name for himself within the Corps of Engineers and the army more generally, and provided him with the skills he later used to great effect in Panama and during the First World War. Notably, however, the army had taken no active measures to ensure Goethals's assignments afforded him with such opportunities. No discerning individual who recognized what experiences Goethals needed to develop properly determined Goethals's assignments during this period in his career.

Instead, a confluence of his own talent, personal connections, and chance—with the latter being the crucial enabling element in the equation—shaped Goethals's early career and provided the foundation upon which all of his future successes would eventually rest. Pure chance placed Goethals in an invaluable assignment under Merrill on the Ohio; the assignment was entirely contingent upon the fact that he happened to anger Miles by refusing an Alaskan expedition at the exact moment that the army created a vacancy at Cincinnati by promoting and transferring Merrill's long-serving deputy. Chance alone also put Goethals in a position to gain an independent command with all its fruitful experiences. Although the command was the direct result of the success he forged in a difficult situation, he arrived in Nashville in the first place not by any purposeful army design but because poor Lt. Graham Fitch fell gravely ill and needed to be replaced at a moment when Goethals was an expendable officer filling a thoroughly trivial position. His earlier assignment at West Point, where he had to immerse himself in a newly adopted textbook that reflected the most recent advances in civil engineering and likely learned the principles he applied in Florence, resulted in part from a similar state of temporary expendability. Goethals was very lucky to receive the opportunities he did. Because of his talents, he consistently rose to the occasion and took maximum advantage of his good fortune. In doing so, important people noticed and began to open doors that led to other particularly valuable experiences unavailable to the vast majority of his peers.

Goethals, however, never understood that the effectiveness of his own experiential development was both exceptional and highly contingent. As he continued to excel within the army, he believed that his success was the result of a well-designed and well-executed experiential model of officer development that shaped his early career. His faith in that model only grew stronger as his career progressed.

Finding success despite an unstandardized and highly contingent system of development that relied upon loosely controlled notions of experiential development, Goethals became conditioned to believe that such a system necessarily breeds success. He placed great value in learning by experience, which he described in 1922 as "the only school that is worth anything."[87] This was not a unique thought; it reflected the views of many of those officers who entered the army between 1870 and 1890 and went on to become its senior leaders in the early twentieth century. One such officer used his required officer's lyceum essay to offer a full-throated rejection of formal education and classroom training, characterizing it as "wisdom crammed down our throats like food down the necks of Strasbourg geese."[88] Another gave more romantic expression to the objection against formal training and education, claiming that true officers were "captains by spiritual commission," and that any single officer "cannot be educated into a commander of men any more than he can [be educated] into a poet, or an artist, or a Christian."[89]

Such views reinforced older and increasingly outdated attitudes about professionalism and officer development that continued to affect the army. As a result, the army developed and reinforced an institutional culture within its officer corps that was generally conditioned to reject the value of formal training and education and to resist reforms meant to forge a legitimate place for education within the institution.

This cultural preference was rooted in the disposition of the frontier army, which sharply limited the extent to which its units could train and prepare for war. Spread out among a network of small outposts and at peace more often than it was at war, the army rarely had the opportunity to mass units of any appreciable size in the same place and at the same time. This meant that soldiers usually did not have the opportunity to participate in large-scale maneuvers against a peer or superior opposing force, or operate in cooperation with other branches of the army—infantry, cavalry, artillery, engineers, etc. There were, however, more significant consequences at the institutional level. The army was never able to test its systems for mobilizing and sustaining a large force in a time of war, nor could it provide the vast majority of its officers with any exposure to or experience in commanding and coordinating the operations of large bodies of troops. As one historian has rightly noted, echoing the sentiments of officers who experienced it, the army in the late-nineteenth century "appeared a place where officers learned all about commanding fifty dragoons on the western plains but nothing about anything else."[90]

Consequently, the reduction or elimination of its frontier mission was a necessary condition for reform in the US Army. It was no mere coincidence that the most significant elements of military reform in the late nineteenth century occurred in concert with the "closing" of the frontier. When a reluctant Congress allowed the army to begin closing its smaller outposts and consolidating larger units onto larger bases, a few leaders began experimenting with training maneuvers on scales not seen since the Civil War. At the same time, a cadre of energetic and reform-minded officers began to remold the Leavenworth schools, laying the groundwork for Ft. Leavenworth's rise as one of the nerve centers of military education in the twentieth century.[91]

But it was also no coincidence that even the most significant elements of military reform were fragmented, ill-coordinated, and unable to effect lasting institutional change. Experimentation with large-scale tactical maneuvers was a fairly limited practice in the late nineteenth century. And despite notable efforts by Arthur Wagner and Eben Swift, the Leavenworth Schools would not begin to fully mature until the 1910s.[92] While the US Census Bureau declared the American frontier to be "closed" in 1890 and the last of the army's campaigns against Native Americans concluded in 1891, the effect of the frontier upon the army was more lasting, having defined the army's identity for more than a century. Multiple generations of officers shaped, ratified, and internalized the methods and systems the army had adopted because of its disposition and mission on the frontier, making such methods and systems institutionalized habits firmly embedded within the very core of the service. With the frontier inextricably woven into its identity and its institutional culture, the US Army was reluctant to accept the fact that although born of necessity, changing conditions and the passage of time had rendered some of its most important systems and processes unnecessary and arcane.

Consequently, the army's institutional culture—defined by its frontier requirements and experiences—failed to adapt as conditions outside the institution changed. But perhaps this is unsurprising. Any human institution is subject to human nature, and humans are creatures of habit. Furthermore, such habits are made even stronger within institutions that promote and select their leaders from within. The army's institutional culture failed to keep pace with external conditions because its leaders were not only accustomed to the habits of the frontier army, but also convinced that these habits were in fact best practices. In a self-generating cycle, leaders who believed they owed their successes to old habits preserved arcane habits, systems, and processes that were no longer justifiable in the absence of the conditions that spawned them, sharply limiting the effect of an ambitious program of reform that would be undertaken as the nineteenth century gave way to the twentieth.

3

War, Reform,
and Resistance

After departing Alabama in 1894, George W. Goethals embarked upon a new phase in his career. The next thirteen years exposed him to larger issues facing the Corps of Engineers and the army as a whole, issues on a level that made much of his previous work and concerns seem trivial and parochial. By consistently challenging him to think beyond immediate priorities and the relatively local problems of one major project, Goethals's assignments between 1894 and 1907 placed him squarely within the intersection of external conditions forcing change within the army, those parts of the army responsible for implementing change, and the stifling response of the army's increasingly outdated institutional culture.

Although the army insulated itself from new trends in education and training emerging within civil professions and American society more broadly, it remained relatively well connected to the society it served. Try as it might to control its own environment, external influences over which it had no control did much to shape the army. One such influence was the closing of the frontier, a gradual process that Americans widely considered to be complete by 1890, when Goethals was working on the Tennessee River. Despite the lasting influence the frontier held upon the army's institutional culture, a drastic change to the context within which the army had existed for more than a century necessarily meant that the army had to change. For most of its existence, the purpose of the army had been to defend the coasts and police the frontier. Now that there was no frontier to police, the very purpose of the army was an open question.

Progressivism influenced the way the army addressed that question. A diverse reform movement, "progressivism" refers to the collective body of public and private responses to social, economic, and political problems springing from and related to the complex and intertwined processes of urbanization, industrialization, and modernization that characterized American life in the late nineteenth and early twentieth centuries.[1] Buoyed by advancements in science, technology, and managerial systems and theories, as well as a rapid exchange of ideas among American and European activists grappling with the similar issues, American society adopted what one historian has described as a new spirit of "active interventionism." Individual and collective intervention characterized a reformist impulse that pervaded the United States from the 1890s through the 1920s. People and organizations intervened on an unprecedented scale to reform urban social conditions, business regulation, business management, government institutions, and government oversight. The reformist impulse so electrified society that even reactionaries were moved to channel it toward agendas of social control like the promotion of eugenics and the "Americanization" of immigrants.[2]

As the army grappled with the completion of westward continental expansion and all of its implications, progressivism and its reformist impulses were in the air. Paralleling trends in civil society, military reform stalled in the absence of a systemic shock. Just as Jacob Riis's widely publicized photographs of the urban poor in New York imparted a shock that lent significant momentum to municipal and social reformers in the 1890s, the war with Spain in 1898 provided a shock significant enough to give military reformers an opportunity to implement their ideas. But in the end, that shock was not quite severe enough. Ultimately, army reform was visionary in scope and intent but faulty in execution. Like progressive activists striving for reform in social, political, and commercial spheres, military reformers assumed that structural change within the institution would effect a more general and thorough institutional transformation. By focusing only on institutional structures, reformers unintentionally created a schism between those structures and the army's institutional culture, blunting the effect of reform and preventing reformers from achieving their goals in the early twentieth century.

But all of that remained to be seen when Goethals reported for duty in the office of the chief of engineers in October 1894. That office was the central administrative authority for the Army Corps of Engineers. It programmed and managed congressional appropriations totaling nearly $35 million and coordinated the efforts of 118 engineer officers engaged in the construction and improvement of coastal fortifications, river and harbor improvements, various bridging and aqueduct projects, and the construction and renovation of public buildings throughout the country. It was also the higher headquarters for the army's only engineer battalion and the Engineer School of Application.[3]

Aside from a handful of civilian clerks, only four officers directly assisted the chief of engineers, and their duties varied widely. Some work was completely administrative, such as disbursing funds, producing orders, and printing manuals. Other duties were more technical in nature. As needed, these officers sat on engineering boards and commissions, reviewed plans and contracts, and advised congressional committees. Frequently, they served as a brain trust for the chief of engineers, informally weighing in on special projects and questions of general policy.[4] These officers were overburdened to the point that Brig. Gen. William P. Craighill, who replaced Thomas L. Casey as the chief of engineers in May 1895, successfully lobbied the secretary of war to authorize an additional engineer officer to be assigned to his office staff. Considering the relatively small size of the corps and the expansive mission for which it was responsible, this was no small feat.[5]

In the fall of 1894, Goethals was the most junior officer assigned to that office, so many of his duties were menial administrative tasks.[6] Occasionally, however, he also weighed in on important policy matters and served on various civil-military boards. On the strength of his record in Alabama, the chief of engineers assigned Goethals to provide technical advice to a Senate select committee considering the possibility of constructing an interoceanic canal in Nicaragua. In 1897, a new chief of engineers directed Goethals to confer with the Civil Service Commission to ensure that civilians hired by the Corps of Engineers adhered to rules and regulations established by the commission. Finally, in April 1898, Goethals was assigned to represent the Corps of Engineers on a board convened by the secretary of war to designate articles that would be prohibited for export as the nation mobilized for war against Spain.[7]

Each of these duties exposed Goethals to the nature and mechanisms of the relationship between the army and civil government, a rare opportunity given to very few junior officers in the late nineteenth-century army. Despite this, Goethals was quite unhappy with his assignment in Washington. Like most of his peers, Goethals subscribed to a vision of leadership based on a romantic perception of Civil War officers marching calmly into danger at the front of their units, an image that was growing ever more at odds with the ever more dominant managerial theories and practices embraced by an increasingly industrialized society and economy. Like many of his contemporaries, Goethals was not an easy convert to the idea that an expeditionary army capable of operating in an industrialized world required talented officers in offices and headquarters coordinating myriad logistical and administrative requirements as much as it required talented officers in the field inspiring their troops, if he ever truly came around to the idea at all.[8] In later years when others mentioned him as a candidate to become the chief of engineers in recognition of his work in Panama, Goethals could reply with complete honesty, "I am not an applicant, nor do I care of the position, the work not being to my liking." Continuing, he explained, "These views are not new, for I held them during my service as Assistant to the Chief, and have not changed my mind."[9]

Goethals did not hide his displeasure. In the fall of 1897, Brig. Gen. James Wilson knew his most junior assistant was getting restless. Accordingly he arranged for Goethals to relieve the instructor of practical military engineering at West Point when that officer's assignment expired the following summer. The secretary of war agreed, and Goethals prepared to depart for West Point.[10] But the move would not happen on time. It was interrupted by events in Cuba.

Tensions between Spain and the United States had been rising since the outbreak of the Cuban Insurrection in 1895. While the American public generated vocal and occasionally material support for the Cubans, the United States officially maintained a neutral position.

At the same time, the successive administrations of Grover Cleveland and William McKinley pressured Spain to pacify Cuba and grant it political autonomy. Sensing that the point of victory was near, Cuban revolutionaries rejected autonomy, opting instead to fight for complete independence. An ineffective and heavy-handed Spanish response fueled increasing and genuine support among the American public for Cuban revolutionaries. Tensions escalated into a full-blown crisis in a single week in early February 1898. First, American newspapers published a stolen letter written by the Spanish ambassador to the United States that insulted President McKinley, calling him a weak and pandering leader. Then the USS *Maine* mysteriously exploded while in Havana's harbor, killing more than two-thirds of the ship's crew. As the American public clamored for war and Spanish officials convinced themselves that a war abroad was the only way to avoid political upheaval at home, policymakers on both sides lost the ability to pursue effective diplomacy. On April 25, 1898, the United States declared war against Spain, and its army began to mobilize.[11]

The army expanded rapidly through a congressional authorization to increase the strength of its regular forces, a presidential call for volunteers, and broad popular enthusiasm for the war. Units mustered into service so quickly that they outpaced efforts to organize headquarters staffs to command and control them. The frontier army had no need for the division or corps headquarters necessary in wartime, leaving it in the awkward position of simultaneously raising a large army and building the means to command it. Organizing their headquarters haphazardly in an attempt to catch up to their subordinate units, division and corps commanders took individual initiative on assembling their headquarters, calling for officers with whom they were personally acquainted as they realized certain specialties and skill sets were missing from their staffs.

In early May, Maj. Gen. John R. Brooke, the recently designated commander of the First Army Corps, cabled General Wilson to ask for Goethals's services as his chief engineer. Wilson needed no convincing, endorsing the request with a notation that the position of chief engineer for a corps was "a position for which [Goethals] is thoroughly qualified by his high character, soldierly ability, and scientific attainments."[12] On May 20, 1898, Goethals received orders to report for duty under Brooke at Chickamauga National Military Park, the designated mobilization center for the First Army Corps. The assignment came with a temporary promotion to lieutenant colonel of volunteers.[13]

Wartime exigencies heightened the degree to which personal connections influenced officers' assignments. Commanders held more sway over a given officer's assignment than any centralized authority in Washington. Since 1894, Goethals's reputation had put him in high demand. Shortly after Brooke secured Goethals's assignment with the First Army Corps, the newly designated chief engineer of all armies in the field requested that Goethals be assigned as his own assistant and sent to accompany the Fifth Army Corps on its campaign in Cuba.[14] Not long afterward, the chief of engineers nominated Goethals to serve as a lieutenant colonel in the first of three regiments to be raised to form a brigade of volunteer engineers that Congress had belatedly authorized.[15]

Ultimately, the decision fell to Brooke and Goethals themselves. Goethals learned of the competing requests shortly after reporting to Brooke at Chickamauga on May 30. In a passive refusal of Ludlow's request, the adjutant general—the ultimate authority on officer assignments and transfers—replied that while Goethals was assigned to the First Army Corps, a transfer to Ludlow's staff was possible only if Brooke agreed and wrote the orders. Predictably, Brooke was unwilling to let him go.[16] The chief of engineers left the transfer to the volunteer engineer regiment up to Goethals himself. He was torn, commenting to his son that "Genl. Brooke doesn't want me to go and I don't reckon what to do." Ultimately, he acceded to pressure from Brooke and declined the appointment in favor of maintaining his position as chief engineer in the First Army Corps.[17]

Goethals likely regretted that decision upon arriving at his assigned campsite, which he was surprised to find only a short distance downhill from a slit trench that was used as a latrine. "During the heavy rains," he testified after the war, "our sink [latrine] was flooded out, and naturally the drainage was toward the tents."[18] Such amateurish and unsanitary mistakes characterized the army's mobilization for war in 1898. Poorly sited mobilization camps became pestilent breeding grounds of disease. The First and Sixth Army Corps mobilized at Chickamauga Park, which became one of the more notorious mobilization centers of the war as scandalous reports, some accurate and some exaggerated, filled the pages of widely read newspapers during the heyday of muckraking journalism.[19]

For Goethals, experiences at Chickamauga underscored the importance of preventive health measures and strict enforcement of sanitation regulations. To his family, Goethals reported only, "It is awfully dirty out here."[20] He was considerably more candid to postwar investigators, recalling that rides through the woods revealed "evidences of the men having defecated all through the woods without reference to sinks [latrines]" and that his "attention was particularly called to our own headquarters, which were not in a very good condition as far as policing was concerned."[21] Goethals further testified that many commanders at the camp selected bivouac sites in unhealthy locations because they deemed healthier locations to be more useful as training and drilling grounds. Such sites became dangerously overcrowded as inexperienced leaders failed to comprehend the relationship between dispersion and sanitation. Units were encamped in and among their own filth or upon ground that was too rocky to permit the excavation of sufficiently deep latrines to prevent unsanitary runoff from contaminating entire campsites. Beyond this, Goethals's testimony suggested that officials had made a fundamental error in selecting Chickamauga Park as a mobilization site for two entire corps, as the sole uncontaminated water supply that was available to provide water to the camp could not support both corps once they were fully manned.[22]

Despite such poor and inexcusably preventable conditions, Goethals found the mobilization at Chickamauga somewhat mundane. He spent much of June working to improve the water supply. Goethals conducted the necessary surveys and ran a line to a supplemental source at a nearby spring, but General Brooke ordered work on the water supply to be stopped when he heard a rumor that 15,000 of his soldiers were to be diverted to the Fifth Army Corps at Tampa, Florida.[23] With newfound downtime, Goethals indulged an interest in Civil War history perhaps nurtured by the fact that he was encamped on an old battlefield of that war, venturing out to visit nearby battle sites in and around Chattanooga and Lookout Mountain. He also began visiting the camps of various volunteer regiments at Chickamauga and took the initiative to instruct their officers on how to conduct reconnaissance, continuing this improvised training program throughout late June and July.[24] Seeing that his reliable assistant from Florence, Sydney B. Williamson, had been commissioned as a captain in the Third Regiment of Volunteer Engineers, which also mobilized at Chickamauga, Goethals persuaded Brooke to assign Williamson as his assistant. Otherwise, he watched the war unfold in newspapers, following the Santiago campaign and the decisive attacks up the San Juan and Kettle Hills with great interest and waiting for the First Army Corps to receive orders that were painfully slow to arrive.[25]

Confusion, disorganization, and muddle characterized the American war effort, particularly at higher levels of command. Goethals and the rest of the First Army Corps headquarters staff learned that they were to plan and lead the invasion of Puerto Rico not from a War Department directive but from the newspapers.[26] Fortunately, Brooke had acted upon rumors suggesting such a possibility and had asked Goethals to procure maps and information concerning Puerto Rico. Goethals sent a request for both maps and information to the chief of engineers on June 29, who promptly forwarded the request to the War Department's Bureau of Military Information. Receiving no helpful response, Goethals telegraphed the bureau directly on July 8 and shortly thereafter "received by return mail a copy of a map of Puerto Rico, but no information whatever concerning that island."[27] The corps continued to prepare blindly until the War Department confirmed in the middle of the month that Brooke would lead a detachment of approximately 5,000 men from the corps in the Puerto Rico Campaign.[28]

Following the surrender of Spanish forces defending Santiago de Cuba on July 17, 1898, Secretary Russell Alger ordered Gen. Nelson Miles to assume command of a previously planned expedition to Puerto Rico. Ravaged by disease from their operations in Cuba, Shafter's Fifth Army Corps was in no shape to participate in the campaign. Accordingly, the War Department selected a conglomeration of units from the First and Fourth Army Corps, encamped at Chickamauga and near the ports of Charleston and Tampa, to join Miles and nearly 3,000 soldiers who had been assigned to reinforce Shafter on Cuba but had never debarked from their troop transports. These orders cobbled together a force of approximately 17,000 men. Although the War Department had directed Miles to land at Cape Fajardo on the northeast coast of Puerto Rico and make a quick strike west to capture San

Juan, Miles elected to change course after sailing out of Guantanamo Bay. Suspecting that the Spanish expected him to land as close to San Juan as possible, Miles chose instead to land on the southern coast.[29]

As Miles sailed from Cuba, the War Department coordinated the movement of the remainder of his invasion force to their ports of embarkation and transported them to Puerto Rico. The portion of First Army Corps selected to participate in the campaign departed Chickamauga Park on July 23, 1898, to await transportation at Newport News, Virginia. They were fortunate; cases of typhoid fever in the unsanitary camp climbed dramatically beginning in late July and doubled by the middle of August.[30] But Goethals was unaware of his comparatively favorable luck. When he boarded the USS *St. Louis* at Newport News on July 28, he noted that "the bedding was foul, very bad; ventilation, none at all, and the meals were simply abominable."[31]

Brooke's corps had a woefully inadequate understanding of the island. The War Department had failed to send anything more than a single map of the island in response to Goethals's requests in July. General Brooke, however, noticed that a small detachment of Puerto Ricans who were to serve as scouts and guides for General Miles had also embarked on USS *St. Louis*, and he sent his engineer to interview them. Goethals spent most of the voyage collecting from them "all the information concerning the island, roads, etc., needed by the Commanding General for intelligent operations."[32] Rumors, newspaper accounts, a map sent by an apparently indifferent War Department clerk, and hurried interviews with a group of expatriates of unknown reliability were all that Brooke, Goethals, and the rest of the staff had to inform their actions. Many disastrous campaigns have begun with a similar lack of intelligence and preparation.

Landings had commenced on Puerto Rico's southwest coast at Guánica on the morning of July 25, 1898. After a minor skirmish, American soldiers established a secure beachhead. The next day, Miles expanded the beachhead at Guánica and landed a division at Ponce near the center of the island's southern coast. More reinforcements landed on July 31 at both Ponce and Guánica. Recently abandoned by Puerto Rican militiamen who either left the front lines for their homes or defected outright to the American side, the outnumbered Spanish troops began to retreat inland after a few small-unit actions. When the *St. Louis* and accompanying transports steamed into Ponce on July 31,

Miles directed Brooke to collect his forces and prepare to land forty miles to the east, near a village named Arroyo.[33]

Goethals splashed ashore with the lead elements of the First Army Corps on August 2, 1898, meeting no opposition. During the time that it took Brooke to disembark all of his men, Goethals's duties ranged widely. In the nineteenth century, the engineer on a headquarters staff was a genuinely multipurpose officer, responsible for a wide range of duties including intelligence, reconnaissance, relaying messages for the commander, preparing defensive positions, and establishing or improving lines of communication. For the first two days, Brooke placed Goethals in command of the perimeter of outposts securing the beachhead.[34] Once the corps was mostly ashore, Goethals, along with Williamson, received orders to return to the beach, "charged with building a wharf to facilitate landing supplies—the rough surf was preventing landing supplies on the beach itself." The dock was a relatively simple project and took little time to complete.[35]

By August 5, all of Brooke's soldiers had landed and supplies were starting to move ashore in bulk. Expanding the base of operations, one of Brooke's regiments had seized the nearby town of Guayama after a brief skirmish. Although now poised to support a general offensive, Brooke still lacked intelligence about the position and disposition of the Spanish.[36] With the dock complete, Brooke ordered Goethals to scout ahead of the corps and develop the intelligence needed to prepare for the pending offensive. Taking along his trusted friend Williamson, Goethals executed several thorough reconnaissance missions, finding that the Spanish had "occupied the heights three or four miles inland from the town that commanded the highway leading to San Juan." It was risky work on both ends of these missions. Williamson later recalled that "the most dangerous feature of the reconnaissance was getting back through our own outpost composed of green volunteer troops that were liable to shoot first and investigate afterwards."[37]

Meanwhile, Miles had completed his plan for the conquest of Puerto Rico. He envisioned four assaulting columns converging on San Juan. In the west, two columns starting from Guánica and Ponce would move from south to north, converging at the town of Arecibo on Puerto Rico's northwest coast and then moving east against San Juan. In the center of the island, one column would move northeast from Ponce against the main Spanish defensive position at Aibonito, a village well situated upon high ground in a mountain range that bisects the interior of the island from east to west. There, 1,300 Spaniards blocked the main highway leading to San Juan. The First Army Corps constituted the fourth assaulting column, under orders to support the attack against Aibonito by moving against Cayey from Arroyo and Guayama, then cutting across the highway behind Aibonito in order to isolate its defenders. After Aibonito fell, Miles intended the two columns to move north along the main road to San Juan.[38]

The offensive began on August 9, 1898. What neither Miles nor Brooke knew, however, was that the Spanish were ill-prepared to mount an effective defense. Because the Puerto Rican militia had gone home or defected, the Spanish mustered only 8,000 defenders, less than half the strength of the American forces under Miles. Furthermore, despite their comparatively small force, the Spanish attempted to defend too many points at once. Consequently, they were unable to mass enough combat power at any point to defend effectively against any of the four assaulting columns.[39]

The First Army Corps watched idly as the three columns to its west opened the offensive, with the westernmost units making the most rapid progress. Readying his corps to move, Brooke sent the Fourth Ohio Volunteer Infantry Regiment out on a reconnaissance in force that ended with a skirmish that indicated Spanish forces were entrenched in the high ground near Cayey.[40] Brooke spent the next few days planning his attack. He hoped to delay the action until his corps could be reinforced by an additional regiment of volunteers, but opted to take earlier action when he learned that the center column was making unexpectedly rapid progress toward Aibonito.[41]

On the evening of August 11, Brooke issued orders to advance on Cayey shortly before dawn the following morning. But inexperienced leaders of his volunteer regiments failed to coordinate their movements properly, and the corps began its movement two hours behind schedule. Brooke sent Goethals and Williamson ahead to conduct a final reconnaissance of the Spanish lines, then relied on them to post the lead battalion of skirmishers. With this task accomplished, and with anxiety mounting as his first taste of combat drew near, Goethals returned to his commander, who was positioning a battery of light artillery that he intended to use to open the battle. Satisfied with the battery's position, Brooke directed Goethals and the rest of his staff to

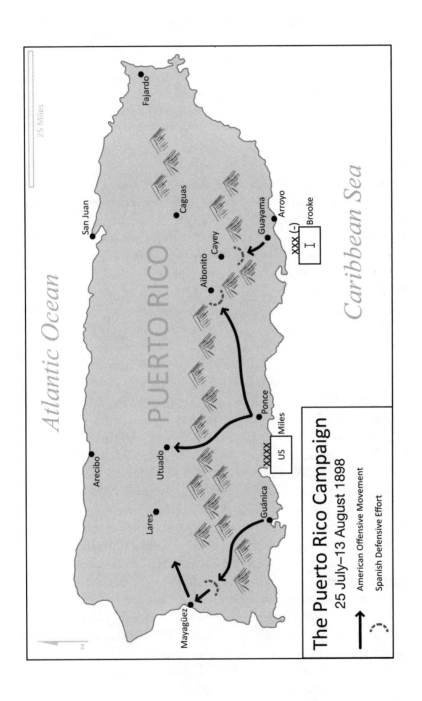

Atlantic Ocean

PUERTO RICO

Caribbean Sea

25 Miles

N

Fajardo

San Juan

Caguas

Arecibo

Lares

Utuado

Ponce

Guánica

Mayagüez

Aibonito

Cayey

Guayama

Arroyo

XXX (-)
I
Brooke

XXXX
US

Miles

The Puerto Rico Campaign
25 July–13 August 1898

American Offensive Movement

Spanish Defensive Effort

observe the artillery and adjust it as needed. It was then early evening, and the moment of battle had finally arrived as soldiers unlimbered the last artillery piece and hauled it into position. But the moment passed as quickly as it came. Just then, "a messenger came galloping up and shouted that he had an important dispatch." After reading the message, Brooke "abused the messenger for not caring more for his horse and telling him never to ride so hard again, after which he told us there would be no fight as peace had been declared."[42] With that, the battle was over before it even began.

Rather than feeling relieved to be out of danger, Goethals felt cheated. "Five minutes more," he lamented, "and the first shot would have been fired and then there could have been no stopping until after the Spaniards had been driven away . . . thus ends the war, I expect, and I haven't been under Spanish fire at all, I'm sorry to say, for the outpost firing doesn't count for anything as there were only a few shots fired on us."[43] While it seems inconsistent with any rational sense of self-preservation, Goethals's sentiments were genuine. His generation of officers had been educated at West Point and reared as junior officers by Civil War veterans in a time when veterans and society alike were constructing an idealized and romanticized memory of the war.[44] Like his peers, therefore, Goethals clung to a sense of war and military service that was more closely related to the Victorian Era than to the realities of modern industrialized warfare.

Describing the battle that wasn't, he wrote to his wife celebrating Brooke's performance in directing the emplacement of a single gun from a single artillery battery as the corps deployed for action. He wrote in terms reminiscent of the earliest phases of the earlier war, commenting, "The General was just magnificent; he was in khaki uniform, in the front, and had no fear for anyone but his staff."[45] Goethals's interpretation of the aborted battle is telling. Like many officers of his generation, he perceived the ideal officer to be a seasoned veteran in the thick of the action, undisturbed by imminent danger and calmly directing a seemingly small task rather than commanding his forces from a point farther to the rear that was more suitable for seeing, understanding, and effectively responding to what was happening to and around his entire corps.[46] Furthermore, in Goethals's view, a failure to experience battle cheapened his wartime service. This would be a constant source of insecurity throughout his career.

Goethals's perceptions reveal much about his generation of officers. Having entered an army that consciously idealized and idolized the Civil War, and having been nurtured early in their careers on war stories and advice from commanders and other senior officers who were veterans, Goethals's generation of officers thought about warfare and military service in outdated forms and terms of a bygone era. This was the essential feature of that generation's mindset. And it was that mindset that came to frame and define the incongruity between the army's institutional culture and its structures once change was under way to better prepare the army for the managerial and logistical requirements of modern industrialized warfare.

But for time being, Goethals stewed in Puerto Rico with no war to fight and with very little to do. He passed time by touring the island and collecting Spanish stamps and other relics to send back home to his sons. He was not enamored with the inhabitants, whom he viewed in racialized and racist terms. In a letter home, he observed that "the little boys and girls about here run around naked until they are about 7 or 8 years old—nearly all the men and women go barefooted." Continuing, he explained, "They are awfully dirty too, and I don't think there are any full blooded whites."[47] When Miles returned to the United States, Brooke assumed command of the occupation of Puerto Rico and brought Goethals with him to serve on his staff in this new capacity. There remained, however, little for Goethals to do. Always uncomfortable with idleness, Goethals wrote home, "Genl. Brooke wants me to stay here with him, but I don't care to unless I have something to do and to keep busy."[48] By the middle of September, he was miserable. "I want to get back very much," he wrote to his family. "I have no work to do, [and] everything is so filthy and dirty that I just cannot stand it here for any length of time."[49]

Goethals did not have to wait long for a reprieve. In the second week of September, General Wilson, still serving as chief of engineers, began taking steps to move his former subordinate to the Department of Practical Military Engineering at West Point, as originally planned. The Department of Practical Military Engineering was an important part of cadets' military training at West Point. It ran exercises that taught cadets how to design and dig field fortifications and entrenchments, conduct reconnaissance, execute topographical surveys, construct pontoon bridges, operate signaling and communications equipment, and employ siege materials and equipment.[50] Brooke opposed losing his engineer, forcefully but unsuccessfully protesting the transfer. Goethals relinquished his responsibilities in Puerto Rico on October 20, 1898, and was soon on his way back home to move his family to the Military Academy once again.[51]

Because much of the cadet training for which the Department of Practical Military Engineering was responsible occurred outdoors, it generally happened in the spring and summer. Goethals therefore had several other duties that kept him busy. Having reverted back to his regular army rank of captain, he was the commander of Company E of the army's sole engineer regiment. Company E provided a daily guard for the West Point garrison, maintained the artillery batteries and their emplacements, and supported field training for the cadets. In addition, Goethals served directly under the superintendent's command as the post engineer. In this capacity, he increased and improved West Point's water supply by identifying new local water sources and adding more pipelines and purification systems to handle the additional water they provided, and he supervised the renovation of the building that housed the academy's library.[52]

Goethals did not remain at West Point for long. General Wilson ordered him to appear before an examination board scheduled to convene in New York City on December 6, 1899. The board recommended him for promotion to major, with an effective date of rank of March 6, 1900.[53] Because the head of the Department of Practical Military Engineering was a captain's position, Wilson recommended that the new secretary of war, Elihu Root, approve orders to transfer Goethals to the engineer district based at Newport, Rhode Island, where he would be responsible for the maintenance and improvement of fortifications, rivers, and harbors in Rhode Island and southeastern Massachusetts.[54]

The experiential model of officer development informed Wilson's decision to send Goethals to Newport. Gen. Leonard Wood, a future army chief of staff who then commanded the forces still occupying Cuba, had requested Goethals's services on his own staff. He explained to Wilson, "I want a moderately young man, active and thoroughly tactful" to employ in a situation that "is difficult and requires great judgment and tact." Continuing, he wrote, "I should prefer above all others Major George W. Goethals if he is available." He then explained that his "next choice would be Captain David DuBois Gaillard, then Captain H. F. Hodges, Captain J. J. Morrow, and Captain McKinstry." Wilson replied, "Of the names you sent me, I have selected Capt. Hodges; he has had every class of duty nearly, river work, harbor work, fortification work, canal work, and was Lt. Col. of one of the Volunteer Engineer regiments during the Spanish war."[55] Perceiving service under Wood to carry little to no experiential value, Wilson refused to send Goethals—whom he thought still needed experiential development, especially in coastal defense and harbor improvements—and instead selected an officer whose more complete base of experience meant that the assignment in Cuba would do no harm to his professional development.

Wilson's actions demonstrate that the army's experiential model of officer development could have some merits if it was managed by perceptive leaders with effective oversight of the assignments process. The general saw a shortcoming in Goethals's base of developmental experience and deliberately acted to correct it. Leaders like Wilson, however, were not particularly common. Such active institutional-level measures to mitigate developmental deficiencies were rare, as Goethals's own career shows. Then in the third decade of his career, this was the first time that the Corps of Engineers ordered Goethals to a duty assignment specifically because it offered experiences in an area of engineering to which he had not yet been exposed. Despite the army's lingering reliance upon the experiential system of officer development, it rarely did anything to ensure its officers were exposed to the right experiences. While laudable, Wilson's carefully considered intervention was unusual.

Goethals reported for duty in Newport on August 31, 1900.[56] His new engineering district was large and multifaceted, responsible for both coastal fortifications and improvements of rivers and harbors throughout Rhode Island and southeastern Massachusetts. As district engineer, Goethals managed simultaneous efforts to establish or deepen anchorages and create more navigable channels in and around harbors in Martha's Vineyard, Nantucket, Cape Cod, and Rhode Island's Narragansett Bay, as well as to dredge river channels in the Taunton River in Massachusetts. In addition to this, routine work in the district included removing wrecked or sunk vessels that obstructed navigation in channels frequently used by fishermen and commercial shipping, especially near Buzzards Bay, Nantucket, Martha's Vineyard, and Block Island. Contractors did most of the work. While Goethals and his supporting staff—including the ever-present Sydney B. Williamson—monitored progress and disbursed funds for the contracted projects, they directed most of their effort to the coastal fortifications near Newport, Rhode Island, and New Bedford, Massachusetts.[57]

Contrary to Wilson's intentions, however, this became a worthwhile assignment for Goethals despite rather than because of its focus on coastal fortifications. Beyond late nineteenth-century technological improvements that allowed for the use of electricity and "disappearing" guns that could be raised to fire and lowered behind cover to load, there was little that was truly cutting-edge about the army's coastal defense programs, which were always engaged in a losing battle with time and technology. Systems of coastal defense planned before and after the Civil War were based on unrealistic appraisals of available resources and funds. Congress rarely funded fortification programs to the extent called for by planners, and construction could progress only at the rate that available labor, funds, and resources allowed.

Plans took decades to complete, while naval technology advanced at an exponentially greater pace in an increasingly industrialized world. Once finally complete, most new forts were already obsolete monuments to futility that had been designed to face decades-old naval threats that existed when the fortification systems were planned, but were woefully inadequate for the threats that had materialized in the intervening years. For example, the Endicott Board had convened in 1886 and was still the basis of coastal defense in 1900. The board had based its entire concept of defense around rifled artillery powerful enough to pierce twenty inches of armor on a warship at ranges of up to 1,500–2,000 yards. At the time Goethals reported for duty at Newport, however, the leading navies of the world already possessed ships armed with heavy cannon that were effective at ranges exceeding 3,000 yards and were only a few years away from beginning work on a new class of battleship that would boast heavy guns that could accurately engage targets nearly a mile away. American forts, then, would find themselves helpless against ships that could pound them into submission while loitering well out of range of defensive coastal artillery. Although considered to be one of the most important missions for the Corps of Engineers in the late nineteenth century, and although new technology that could be brought into coastal defenses offered some genuinely unique opportunities, an assignment focused mainly on coastal fortifications was inherently backward-looking.[58]

Nevertheless, the Newport assignment allowed Goethals to improve his already strong reputation as an energetic officer and a talented engineer. The army and navy planned to hold joint maneuvers near Newport in late September 1900, just one month after Goethals arrived in the city. The navy intended to exercise its North Atlantic Squadron and test tactics for penetrating coastal defenses while raiding a port. At the same time, the army wanted to test its defenses at the mouth of Narragansett Bay and was particularly interested in testing its use of the electric searchlight as a defensive weapon.[59] Goethals observed the exercise and sent a lengthy report to the chief of engineers. The report focused on possible uses of searchlights, strongly recommending that fortifications be equipped with multiple lights. "That there cannot be too many searchlights was very evident," he reported.[60] He emphasized the diverse roles they could play in the defense. In addition to searching for ships approaching a minefield, he experimented with a more active tactical role for the searchlights, using one to blind the pilot of the torpedo boat *Stiletto,* which caused that unfortunate sailor to lose his bearings and run the ship into a nearby wharf. According to Goethals, this action led naval officers to "assert that an additional light would have been as good as another battery" of artillery.[61]

General Wilson received Goethals's report enthusiastically, circulating it widely within the Corps of Engineers.[62] But its recommendations created a complicated problem. The existing power demands of forts' artillery emplacements—whose range-finding equipment, auxiliary ammunition hoists, and disappearing gun carriages were by then electrically powered—and of the buildings within the garrisons themselves consumed all of the generating capacity of the forts' simple power plants. Engineers had originally designed those plants to provide intermittent power to artillery emplacements alone, and only when they were actively in use. Existing power generation systems were therefore insufficient to support the extended use of multiple high-power searchlights in the forts.

To address the problem, Wilson created a board of engineers consisting of Goethals and two other officers. Together, the three officers created a larger central power station that became the new standard for coastal fortifications.[63] As the board's leader, Goethals wrote and presented a paper entitled "Electricity in Permanent Seacoast Defenses" to the American Institute of Electrical Engineers in May 1902. Well received within both the engineering community and the larger coastal defense community, the paper was reprinted in the *Journal of the United States Artillery* in 1903.[64] This improved Goethals's already excellent reputation at exactly the right time. In the spring of 1903, President Theodore Roosevelt and Secretary of War Elihu Root ordered Maj. Gen. Samuel B. M. Young to convene a board to select forty-two officers for service in the army's newly authorized General Staff Corps. On the strength of his well-known innovations—even if the effect of those innovations was limited due to the inherently regressive nature of the coastal defense mission—Goethals made the cut.[65]

Power and authority within the army had long been split between the commanding general and the powerful chiefs of autonomous supply and administrative bureaus, such as the adjutant general, quartermaster general, chief of ordnance, judge advocate general, and chief of engineers. The relative power of the commanding general waxed and waned throughout the nineteenth century according to shifting political winds and the personalities of successive commanding generals and secretaries of war. Politics and the relationship of the individuals holding those two offices twice made the relationship so tense and awkward that it drove the commanding general to remove his headquarters from Washington, DC.[66]

The bureau chiefs were more constant and consistent forces within the War Department. Generally less hierarchical than their colleagues of the line branches—over whom the commanding general reigned supreme—the bureau chiefs were more comfortable with a broadly consultative approach to managing the military, and they jealously guarded their respective spheres of expertise, influence, and authority. The bureau system was mired with inefficiency because of significant overlaps among the responsibilities of the several bureaus. For example, when Goethals worked on the problem of power generation in coastal fortifications, different aspects of his work fell under the purview of five bureaus: the Corps of Engineers for construction and power generation, the Quartermaster Department for lighting the

buildings of the forts' garrisons, the Signal Corps for power requirements of communications equipment, the Ordnance Department for
power requirements of the ammunition hoists, and the Artillery Bureau for power requirements of the gun emplacements, range-finding
equipment, and battery commanders' stations.[67] The old system had
not aged well. In the nearly four decades that had passed since the end
of the Civil War, the army ambled toward a critical turning point. Previously, except in times of war, the regular army's mission was to serve
as a frontier constabulary and as a coastal defense force. By the end of
Reconstruction, it was clear that the day was rapidly approaching when
there would be no frontier to police. Forced to reconsider the proper
role of the army, many officers came to believe that the proper role of
an army at peace was to prepare for war. Reflecting the trends of a society whose conception of professionalism was evolving, officers began
to debate the future of their profession in newly established professional associations and journals. Some looked to European nations as
potential threats and future adversaries and determined that the army
was structurally and doctrinally ill-prepared for modern warfare.[68] A
faction led by Civil War hero and William T. Sherman protégé Emory
Upton pushed for a centralized system of command and administration headed by a chief of staff and a general staff corps, modeled after
Upton's interpretation of the Prussian military's system of command
and administration.[69]

Upton and those of his followers who carried the argument forward after his untimely death in 1881 failed in their endeavors to alter
the existing American system of command and administration. Their
ideas did not gain enough traction because they exceeded the parameters of what was then considered possible and acceptable. Although
American society generally accepted the consolidation of professional
authority in civil professions such as medicine and law, it had not
shaken off its long-held distrust of centralized military authority. Furthermore, nothing had occurred to shake the army's confidence in
the bureau system. For much of the late nineteenth century, officers
and political leaders alike basked slothfully in the afterglow of Union
victory in the Civil War, seeing little reason to modify systems that
they believed had led to success. Compounding this, reformers' ideas
met a cold reception from congressmen who viewed traditional army
structures, systems, and processes as significant sources of political pa-

tronage, and they failed to win the unconditional support of an officer corps raised on the notion that the Civil War proved the value and efficacy of the army's traditional means and modes of operation. Crisis is the mother of all motivators, and it took a severe one to shift the parameters of both internal and external debates over military modernization and professionalization.[70]

That crisis came in 1898. Goethals's experience of a problematic mobilization for war was all too common. Mobilization camps were badly sited, supplied, and supervised, leading to scandalously preventable epidemics of disease. The War Department selected ports of embarkation serviced by limited, sometimes solitary, and generally underdeveloped rail lines, leading to congestion and confusion at the ports and scandalously ill-supplied troops embarking for operations in Cuba, Puerto Rico, and the Philippines. Much like Goethals's experience in the First Army Corps, most units departing the United States found that the War Department could not supply them with adequate maps or even the most rudimentary information about their objectives or the disposition of Spanish forces. Furthermore, war plans were virtually nonexistent, and events in both the Caribbean and the Pacific theaters took on a strikingly improvisational air. In fact, the War Department instructed Capt. Peyton C. March, who would later serve as chief of staff of the army during World War I, to decide for himself to which theater of the war his light artillery battery would be deployed.[71]

These real and significant blunders, as well as plenty of fabricated ones, came to light in almost real time in the age of muckraker journalism. Public opinion turned decidedly against the War Department, leading President McKinley to appoint a commission led by Grenville Dodge, a former Union general turned railroad executive who had previously served in Congress, to investigate the conduct of the war. Although the Dodge Commission's report balanced criticism of the War Department's most blatant errors with praise for what it accomplished in managing the country's first substantial overseas military expeditions, the public continued to demand accountability for the department's mismanagement. In the summer of 1899, McKinley acted, sacking Secretary of War Russell Alger and appointing in his place Elihu Root, a corporate lawyer from New York.[72]

That Root would implement the most significant institutional and organizational reforms in the army's history to that date came as a surprise. Root had no prior experience in or association with the military. McKinley selected him because he believed Root's excellent reputation as a lawyer made him well qualified to run a War Department wading into unprecedented legal territory, charged with administering the military occupation and civil reconstruction of Cuba, the Philippines, Puerto Rico, and Guam in the wake of the war with Spain. But a close study of the Dodge Commission's report and a closer association with the influential and reform-minded Adj. Gen. Henry C. Corbin and his assistant Lt. Col. William H. Carter made Root a devoted convert to the cause of military reform. Perceptively, Root recognized that the controversies surrounding the war with Spain and the possibilities suggested by various progressive reforms elsewhere in American society had shifted the parameters of what both the army and the American public considered possible and acceptable and that conditions both favored and necessitated reform. Furthermore, his legal background and excellent relationships with the nation's political elite gave him the political acumen to manage the legislative effort to turn reformers' theories into policy.[73]

The most important reforms of Root's tenure were the establishment of the Army War College, the overhauling of the nation's outdated and unreliable militia system, and the establishment of the General Staff Corps. The War College came first, as Root discerned that this would be not only the least controversial of the major reforms he had in mind but also the only one that he could institute without seeking the approval of Congress. Next, with the passage of the Dick Act in January 1903 came the first fundamental overhaul of the militia system since 1792. It imposed standardized tables of organization and equipment upon the National Guard, as well as established a formal training and support relationship between the regular army and the National Guard. The crowning achievement of Root's program of reforms came a few weeks later with the passage of the General Staff Act of 1903.[74]

Early in his tenure, Root came to the conclusion that modern warfare demanded a general staff. From his vantage point, the most important lesson of the war with Spain was that it revealed the need for an agency responsible for developing war plans and coordinating the complex array of activities and resources required to mobilize and deploy the army. In 1902, his first attempt at legislation for such a body failed due to an excess of ambition. Root had not only attempted to create a planning and coordinating agency in the form of the General Staff but also directed the closure or consolidation of several powerful bureaus. At the same time that Commanding Gen. Nelson A. Miles railed to a sympathetic Senate Military Affairs Committee filled with veteran volunteer officers of the Civil War that the General Staff would be a useless and unnecessary appendage because the existing system had succeeded in defeating the Confederacy, the bureau chiefs—with the notable exception of Adj. Gen. Henry C. Corbin—closed ranks and argued that the proposal would deprive the army of the benefit of their technical expertise. Root remained committed to the cause and orchestrated an intensive lobbying campaign in support of a second attempt. Securing the support of a critical mass of senior officers and political leaders, and masterfully dividing the opposition by backing away from his proposal to consolidate the bureaus, Root finally secured passage of the General Staff Act in February 1903 despite continued vocal opposition from Miles, whom Root conveniently sent on an tour of inspection in the Philippines when Congress considered the legislation.[75]

In a generous nod to Miles, the act that finally abolished the office of the commanding general, replaced it with the chief of staff, and established the General Staff took effect on August 15, 1903, exactly one week after Miles's retirement. In the meantime, Secretary Root directed the War College Board to prepare recommendations on how to select officers for detail to the General Staff. Although the War College had been formally established a year and a half earlier, it was not yet anything more than a small administrative board that Secretary Root had appropriated as an informal staff until such time as he was able to formally establish the General Staff Corps. The board recommended that "the personnel of the General Staff Corps should be selected with great care and should comprise the most competent officers in the Army at large." Root was only too happy to accept this recommendation, as he viewed the General Staff and a rationalized education system as the means of advancing talented officers through the ranks more quickly. With his excellent reputation, Goethals was widely considered to be among the best officers of his generation and was a natural selection for the new organization. With orders in hand to report for duty as part of the new General Staff Corps, Goethals formally transferred charge of the Newport District to his successor on May 22, 1903, and moved his family to Washington.[76]

As Goethals could heartily attest, establishing the General Staff did not end the bureau system. After the failed legislative effort in 1902, Root knew that he would have to accept some level of coexistence between the General Staff and the bureaus in order to secure support for the act within both Congress and the army. In fact, he came to believe that coexistence would be a good thing, as it would enhance the General Staff's ability to plan for war by freeing it from the minutia of daily administration. As drafted by Root and his advisors and approved by Congress, the General Staff Act stipulated:

> The duties of the General Staff Corps shall be to prepare plans for the national defense and for the mobilization of the military forces in time of war; to investigate and report upon all questions affecting the efficiency of the Army and its state of preparation for military operations; to render professional aid and assistance to the Secretary of War and to general officers and other superior commanders, and to act as their agents in informing and coordinating the action of all different officers who are subject, under the terms of this act, to the supervision of the Chief of Staff; and to perform such other military duties not otherwise assigned by law as may be from time to time prescribed by the President.[77]

Root intended the General Staff to be a planning and coordinating agency, but the extent to which it could coordinate anything was largely dependent upon the extent to which the bureaus felt that they were "subject . . . to the supervision of the Chief of Staff." Events in the early years of the new organization proved that this was highly contingent upon individual personalities, mostly because of a remarkable lack of guidance and direction from the secretary of war.[78]

Root relaxed his grip on the reins after formally establishing the General Staff. Perhaps he recognized that while he had the ability to change the army's systems and organization, he could do little to reshape the culture of the officer corps. Beyond what was specifically stipulated in the legislation, he refused to dictate how the General Staff would organize, operate, or relate to the other agencies of the War Department. The officer corps had to figure out on its own how to integrate this new organization into the army. As William H. Carter later recalled, "The General Staff Corps was established and began to function officially, but without expectation of reaching its full usefulness in the immediate future," and the General Staff took on a remarkably uncertain and improvisational character in its early years.[79] Accordingly, Secretary Root reported to Congress in the summer of 1903 that Goethals and the other General Staff officers first assembled in Washington "were then organized as an experimental or provisional general staff, and directed to work out a permanent organization and distribution of duties for the General Staff Corps, a draft of new regulations, and a revision of old regulations made necessary by the new departure." Illustrating the bureaucratic tightrope that was his to walk, Root said that "this work was done upon full consultation with the chiefs of bureaus and taking the opinions of general officers commanding departments" in an effort to encourage some investment from those quarters in establishing the General Staff, so "they might become familiar with their work, and test by experiment the best methods of accomplishing it."[80]

The newly established General Staff organized itself into three divisions. The First Division considered problems and policy related to organization, doctrine, and training for infantry, cavalry, and field artillery units, regulations, training maneuvers, and mobilization. The Second Division, also known as the Military Information Division, collected and developed intelligence on foreign armies, procuring and producing maps for potential theaters of war, and coordinating the efforts of military attachés stationed abroad. The Third Division studied possible theaters of war, developed war plans, and also dealt with coastal defense, combined maneuvers with the navy, and organization and doctrine for the army's technical branches. Given his recent experience in coastal defense, Goethals was assigned to the Third Division.[81]

In short order, Goethals and the rest of the Third Division became an arm of the Army War College, and his experiences in that institution reflected more continuity than change in an institutional culture that generally rejected formal training and education. The army's resistance to the educational mandate incorporated into Secretary Root's sweeping reforms in 1903 illustrated the rigidity of its institutional culture and its discomfort with formal education. From his first year in office as secretary of war, Root had envisioned War College to be a dual-purposed institution. On the one hand, Root intended the War College to "direct the instruction and intellectual exercise of the army, to acquire the information, devise the plans . . . and to advise the Commander in Chief upon all questions of plans, armament, transportation, mobilization, and military preparation and movement." On the other hand, it would serve as a school in which officers would "receive instruction . . . in the science of war, including the duties of the staff, and in all matters pertaining to the application of military science to national defense."[82] Development of the War College stalled in 1902 and early 1903 as its board functioned almost entirely as an informal staff for Root, aiding in the effort to secure passage of the General Staff Act. Afterward, the War Department put more thought into the War College and its relationship to the General Staff, and eventually it determined that because both organizations were at least partly intended to consider and develop war plans and mobilization systems, the War College would be an adjunct component of the General Staff. Given the fact that its scope of responsibility included developing war plans, the Third Division was the natural selection to carry out the mission of the War College. By October 27, 1903, then, Goethals and his colleagues in the Third Division were assigned to the War College. But rather than being a symbol and engine of change, the War College soon steered in a far more traditional direction.[83]

In 1903, Root assigned the newly promoted Brig. Gen. Tasker H. Bliss to serve as the first president of the Army War College. This placed Bliss in the unenviable position of negotiating the inherent tensions between the theoretically educational nature of Root's mandate and the immediately practical implications of the board's decision to situate the War College within a new and active staff organization dedicated to planning and coordinating the army's myriad activities and operations. Surprisingly, he failed.

Bliss was an uncommon officer. He was raised by academics and inherited their intellectual nature. He entered West Point after having already studied for a year at Lewisburg University, where his father was a professor of classical languages. He graduated from West Point in 1875 with a commission as an artillery officer and spent only three

of the next twenty-three years with his regiment. His next two decades
of service brought a series of unconventional assignments teaching
French and artillery at West Point, teaching strategy at the Naval War
College, serving as an aide to the commanding general and the secretary of war, and serving as the military attaché to the US ambassador
to Spain prior to the war with Spain in 1898. Once the war came, he
returned from Spain for wartime service, eventually joining the First
Army Corps in its expedition to Puerto Rico as the chief of staff of
one of its divisions—an assignment that undoubtedly first introduced
Goethals and Bliss to each other. Subsequently, he served as the col-
lector of customs for Havana, where his herculean efforts reformed a
corrupt bureau and increased the revenue for the military-run government of Cuba during the postwar occupation. Bliss's service caught
the attention of Secretary Root, who in 1902 rewarded him with a
promotion to brigadier general, despite the fact that he was then only
a major in the regular army. Bliss was an intellectual whose career experiences had kept his mind occupied with matters on a much higher
plane than most of his peers. Root therefore believed he was the perfect officer to lead the new War College.[84]

Unexpectedly, Bliss countered Root's vision for the Army War College with a somewhat anti-intellectual plan of his own. As president of
the new institution, Bliss was responsible for all professional education
in the army. When he issued orders in November 1901 establishing the
Army War College, Root helped consolidate a formally rationalized
and tiered system of professional education that began at West Point,
progressed to schools of application for technical training, continued
onward to post schools and lyceums for regimental officers, advanced
to the more advanced tactical and staff training at schools based at Ft.
Leavenworth in Kansas, and ultimately culminated at the War College.
In formalizing this system, Root initiated a fundamental change in the
processes of officer development within the army by tacitly acknowledging that formal education was a more legitimate component of professionalism and means of professional development than self-study.
Despite his deeply intellectual nature, nearly thirty years of experience
in an army that valued experiential learning far more than formal
education had conditioned Bliss against a wholehearted embrace of
Root's new model for professional military education. Accordingly, he
designed and ran the War College not as an educational institution

but as an organization that provided a practical apprenticeship for officers newly inducted into the General Staff Corps.[85]

Bliss first broached the subject in a lengthy memo to the secretary of war in August 1903. He opined that "an examination of the curricula of" post schools, schools of application, and the Leavenworth schools "show that they go, or are intended to go, to the limit in the matter of direct theoretical instruction of officers." He then reasoned, "It is evident that if instruction is to be continued on this general line at the War College, it will involve a repetition of what has been given at the other service schools," and that "manifestly all this will be a waste of time and a degradation of the institution from its true function." More to the point, he declared, "When an officer has passed through the course to which he must have been subjected before he comes to the War College he must have learned (unless there be a great fault somewhere) all that he needs to know of the *theory* of the art of war," and that "from that time on he should *learn things* by *doing things.*"[86]

Either Bliss was successful in convincing the secretary of war, or he was allowed to carry on because Root was preparing to leave the War Department in early 1904 and had concluded that his imminent departure from office precluded further efforts on behalf of his grander vision for the War College. Bliss received no argument from William H. Taft, Root's successor, when he made a similar argument in another report early the following year. Bliss stated that the components of the education system below the War College "go to the limit of useful training by the ordinary scholastic methods," and that "after passing them there is no further need for professors, instructors, and text books." Continuing, he described collaborative planning with experts from various branches as "an essential part of the art of war and which can be learned not from books and professors but only by patient and unostentatious labor in doing these things themselves." Bliss believed the primary purpose of the War College was to serve as a planning and supplemental staff agency, with a useful side effect of allowing its members to train in planning and problem solving through sheer repetition. "Thus," he concluded, "the scholastic work of the War College will not consist in the study of general principles but in the application of these principles to the details of a specific plan."[87] The War College therefore spent its first few years functioning more as an apprenticeship for General Staff officers than as a truly educational institution.

Goethals was a member of the War College during its first year. Under the leadership of its president and directors, Col. Arthur Wagner, and Lt. Col. William W. Wotherspoon, nine officers were detailed as students, and five officers, including Goethals, were detailed as War College faculty, with an additional two officers detailed for administrative duties.[88] That he was assigned to serve on the War College staff rather than for administration was likely due to his by-then excellent reputation and a probable prior working relationship with Bliss in the First Army Corps during the war with Spain. Goethals's achievements earlier in his career had shaped his reputation for having a sharp and inquisitive mind. As an intellectual, Bliss likely would have recognized and appreciated this quality and sought to use it to maximum advantage in the War College.

The first session of the War College proceeded very much according to Bliss's concept of how it should function. Its officers worked on several of the army's most vexing problems, most of which related to President Roosevelt's active Caribbean policies. War College officers developed plans to prevent foreign intervention in Haiti and mobilize expeditionary forces between 5,000 and 30,000 soldiers strong for operations in Santo Domingo, Venezuela, and Panama. Additionally, they attended a series of fifteen lectures in which fellow students, faculty, and other General Staff officers addressed the War College on current events or their areas of technical specialty within the army. The ongoing Russo-Japanese War was the topic of seven of these lectures, each delivered by officers recently returned from assignments as attachés or observers with the belligerent armies.[89] For his part, Goethals served as a member of the strategy board, the chairman of the committee considering problems related to the defense of the Philippines and military operations in the Pacific, and a member of a special committee planning joint army-navy maneuvers scheduled for 1905. Demonstrating the nonacademic nature of the War College, its students and faculty alike were designated as graduates of the inaugural class of 1905.[90]

The practical nature of the early Army War College was reinforced by the fact that it operated quite literally in the shadow of the War Department and the General Staff. Because its permanent home at Washington Barracks was not yet complete, officers assigned to the War College between 1903 and 1907 crammed into whatever office space they could improvise in a home the army rented from a well-known Washington socialite. The four-story brick townhouse at 22 Jackson Place sat at the northwest corner of Lafayette Square, mere yards down the road from the White House and its more sprawling, dourly Victorian neighbor—the State, War, and Navy Building—where the rest of the War Department and General Staff were ensconced. Although those who secured workspace in one of the townhouse's rooms whose tall, slender windows gave excellent views of the park outside may have been content, the officers of the War College, especially the unlucky four who were confined to the attic, found that the pleasant home made for an uncomfortably cramped workspace.[91]

For Goethals, the work environment was especially uncomfortable because it exacerbated deeply held insecurities about his lack of combat experience. The reformers who organized the General Staff Corps, of which the War College was a part, were careful to select for its first cohort of officers only those officers who represented the cream of the crop. As Maj. Gen. William H. Carter recalled in later years, "The type and character of officers detailed in the General Staff . . . was of the highest, and were, I am sure, unexcelled in any other army."[92] Nearly three-quarters of officers assigned to the first General Staff were officers from line branches whose only opportunities to stand out as junior officers were in combat in the West during the Indian Wars, in Cuba or the Philippines during the war with Spain and the subsequent Philippine Insurrection, or in China during the Boxer Rebellion in 1900.

Many of Goethals's Third Division colleagues had distinguished combat records. The first General Staff included Carter, a Medal of Honor recipient from wars with the Native Americans, and many officers who had been cited for bravery in more recent conflicts, including Maj. Gen. Adna Chaffee, Capt. John J. Pershing, Capt. Peyton C. March, and Capt. Joseph T. Dickman.[93] Like most officers of his generation, Goethals maintained a heroic concept of the ideal officer, heavily influenced by their collective memory and idolization of the Civil War generation. Surrounded daily by combat veterans and undoubtedly subject to their stories, reminiscences, and yarns, Goethals found his lack of combat experience to be utterly discomfiting, even embarrassing. He even went so far as to write in his own service report in 1903 shortly after reporting for duty with the General Staff that he "had participated in no battles, engagements, or actions" in a section in which he was supposed to describe his areas of expertise and special qualification.[94]

Goethals's insecurity turned out to be unfounded. If any of his colleagues or superiors thought any less of him because he had not seen combat, they were quickly won over by his engineering expertise and his dedicated and energetic work ethic. The prominent military reformer Col. Arthur Wagner found Goethals to be "well informed on all military subjects, and especially in regard to Military Engineering."[95] William W. Wotherspoon, then a lieutenant colonel who would briefly serve as chief of staff in 1914, reported in 1905 that Goethals "had shown marked ability in all the work entrusted to him."[96] In private correspondence, Brig. Gen. James Franklin Bell, another soon-to-be chief of staff, included Goethals in a list of a select group of individuals "who, by application and industry, have acquired such special qualifications that their services are always in demand, because those who want them really need their assistance and talent."[97] By 1905, Goethals had more than proven himself and was rewarded by being designated to serve as the junior director of the Army War College for its 1905–1906 session.[98] It is telling that none of these glowing reports attested to Goethals's qualities as either a student or a teacher. Reflecting an institutional culture that continued to reject the relationship between formal education and professionalism that increasingly helped define broader American concepts of professionalism, the new pinnacle of professional education in the army operated in a manner that avoided its educational mandate.

Goethals's affiliation with the Army War College, however, did not last long. Despite his appointment to the position of junior director for the 1905–1906 session, a new coastal defense board had begun to take up most of his time that winter.[99] In 1904, President Roosevelt halted appropriations for the construction and improvement of seacoast fortifications because it had finally become apparent that technological advances had rendered obsolete crucial aspects of the post–Endicott Board program that had shaped American coastal defense since the mid-1880s. He ordered Secretary Taft to convene a board of general officers in early 1905 to come up with recommendations for changes to be made in order to address the implications of two decades of technological innovation. Due to his work in the Newport District, Goethals was the General Staff's coastal defense expert, having been designated under the original plan of organization in 1903 as the head of a section within the Third Division responsible for considering problems and questions related to permanent fortifications and submersible mines. Later, Tasker Bliss had assigned Goethals to deliver a lecture to the officers of the War College titled "The Tactics of Coast Defense, with Special Reference to Submarine Defense." Therefore, when Taft asked the General Staff to provide him with an officer to serve as the board's secretary and recorder, Goethals seemed to be the natural choice. This proved to be the end of Goethals's tour of duty with the General Staff. His close association with Taft on coastal defense matters ultimately sent him to the Panama Canal.[100]

Goethals left the General Staff an unrepentantly unchanged officer. He later demonstrated in Panama that despite his four-year tour of duty with the General Staff, he was skeptical of the new systems and structures that Root had imposed. Although he had been an integral member of the division of the General Staff that was the foundation of the early Army War College, he wasted no time in undermining the principles of a tiered and rationalized system of officer education by advocating for new engineer lieutenants to undergo a practical course of instruction under his supervision in Panama before attending the Engineer School of Application.[101] Furthermore, Goethals directed the preponderance of his correspondence with the War Department during the busiest construction years in the Canal Zone around the General Staff and to the bureaus rather than to or through the General Staff. From his appointment until the completion of the Panama Canal, Goethals was far more likely to seek assistance from a bureau chief or from the secretary of war himself than from the chief of staff or a member of the General Staff.[102] Even though he had helped to organize and implement the army's new structures, he never wavered from the stubbornly traditionalist mindset that doggedly continued to shape the army's institutional culture.

On an individual level, Goethals embodied the schism between institutional structures and institutional culture that defined the army in the wake of the Root reforms. He was certainly not the only officer whose experiences on the first General Staff failed to inspire confidence in the new organization. While many coveted the prestige of being selected for General Staff Corps service, few were eager to return to it later. John J. Pershing, for example, was not at all enamored with the early General Staff despite being included in its first cohort of officers. Analyzing the army's troubled entrance into the First World War years later, admittedly with a significant ax to grind, Pershing placed all blame squarely on the General Staff. He found faults in its structure, arguing that even by 1917 it "had not yet been properly organized." More tellingly, he found that its implementation was fundamentally flawed. In its first decades, according to Pershing, the General Staff "was too much the inarticulate instrument of the Chief of Staff, who often erroneously assumed the role of Commanding General of the Army."[103]

Looking beyond Pershing's motives and biases, as blame for any problems in the American war effort cast anywhere other than squarely on the General Staff would ultimately lead back to Pershing himself as commander of the American Expeditionary Forces, there remains an interesting indictment of the General Staff in its earliest years. Reformers assumed that implementing the General Staff was the natural end of reform, and therefore they stopped short of ensuring the General Staff proved its worth to the broader army. Accordingly, its modes of organization and operation were not standardized and took on an improvisational air that officers who were accustomed to traditional systems and methods of managing the army found distasteful. As Pershing pointed out, even those who led the new General Staff looked to traditional offices of the past as their model.

Perhaps typically, then, Goethals's experience of the General Staff was rooted firmly in old concepts. He earned his place on it by excelling in the living anachronism that was late nineteenth-century American coastal defense. Once on the General Staff, he served under Bliss in a War College that rejected its own educational mandate in favor of more traditional forms of experiential learning. Outside of the War College and the Third Division, Goethals once again returned his focus to inherently obsolete coastal defense problems. With a gaze fixed firmly on a traditional and outdated mission despite his status as an original member of the new and ostensibly modern General Staff, Goethals ultimately earned much praise and the promotion of a lifetime to lead the construction effort at the Panama Canal.

Above all, Goethals's experience demonstrates that Elihu Root's reforms created a schism between institutional structures and institutional culture within the army. Although he personally experienced and recognized the shortcomings of the war effort in 1898 that constituted the most significant stimulus for reform, Goethals did not fully understand the implications of those shortcomings. He was, in that regard, unexceptional among his generation, which remained decidedly traditional in its outlook. In the end, the promise of reform would remain unfulfilled until the army's institutional culture caught up with its new institutional structures. And that required the cumulative effect of years of pressure from external forces.

4
Making the Dirt Fly

Chief among sources of gradual external pressure on the army was an abiding and widespread faith in the power and propriety of the intricately rationalized managerial systems and practices that reshaped both public and private institutions in American society during the managerial revolution of the late nineteenth and early twentieth centuries.[1] The popularity of the managerial revolution was amply on display when, through Goethals, the army took charge of the construction of the Panama Canal in 1907. Although the Panama Canal was a marvel of modern engineering, Goethals thought of it above all as a managerial problem. That perception informed his approach to leading the construction effort in Panama from 1907 until the canal opened in 1914. Similarly steeped in and subscribing to modern managerial theories, army officers in line and technical branches alike applauded Goethals's leadership in the Canal Zone.

Ultimately, the popularity of the managerial revolution within the army made the Root reforms at least tolerable despite the fact that the notion of a rationalized system of professional education appeared to many officers to be contrary to established wisdom and practice. The officer corps' embrace of the managerial revolution influenced it to accept the notion of a general staff even if it could not come to a consensus on the proper form, role, and scope of the General Staff as it was established in 1903.[2] Furthermore, the army's embrace of the managerial revolution marked the beginning of a long process of cultural change that would ultimately repair the schism between its institutional culture and institutional structures caused by the Root reforms.

***

84

Dreams of a canal in Panama were by no means new in the first decade of the twentieth century. For centuries, the Isthmus of Panama had been viewed as a strategic conduit between the Atlantic and Pacific Oceans and had inspired schemes wildly varying in quality and prac-ticality to join the two oceans. In the sixteenth and seventeenth cen-turies, the king of Spain dreamed of building a canal across Panama, a dream never realized due to the limitations of existing technology. In place of an interoceanic waterway, Spanish officials settled for the construction of two major roads, over which passed approximately one-third of all minerals and revenues that colonial officials extracted from Peru between 1600 and 1660.[3] Panama's strategic value to Spain was neither unnoticed nor unchallenged, inviting dramatic attacks by privateers and the English navy alike. Under increasing military and economic pressure, Spain's interest in Panama faded in the late seven-teenth and early eighteenth centuries. The gradual collapse of the Pe-ruvian silver economy, the opening of a viable and less disease-ridden overland route via Buenos Aires, the beginning of the slow decline of Spanish military and political power in the Americas, and improving maritime capabilities that made the passage of Cape Horn more vi-able combined to render Panama insignificant to global trade in the eighteenth and early nineteenth centuries.[4]

That changed after the Mexican-American War (1846–1848). Hav-ing taken California from Mexico, the United States had a decided interest in shortening and better securing its communications routes between port cities on the Atlantic and Pacific coasts. Lacking trans-continental telegraph or rail services, Congress authorized contracts for American steamship companies to carry mail on the Pacific route between San Francisco and Panama, and between Panama and both New Orleans and New York on the Gulf of Mexico and Atlantic routes. William Henry Aspinwall won not only the contract for the Pacific route but also control of overland transportation connecting the Atlantic and Pacific routes, financing the construction of the Pan-ama Railroad from 1850 to 1858. Fueled by government contracts to move mail between steamship packets and troops to western garrisons, and also by residual private demand from the California gold rush, the railroad became a profitable venture even before it was completed. Passengers would ride a train for as much of the railroad existed at the time of the journey, and then completed their trek on foot, mules, and a rollicking journey down the Chagres River on small boats and rafts.[5]

Americans soon learned from painful experience that the environment in Panama was deadly, especially after tropical rains. Believing that American laborers were too expensive and too vulnerable to tropical diseases, the Panama Railroad Company opted instead to contract Chinese laborers, who proved equally susceptible to environmental hazards. Nearly 80 percent of contracted Chinese laborers either deserted the railroad or perished from disease and suicide, leading the company to recruit thousands of West Indian laborers to complete the job. Beyond the workforce, the unforgiving environment was also fatal for those merely passing through. Even after the horrors of the Civil War, the memory of the Fourth Infantry Regiment's transit from New York to California in 1852 remained visceral for Ulysses S. Grant, who noted in his memoirs decades later that "about one-seventh of those who left New York harbor with the 4th Infantry on the 5th of July, now lie buried on the Isthmus of Panama or on Flamingo [Flamenco] Island in Panama Bay."[6]

Later in the nineteenth century, there emerged a growing consensus that technology had progressed to the point that an interoceanic canal across Central America was feasible. While the United States devoted considerable energy to exploring possibilities in Nicaragua, the French Compagnie Universelle du Canal Interocéanique successfully negotiated to construct a canal across the then-Colombian province of Panama. The company and the canal were pet projects of Ferdinand de Lesseps, who had previously led the construction of the Suez Canal.[7]

Work on de Lesseps's new project began in 1877 and quickly devolved into an unmitigated disaster. De Lesseps's plans called for a sea-level canal, an ill-advised concept given Panama's rugged topography, geology, propensity for mud slides after tropical rains, and tidal patterns that create a twenty-foot difference between the sea levels on Panama's Pacific and Atlantic coasts. Compounding these problems, de Lesseps's engineers inadvertently caused monumental mud slides and created large malarial swamps by dumping all the soil they removed from the canal into valleys adjoining their work sites, effectively blocking natural courses for runoff water during the rainy season. The pace of work slowed to a crawl, and the incidence of disease among workers skyrocketed. Between disease and accidents, at least 22,189 workers died during the French construction period in Panama. As its failures became a national scandal, the French government refused to intervene to save de Lesseps, his company, and the canal. In 1889, the Compagnie Universelle du Canal Interocéanique went bankrupt, forfeiting its assets and rights to a new French company that thereafter took the bare minimum actions required to prevent Colombia from seizing the French equipment and revoking the canal concession.[8]

While the French effort was under way, the United States explored options to compete with and balance against the French by building its own canal through Nicaragua. American political leaders failed to achieve a consensus on the issue, and efforts to build a Nicaraguan canal were limited to an ill-supported private venture by the Maritime Canal Company that began in 1887 and secured a formal charter from Congress in 1889. By 1893, however, political and financial supporters realized that the company had drastically underestimated the amount of effort, resources, and money it required. With public and private investment drying up, the company dissolved.[9]

The war with Spain in 1898 fundamentally altered the American outlook on the need for a canal across the isthmus. Docked at San Francisco when the USS *Maine* sank in the Havana harbor and war began to seem more likely, the battleship USS *Oregon* received orders to steam for the East Coast to join the Atlantic squadron for possible operations against Spain. After the *Oregon* set off on March 9, the public watched breathlessly as its dramatic voyage played out in the newspapers. In the absence of a canal, the *Oregon* had to steam for 12,000 nautical miles, often out of communication and potentially in danger of being intercepted by the Spanish navy, in a nearly complete circumnavigation of Central and South America in order to move into position as ordered. There was much relief when the *Oregon* appeared off Florida at the end of May—sixty-seven days and one declaration of war after it had left San Francisco. If the long and tense journey of the *Oregon* conditioned Americans to begin to think beyond economic ambition and consider military necessity, the annexation of Hawaii and occupation of the Philippines completed that shift in mindset. Given its new possessions in the Pacific after the war with Spain, the United States considered a Central American canal to be a strategic imperative.[10]

Politically contentious issues surrounding the problem of exactly

where and how to build a canal were resolved only after decisive interventions by Theodore Roosevelt. Although the Maritime Canal Company's Nicaraguan venture had failed, powerful financial and political
backers continued to advocate for a canal in Nicaragua. They were
quite persuasive, and for a time it seemed the Nicaragua route would
prevail. Because of his canal experience on the Tennessee River, one of
Goethals's duties while assigned to Washington as an assistant to the
chief of engineers from 1894 to 1898 was to provide technical advice
to a Senate select committee investigating proposed routes and plans
for a Nicaraguan canal.[11] The appeal of Nicaragua, however, declined
sharply after the turn of the century when Philippe Bunau-Varilla—one
of the leading engineers of the French effort in Panama—persuaded his
countrymen to sell their property, assets, and equipment in Panama to
the United States at a significantly reduced price. Given this development, Theodore Roosevelt prodded his allies in the House of Representatives in January 1902 to authorize and appropriate funds to open
negotiations with Colombia to build a canal across Panama. But when
the Colombians balked, Roosevelt acted swiftly.

Giving assurances of American support to separatists in Panama
through the keenly interested and apparently omnipresent Bunau-
Varilla, Roosevelt played a decisive role in prompting the Panamanian
Revolution of 1903. With American warships and a detachment of US
Marines impeding an effective Colombian military response, Panama
declared independence in November 1903. Honoring a prior agreement, the new republic appointed Bunau-Varilla as its agent in Washington to begin negotiations for a canal treaty with the United States.
Duplicitously and underhandedly rushing to complete negotiations
before the Panamanian members of the new republic's delegation
could reach Washington, Bunau-Varilla and Secretary of State John
Hay completed the Hay–Bunau-Varilla Treaty on November 18, 1903.
In return for an upfront payment of $10 million and an annual pay-
ment of $250,000 beginning in 1913, the treaty granted the United
States political and legal control of the Panama Canal Zone. It defined
the Canal Zone as a swath of land twenty miles wide, with a ten-mile
buffer zone on either side of the canal along its entire forty-eight-mile
route, except for Panama City and Colón at its Pacific and Atlantic
terminals, respectively, both of which remained sovereign Panamanian
territory.[12]

Using a vague threat of severe consequences if Panama failed to act expeditiously, Secretary Hay successfully pressed the new Panamanian government—which quite understandably felt equally bullied, betrayed, and helpless to do anything more than acquiesce—to ratify the treaty before it had even been translated into Spanish. Thus began the distinctly American experience of the Panama Canal. And although he would write in his autobiography that "no one connected with the American Government had any part in preparing, inciting, or encouraging the revolution," Roosevelt privately considered his role in the affair to be his most significant foreign policy achievement. Moreover, he believed that the vast majority of Americans approved. The only opposition, he wrote to a friend in characteristically Rooseveltian terms, came from "a small body of shrill eunuchs" who failed to recognize the immense value of the opportunity that he had seized.[13] Vivid metaphors notwithstanding, Roosevelt's perception of popular opinion was generally correct. Although many were uncomfortable with Roosevelt's methods, the notion of an American canal in Panama was overwhelmingly appealing at the time. Accordingly, the Senate ratified the Hay–Bunau-Varilla Treaty on February 23, 1904, by a lopsided vote of sixty-six to fourteen, and the administration established the Isthmian Canal Commission (ICC) to organize and execute the work.[14]

In its first few years, the ICC's record in Panama was mixed at best. Led throughout much of 1904 and 1905 by Rear Adm. John G. Walker as chairman and John Findlay Wallace as chief engineer, the Americans fared little better than their French predecessors. The French canal effort under de Lesseps, a proven engineer and formidable leader, had failed due to an inexplicably inappropriate plan, a lack of medical knowledge, and a state of technological development not quite sufficient for such a venture. By the time of the American canal effort, the last two problems had been resolved. The medical community had gained the crucial insights into tropical diseases needed to make a Central American canal possible, while the methods and means necessary for the construction of grand projects had also advanced considerably. Yet poor leadership and an obtuse refusal to put the new medical knowledge to use brought the American effort unnecessarily close to disaster.

The most significant problem was Walker's and Wallace's refusal to believe that yellow fever was a mosquito-borne illness. Yellow fever had been attributed to poor sanitary conditions until Cuban and American doctors demonstrated the link between yellow fever and the *Aedes aegypti* mosquito during the American occupation of Cuba following the war with Spain. Many laymen were unconvinced, Walker and Wallace among them. They denied requests from Col. William C. Gorgas—the commission's chief sanitary officer and an army doctor with considerable experience fighting the disease in Cuba—for adequate supplies, funding, and manpower for a mosquito eradication campaign. Instead, they ordered Gorgas to direct his efforts toward general sanitation of the Canal Zone, still adhering to the disproven former consensus that yellow fever was a product of unsanitary living and working conditions. An entirely avoidable, if comparatively mild epidemic then hit the Canal Zone in late 1904 and early 1905. As deaths and fears of a return to the nightmarish epidemics during the French construction period mounted, American employees in the Canal Zone panicked, with three out of every four opting to resign and return to the United States in April, May, and June 1905. That exodus included Chief Engineer Wallace, whose resignation was accepted by a thoroughly disgusted Secretary of War William H. Taft on June 25, 1905. As Admiral Walker had resigned a few months earlier, the Isthmian Canal Commission was adrift and rudderless in the middle of a possibly existential crisis, and work in Panama ground to a halt.[15]

Succeeding Wallace as the ICC's chief engineer, John Stevens set a firm foundation for the successful completion of the canal. His tenure in Panama was marked by two distinct achievements: the practical elimination of yellow fever from the isthmus and the completion of the critically important railroad phase of the canal construction. Success on the yellow fever front required Theodore Roosevelt's intervention. Like their predecessors, Stevens and Theodore Shonts—who

---

Right: *Published in the January 31, 1906, edition of* Puck *magazine, this cartoon's full title is, "Opening of the Panama Canal—At Which Distant Day Ocean Navigation Will Be a Trifle Out of Date." In its depiction of tourists flying above the canal in a variety of aircraft, it gives artistic expression to a sense of doubt about the American effort at the Panama Canal in the early stages of construction. (Library of Congress, Prints and Photographs Division, LC-DIG-ppmsca-26030)*

OPENING OF THE PANAMA CANAL.

AT WHICH DISTANT DAY OCEAN NAVIGATION WILL BE A TRIFLE OUT OF DATE.

had succeeded Walker as chairman of the ICC in April 1905—did not subscribe to the emerging scientific consensus that yellow fever was a mosquito-borne illness, and they were ill-disposed to support Gorgas in his efforts to fight yellow fever by eradicating the *Aedes aegypti* mosquito. After the outbreak of 1904–1905, however, Roosevelt consulted with his most trusted medical advisors, whose persuasive arguments and recommendations led him to order Shonts and Stevens to fully support Gorgas and his Department of Sanitation, sparing no expense or resource to eradicate the Canal Zone's deadly mosquitos. Beginning in July 1905, Gorgas's teams meticulously fumigated and screened buildings throughout the Canal Zone, and attacked the *Aedes aegypti* in its larval stage by removing as much standing water as possible, then spraying kerosene over pools of standing water that could not be removed. The campaign was astonishingly successful: the ICC recorded no deaths from yellow fever after November 11, 1905.[16]

With the most deadly disease on the isthmus tamed, Stevens organized and completed the railroad phase of the construction of the Panama Canal in just under a year and a half. His experience building railroads throughout the American West, Canada, and Mexico arguably made Stevens the foremost American railroad engineer of his time. That expertise served him well. Shortly after arriving in Panama, he determined that whatever the result of debates in Washington about the relative merits of a sea-level canal versus a lock canal would be, work could proceed on two fronts: building the logistical infrastructure needed to sustain construction of a canal of either type for years to come and attacking the Culebra Cut, a gorge nine miles long that would have to be carved out of the Panamanian landscape.

Stevens set all the right conditions for a lengthy construction effort. His crews built living quarters, docks, and storehouses, moved the Panama Railroad, and created an intricate railroad system to bring supplies from the storehouses to construction sites throughout the Canal Zone. Perhaps most important, Stevens established an ingenious and intricate rail system inside the Culebra Cut. The experienced railroad engineer intuitively understood that moving millions of cubic yards of earth out of the Culebra Cut was at least as important as the digging operation inside the Cut. In later years, Stevens could justifiably claim that he had "handed over to the army engineers a well-planned and well-built machine" that "ran, comparatively speaking, like a high-grade watch."[17]

In the meantime, George W. Goethals has been assigned in 1905 to serve on the National Coast Defense Board, informally known as the Taft Board. Goethals and Secretary of War Taft quickly developed a close personal bond. Generally prejudiced against overweight people—later in life, he would tell his daughter-in-law that Taft "was the only clean fat man he had ever known"—Goethals was genuinely surprised to find that he enjoyed the jocular and famously rotund secretary of war's company so much.[18] The two shared similar senses of humor and found common ground in their jokes, often at the navy's expense, while on tours of inspection of coastal fortifications in 1905 and 1906.[19] For his part, Taft was deeply impressed by the knowledgeable and hard-working engineer, who in addition to his duties with the board wrote and presented a paper on fortifications for the International Congress of Engineers and published it in the journal *Transactions of the American Society of Engineers.*[20]

Accurately gauging Goethals's abilities and potential, Taft began to see a role for him in the nation's most significant engineering project. "I am convinced," he wrote to the chief of staff and the chief of engineers in the summer of 1905, "that Major Goethals can be of great use in the construction of the Panama Canal. . . . I desire that he be retired from the General Staff and be assigned to this work in any capacity that the [Isthmian Canal] Commission may designate."[21] The commission did not request Goethals's services. A year later, Taft pressed the case again. Writing to Roosevelt, Taft called attention to "Major Goethals, one of the ablest of our army engineers," whom he wanted to send to Panama because the chief engineer of the Isthmian Canal Commission, John Stevens, "would find him so useful that they could work together, and that Goethals might be Stevens' understudy, should he for any reason fail us."[22] Still the commission expressed no interest, and Goethals was not sent to Panama.

Only a few months later, however, the commission slid into crisis. For reasons he never fully disclosed, Stevens grew irritable and dissatisfied in Panama in the winter of 1906–1907. When Theodore Shonts resigned from his position as chairman of the Isthmian Canal Commission on January 22, 1907, Stevens became more de-spondent, appearing to crack under the strain of his duties.[23] On January 30, 1907, he sent a letter to Roosevelt. "I never sought this position," he complained, "on the contrary, [I] declined it twice, and finally accepted it against my better judgment." Continuing, he stated that "the idea of being constantly before the public, whether in a favor-able or unfavorable light, is extremely distasteful to me . . . continually subject to attack by a lot of people, and they are not all in private life, that I would not wipe my boots on in the United States." Stevens went on to complain that his salary was too low, that the job required too much time away from his family, and that he was rapidly losing inter-est in the work. "The 'honor' which is continually being held up as an incentive for being connected with this work," he declared, "appeals to me but slightly," as "the canal is only a big ditch, and its great util-ity when completed, has never been so apparent to me, as it seems to be to others." Summing up after six meandering pages, Stevens stated unequivocally that he was "not anxious to continue in the service" and that there were other "men as competent and far more willing to pick up and carry the burden." "My desire," he concluded, "is to take a rest, and then to re-enter railway service, for which I know I am best fitted by training and inclination."[24]

The letter took Roosevelt completely by surprise. He had seen Ste-vens in Washington only one month earlier and had told the engineer to expect to be named chairman of the commission if Shonts stepped down, receiving no objection or complaint at the time.[25] After read-ing the letter and digesting it, Roosevelt forwarded it to Taft, whose department was nominally responsible for overseeing all work on the isthmus. He enclosed a cover letter that simply stated, "There is of course no question that Stevens must get out at once," and "if he should now alter his mind, as he has so frequently altered it in the past, and wish to stay, I should not consider it for a moment given the tone of his letter." He then called Taft to a meeting at the White House on the morning of February 13 to discuss the matter further.[26]

Roosevelt wanted a drastic change. The resignations of Shonts and Stevens constituted the end of the Isthmian Canal Commission, mark-ing not only the demise of the second commission but also the sudden departure of the second chief engineer from the Panama Canal, both in as many years. Wanting the project run by people who could not

*Goethals and President William H. Taft during Taft's visit to the Panama
Canal Zone in December 1910. Goethals would likely not have been assigned to
lead the construction effort at the Panama Canal without an earlier assignment
on the General Staff that brought him into Secretary of War Taft's orbit and
good graces. (Library of Congress, Prints and Photographs Division,
LC-USZ62-53972)*

quit unless they were fired or relieved, Roosevelt had decided to place a
soldier in charge. The president relayed his decision to Taft and asked
for his recommendation on whom to select to serve as both chairman
and chief engineer of the next Isthmian Canal Commission.[27]

Although Taft had already spent a year and a half trying to assign
Goethals to Panama, he asked to be excused to consult with Alexander
Mackenzie, who by then had been promoted to brigadier general and
chief of engineers. Mackenzie held a high opinion of Goethals from
repeated professional encounters, first during their service together
in the chief of engineer's office from 1894 to 1898, and subsequently
during their service together on the first General Staff in 1903. He
echoed Taft's assessment that Goethals was the officer most fit for the
job. The two brought their recommendation to Roosevelt, and the
matter was settled.

Although he had accomplished much during his short tenure, Stevens departed at the right moment. He was an experienced railroad engineer with little knowledge of and no experience in canal engineering. Once the railroad phase of the construction was completed, he no longer had the technical expertise needed to lead the effort. The administration had decided upon a lock canal in February 1906, and Congress gave its approval four months later.[28] The project required an engineer knowledgeable of and experienced in the construction of lock canals. Moreover, as his letter to Roosevelt clearly revealed, Stevens was burned out and near his breaking point. Just as he was ill-equipped for the technical problems of canal's construction moving forward, he was not in the proper mental state to handle the extraordinary problems of leadership and management that defined Goethals's tenure in Panama.

Roosevelt, who felt a keen sense of ownership and personal investment in the Panama Canal, had come to frame the canal as a managerial problem well before appointing Goethals to lead the effort.[29] In 1906, the president had complained to Taft that although Shonts and Stevens were "the very best men we could get for actually digging the canal," he believed that "their phenomenal administrative and engineering qualities are not accompanied by any appreciation of the exact qualities necessary in dealing either with a foreign power, especially a small Spanish American power, or with Congress or with the labor situation." Despite his famous admonitions to "make the dirt fly," Roosevelt correctly believed that "actually digging the canal" was but one of several complicated issues with which the leadership of the ICC had to contend.[30] He became even more convinced of this when Stevens resigned, and he likely emphasized managerial issues in his subsequent meetings with Goethals.

Seizing the opportunity to repair an organizational problem he believed the other commissions had suffered from, Roosevelt appointed Goethals to serve as chairman and chief engineer of the ICC. He had floated a more radical idea one year earlier, testing among his close associates an idea that would reduce the commission to just one member and would fill all other significant positions in the Canal Zone with appointees serving at the president's discretion who would report to rather than serve with the sole commissioner.[31] Although Roosevelt's inner circle advised that such a policy was politically infeasible, Stevens's resignation prompted Roosevelt to reorganize the ICC to make one commissioner, Goethals, much more powerful than the others. In doing so, he did not intend to facilitate Goethals's work as an engineer, but to facilitate his work as an executive managing a mammoth undertaking. As Roosevelt later explained in his autobiography, "I tried faithfully to get good work out of the commission, and found it quite impossible; for a many-headed commission is an extremely poor executive instrument."[32] As would his successors in subsequent reorganizations of the ICC until the canal was complete, Roosevelt opted to concentrate power in Goethals's hands. He took this course neither for power's sake nor to satisfy Goethals's ego but to improve the efficiency of the executive management of the construction effort. This was a massive gamble on Roosevelt's part. Nearing the end of his presidency, he had by then come to regard the canal as a major part of his legacy. Rightly or wrongly, he believed that his reputation in posterity would rise or fall with the success or failure of the canal, and he was about to entrust it all to a lieutenant colonel of engineers.[33]

February 18, 1907, began ordinarily enough for George W. Goethals, but the day soon took a more interesting turn. Having arrived at the usual time, he was by the late morning ensconced in his office off Washington, DC's Lafayette Square attending to routine staff work when he received a message from Secretary Taft asking for a meeting. Goethals dropped what he was doing and walked half a block to the simultaneously grand and dour monument to Victorian architecture that was the State, War, and Navy Building to see Taft, who proceeded to quiz Goethals on his background and his previous experiences in the army. The conversation revolved—unusually, it seemed to Goethals—around matters that they had discussed at great length on their many recent tours of inspection of fortifications throughout the country. Finally, Taft intimated that President Roosevelt had accepted Stevens's resignation, and that with the concurrence of the army's chief engineer, Taft had urged Roosevelt to appoint Goethals as chairman and chief engineer of the Isthmian Canal Commission. "He could not assure me I would be selected," Goethals recalled eight years later, "but [said] I probably would be summoned to the White House that evening and should be prepared for such a call" and that "in the meantime nothing was to be said concerning the matter to anyone."[34]

Later that night, Goethals and his wife were at their Washington home three blocks north of Dupont Circle, entertaining Gustav Fiebeger and his wife. Well into the evening, a message arrived from the president's personal secretary asking Goethals to come to the White House at 9:30 the next morning.[35] Remembering what Taft had told him, Goethals immediately called the secretary, who then told Goethals not to wait until morning. Fully aware of what was about to happen, Goethals slipped into a dress uniform and out the front door.[36]

It was around 10 p.m. on a Monday. Goethals would have found his most direct route to the White House—a twenty-minute walk from his townhouse on the corner of S and 19th Streets—relatively unpopulated save for a few nocturnal passersby and occasional stony, unmoving figures on monuments to Civil War heroes he and his colleagues so exalted. He would have been alone to his thoughts, torn as they may have been between the excitement of a consistently ambitious man and the nervousness of an experienced and pragmatic engineer who was well aware of how enormous the job ahead of him was. His reception and the chaotic few weeks that followed did little to calm those nerves. Goethals had little time for anything more than getting his affairs in order before he and his wife boarded a ship for Panama, arriving in early March 1907.

Assessing progress in the Canal Zone shortly after his arrival, Goethals was impressed with what had already been accomplished. During his first weeks in the Canal Zone, he wrote home that "Mr. Stevens has done an amount of work for which he will never get any credit—or if he gets any, will not get enough." Delighted that Stevens had accomplished so much, Goethals reported that the railroad "part of the problem is practically solved, and being the part with which we are least familiar, it is going to be an advantage that he has been here in advance and taken hold as he has done." Continuing, he explained that "Mr. Stevens has perfected such an organization so far as the R.R. part of the proposition is concerned, that there is nothing left for us to do but just have the organization continue in the good work it has done and is doing."[37] A year after the canal opened to commercial traffic, Goethals remained grateful. He wrote in *Scribner's Magazine* that he had been "fortunate in falling heir to the organization that had been perfected for excavating the Culebra Cut, for no one not thoroughly familiar with railroad transportation and not possessed of organizing ability could have succeeded in this part of the work."[38]

Turning to the work remaining to be done, Goethals identified management as the largest and most critical problem he faced, and he surmised—probably accurately—that it was the problem that broke John Stevens. "The magnitude of the work grows on me; it seems to get bigger all the time," he wrote home in the middle of March. Goethals found the chief engineer's work to be "lonely and isolated," and concluded that Stevens had "broken down with the responsibilities and an evident desire to look after too many of the details himself." He confided to his son that Stevens lacked "any assistants on whom he can throw off matters, preferring, as I understand the situation, to decide everything himself, and in this respect the job is too great."[39] The problem of management was still looming foremost in Goethals's mind in his next letter home. "The work," he wrote, "is all absorbing and its magnitude enormous." Reflecting on the task ahead, he described to his family exactly how he perceived his role as the newly appointed chairman and chief engineer of the Isthmian Canal Commission. "As the head of everything here," he wrote, "I will not be able to do much with the details of the engineering, but I'm going to make the others work."[40] By the end of his first month in the Canal Zone, Goethals had also come to frame the construction of the Panama Canal exactly as Roosevelt had—not as a technical engineering problem but as a managerial problem.

None of his subsequent experiences in the Canal Zone changed his mind. Later, in retrospective writings and public statements, he insisted that the Panama Canal was more of a managerial triumph than a marvel of engineering or technology. A year after the canal opened, Goethals wrote, "The construction of the canal involved the solution of no new engineering problems—simply the application of known principles and methods which experience had shown would give satisfactory results, for the very magnitude of the work precluded trying out anything new or experimental." Continuing, he asserted that "the task was a formidable one, therefore, because of its size, rather than because of the engineering difficulties overcome."[41] In a different forum, he claimed that when comparing the managerial problems of the canal to its engineering problems, "they made the latter appear relatively small."[42] Goethals addressed this point most clearly in a 1922 inter-

Three steam shovels (lower right) and a crew of laborers (lower center left) near the Culebra Cut in 1913. This picture gives a glimpse of the problems of scale inherent in constructing the Panama Canal. Goethals, however, always believed that problems related to managing the work and the workforce in the Canal Zone were more complex and significant than any technical engineering problem associated with the canal's construction. (Library of Congress, Prints and Photographs Division, LC-DIG-hec-03148)

view in which he insisted that his "chief interest at Panama was not in the engineering, but in the men," because he firmly believed "that the canal would be built if the men could be managed." Explaining his success, Goethals stated with characteristic curtness, "We managed the men and the canal was built." He went on to opine that the greatness of the Panama Canal was not in its massive locks, but rather "in the forming of a good-sized principality solely devoted to fighting the jungle, the Culebra Slide, and the Chagres River—and having them finish the fight on time."[43]

Such statements were somewhat too categorical and certainly unfair to his subordinate engineers, whose excellent work at the canal involved a daily struggle with monumental technical difficulties, and perhaps reveal an inability to empathize with and appreciate the difficulties and challenges that others faced. In his own position, however, Goethals was right to focus above all on the problem of management. The scale of the project was immense. Although it had to be led by an engineer who was an expert in the technical aspects of canal construction, the engineer in charge could not afford to dive into the technical work and had to act in an executive capacity. When Goethals arrived on the isthmus, the workforce in the Panama Canal Zone was more than 29,000 strong and the Isthmian Canal Commission had an operating budget that exceeded $79 million.[44] By contrast, the entire army consisted of fewer than 54,000 soldiers and had an operating budget of over $143 million.[45]

Upon his appointment as chairman and chief engineer of the ICC, then, Goethals assumed control of an organization that was roughly equivalent—in both manpower and operating budget—to half of the entire army. At its peak in 1913, the canal workforce would swell to almost 45,000 employees and contractors, a force slightly greater than three-quarters the size of the army.[46] While his limited training and extensive professional experiences to that point had given him the technical knowledge to lead the construction effort, nothing in his training and experience had prepared Goethals to manage an organization that large. After all, he was at the time of his appointment only a lieutenant colonel, and a newly promoted one at that. The turn-of-the-century army certainly did not train its lieutenant colonels to be able to assume command of organizations roughly the same size as an army corps. It lacked a system to train even its generals to do so.[47]

Goethals consciously framed the construction of the Panama Canal in managerial terms that would have been familiar in any corporate boardroom at that time. The managerial revolution had taken hold of American society in the late nineteenth century. It was a process that took place in the decades after the Civil War when large, multiunit, and multifunctional businesses supplanted traditionally small, individual enterprises as the central driving force of the American economy, generating an expanding class of managers to fill the administrative and executive apparatuses at the heart of these new businesses and corporations.[48] The jobs that were a part of these managerial hierarchies were increasingly professional and technical and came with respectable status and salaries. The growth of such positions fueled a considerable expansion of a middle class that was increasingly enamored with concepts of efficiency and "scientific management."[49] As the reformist spirit of the Progressive Era swept over the country in the 1890s and early 1900s, such concepts were applied to problems beyond the economic sector, extending their influence to many aspects of American society.[50]

The army was not immune to the managerial revolution. In part, this was because of the naturally symbiotic relationship between an army and American society. It is unsurprising to see that as the economy became increasingly corporate and the middle class expanded, many of its values and trends found their way into the army by way of its largely middle-class officer corps. More important and less obvious, the managerial revolution's values and trends were easily transferred to the army because they did not clash with its institutional culture. In fact, they seemed strikingly and comfortably familiar to the army, as the seeds of the managerial revolution had been planted during the Civil War.[51]

Historians of American business have identified mid-nineteenth-century railroads as the foundation upon which the managerial revolution was built. Railroads were the original large American corporations whose size and complexity demanded sophisticated systems of management and administration.[52] Many railroad managers and executives had served in the war in civil or military capacities, often having performed valuable service in mobilizing and supplying armies in the field. The Union in particular made notable achievements in efficiently financing and resourcing its war effort and crafting an intricate system to move supplies over an extensive rail network to sustain its armies. With a massive postwar demobilization, those who perfected the Union's financial and logistical systems transitioned to civil society, bringing with them the ideas, organizational concepts, and techniques the army put to such effective use during the war.[53] With the growth of large corporations in the 1870s to 1890s, these ideas, concepts, and techniques—as well as plenty of new ones—were repeatedly tested and improved upon in the corporate world of late nineteenth-century America. Meanwhile, the organizational concepts and skills developed during the Civil War atrophied and faded in the postwar army that neither used nor needed them after completing its drawdown and returning to the peacetime routine of a traditionally small army.[54]

After the turn of the century, however, army officers were particularly receptive to managerial trends which were both increasingly popular in middle-class American society and firmly rooted in much-celebrated Civil War antecedents. The Corps of Engineers was especially attuned to these developments, as its mission necessarily brought its officers into more frequent and direct contact with the business community than their colleagues in the line.[55] In the absence of any other relevant frame of reference from his previous training and experience, then, it was quite natural for Goethals to think of the Panama Canal as a complex and multifaceted managerial problem.

In addition to shaping how he thought about the canal, the managerial revolution influenced how Goethals organized the work in Panama. In the late nineteenth century, corporate mergers and consolidation gave rise to large, multifunctional firms. Seeking maximum profit, executives developed thoroughly integrated systems of management defined by centralized power and decentralized operations. Executives retained all power and responsibility, but delegated considerable authority to managers of subordinate organizations formed along well-defined functional or geographic lines, as circumstances dictated.[56]

Goethals had long embraced this managerial approach, as he had clearly demonstrated at the Florence District from 1891 to 1894 by dividing his district into four divisions, each organized to work on one of the district's distinct but related major projects.[57] Having succeeded with that approach before, Goethals applied it again in Panama. Because "the work is all absorbing and its magnitude is enormous," he wrote to his son, "I will not be able to do much with the details of the engineering, but I'm going to make the others work."[58] In a different letter, he explained, "I am going to divide up the supervision of the work among the other three Engineers on the commission, let them look after the details of the work, and just maintain general supervision over the whole."[59] In the end, that is exactly how Goethals organized the ICC workforce. When he assumed control, the ICC's construction department was in disarray, having been organized in twelve divisions, each with independent clerical, administrative, and logistical units. "Recalling the President's desire to continue intact the existing organization," and convinced "that it would be madness to attempt any change" until he had a more firm understanding of the job, Goethals did not make immediate changes. He believed that premature reorganization "would have resulted in nothing short of chaos."[60]

Goethals settled on a scheme of organization in 1908 that would remain in place, for the most part, until construction was complete. He divided the canal into three segments and created three corresponding engineering divisions. The Atlantic, Central, and Pacific Divisions were each responsible for one segment. Additionally, because he considered the locks to be complex enough to require one senior engineer's full attention, he created a separate division responsible only for planning and designing locks. The same general principle informed how he organized portions of the workforce dedicated to the various administrative and logistical tasks that supported the work. Goethals ensured he had a body of employees and a supervisor dedicated to each of the Canal Zone's many functions, and he assumed a role that was more closely related to a modern executive of a large corporation than a nineteenth-century general leading his troops in the field.[61]

The Atlantic Division was responsible for all canal construction work from deep water in Limón Bay at Colón to the Gatún Dam. Goethals placed this division under William L. Sibert, an army engineer who had considerable canal experience. Assisting Sibert were several other officers from the Corps of Engineers. The Atlantic Division was responsible for constructing breakwaters to protect the Atlantic entrance to the canal from storms, dredging a channel from Limón Bay to Gatún Dam, emplacing three flights of double locks known as the Gatún Locks, and building the Gatún Dam. The dam was the most important project assigned to the Atlantic Division, consuming the bulk of its resources and effort until early 1912. Over 100 feet high and approximately a mile and a half long, its size was unprecedented for its time. The dam was designed to block the powerful Chagres River, thereby flooding 162 miles of jungle to make Gatun Lake large enough and consistently deep enough to serve both as a twenty-one-mile section of the Panama Canal and as a reservoir capable of providing water for the canal's locks.[62]

To the Central Division, Goethals assigned responsibility for all construction from a point just south of the Gatún Dam to the

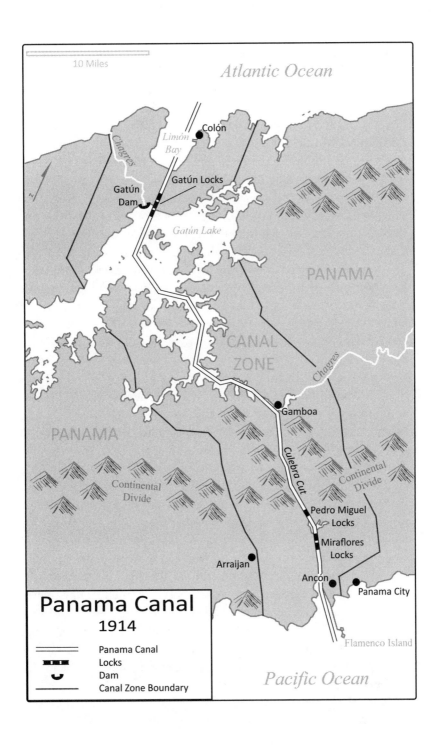

10 Miles

Atlantic Ocean

Chagres

Colón

Limón
Bay

Gatún Locks

Gatún
Dam

Gatún Lake

PANAMA

CANAL
ZONE

Chagres

Gamboa

PANAMA

Continental
Divide

Culebra Cut

Continental
Divide

Pedro Miguel
Locks

Miraflores
Locks

Arraijan

Ancón

Panama City

Flamenco Island

Pacific Ocean

Panama Canal
1914

Panama Canal	
Locks	
Dam	
Canal Zone Boundary	

Continental Divide at Pedro Miguel. Leading the Central Division was David DuBose Gaillard, a well-regarded army engineer. The division's principal tasks were to dig and dredge a channel through what would become the expanded Gatún Lake after the completion of the Gatún Dam and to excavate the Culebra Cut. The latter was the most technically difficult project on the isthmus, even more difficult than designing and building the canal's monumental locks. The Culebra Cut—renamed the Gaillard Cut after that engineer's untimely death from a brain tumor in December 1913—was a nine-mile stretch of the canal that had to be blasted and dug out of mountains near the Continental Divide. Although initial estimates figured that excavating the Cut would involve removing 53 million cubic yards of earth, Gaillard's division had excavated more than 100 million cubic yards by the time the canal opened in 1914, nearly half of the total volume of excavation in the entire Canal Zone during the decade-long construction effort. The volume of excavation in the Culebra Cut was significantly greater than expected because its topography, soil, and weather frequently combined to produce catastrophic mud slides throughout the construction period and even after the canal opened in 1914. These slides bedeviled Goethals, Gaillard, and the entire Central Division, accounting for nearly one-third of all excavation in the Cut.[63]

The Pacific Division's area of responsibility began at the end of the Culebra Cut and stretched to the canal's Pacific terminus near Flamenco Island south of Panama City. This division's major tasks included digging, blasting, and dredging a channel from the Culebra Cut to the Pacific and constructing locks at Pedro Miguel and Miraflores. Goethals placed his close friend and associate Sidney B. Williamson in charge of the Pacific Division and appointed other civilian engineers to serve as his assistants. In doing so, he fostered a productive rivalry between the Atlantic and Pacific Divisions. Because the former was led and staffed by army engineers and the latter by civilian engineers—and because the two had very similar scopes of work—the Atlantic and Pacific Divisions competed to outperform each other, especially after Goethals decided to publish the statistics of each division's progress in excavation and concrete emplacement in the weekly ICC newspaper, the *Canal Record*.[64]

While the three engineering divisions built their foundations and managed their physical construction, Goethals considered the canal's massive locks to be complex enough to demand an independent department equal in stature if not in size to the engineering divisions. When President Roosevelt and Congress decided in favor of a lock canal, John Stevens had opened an office in Washington to design the locks. Goethals moved that office and its staff to the isthmus as a subordinate organization within the office of the chairman and chief engineer, placing Harry Foote Hodges at its head. Hodges was an army engineer who had graduated from West Point one year later than Goethals and who enjoyed an excellent reputation from previous work on the Soo River. He and his staff were responsible for designing not only the massive lock gates but also—and more important—the intricate array of valves and conduits needed to make the locks electrically powered and capable of raising and lowering ships twenty-eight feet in fifteen minutes or less. Hodges was also responsible for monitoring the manufacture of the lock gates, which was the only major aspect of the construction of the Panama Canal that was subcontracted to a private firm.[65]

Goethals applied the same organizational principles to the medical, administrative, and logistical dimensions of the work. He left the Sanitary Department in William C. Gorgas's hands. By the time Goethals arrived, the problem of yellow fever on the isthmus had been resolved. "By the fall of 1907," Gorgas recalled, "our fight against disease in Panama had been won, and from that time on, our attention was given to holding what had been accomplished."[66] But that blithe statement belied the scale and scope of medical work that remained. Although the commission recorded its last death from yellow fever on November 11, 1905, the Sanitary Department could not become complacent. Gorgas's inspection teams, oil slickers, and fumigation teams had to continue their work in order to keep the *Aedes aegypti* mosquito at bay.

But since 1905, Gorgas's principal nemeses had been the *anopheles* mosquito and malaria. The *anopheles* presented a much more difficult problem, as it was far more resilient than the *Aedes aegypti*, proving remarkably impervious to attempts to eradicate it at the larval stage. While Gorgas could not eliminate the threat posed by the *anopheles*, he thought he could drastically reduce it. His teams fanned out across the Canal Zone to drain swamps, spread oil in standing water that could not be drained, clear overgrown land near the canal and the cities and camps along the line of the canal, treat the entire Canal Zone with in-

secticide deemed so essential that the ICC built a special plant to produce it locally, and introduce into the environment imported natural
predators of the *anopheles* mosquito. Additionally, Gorgas's Sanitary
Department administered roughly 40,000 doses of quinine per day in
the hopes of mitigating the incidence of malaria in an environment in
which the very best efforts could only reduce the *anopheles* population,
not eradicate it altogether.[67] The department's work brought significant results. In June 1907, the Isthmian Canal Commission reported
an average daily sick rate of 31.1 per thousand employees and an annual total of 205 deaths from malaria. By June 1912, the average daily
sick rate was down to 22.91 per thousand employees and an annual
total of only 21 deaths from malaria.[68]

Goethals used a similar departmental structure to address the
administrative and logistical functions of the Isthmian Canal Commission. He charged the Quartermaster Department with recruiting
skilled and unskilled labor, assigning all quarters for ICC employees,
constructing, furnishing, and maintaining residential and office buildings, and acquiring and distributing fuel, food, distilled water, and
supplies throughout the Canal Zone. He organized the Department
of Commissary and Subsistence to manage the ICC's commissaries,
hotels, kitchens, and messes. Goethals also assembled an office and
staff for the examiner of accounts and disbursements to manage finances and claims throughout the construction of the canal. Finally,
he organized the Department of Civil Government, which managed
the Canal Zone's post offices, police force, prisons, schools, fire department, and courts.[69]

Goethals relied upon a departmental system of organization in part
because it was the only way he could attempt, with varying degrees
of success, to keep his own workload down to a manageable level.
Even though he was conscious of the need to delegate and therefore
organized the work in geographic and functional divisions and departments, Goethals's personal share of the work was still enormous. In
his second month on the job, he reported to his family, "Since I came
here, I have been confined to the office almost continuously from
7:30 AM to 10 PM."[70] A few days later, he reported that his office hours
began at the same early hour and lasted "till we shut up, and though
I have stopped for lunch & dinner, I have been spending evenings at
it as well." He then expressed a determination to set an office routine

A Sanitary Department worker applies oil to a drainage ditch near Miraflores in June 1910. Spraying pools of standing water with oil to eradicate mosquito larvae was an essential tactic in the battles against yellow fever and malaria. (National Archives, 185-G-1973)

that allowed him to get out to personally observe "some part of the work" at least every other day.[71]

By all accounts, he succeeded in setting such a routine and even increased the frequency of his inspection tours along the line of the canal to six mornings a week. But that did not in any way alleviate the length of his work days or the weight of his duties. Observers through-

out Goethals's tenure in Panama commented on his almost ubiqui-
tous presence in the Canal Zone, the consistently late hours he kept at
his office, and the eventually fatal chain-smoking habit he developed
in Panama as a means of dealing with the stress of the job.[72]

The departmental system was absolutely essential to the successful
completion of the canal. Goethals realized that he needed to harness
the expertise and creativity of his subordinate engineers and officers in
order to get the job done. He immediately perceived the advantage of
the organization adopted in 1908 and maintained it, with some modifications, for the rest of the construction period. "The more I think of
this organization the more it appeals to me," Goethals wrote to David
DuBose Gaillard at the Central Division. He believed that such an
organization would "throw responsibility" on those subordinate leaders in charge of the various new divisions who had been designated
members of the Isthmian Canal Commission "to a greater extent than
they now have."[73]

Later and in a more public forum, Goethals explained what he believed were the most important virtues of the mode of organization he
used in Panama. "In addition to definitely fixing the work in charge
of each subordinate," Goethals wrote in *Scribner's Magazine*, "an effort
was made to give him full authority and hold him responsible, thus
securing the best that was in him." And in his view, it worked. He reported that "each individual took a personal interest and pride in the
work, feeling that the particular work on which he was engaged was
the important piece; it therefore became *our* Canal and *we* were doing
it."[74] Managing leaders at multiple echelons in the organization was a
critical piece of Goethals's solution to the managerial problem that he
perceived the Panama Canal to be. Managing leaders, however, was a
particularly thorny issue for Goethals.

On this point, many commentators have depicted Goethals as either
an all-powerful czar or a despot concerned at least as much with increasing or preserving his own power and authority within the Canal
Zone as with completing the canal.[75] Such interpretations are founded
upon a misinterpretation of contemporary commentary. Goethals's
own friends referred to him as "the Czar of Panama," and a reporter's
remark that Goethals, "with his immense capacity for work and the
restricted area of his domain . . . succeeds in the role of an autocrat

after a fashion that must cause no little envy to Nicholas II," was representative of depictions of Goethals that appeared in the press during the construction period.[76] Goethals himself agreed, writing in his account of governing the Canal Zone that President Roosevelt's executive order of January 8, 1908, which unquestionably declared that all other members of the Isthmian Canal Commission were subordinate to the chairman and chief engineer, "permitted the subordination of everything" and placed him at the head of "an autocratic form of government for the Canal Zone."[77]

But as Goethals's statement shows, these characterizations referred to the form and extent of Goethals's power and authority, not to the manner in which he exercised power and authority. In referring to him as a czar, Goethals's friends were remarking on the fact that he controlled not only the construction of the canal but also the "civil government, courts, schools, post office, municipal governments that are scattered all along the line, the police, [and] the battalion of marines."[78] The reporter who characterized Goethals as a successful autocrat also wrote that "such an absolutism would not be endured except for the almost universal feeling that Goethals is just."[79] Although that claim somewhat overstates the case, it accurately captures a widely held contemporary opinion that Goethals did not abuse the vast power and responsibility he held. While he was given autocratic powers, he did not behave as a tyrant.

In fact, Goethals delegated considerably more authority to his subordinate leaders than one reasonably could have expected from an army officer of his generation. As Williamson recalled, "While Col. Goethals was always willing to discuss the work with his Division Engineers in any or all of its phases and was thoroughly familiar with it from the ground up, he left the administration and details of the work to the respective division heads and held them strictly responsible for the results."[80] Goethals retained responsibility for planning the canal's locks and the Gatún Dam within his office, delegating that considerable task to Harry F. Hodges and his department staff. Otherwise, according to Williamson, "other features such as the smaller dams, municipal improvements, docks and foundation plans for the locks were prepared in the division offices," then approved by Goethals.[81]

An example of this style of management occurred in 1908 when Goethals and the military engineers on the ICC determined that the original plan placed the locks on the Pacific side of the canal in a location that would be unacceptably vulnerable to hostile naval gunfire in the event of war. Williamson surveyed and selected new locations for the locks and forwarded his findings and recommendations to Goethals for approval. Williamson then created the general schematics for a flight of two locks at Miraflores and a single, final lock at Pedro Miguel. When a disagreement arose among the three division engineers as to the feasibility of Williamson's plan, Goethals asked Sibert, Gaillard, and Williamson to conduct a technical study of the issue and forward their written opinions to him. Unsurprisingly, Williamson argued in favor of his plan. Sibert and Gaillard advocated for a triple lock at Miraflores and the elimination of the Pedro Miguel Lock. After studying both options, Goethals approved Williamson's plan, which informed the Pacific Division's work through 1913.[82]

On this issue, Goethals allowed his subordinates much discretion. At no point did he unilaterally direct any action or create technical plans of his own. His interventions into the matter occurred at only two points: the initial identification of the problem and the final decision on its resolution. In between those interventions, his subordinates developed and advocated for their own plans. This is particularly noteworthy on an issue as important to the construction of the Panama Canal as the location and general plan for three of its six locks.

Despite his ability to delegate, Goethals was by no means an easy person to work for. He was an incredibly demanding boss, especially to his principal subordinates. Some of those who reported directly to Goethals found him to be an acerbic taskmaster. Robert E. Wood served in Panama as the ICC's assistant chief quartermaster and eventually as its chief quartermaster throughout Goethals's tenure. He went on to serve as the acting quartermaster general of the army in 1918 before becoming a successful businessman who held the presidency of Sears, Roebuck from 1928 to 1939 and serving as chairman of its board until 1954. Reflecting upon his many experiences and accomplishments, Wood remarked of Goethals in 1963, "I was his assistant for seven years, and I might say that everything in my life since has seemed comparatively easy." To Wood, Goethals was "stern and unbending—you might say a typical Prussian."[83] Williamson remembered that while Goethals's leadership style was to delegate authority and then hold subordinate leaders "strictly responsible for the results," his personality was such that "this made a man do his best and carry on his work so that he was damned certain of the results."[84]

In holding his principal subordinates "strictly responsible for the results," Goethals spared no feelings and took little account of pride or ego. He did not attempt to rule by committee, nor did he attempt to build consensus once he had made up his mind. As he said after opening the canal, "I doubt if this result could have been accomplished in any other way than by a single responsible head."[85] While he delegated and consulted freely, Goethals was quite firm and unbending once he came to a definite decision about a problem. He was equally firm and unbending when he felt a subordinate was underperforming or when he was not satisfied by the results attained by a particular department or division. At times this was a source of considerable friction.

Although they maintained a functioning professional relationship, Goethals and Gorgas had a major falling out in Panama that affected their personal relationship for the rest of Gorgas's life—and beyond, as it influenced a particularly villainous depiction of Goethals in Marie Gorgas's 1924 biography of her late husband.[86] At first Goethals and Gorgas got along well enough. For the entirety of March 1907, while Goethals was in the Canal Zone getting acquainted with the work and John Stevens had not yet departed, the Gorgas family cheerfully hosted Goethals and his wife, Effie, at their home.[87] In late 1907 and early 1908, however, Goethals grew concerned with the way Gorgas managed the Sanitary Department. As brilliant a doctor and scientist as he was, Gorgas's organizational skills were subpar. Goethals, Williamson, Sibert, Gaillard, and Secretary of War Taft noticed that Sanitary Department operations were somewhat inefficient, suffered from inadequate coordination with the engineering and quartermaster divisions, and reported expenditures that appeared unreasonably high. As Williamson put it in his own characteristically colorful way, Gorgas was "too easy going and of too pleasant a disposition to be a good executive . . . and his subordinates took advantage of this and spent money like drunken sailors."[88]

Taking action, Goethals decided to reallocate certain Sanitary Department functions to other organizations within the ICC. While the Sanitary Department retained direct responsibility for the hospitals and the sanitary inspectors, the crews that performed the drainage, ditching, and fumigation work related to the antimalarial campaign would be managed by the Atlantic, Central, and Pacific Divisions. This was a matter of redistributing control of work crews, supply management, and disbursement of funds, not a matter of transferring responsibility for the fight against malaria. Gorgas and his sanitary inspectors still maintained full control over antimalarial work throughout the isthmus. Nevertheless, Gorgas interpreted the new measures as a personal and professional affront. Goethals consulted him on the decision and secured the doctor's acquiescence to a six-month test of the new system. At the end of the trial period, Gorgas requested a return to the old system. Observing a reduction in expenditures and new malaria cases, Goethals rejected that request. Whenever Gorgas revisited the issue, as he did in 1909 and 1910, Goethals's curt reactions betrayed rising levels of frustration and commensurately decreasing levels of patience. As the two drifted further apart, he came to view Gorgas's continued objections as a sign of disloyalty.[89]

Relations with Atlantic and Central Division Engineers Sibert and Gaillard were similarly strained. A member of West Point's class of 1884 whose subsequent canal and river work was both well known within the Corps of Engineers and a source of great personal pride, Sibert believed he was more qualified than Goethals to lead the construction effort in Panama. He resented his subordinate status to an engineer whom he considered to be less adept at canal work, and he rarely passed up an opportunity to directly or indirectly express his frustrations to Goethals and others, including members of Congress whom Sibert thought he could prod to arrange for Goethals's removal.[90] As early as June 1907, after Sibert made a petty issue of seniority in rank with Gaillard—both army majors at the time—because an executive order had mistakenly listed his name before Gaillard's, Goethals reported home that "Sibert . . . gets cantankerous and hard to hold at times."[91] His opinion hardened after years of Sibert's scheming. In the summer of 1911, Goethals wrote in a response to a congratulatory letter from Col. Albert Todd, the army attaché to the American legation in Berlin, "I was somewhat amused by your remark that I am 'seconded so efficiently and loyally by Gorgas and Sibert.'" He continued, "This is neither true in spirit nor in fact."[92]

David DuBose Gaillard was also a member of the class of 1884 at West Point, where he had been Sibert's roommate. Gaillard was a brilliant engineer who struggled mightily with the problems in the Culebra Cut, especially the infamous mud slides. He too bristled under Goethals, believing that Goethals lacked confidence in him and was too demanding. Goethals had full confidence in Gaillard's engineering abilities, but he did have some concerns about Gaillard's management of his division. The problem, as Goethals reported in a letter to his son in April 1907, was that Gaillard alienated his workers almost immediately after arriving on the isthmus. "For some reason or other, the men don't take kindly to Gaillard," he noted. Because of the nature of the work in the Culebra Cut, he explained, most of Gaillard's workers were railroad men who were "rough and outspoken & they are all anxious to deal directly with me." Given the circumstances, Goethals concluded, "If things don't improve—as I hope they will when the men find that his talk is after all harmless, I shall ask to have him relieved."[93]

Goethals therefore gave extra attention to Gaillard, which Gaillard perceived to be undeserved micromanagement. Between Goethals holding him "strictly responsible for the results" in the Culebra Cut and within the Central Division, and the mounting strain of the recurring slides in the Cut, Gaillard was constantly stressed, almost to the point of a mental breakdown. Although he died from a brain tumor on December 5, 1913, his widow believed his demise was due to the pressure Goethals had put on Gaillard. Upon encountering Goethals's youngest son, Tom, who as a medical student had been invited to observe Gaillard's unsuccessful brain surgery, Katherine Gaillard remarked coldly, "Your father has killed my husband." She never swayed from her belief that it was the work and not cancer that killed her husband, whom she described as "a man, who in the accomplishment of the conquest of the slides, absorbing their cost into that of the regular excavation, finishing the work ahead of scheduled time—did so at the cost of his life."[94]

While Goethals was in no way responsible for Gaillard's death, he was not exactly blameless in these disputes. He maintained coldly adequate professional relationships with his detractors. But at the same time, he took some amount of vindictive pleasure in frustrating them on relatively insignificant matters that did not impact their work in the Canal Zone. Disapproving requests for leave appears to have been one of his preferred means of revenge. Gorgas was on the receiving end of this tactic at least twice. And Katherine Gaillard at one point felt compelled to pay a personal visit to the secretary of war in Washington in order to preempt Goethals's rejection of her husband's request for leave.[95]

Despite such tension—for which he was at least as responsible as any of his antagonists—Goethals continued to work effectively with and delegate authority to his subordinates throughout the construction period, even those among the decidedly anti-Goethals faction in the Canal Zone. However much he was tempted to do so, he did not lobby for the relief of Sibert, Gaillard, or Gorgas until he began to make plans for the post-construction organization of the Canal Zone and its workforce, when he determined that the remaining work no longer justified their positions. In fact, he intervened in 1908 and persuaded Secretary Taft to refrain from relieving either Sibert or Gaillard in an attempt to make room on the commission for the newly designated head of the ICC Quartermaster Department, Maj. C. A. Devol. According to Goethals, "Such a course would have discredited the officer suggested for relief by the secretary, and this I wished to avoid."[96] Similarly, "the question of getting rid of Gorgas," attested Sydney B. Williamson, "never entered Goethals's head."[97]

Goethals's professional and personal relationships with his principal subordinates in the Canal Zone were not all fraught with the tension and controversy that was part of the fabric of his relationships with Gorgas, Sibert, and Gaillard. Williamson remained a friend to and defender of Goethals for the rest of his life. Harry F. Hodges and his naval counterpart in the Canal Zone, Rear Adm. H. H. Rousseau, remained close and eventually served as honorary pallbearers at Goethals's funeral.[98] And Robert E. Wood admired the man he had described as a tough and demanding boss, remarking almost fifty years after the canal's opening that Goethals's "iron will and energy were responsible for driving the work to conclusion in record time."[99]

Wood's view was shared by many of the rank-and-file workers. For Goethals, managing the work in the Canal Zone extended well beyond his principal subordinates. In addition to his deputies, Goethals devoted considerable time and energy to managing the entire workforce. Although he recognized this as one of his two most significant managerial problems, Goethals had no consistent example to guide his approach to labor management.

The managerial revolution offered no uncontested model for the relationship between a leader and the led. Some civilian executives were strict disciplinarians—either out of an obsession with efficiency rooted in a belief that maximum efficiency led to maximum profits, or because new technologies demanded firm discipline in order to minimize accidents and work stoppages. Others were more benevolent, focusing more intently on workers' morale out of a belief that a content workforce was more productive and therefore was good for business.[100] Goethals was more inclined toward the morale-centric approach, as it accorded well with lessons he internalized during his service in Florence, Alabama. He firmly believed that "contentment leads to efficiency" and that "the best results are secured through co-operation of men who are contented and who have respect for and confidence in their leader."[101] But as his inclusion of "respect for and confidence in their leader" vaguely suggests, Goethals saw value in the disciplinarian approach as well.

The common theme in these two distinct approaches to labor management is that they were informed by perceptions of what was best for business. Similarly, at his core, Goethals firmly believed that "everything should be subordinated to the construction of the canal." More than anything else, that singular notion informed his management of labor in the Canal Zone. He alternated between being a stern disciplinarian wielding absolute power and authority in the Canal Zone and being a conscientious steward of workers' morale as he felt the good of the canal required.[102]

The workforce that built the Panama Canal was enormous and diverse. When Goethals arrived in 1907, it consisted of 29,446 employees of the ICC and the Panama Railroad Company. Almost 19 percent came from the United States and 15 percent came from Europe, while approximately two-thirds came from the West Indies.[103] Three years later, the workforce in the Canal Zone included 38,676 employees of the ICC and the Panama Railroad Company, with roughly the same demographic composition.[104] Goethals quickly realized that in such a large and diverse workforce was an equally diverse set of cultures, norms, and expectations of how the work should be conducted and how labor should be managed. He wrote in 1915 that the presence in the Canal Zone of "40,000 men gathered from all parts of the world," who were "many miles from home and away from the ties and associations which have more or less guided and restrained them," made the "human element" of his job "charged with uncertainties and difficulties."[105] To Goethals, managing the workforce was at least as significant and complicated as the technical aspects of canal construction, if not more so.

Goethals believed that the first step to managing a civilian workforce somewhat reticent about military control of the project was to establish his authority decisively. He chose to do so over the issue of unions in the Canal Zone. In March 1907, Goethals arrived in Panama in the midst of an ongoing labor dispute over wages for steam shovel and locomotive engineers and conductors. Hoping to strengthen their negotiating position, these men pressed their demands through union leadership. The International Brotherhood of Steam-Shovel and Dredge Men took the issue straight to the White House in January 1907. When President Roosevelt referred the matter to the ICC, the local chapters of the unions representing steam shovel and locomotive engineers and conductors in the Canal Zone took up the issue with John Stevens. While Stevens was willing to meet a few of their demands, the deal he offered fell far short of their expectations. Still unsatisfied, they formed a committee to approach Goethals, who refused to take any action on the grounds that the union had already brought the matter directly to the Roosevelt administration, thus requiring a decision from Secretary Taft.[106]

News of Taft's decision arrived on the isthmus on May 6. Based on changes to the average wages in the United States, Taft agreed to raises for the locomotive engineers and conductors, but refused all of the steam shovel crews' demands. Furthermore, Taft decreed that future labor disputes would be addressed to and adjudicated by ICC officials in the Canal Zone. Goethals applauded the decision, writing that "so long as recourse could be had to the authorities in Washington, it would be useless to attempt an adjustment with a view to prompt settlement unless the men were given what they demanded, for, if denied, they would immediately take it to Washington." Taft's decision bolstered Goethals's ability to manage the workforce, not only avoiding a repetition of the labor dispute with the steam shovel and locomotive engineers and conductors but also "materially strengthening the hands of the isthmus authorities."[107]

Goethals wasted no time in leveraging his newly strengthened position. The steam shovel crews were particularly displeased with Taft's decision and opted to escalate the situation. Union leaders planned to force the issue through mass resignations. Assuming that their services were too important to the construction effort for ICC officials to allow them to leave, union leaders reasoned that the threat of mass resignations would move the ICC to meet their demands. Most crews adhered to the plan. As Goethals recalled, "Out of a total of forty-eight steam-shovels that had been at work, in two days' time only thirteen shovels were left with crews."

To the surprise of his disaffected crews, Goethals refused to negotiate and allowed them to leave the isthmus. He filled many of the vacancies on the steam shovels with mechanics and junior clerks who had listed any amount of previous mechanical training on their employment records. Having given the equivalent of promotions and pay raises to the replacement steam shovel crews, and with the locomotive engineers and conductors having received part of the increase in wages they had demanded, Goethals created a situation in which "the sentiment was against the steam-shovel men." He assessed that "the disturbance affected the work and reduced the output for the time being, but the action taken had a wholesome effect on all classes of employees, for the steam-shovel crews had appeared to be indispensable, yet the outcome showed conclusively that the defection by them or any other one class of men would not tie up the whole work."[108] He put it more bluntly and more revealingly in a letter home shortly after the ordeal, reporting that the resolution of the issue left the workforce "so tame that they now meekly eat out of our hands" and that "the men have learned that it doesn't pay to bluff."[109]

After the dust settled, a committee of locomotive engineers and conductors requested a meeting with Goethals. They hoped to persuade him to sign a written agreement guaranteeing them not only the concessions that Taft had granted but also the right to collectively represent any individual engineer or conductor with grievances in the future. Goethals refused, electing to make a stand on this issue. His goal was not to challenge Taft or Roosevelt but to keep unions out of the Canal Zone and strengthen his own authority in resolving future labor grievances. Goethals told the committee that their proposed agreement was not "in accord with government practice, and the Canal, as government work, so far as concerned the various classes of employees, was an 'open shop.'"

He also curtly informed the committee that "it was ill-advised to make *demands*," and "thereafter none would be given any consideration." Making what he considered to be the all-important distinction, he explained that "requests, if properly made, would be received and acted on according to their merits." Finally, he "declined to take up with any committee a grievance of any individual of the order that it represented, for the best party to present it and with whom to discuss it was the person aggrieved." He promised the committee that any member of the workforce could raise any grievance to their immediate supervisor, and if that failed to bring a resolution that satisfied the aggrieved worker, he could then see Goethals about it, confident that the matter would be investigated and adjudicated if the investigation showed that the complaint had merit.[110]

Through these early decisions and actions, Goethals strengthened his authority and ability to manage the workforce. By keeping unions out of the Canal Zone and rejecting collective bargaining, Goethals simultaneously removed the mechanism by which zone-wide strikes could occur and averted subsequent incidents in which local chapters could appeal over his head by pushing national and international trade unions to lobby the White House directly. Perhaps most important, by denying individual workers any recourse other than appealing directly to him to resolve labor disputes, Goethals exponentially increased his influence over the workforce by maximizing both his contact with individual workers and the extent to which workers felt he was invested in them personally. In this way, the policy increased both Goethals's authority and the morale of the workforce, in which many—though certainly not all—appreciated the quick access to the ultimate authority in the Canal Zone in the event of labor disputes and grievances.

Throughout his tenure, Goethals consistently strove to maintain his singular authority, which he considered to be critically important to the construction effort. When Taft, as president-elect in early 1909, ordered him to adjust his stance on unions and "receive committees," Goethals persuaded Taft to modify the order. A revised directive mandated that Goethals permit collective representation for collective issues affecting any "class of labor," but granted him the authority to refuse collective representation for any individual worker.[111] Subsequently, there were few large-scale labor disputes in the Canal Zone, and those that did arise failed to affect the work to any substantial degree.

Although prohibiting collective bargaining played a significant role in the relative absence of major labor disputes in the Canal Zone between 1907 and 1914, a more important factor was Goethals's effective and well-publicized campaign to improve and sustain the morale of his workforce. This is certainly not to say that the ICC rank and file worked in an idyllic paradise. Most toiled for little pay under extraordinarily austere conditions, and all were subjected to a hostile disease environment. As Gorgas's efforts bore fruit, deaths from disease decreased. However, as improving sanitary conditions enabled more focused attention on excavation, deaths from preventable accidents increased dramatically. But at no point did an exodus of labor occur as it did during the yellow fever epidemic in 1904–1905. In fact, so much of the workforce opted to remain on the job that Goethals's labor agents had to suspend recruiting unskilled laborers in 1910. Despite glaring injustices in the pay and privileges afforded to different groups of workers, particularly nonwhites, the workforce remained generally content and committed to building the canal.[112]

That apparent contentment and commitment, however, is surprising. Although the vast majority of the workers who built the Panama Canal were people of color, racial discrimination was rampant in the Canal Zone. From the outset, American attitudes and perceptions about race shaped ICC labor policies to an incredible extent. Aware of the comparatively high wages in the United States, canal officials made a deliberate decision to fill nearly all of its unskilled labor force—by far the largest class of work on the isthmus—with foreign workers. Popular yet bizarrely pseudoscientific theories about the work ethic, strength, subservience, honesty, and relative immunity to tropical diseases of various races and ethnicities informed officials' decisions on where and whom to recruit to build the canal. During his tenure as chief engineer, John Stevens was frustrated that he failed to persuade officials to send Chinese laborers, whom he believed were highly efficient workers and immune to all tropical diseases. While he had immediate access to a pool of willing West Indian laborers, he was unable to reconcile his racist prejudices and accept them. In fact, he wrote that it was "useless

"Silver roll" employees hard at work on compressed air drills in the Culebra Cut in 1913. During the American construction period, the gold and silver rolls were used as a vehicle to bring segregation and other Jim Crow laws to the isthmus. As is evident in this photograph, silver roll employees were almost exclusively nonwhite unskilled laborers. (Library of Congress, Prints and Photographs Division, LC-DIG-hec-03147)

to think of building the Panama Canal with native West Indian labor," and he did not "believe the average West Indian nigger is more than equivalent to one-third of an ordinary white northern laborer."[113]

Stevens's prejudices influenced the racialization of the so-called silver and gold system, the hallmark of structural and officially sanctioned racism in the Canal Zone.[114] "Silver" and "gold" referred to the ICC's two payrolls, the gold roll and the silver roll, and the distinction between the two was implied by their terms. Gold roll employees were paid in American gold-backed currency. Silver roll employees, on the other hand, were paid in local silver-backed currency. Originally, a laborer's classification was determined by the distinction between skilled and unskilled labor, with the former filling the gold roll and the latter relegated to the silver roll. Although most of those listed on the gold roll were white Americans or Europeans, nearly a thousand

Americans exported Jim Crow laws and norms to the isthmus of Panama. "Silver roll" employees were segregated and relegated to substandard living conditions in the Panama Canal Zone. While their white colleagues lived in spacious homes in well-planned and supplied cities, workers of color lived in houses and communities they constructed on their own throughout the Panama Canal Zone. (National Archives, 185-G-1442)

West Indians had been classified as skilled laborers and listed on the gold roll.[115]

Stevens, however, brought Jim Crow laws to the Canal Zone. As he supervised the construction of housing, hospitals, hotels, and kitchens to prepare the Zone for construction, he took measures specifically designed to avoid racial intermingling. Accordingly, the distinction between the gold and silver rolls was gradually racialized, with "gold" becoming a euphemism for white Americans and northern Europeans and "silver" becoming a euphemism for workers of color. Those familiar with the means and modes of racial segregation in the United States in the late nineteenth and early twentieth centuries felt quite at home with the implications of separate commissary entrances labeled "gold" and "silver," gold-only hotels, and silver-only kitchens.[116] One astute observer correctly noted that through the silver and gold system, "the I.C.C. has very dexterously dodged the necessity of lining the Zone with the offensive signs 'Black' and 'White.'"[117]

Goethals inherited this system from Stevens and did nothing at all to change it during his tenure. He convinced himself that the silver and gold system continued to be defined by class of labor and not by color. He maintained that position even after construction was complete, going so far as to say that the silver and gold system "was found not only convenient but politic, since it avoided all reference to the color line." This was no mere rhetoric; Goethals genuinely believed that the silver and gold system was color-blind. He even made some attempts to enforce distinctions along classes of labor rather than color, going so far as to reprimand commissary clerks who treated black Americans differently than white Americans, pointedly reminding them that American citizens of any color were American citizens. But while he would from time to time address the grievances of individuals who had been discriminated against because of their race, he took no steps to repair a system that enshrined inequality and segregation in the Canal Zone, nor did he ever recognize that the system was consciously designed to preserve and even promote inequality and segregation.[118]

Goethals's cognitive dissonance on this issue was rooted in his own racism. Longtime friend and colleague Sydney B. Williamson, who was profoundly racist in his own right, accurately described George Goethals as "a man of strong prejudices."[119] Evidence of such prejudices is readily apparent in surviving correspondence from various stages in his career. In 1877, he exchanged letters with a friend in which he referred to Cadet Johnson C. Whittaker—an African American member of Goethals's class who was brutally assaulted two months before graduation in 1880 and, in perhaps the worst chapter of West Point's history, subsequently expelled under false charges of feigning the entire incident—as "the Darkey." Going further, Goethals applauded an incident in which a fellow cadet had assaulted Whittaker and reported that he and his colleagues were watching Whittaker's progress in mathematics, rooting for him to fail and be dismissed by the academic board.[120]

Goethals's views did not temper over time. In response to the army's decision to station an all-black cavalry detachment at West Point in

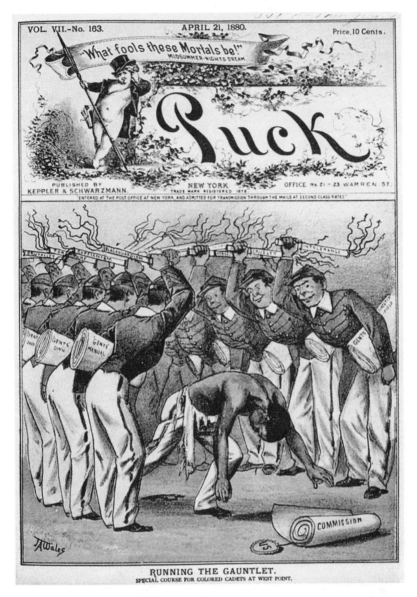

This April 21, 1880, cover of Puck magazine—depicting a black cadet being beaten by white cadets as he tries to obtain a commission as an officer in the US Army—is a direct response to the Charles Whittaker case, which justly earned West Point a fair amount of infamy. Whittaker's ordeal showed that systemic racism was a significant problem not only at West Point but also among the officer corps writ large. George Goethals was not immune to its influence and likely cemented his views on race while attending West Point. (Library of Congress, Prints and Photographs Division, LC-USZC2-1231)

1907, Goethals wrote to his son, "I am sorry that they have sent the negro troopers to West Point." He explained, "I can appreciate the feeling of the Southerners on that score, and the powers that be ought to have considered that point."[121] Later still, and despite their vital contributions as the vast majority of his workforce in Panama, Goethals claimed that "West Indian laborers were never entirely satisfactory." He wrote, "Their standard of living is low, and as a class they are sluggish and lack vitality; but their efficiency was increased by introducing competition through the European laborer, by supplying them with proper food, by training, and by familiarizing American foremen with their peculiarities."[122]

In his racism, Goethals was unexceptional for his time. American society during the Gilded Age and Progressive Era was unabashedly racist. Where he was exceptional, however, was in his willingness and capacity to temporarily put aside deeply held racial prejudices to deal fairly on an individual basis with those against whom he was prejudiced. This too was a trait that Goethals carried throughout his career after his cadet years at West Point. Later, his ability to deal fairly on an individual basis despite his prejudices was a hallmark of his tenure in Panama, and it was one of the most significant factors in his ability to keep the canal workforce content and stable enough to finish the canal.

Goethals demonstrated it most clearly by intervening in Cadet Charles Young's case at West Point in 1889 while serving as an instructor of engineering. Never gifted in the technical subjects, Young finished the first semester of his final year at West Point ranked second to last in his class in civil and military engineering, which Goethals taught. In the spring examinations at the end of his final semester, Goethals declared him deficient in engineering, endangering Young's ability to graduate and receive a commission. In its initial deliberations in June 1889, the Academic Board reviewed Young's files, found him deficient in engineering, and recommended him for dismissal. At that moment, however, Goethals's "sympathy was aroused."[123]

He intervened and prevailed upon the board to grant Young a reprieve to study further and undergo a reexamination prior to September 1, 1889. While preparing to leave West Point for his next assignment on the Tennessee and Cumberland Rivers, Goethals set aside one or two hours every day for the entire summer to tutor Young to assist him in preparing for his reexamination. Two days after Goethals left West Point, Young passed the examination and was commissioned as a second lieutenant of cavalry, the last cadet in the class of 1889 to graduate.[124] Young was profoundly grateful for Goethals's efforts. He would proclaim in later years that he could never forget "the disinterested help of . . . General Goethals." Thinking about those who treated him well during his cadet years, Young went on to say that "the world is better and only worth living perhaps, because it has its Skerretts, Bethels, Goethals, Gordons, Barnums, Haans, and Langhornes with the others of that stripe."[125]

Goethals made a point of offering both access and similarly "disinterested help" to workers in Panama regardless of race. In his weekly routine, he set aside five hours on Sunday mornings to hear their complaints and grievances. He frequently launched formal investigations to determine the validity of what he heard, taking swift and decisive action when his investigators determined that a worker had been wronged. "Sunday court," as it came to be known, attracted so many visitors that in order to allow all to be seen, Goethals had to devise a system in which "gold" employees could go straight to Goethals's office and "silver" employees only reached Goethals if they first met with his secretary or chief clerk and remained unsatisfied after that meeting. Despite this extra hurdle, nonwhite workers regularly got through to air their grievances to Goethals, who proved just as willing to investigate their claims and redress legitimate grievances as he was with white workers.[126]

That Goethals accommodated such diverse groups in his Sunday morning sessions stood out as particularly noteworthy to his admirers and critics alike. The latter saw Goethals's Sunday routine as an exercise in paternalism carried out by a "Venetian doge" and a "patriarchal despot." But there is far more evidence of contemporary observers viewing Sunday court in an unreservedly positive light. Journalist Albert Edwards described one such Sunday morning in which "the first callers were a Negro couple from Jamaica" arguing about money, after which "came a Spanish laborer who had been maimed in an accident," who was followed, respectively, by a man who had been recently fired, a committee of machinists, a nurse, a foreman, and then an African American laborer before there had been so many visitors that Edwards stopped taking note of individual cases. "It is as remarkable a sight as

I have ever seen to watch him at it," Edwards wrote, explaining that Goethals was "a good listener until he is quite sure he has got to the nubbin of the matter, and then, like a flash, the decision is made and given."[127]

Some of Goethals's contemporaries ascribed his commitment to holding court every Sunday that he was on the isthmus to a strong sense of fairness to which Goethals consistently adhered. Pacific Division engineer Sydney B. Williamson insisted that Goethals was "absolutely fair in his dealings with his organization from the highest to the lowest laborer on the work."[128] While Goethals prided himself on treating the workers fairly, he would not have agreed that this was the underlying motivation for his Sunday routine. Although he did have a strong commitment to fairness when dealing with people on an individual basis—precisely the quality that allowed him to move beyond his racial prejudices in one-on-one interactions—his Sunday morning sessions were motivated above all not by empathy but by his interpretation of the relationship between the morale of the workforce and workers' efficiency. According to Goethals, conditions in Panama "were not conducive to contentment; on the whole, a general clearing-house became an important factor in the common desire to secure harmony, and the 'Sunday court,' which seems to have attracted attention, was established more for this purpose than with the idea of meting out justice."[129]

The relationship between workers' morale and efficiency informed all of the actions Goethals took on behalf of the workforce. "That contentment leads to efficiency was fully recognized at the beginning of the enterprise," he wrote in 1915, "and had resulted in the adoption of a broad, generous, and what seemed to me a very wise policy in regard to the force." That belief influenced Goethals's decisions to improve housing, improve the quality of food served to the workforce, and open YMCA clubhouses in all of the ICC towns along the line of the canal. It even inspired the establishment of a baseball league in the Canal Zone that became so popular and competitive that Goethals at one point had to launch an investigation because various divisions and departments were giving temporary contracts to professional baseball players during their off-season in order to gain a competitive advantage. His concern for and actions on behalf of workers' morale extended to their families. "If Mrs. Smith were dissatisfied," he explained, "Mr.

Smith was apt to be dissatisfied also, with a consequent loss of interest in his work and lack of efficiency." Going further, Goethals wrote that "if these little grievances and dissatisfactions had been allowed to smolder, they would have spread and become general throughout the force, seriously affecting the whole human machine."[130]

Goethals succeeded in sustaining the morale of his workforce, though not necessarily in the ways that he intended. Most of his efforts to improve morale in order to generate and maintain a stable and efficient workforce were directed at the gold workers. His housing initiatives were generally limited to towns built for gold roll employees and families, while their silver roll counterparts lived in barracks, dormitories, or ramshackle settlements along the line of the canal. The YMCA clubhouses that were established throughout the Canal Zone were gold roll establishments. And while silver workers could watch baseball games put on by the Canal Zone's league, they were not allowed to play. And yet although it was generally efficient, the gold force was never stable, constantly subject to high turnover as its workers grew restless or homesick and left the isthmus. The silver force proved far more reliable and stable.[131]

This suggests that of all the actions Goethals took on behalf of workers' morale, his accessibility to workers was the most effective. His Sunday morning sessions and random encounters with laborers during his routine travels throughout the Canal Zone certainly were the most color-blind and the most applicable to the entire workforce. Much celebrated during the construction period and long remembered afterwards, "Sunday court" was immensely popular with canal workers, among whom a song called "Tell the Colonel" had become popular by 1911. "Don't hesitate to state your case, the boss will hear you through," the third stanza began. "It's true he's sometimes busy, and has other things to do, but come on Sunday morning, and line up with the rest—you'll maybe feel some better with that grievance off your chest."[132]

Ultimately, Goethals's belief that "the canal would be built if the men could be managed" was correct. The results reveal that his management of the work—improving its organization, managing his principal subordinates, and managing the workforce—was an absolute success. In his first year on the job, Goethals pushed the Isthmian Canal Commission to excavate an amount of material that tripled what had been excavated between 1904 and 1907. The output of the ICC under Goethals only became more impressive over time, leading inexorably to a completed canal.

On August 15, 1914, the greatest engineering triumph of the twentieth century opened with little fanfare or acknowledgment. Although a grand multinational parade of ships had been planned for the occasion, events in Europe overshadowed any ceremonies in Panama. As the Belgian garrison at Liège fell to the German army in the opening campaign of the First World War, the world hardly noticed that the small steamer *Ancon*, filled to capacity with the longest serving canal workers, successfully traversed the Panama Canal and formally opened it to commercial shipping. The *Ancon*, however, commanded all of Goethals's attention. Having led the construction effort in Panama for more than seven years, the chief engineer watched its progress from shore, shadowing the ship in a railcar adjacent to the canal. Watching the *Ancon* exit the final lock and make its way to the Pacific Ocean marked the culmination of the project that consumed all of his thoughts and energies for the better part of a decade. Under Goethals's leadership, the Panama Canal was at last open to commercial traffic—a result that was very much in doubt when he arrived on the isthmus in 1907.[133]

While effective, Goethals's managerial philosophies and techniques were not original. Instead, they reflected both managerial practices then popular within corporate America and what American society then celebrated as "scientific management." Like the major railroads of the mid- and late nineteenth century, Goethals organized his major engineering divisions geographically. Like the large multidivisional corporations that succeeded the railroads as the largest private enterprises in the United States, Goethals organized supporting engineering, medical, administrative, and logistical departments and divisions along functional lines.

Just as turn-of-the-century executives ran their corporations, Goethals delegated considerable authority to subordinates he selected to lead departments and divisions, while at the same time closely monitoring their progress. He maintained firm control over the general direction of the entire project and retained enough power to be the final arbi-

By 1913, the completion of the Panama Canal had become a forgone conclusion, and Americans eagerly anticipated its opening. This illustration from the January 22, 1913, edition of the magazine Puck shows Uncle Sam holding the American flag raised in his right hand and George W. Goethals sitting on his left shoulder, standing astride the Panama Canal, which he is presenting as the eighth wonder of the world to the other seven wonders (as recorded by Puck): "The Tomb of Mausolus, The Pharos of Alexandria, The Statue of Jupiter, The Pyramids of Egypt, The Hanging Gardens of Babylon, The Colossus of Rhodes, [and] The Temple of Diana." Little did they know that the next year's grand opening would receive scant notice from a world consumed by the opening campaigns of World War I. (Library of Congress, Prints and Photographs Division, LC-DIG-ppmsca-27913)

ter of major decisions in order to keep all divisions and departments functioning coherently and cohesively along schedules and plans he established or approved. With the work organized in that manner and a system in place that simultaneously facilitated centralized control and decentralized operations, Goethals focused on supervising his principal subordinates and maintaining the morale of his workforce in the hopes of maximizing its efficiency.

Goethals's embrace of the managerial revolution was by no means unusual within army circles. His leadership and style of management in Panama were widely applauded throughout the army, not just the Corps of Engineers. In personal letters received during a two-month span in 1910 alone—four years before the canal was completed—Goethals received high praise from a general commanding a division in the Philippines, the army quartermaster general, two majors of cavalry, and the general then serving as the president of the Army War College. Even the antireform stalwart Nelson A. Miles, who in an earlier time had banished Goethals from his command, expressed similar sentiments as early as 1908. Apparently, even those officers who most actively resisted the Root reforms saw merit in new managerial theories and techniques.[134]

Furthermore, Goethals's fellow officers revealed an increasing investment in the managerial revolution by regularly using its language in a military context and advocating for its methods in professional military journals during the early twentieth century. Brig. Gen. Robert K. Evans argued that the army needed to adopt more "businesslike" recruiting practices in the *Infantry Journal* in 1911.[135] A year earlier, another infantryman described the armies of the great powers as "huge machines" that had rendered war "a scientific affair" that could only be managed efficiently by professional soldiers.[136] Such thoughts and language appear in works produced by line officers, revealing that the army's acceptance of the managerial revolution was not limited to the Corps of Engineers, whose mission necessarily involved frequent contact and cooperation with American industry. The influence of the managerial revolution upon the army was much broader and cannot be ascribed to one branch alone.

Embracing the managerial revolution was the first stage of a gradual process that would eventually repair the schism between the army's institutional culture and its institutional structures wrought by the Root reforms. Subscribing to contemporary managerial theories allowed the officer corps to accept the notion of a general staff, even if it could not agree on the form and function of the General Staff as established in 1903. Most important, the managerial revolution provided the army with an effective theoretical framework to conceptualize and resolve many of its systemic weaknesses revealed during the first year of the American intervention in the First World War.

5

Crisis

The United States entered the First World War when it declared war on Germany on April 6, 1917. Despite Elihu Root's series of reforms in the wake of the War Department's scandalous performance in mobilizing for and managing the war with Spain, the army's readiness for war was only marginally better than it had been in 1898, a condition made abundantly clear by another troubled mobilization in 1917–1918. As a result of shortages of trained soldiers, robust mobilization centers, supplies, and ships, comparatively few American soldiers crossed the Atlantic in 1917. In fact, by April 1918—a full twelve months after declaring war—the United States had managed to ship only 320,000 soldiers overseas to join the American Expeditionary Forces (AEF), of whom approximately 4,600 had engaged in combat on the Western Front. At that time, the Germans had approximately 1,569,000 riflemen fit for service. Opposing them, the Allies mustered 1,245,000 riflemen. By lending only 4,600 soldiers to front-line combat by the end of its first full year of belligerency, the United States contributed only 0.37 percent of Allied combat power on the Western Front as the last major German offensives were getting under way.[1]

In light of these facts, few contemporary observers thought the United States was particularly successful in its first year of belligerency. In fact, it had been nearly disastrous for the army. Despite heady optimism in the spring, by the end of 1917 the army had mobilized more soldiers than it could supply, and it had yet to deploy enough forces to the western front to make a substantial impact on the battlefield. In combination, poor strategic direction and institutional dysfunction stemming from the schism between the army's institutional structures and institutional culture in the wake of the Root reforms brought the

American war effort uncomfortably close to failure. Thought to be a panacea, civil boards composed of zealous citizens of varying levels of qualification were unable to ameliorate the shortages of shipping and supplies that so plagued the war effort. Through it all, the army learned painfully and publicly that its deeply ingrained habits and preferences were wholly unequal to the problems posed by modern industrial warfare.

The army learned as it struggled with serious issues, some forced upon it and some self-inflicted. In addition to being too small to bring significant forces to bear on the battlefield, the AEF at the beginning of 1918 still relied on France and Britain for essential equipment ranging from helmets to tanks, artillery, and airplanes. Additionally, it was poorly trained and wedded to a tactical doctrine that blithely ignored many of the lessons learned by the Allies at great cost since 1914. Although both the AEF and the War Department proved to be learning organizations that were capable of resolving enough of their shortcomings to influence the course of the war in the latter half of 1918, their experience in 1917 was at best a long and perhaps unnecessarily problematic stumble into war.

The army's shortcomings in its first year at war served as a vital shock to its system. Although it did not identify all of its weaknesses, the army had recognized that its war effort was in danger of failing by the winter of 1917. This was a frightening thought, given Allied prospects after Russia withdrew from the war, allowing Germany to focus almost exclusively on the Western Front. Significantly, the points of failure in the American war effort that officers and the wider public alike identified and addressed were weaknesses in War Department organization and logistics. By its first winter, the AEF had not yet seen enough combat for its flawed training and tactical doctrine to be evident. But inadequate stocks of war materiel, ill-supplied units and training camps, congestion on the railroads, and a critical shortage of coal were failures that both soldiers and civilians could see plainly and understand.

On an institutional level, the army perceived its shortcomings to be failures of management. Because the managerial revolution had become well embedded within the army's institutional culture, War Department officials and army officers alike framed shortcomings and considered solutions in terms of prevailing theories and systems of management. From this perspective, and with the added weight of the prospect of failure and defeat, key officers and officials finally realized that the army's systems and structures were wholly inefficient and inadequate for the complexities of modern industrial warfare. This realization would ultimately prove fatal for resistance to reform. Thus the first year of the American war effort created a crisis severe enough to shock the army to a degree that made possible the cultural shift needed to realign the army's institutional culture with its structures.

One major cause of the army's lack of preparedness was more than a decade of institutional dysfunction in the wake of the General Staff Act of 1903. During and after Elihu Root's tenure as secretary of war (1899–1904), reformers failed to influence not only the extremely powerful chiefs of administrative and logistics bureaus but also Goethals's generation of officers more generally. Although they acknowledged and accepted modern managerial theories and techniques, many officers would have preferred considerably more moderate reforms to the existing bureau system than to create a general staff endowed with the power to synchronize and coordinate the efforts of the several bureaus, and so they continued to cling to their traditions. Consequently, Goethals and others—including some of those who, like Goethals, served on the General Staff in its earliest years—harbored attitudes about the General Staff that fell somewhere between apathy and contempt. Under pressure from the bureau chiefs and their congressional allies, and lacking clear support from the generation of officers that had risen to lead the officer corps, the General Staff in 1917 was but a faint shadow of what Root had envisioned in 1903.[2]

Root vacated the office a year after passing the General Staff Act, leaving the War Department in the hands of William Howard Taft. Ever the amiable diplomat, Taft placed more value in consensus than decision and preferred to leave the chief of staff and the bureau chiefs to mold their own working relationships. Without firm backing from Taft, the General Staff could only exercise its planning and coordinating functions if the chief of staff could overcome the resistance of the bureau chiefs. None of the first three chiefs of staff overcame them. The fourth, Maj. Gen. J. Franklin Bell, was much more willing to confront the bureaus but still could not preserve the authority of the General Staff.[3]

In this power struggle, the pendulum swung briefly in favor of the General Staff during Maj. Gen. Leonard Wood's tenure as chief of staff from 1910 to 1914. The bureau chiefs, led predominantly by Adjutant General Fred C. Ainsworth, vigorously reasserted their claims to power by resisting what they perceived to be Wood's encroachments upon their rightful prerogatives. Secretary of War Henry Stimson, Elihu Root's former law partner, sided with the chief of staff in a much-publicized struggle over muster roll procedures in 1912 and forced Ainsworth's retirement under the threat of court-martial for insubordination.

Within the War Department, prospects for the new General Staff seemed promising. Ainsworth, however, proved to be as stubborn and energetic as Wood.[4] In retirement, he enlisted congressional allies to continue his efforts to diminish the power of the chief of staff and to sharply restrict the size and scope of the General Staff. Prompted by Ainsworth, the powerful Senate Armed Services Committee drafted legislation to protect the authority and independence of the bureau chiefs. Parts of the National Defense Act of 1916 constituted the apogee of attacks by the bureau chiefs and their allies in Congress. While the act authorized an increase to the total number of officers assigned to the General Staff Corps, it sharply limited the number of General Staff officers who could be assigned to duties in or near Washington, DC.[5]

Institutional resistance to the General Staff envisioned by Root, however, was not limited to bureau chiefs and their congressional patrons. Although officers of Goethals's generation generally agreed on the need for a general staff, they failed to achieve consensus on its form and function prior to the passage of the General Staff Act of 1903. The debate that played out in professional journals offered a wide range of options. Some officers had long advocated for a general staff similar to what the Root reforms created.[6] Many thought that rather than create a new entity altogether, the War Department should simply modify the existing bureau system to assign general staff responsibilities to the Adjutant General Corps and the supply bureaus.[7]

The officer corps remained ambivalent about the new system even after the passage of the General Staff Act. The editors of the *Journal of the Military Service Institution of the United States* felt compelled to publish an editorial in the fall of 1903 to persuade skeptical officers that the General Staff was compatible with army traditions and habits. "The general staff idea," they wrote, "is not a suddenly discovered and flippant innovation, but a broadly conceived and wise business proposition worthy of the honest and fair minded support of all military men." More tellingly, they argued that the new General Staff was not intended "to tear down the system which brought ultimate victory over the armies of the Confederacy, but to improve and render more elastic the methods which, during a long era of peace, had grown to be sufficiently unworkable to be distasteful to many of the general officers who have commanded troops in recent years."[8] As this editorial suggests, significant parts of the officer corps remained simultaneously convinced that military developments should be assessed according to the perceived lessons of the Civil War and obstinately ambivalent about the new General Staff. In the absence of a zealous commitment to reform, officers' perceptions, attitudes, and actions continued to be shaped above all by comfortably familiar traditions.

Consequently, between 1903 and 1917, officers of Goethals's generation often acted in a manner that undermined the General Staff. Aside from its stalwart partisans and those intrigued by its novelty, plenty of company and field grade officers did not look upon General Staff duty as a particularly desirable professional experience. Notably, John J. Pershing, who graduated from West Point in 1886 and went on to lead both the Punitive Expedition in Mexico in 1916–1917 and the AEF during the First World War prior to serving as the army's tenth chief of staff, recalled that the new body "did not meet at once with the full favor of the army" and that some officers "especially took exception to what they called a usurpation of authority" on the part of the General Staff, "and in several instances they had reason for complaint." Continuing, he opined, "The mere designation of members of the General Staff, including the chief is no guarantee of their infallibility; in fact, the first General Staff could have been duplicated several times over from the commissioned personnel of the army, to its improvement in several instances."[9]

Although he joined Goethals as one of the first officers assigned to the General Staff, Pershing fled as soon as possible to serve as an observer of the Russo-Japanese War, and he never returned to General Staff duty until he became the chief of staff in 1921. His skepticism of the new organization colored his view of it for the rest of his career. Pershing found fault with the General Staff's organization and operation, describing it as "too much the inarticulate instrument of the Chief of Staff, who often erroneously assumed the role of Commanding General of the Army."[10]

Goethals's own attitude about and interactions with the General Staff had much in common with Pershing's. He was only too happy when duty with the Taft Board pulled him away from the rest of the General Staff, and he never again sought an assignment to it. Furthermore, while he was in Panama, Goethals tended to work around the General Staff rather than with it. His surviving official correspondence from the Panama years reveals that he preferred to work with the bureau chiefs to obtain whatever support he needed from the army. His correspondence with army chiefs of staff is sparse and unexceptional, and his correspondence with the General Staff is limited almost entirely to issues related to the construction of fortifications to defend the Panama Canal.[11]

In part, Goethals, Pershing, and their contemporaries maintained such traditional attitudes because they saw no significant impetus for change prior to their experience of World War I. Goethals succeeded at Panama by working around, rather than with or through the General Staff—a point which only reinforced his confidence in the bureau system. Similarly, Pershing relied on traditional systems and processes when he commanded the Punitive Expedition (March 1916–February 1917) to pursue Pancho Villa into Mexico after his irregular forces had earned the ire of the United States by killing eighteen civilians and soldiers during a raid on Columbus, New Mexico, on March 9, 1916. The logistics effort to sustain Pershing's campaign showed considerable strain from the very beginning. But although this should have prompted individual and institutional introspection, the expedition itself did not present a shock substantial enough to force changes upon obsolete systems of supplying armies and waging war. In a self-congratulatory spirit at its end, many officers interpreted the Punitive Expedition as a validation of and a reason for confidence in the continued relevance of the bureau system.[12]

Neither Goethals nor his contemporaries anticipated that the First World War would provide just such a shock. In 1914, the army had just over 98,000 soldiers on its rolls and little inclination to become involved in the war then breaking out in Europe. By 1916, it had increased by approximately 10 percent, reporting a total strength of 108,399 soldiers. Although it expected to rely upon augmentation from the National Guard in time of war, this mobilization in 1916 brought only 158,664 additional men under arms. Given the mobilization of millions by European belligerents in 1914, the army clearly was not prepared to play a significant role in the war.[13] Although American public opinion generally sympathized with and supported Britain and France, the administration and Congress alike opposed intervention in the war during its first two years, rejecting the army's requests for appropriations to purchase additional arms, ammunition, and equipment to hedge against the possibility of entering the war. Throughout the period of American neutrality, the army had little reason and fewer resources to prepare for war.[14]

Despite opening the Panama Canal as the war in Europe was only just beginning, Goethals clearly did not anticipate going to war. In recognition of his achievements in Panama, he had been promoted to major general with the thanks of Congress. Rather than maneuvering for a command or senior duty in the War Department that would position him for significant service if the United States entered the war, Goethals remained in Panama. He served as governor of the Canal Zone from 1914 until September 1916, when he returned to the United States to retire from the army.

As governor, Goethals focused above all on transitioning the Canal Zone workforce from a construction organization to a smaller maintenance and operations organization, digging out from the maddeningly persistent landslides in the Culebra Cut that were substantial enough to close the canal for up to six months at a time and completing the construction of fortifications to defend the canal. Beyond the possibility of a European power attacking the canal, war did not weigh heavily on his mind.[15]

Although the army was more attuned to the war than Goethals, its experience of neutrality from 1914 through April 1917 did not produce a clear recognition of the imperative for institutional change. It continued to grapple with the proper role and composition of the General Staff, even as American soldiers deployed to the border and launched the Punitive Expedition into Mexico. While the Preparedness Movement—a national campaign for improved military readiness in anticipation of the possibility of intervening in World War I—became more popular in 1916, it had little impact on the army beyond prompting the sacking of Secretary of War Lindley Garrison, whose enthusiastic embrace of Preparedness was politically untenable at that time within Woodrow Wilson's cabinet. Consequently, the army neither updated its tactical doctrine to account for lessons coming out of the war in Europe nor prepared to mobilize and deploy an army of sufficient strength and capability to have an immediate impact on the battlefield should the United States be drawn into war. Even as late as the end of February 1917, Goethals could accurately note that "Washington is in a state of unrest as to the future, but there seems to be little doing in the way of preparedness for the army."[16]

The most significant step the army took to prepare itself for war was drafting and successfully lobbying for the Selective Service Act. Passed in February 1917, thanks in large part to the considerable efforts of Judge Advocate General Enoch Crowder, Chief of Staff Hugh Scott, and Secretary of War Newton D. Baker, the act laid the groundwork for raising an army in wartime through selective national conscription rather than through a nationwide call for state volunteer regiments. This was a significant success for military reformers, who were still working against the grain of army traditions and public perceptions of how to mobilize for war. Since the American Revolution, the army had relied on state volunteers to meet wartime demands for military manpower. The volunteer system continued to bear considerable weight in an officer corps in which junior and senior officers alike saw it as a legitimate opportunity for promotion and fame in war.[17]

Even after the passage of the Selective Service Act, the matter was not completely settled. Ever the active and vocal ex-president, Theodore Roosevelt lobbied strenuously for the right to raise a volunteer division and bring it to France as the first American divisions committed to the war.[18] Although a growing proportion of officers denounced the idea as arcane, dangerous, and completely inappropriate, many officers still applied to serve in Roosevelt's division. Goethals pushed his oldest son—a 1907 graduate of West Point then serving as a captain of engineers—to interview for a position in the division and then leveraged his connection with the former president ensure his son would be selected.[19] Even a young Capt. George C. Marshall—who went on to serve with great distinction on the western front with the First Infantry Division and the AEF's First Army Headquarters—applied, interviewed, and was selected to serve as a regimental commander in Roosevelt's proposed division. Marshall, Goethals, and others like them eventually needed formal releases from Roosevelt when it became apparent that Woodrow Wilson would not authorize the volunteer division.[20]

In sum, despite setting conditions for the first national draft since the Civil War, the army remained egregiously unprepared for war in 1917, a condition for which the army itself bore a significant amount of responsibility. Institutional dysfunction and congressional politics gutted the General Staff, leaving it far too small to plan and coordinate the myriad aspects of mobilization for the type of mass industrialized warfare that characterized World War I. Lingering traditionalism within the officer corps also influenced not only the retention of arcane tactical doctrine but also friction over the best model for expanding the army in the event of war.

Furthermore, inadequate strategic direction severely limited the army's ability to plan and coordinate mobilization for a major war in Europe. Woodrow Wilson's goal had long been to reshape the world order according to his principles and his perceptions of the national interest. From the outbreak of war in Europe in 1914 until early 1917, Wilson believed that the best way to achieve that end would be to keep the nation out of war so that it could not only avoid wasting its power and resources on faraway battlefields but also stand well positioned to serve as a legitimate moral arbiter of peace. He repeatedly offered to mediate an end to the war, hoping that his status as a neutral mediator would allow him to dominate the peace negotiations.[21]

Wilson left few clues that suggest when he irrevocably shifted course. Some historians claim that it was in February 1917, when in rapid succession Germany resumed unrestricted submarine warfare and British officials disclosed the contents of the Zimmerman telegram to their American counterparts. At that point, Wilson came to the conclusion that neutrality was no longer an option and that the best way to ensure American influence in shaping both the peace and a new world order was to intervene and earn influence at the negotiating table by somehow contributing decisively to an Allied victory.[22] Others claim that although he began seriously considering American intervention at that point, he did not arrive at a firm decision until later in March 1917.[23]

Wilson's decision was similarly unclear to his contemporaries. Recounting a meeting at the White House on February 28, the famed activist Jane Addams wrote, "The President's mood was stern and far from the scholar's detachment when he told us of recent disclosures of German machinations in Mexico and announced the impossibility of any form of adjudication." Continuing, she recalled that Wilson addressed his audience that day "as to fellow pacifists to whom he was forced to confess that war had become inevitable."[24] If Wilson thought the war had become inevitable by the end of February, he neglected to tell anyone who would have a hand in the war effort. In his March 20, 1917, diary account of the cabinet meeting in which Wilson had asked for advice about whether or not to go to war with Germany, Secretary of State Robert Lansing concluded that "the ten councilors of the President had spoken as one [in favor of war], and he—well, no one could be sure that he would echo the same opinion and act accordingly."[25]

Like the cabinet, the highest echelons of the military were also unable to discern the president's thoughts about whether the United States would enter the war or what form any potential intervention would take. On the same day Wilson convened his cabinet to consider intervening in the war, the assistant chief of staff of the army, who only two weeks later would begin overseeing the first several months of mobilization, wrote, "I think, therefore, that whenever conditions are such that we are warranted in saying that war is threatening, movements to and from foreign service (except under advice of medical officers) should be temporarily suspended," as though those conditions were somewhere in the distant future.[26] Even the chief of staff was not able to direct his staff to come up with even the vaguest of operational plans until March 27, 1917, just five short days before Wilson delivered his war message to Congress.[27] Only one day earlier, Tasker H. Bliss, then serving as assistant chief of staff of the army wrote with an understandable note of exasperation to a friend, "You can imagine the pressure under which we are working here in the War Department just now." He added, "I do not know whether the work will result in any good or not. . . . We will all be wiser in a few days than we are now."[28] Famously mistrustful of career soldiers and committed to keeping his thoughts to himself and a very small inner circle of close friends and advisors, Wilson offered little clarity on his decision to commit the nation to war until only a few days before his war address to Congress on April 2.

Even after the country was at war, few in or out of the army knew what the American contribution to the war would be. Some anticipated a large army fighting in Europe, while others saw the United States providing only naval and financial assistance to the Allies. Firm plans for the deployment of a major American army did not mature and receive the president's final approval until the summer of 1917. Such delays hindered the development of a coherent program for mobilizing the army. It could not make basic decisions about how many training camps to build, where to build the camps, and how much war materiel to purchase or produce in the absence of a clearly defined strategic construct in which the army had a distinct role.[29]

These delays also retarded the equally important development of an industrial base sufficiently expansive and efficient to sustain a rapid mobilization and a protracted war effort. What ultimately became a 4 million man army would need millions of helmets, rifles, bayonets, bandoliers, and uniform sets; many more millions of bullets; thousands of machine guns, artillery pieces, trucks, wagons, and train cars; hundreds of airplanes and tanks; and enough food, fuel, and fodder to feed all parts of the army. And it would need enough ships to move soldiers and supplies across the Atlantic—a commodity in shockingly short supply.[30]

Shipping presented an immediate problem at the outset of the American intervention, and the administration called Goethals back into public service to address it. Few reliable American ships were available for use as seaworthy military transports in 1917, largely because of a half-century of decline and neglect in the US merchant marine. Navigation acts signed into law by George Washington in 1789 and kept in place with little modification throughout the nineteenth century prohibited the registration of foreign-built ships into the nation's merchant marine fleet. While a superabundance of American timber drove down the costs of shipbuilding in the United States and made American ships attractive options in the nineteenth-century maritime market, European shipbuilders produced ships made of iron and eventually steel. These materials were far superior in quality to America's wooden alternatives, and yet they were priced similarly following the Civil War. Even when a robust steel industry developed in the United States in the late nineteenth century, its monopolistic practices ensured prices remained considerably higher than its European competition.[31]

In the latter half of the nineteenth century, then, American merchants overwhelmingly preferred European-built ships. Accordingly, they were forced to register their ships under foreign flags, and the American merchant marine withered away. Having carried 65 percent of US imports and exports in the mid-nineteenth century, the merchant marine carried less than 10 percent by 1914. Looking for new sources of revenue, shipbuilders reconfigured their construction yards to take part in the massive naval modernization program that the United States undertook around the turn of the century. While this allowed the navy to prepare more adequately for industrialized warfare by producing more and better battleships, destroyers, and submarines, it did little for an army that would need to be transported and sustained over the Atlantic Ocean if it were to have any impact on the war.[32]

The Wilson administration recognized the explicit and implicit problems inherent in a depleted merchant marine. When the Panama Canal was nearly complete, administration officials agreed that the United States had a vested interest in rebuilding a federally owned and operated merchant marine. That sentiment gained momentum with the outbreak of war in 1914. Still committed to peace, Wilson sensed an opportunity to dominate Latin American trade as the war consumed the attention and resources of European competitors. With the passage of the Ship Registry Act of 1914, foreign-built ships could be transferred to the American registry. Further momentum stalled for a time due to formidable political resistance from friends of American shipping companies that feared being pushed out of business by a more robust merchant marine equipped with foreign-built vessels. By September 1916, however, congressional factions with nagging fears of economic isolation united with colleagues who supported the Preparedness Movement to pass the Shipping Act in September 1916. The law established the United States Shipping Board, granting it both regulatory and statutory powers to own and operate a merchant fleet. Additionally, it authorized the creation of the Emergency Fleet Corporation, a public-private corporation established under the Shipping Board to purchase and contract for the construction of merchant vessels.[33]

When the Shipping Act became law, George W. Goethals thought his service to the nation was nearing its end. First as chairman and chief engineer of the Isthmian Canal Commission and then as governor of the Panama Canal Zone, nearly a decade in Panama had taken its toll. The job was wearing, and Goethals was eager to enter private life and open his own engineering firm. By June 1916, he alerted his family that he planned to request relief from the Canal Zone and retirement from the army in July.[34]

This was an unrealistic timeline, partly because of the difficulty in appointing a replacement so quickly, and partly because of Goethals's well-known connections to Roosevelt, Taft, and other prominent Republicans who sustained him during the first several years of his tenure in Panama. It made Wilson uneasy to think about Goethals being in the country and out of uniform during a presidential campaign. And so the president persuaded Goethals to delay his retirement until after the election in November. Goethals departed the Canal Zone, never to return, in September 1916 and began to set up a new home and business in New York City. Placed on the retired list two months later, he opened his engineering firm in January 1917. His retirement from public service, however, was short-lived. Goethals reentered public life three months later when called to serve as chairman of the newly constituted Emergency Fleet Corporation.[35]

He was far from happy to serve in that capacity. Goethals had been approached in February and March 1917 by members of the Shipping Board who hoped to gain not only his endorsement for the emergency construction of a fleet of wooden ships in the event of an American entry into the war but also his consent to manage the construction of that fleet. For the Shipping Board, this was merely a public relations stunt intended to influence policymakers and the American public to accept its wooden ship plan. At no time did the board's leadership intend to give Goethals actual control of shipbuilding efforts. In the end, they gained neither his endorsement nor his willingness to join the effort. Goethals did not believe that wooden ships could be made strong enough withstand the forces of waves on the open ocean while being propelled by the relatively advanced steam engines called for in the Shipping Board's plans. Furthermore, he had "no desire whatever to handle" the Emergency Fleet Corporation. "If we were to enter the war," Goethals later explained, "I preferred military duty" in the traditional sense: in the field with the troops.[36]

Goethals was justifiably skeptical of the Shipping Board and its schemes. In an example of a flaw replicated too often on other civil boards organized to assist in the management and direction of mobilization for war in 1917, officials who lacked expertise in shipping and shipbuilding dominated the Shipping Board. The chairman was William J. Denman, a member of Harvard Law School's class of 1897 who had made a name for himself as a specialist in maritime and admiralty law and as one of San Francisco's leading progressive Democrats. One of his most trusted subordinates was Frederick A. Eustis, an amateur yachtsman and Harvard-educated scion of a wealthy Massachusetts family who taught Denman of the merits of the wooden ship plan. In fact, only one member of the Shipping Board in the spring of 1917 had a legitimate maritime background. The rest were merely political appointees and their friends.[37] Ultimately, then, the nation relied upon a lawyer and a nautical hobbyist to resolve a shipping crisis at least half a century in the making. This bode poorly for the war effort.

Goethals was also justifiably skeptical of his own fitness for the job. Although he could bring his experiences at the Panama Canal and his considerable organizational and managerial talents to the table, he lacked expertise in shipping and shipbuilding. He was sufficiently self-aware to know that ship construction was not his natural element. And as a lifelong soldier, Goethals longed for wartime service in France, not to waste away on a board that he considered to be full of "some excellent hot air artists."[38]

Having been very clear with the Shipping Board officials who approached him, Goethals was surprised to receive a letter from Wilson on April 11, 1917, that informed him of his appointment to lead the construction of the Shipping Board's wooden fleet. In it, Wilson told Goethals that he had approved the Shipping Board's plans and had been reliably informed that the wooden ship plan had received Goethals's "enthusiastic endorsement" and that Goethals had intimated to the Shipping Board that he "would be willing to accept in directing the enterprise in cooperation with them."[39] Apoplectic, Goethals took a train to Washington and demanded a meeting with the Shipping Board in which he bluntly called its chairman a liar. He then requested an appointment with President Wilson to clarify the situation. As a major general on the army's retired list, he acknowledged, "If this was a military duty which the President desired me to take hold of, there was nothing for me to do but accept." Wilson stonewalled. On his third unsuccessful attempt to see the president, he was informed by the president's personal secretary, as he later recalled, "that the President could not see me but expected me to take hold of the work, as I was subject to orders and he had decided that this should be my task in the war."[40]

Although his sense of duty compelled him to accept the president's decision without public complaint, Goethals did not assume control of the project, intending to put aside his differences with the Shipping Board. The duplicitous manner in which William Denman and other members of the board secured his appointment ensured a dysfunctional relationship with Goethals for as long as he was associated with them. In letters to his son, Goethals regularly referred to the Shipping Board as "the fool board."[41] Even its first meeting with the famed engineer serving in his new capacity quickly degenerated into mutual recrimination. "I found the air still hot," Goethals wrote in the aftermath, "but I increased the temperature by giving them my opinion of them, from which they gathered that I couldn't serve under them or with them and I assured them they had drawn correct conclusions."[42]

Despite this, the Shipping Board exercised its right to create a public-private corporation as a separate but subordinate entity to procure and contract for the construction of merchant and transport ships, and it named Goethals as its general manager. The Emergency Fleet Corporation was thus created on April 16, 1917. In a bid to maintain control over Goethals despite the general's insistence upon full control, Denman named himself as the president of the corporation. Goethals, however, did not acknowledge any degree of subordination in his new position. After the articles of incorporation were signed, he told his son, "A separate corporation was formed and I am it." Friction between Goethals and Denman was bound to continue.[43]

The two men immediately became embroiled in a major feud over the nature of the shipbuilding program. Goethals adamantly opposed Eustis's wooden ship plan and moved quickly to thwart it. Discovering upon his arrival that Eustis had arranged for the board to authorize firms in Georgia to construct yards for building wooden ships, Goethals "flew into the air" and countermanded the authorizations, mandating that no further orders for shipbuilding were to leave the offices of the Shipping Board and Emergency Fleet Corporation without his endorsement. "There were objections," recounted Goethals, who told the board that his demands "would stand until they discharged me or secured my relief."[44]

Goethals preferred a steel shipbuilding program to the wooden program that Eustis and Denman had attempted to force upon him through secret deals and arrangements before he arrived in Washington. He believed steel ships were more seaworthy, better able to escape or survive submarine attacks, and would be more useful in a merchant capacity after the war. Accordingly, he developed and advocated for a shipbuilding plan "stipulating the construction of steel vessels, with wooden ships limited to the number that could be turned out by already established yards." Such a program would contract existing firms and yards to construct a small number of wooden ships, but divert the preponderance of funds appropriated to the Shipping Board to orders for the construction of new yards capable of building steel ships.[45]

His proposals met with considerable resistance from the Shipping Board, which was already pushing forward with the wooden program. Goethals complained to his son that his new "job is the most strenuous one I have struck yet," a telling complaint in light of his career to that point. "I am so handicapped," he elaborated, "by the promises that have been made to every Tom, Dick, and Harry who has lumber that contracts would be given them." Continuing, he wrote, "I can't get the Fool Board to ask for permission to build steel ships as well as wood, and though I have been asking for money enough to do something, they haven't submitted their estimates, promising each day that they would do so tomorrow—and as tomorrow never comes neither do the estimates."[46] As Goethals's bitterness grew, his willingness to work with Denman in any constructive manner vanished. The feeling was mutual for Denman, who was more than able to match Goethals's assertiveness and combativeness. Thus began a tit-for-tat escalation of acrimony in which lay the true nature of their feud.

From early May onward, their inability to cooperate was much more about authority and control than it was about the relative merits of

wooden and steel ships. Simply put, Goethals resented what he perceived to be an intrusion upon his prerogatives as the general manager
of the Emergency Fleet Corporation. In one memorable and particularly tense meeting of the Shipping Board, Goethals "drew forth a
letter of instructions which Denman had sent" to him, telling Denman and the rest of the board that he would "flatly refuse complying
with the instructions." According to Goethals, the instructions "were
at variance with the understanding that I was in supreme control, that
I was there by order of the President, that I could be dictated to by no
one but the President and would maintain this position until relieved
by him."[47] Similarly, Denman resented Goethals's intransigence and
frequent challenges to his authority as chairman of the Shipping Board
and president of the Emergency Fleet Corporation.[48]

Mutual animosity blinded both men to the fact that they had gradually arrived at positions that were actually quite similar. Denman began the affair as a stalwart proponent of Eustis's wooden ship plan.
But Goethals's skepticism and a revelation in spring 1917 that wartime demands from Britain and France were leading steel shipyards
to significantly increase their capacity pushed Denman to adopt a
more moderate position that allowed for both steel and wooden ship
construction. Similarly, while Goethals was adamantly opposed to
the wooden ship program, he came to accept the inclusion of some
wooden ships within his own plans due to both fiscal constraints
and the existence of contracts already executed before he arrived in
Washington. Both Goethals and Denman, then, envisioned a hybrid
steel and wooden shipbuilding program by the middle of May 1917.
The only difference between their two positions was in the ratios of
wooden ships to steel ships they had in mind. They were already on
common ground and should have been able to resolve their remaining
differences to work together and contribute something constructive to
the war effort.[49]

But they did not. The feud between Goethals and Denman played
out in an ugly and public manner from May through July 1917. Both
men did much to add fuel to the fire. Goethals was unable to keep the
dispute confined to the offices of the Shipping Board and the Emergency Fleet Corporation. He allowed it to become a press sensation,
with journalists, editorialists, and cartoonists routinely calling attention to the escalating feud.

This poster, produced by the Wilson administration's Committee on Public Information, highlights the work of the US Shipping Board and the Emergency Fleet Corporation, implicitly emphasizing its importance to the war effort. Its statement that "teamwork wins" is particularly ironic, as it was produced in 1917 during the Goethals-Denman feud. (Library of Congress, Prints and Photographs Division, LC-USZC4-9879)

Goethals's uncharacteristic inability to keep his feud with Denman private may have been because, possibly for the first time in his life, immense professional stresses and pressures coincided with powerful personal stresses and pressures. His relationship with his wife had deteriorated, and it is unclear how often they lived together at this stage in their marriage. Goethals family tradition holds that the marriage had gone stale and cold at some point during the Panama years for reasons that remain unclear, and while they never divorced or formally separated, they spent increasing amounts of time apart in the 1910s and 1920s. This seems to be supported by the comparative dearth of references to Effie Rodman Goethals in his personal correspondence. She appeared more regularly in his letters before and during his first few years in Panama.[50] In addition, Goethals was in an unenviable position as a father and an experienced soldier. He had intimate knowledge of the flaws and shortcomings of the American mobilization for war and had to see his sons go off to war.

In his room at the Hotel Astor on the night of May 11, 1917, Goethals attempted to exorcise a gloomy mood by writing a letter to his oldest son, George. A trip to New York City should have allowed brief respite. But he had traveled north to see off to war his youngest son, Tom, a Harvard-trained and Boston-based doctor who was also an officer in a reserve medical unit. In New York, he was surprised to discover that Tom was newly engaged to a young woman named Mary Webb, whom he had never met. She did not make a strong first impression— Goethals reported to George only that "she seems very quiet and I hope they will be happy together." He was similarly succinct in describing his farewell to Tom. "I didn't linger long," he wrote. "[I] bade him goodbye and he's off to England, enthusiastic over the prospect and the future." The eldest Goethals, however, while outwardly cavalier about his son's opportunity for wartime service, was less enthusiastic. Something had unsettled him at the dock. Ruminating over what he saw of Tom's unit, he wrote, "They are illy [poorly] prepared and equipped and yet better so than some of the outfits that are going, I guess."[51] He was right, and the personal weight of that fact compounded the professional stress he was already suffering from.

Still simmering, Goethals also aired his grievances with Denman and the Shipping Board in a very public setting in late May when asked to deliver an impromptu speech at the annual banquet of the American Iron and Steel Institute in New York City, in which he proclaimed that the task he had inherited was "simply hopeless." He joked that he resented his association with the Shipping Board because he regarded "all boards as long, narrow, and wooden" and because it denied him what he believed to be the necessity of "absolute authority in carrying out any important work." For his part, Denman escalated the situation by lobbying incessantly for President Wilson's support in sustaining his authority at the expense of Goethals's and in systematically working to undermine his general manager's contracting initiatives. With their relationship irreparably poisoned, both men appealed to President Wilson for full authority in merchant and transport shipbuilding.[52]

The president supported Denman in the dispute. He was never quite comfortable with Goethals at the helm of the Emergency Fleet Corporation. Given his inclinations against career soldiers and associates of Theodore Roosevelt, Wilson likely would not have appointed Goethals without Denman's lobbying to attach the engineer's name to the wooden ship program to improve public support for the plan. When both Goethals and Denman appealed to him to intervene, the president did not agonize long over whom to support. He composed a diplomatic response to Goethals on July 19, 1917, stating strongly but politely that Goethals and the Emergency Fleet Corporation were subordinate to Denman and the Shipping Board.[53]

Goethals, however, refused to accept this subordinate position. In a reply the next day, he explained that he had accepted his appointment in April under the impression that it came with assurances that he would enjoy "absolute and complete authority for the administration on the constructing side; that everything the Board could do would be done, and that it would act on [his] suggestion and initiative." Goethals then explained, "Believing that a centralization of authority in one man is necessary to carry out the shipbuilding program rapidly and successfully, after mature consideration of the whole subject, I am satisfied that I cannot secure efficient results under the conditions of your letter." Concluding his resignation on a candid note, Goethals wrote, "I am convinced, therefore, that the best interests of the public welfare would be served if I were replaced by someone on whom full authority can be centered and whose personality will not be a stumbling block."[54] Finding that sentiment compelling, Wilson then asked

Denman to also resign from the Shipping Board, hoping to wipe the slate clean and allow officials untainted by public controversy to address the critical shortage of American ships.[55]

Goethals's nearly four months of service with the Shipping Board thus proved fruitless. As newspapers reported on the growing acrimony between Denman and Goethals, the Shipping Board made no progress whatsoever in resolving the shipping crisis. The Emergency Fleet Corporation eventually became a reasonably effective organization, working with the Shipping Board to facilitate the production of enough new ships to increase the gross troop and cargo capacity of American shipping by nearly 1 million deadweight tons, but most new ships entered service between June 1918 and January 1919.[56] As the war ended in November 1918, ships built under the auspices of the Emergency Fleet Corporation had only a limited impact on the American war effort. Almost four months of marking time while Goethals and Denman bickered over authority and the Wilson administration stood idly by cost the American war effort much in lost time and opportunity.

Goethals's experience with the Shipping Board was a microcosm of the American mobilization writ large. Progressives went to war in 1917, carrying with them the managerial theories and faith in bureaucratic structures that were important features of early twentieth-century American society. Aware that industrialized warfare on a vast scale required degrees of a controlled economy and coordination between industry and the military that the country had not previously experienced, the Wilson administration commissioned a number of boards, councils, and committees staffed by civilians to assist in coordinating the military, economic, and industrial mobilization for war. Entirely in keeping with his distinct approach to the presidency, however, Wilson gave these boards, councils, and committees vague instructions and poorly defined authority. The effectiveness of such agencies was entirely contingent upon both their ability to forge amicable and effective working relationships and the willingness of civilian and military officials to cooperate voluntarily. As administration-appointed council, board, and committee members scrambled to define their roles and authorities, the management of the war effort took on a confused and improvisational air.[57]

Such was the case with even the War Industries Board (WIB), which is generally considered to have been one of the most effective civil advisory and coordinating agencies established in 1917 and 1918. Wilson intended the WIB to coordinate American industrial mobilization for war. In 1917, however, the WIB was largely unsuccessful in its mission. Its mandate was unclear—some saw it as a temporary agency organized to meet a wartime emergency, while others assumed its purpose was to establish the systems necessary for the federal government to oversee a planned and coordinated national economy on a permanent basis. Additionally, the military did not perceive a need to listen to or work closely with the WIB prior to April 1918.[58]

Given the internal dynamics of the WIB and its dysfunctional relationship with the army and navy in 1917, even the formidable Bernard Baruch—who would revitalize the WIB in 1918—was sidelined and unable to aid the war effort in any substantial way. Baruch spent much of the last few months in 1917 hounding military and civil officials alike about the need to extract saltpeter from Chile to produce enough gunpowder to sustain the war through 1919 and 1920 and the related need to devote shipping to transport that saltpeter to American nitrate and powder plants. It was a fool's errand. Military officers had more pressing issues to deal with, and the Shipping Board could not find enough tonnage to meet the War Department's needs, let alone dedicate ships to satisfy Baruch's plans for saltpeter. This minor point of friction reveals much about the confused state of the American war effort during its first year. Baruch angrily spun his wheels over saltpeter, blind to the fact that although he had a point about the need for that particular resource if the war were to last into 1919 and 1920, the government and military were deluged with much more immediate needs and problems.[59]

Shortcomings in the civilian boards and agencies were not the only problems in the American mobilization in 1917. The army's performance was similarly improvisational and lackluster. With the General Staff so sharply restricted and the bureaus once again ascendant, many of the conditions that led to a problematic mobilization in 1898 still existed in 1917. Tasker H. Bliss foresaw the complications ahead. He wrote a memorandum to the chief of staff on March 31, 1917, recommending immediate changes to the War Department's management of logistics in order to avert disaster should the army be called upon to mobilize for war with Germany. Bliss foresaw a situation in which "the War Department may be placing huge orders for supplies of all kinds," but that the several bureaus of the department could inadvertently compete with each other for the same limited resources. "If the matter is not properly coordinated," he explained, "it may result that one bureau of the War Department requiring great quantities of such material will find that the manufacturers supplying it have tied themselves up for a long time in contracts with another bureau of the War Department." Bliss recommended "that this matter should be brought to the attention of bureau chiefs with the view to their arranging some sort of a 'steering committee' among themselves to ensure an orderly and uniform acquisition of supplies."[60]

Although it was not acted upon at the time, Bliss's warning was remarkably prescient. Only weeks later, the well-meaning commanding officer of the army arsenal at Rock Island, Illinois, cornered the market on the nation's leather supply, without regard for the needs of other arsenals or other supply bureaus. "Well, that was wrong, you know," he explained after the war, "but I went on the proposition that it was up to me to look after my particular job, and I proceeded to do so."[61] The problem was that many people were looking after their particular jobs, and nobody was coordinating them. By the summer of 1917, a national draft was in progress, and more than 150 distinct committees, agencies, and bureaus were requisitioning, purchasing, and transporting supplies in support of the mobilization. As each one zealously seized the initiative and went about its work, it was impossible for the secretary of war and the chief of staff of the army to be aware of all of the independent initiatives and efforts, let alone to synchronize them.[62]

Part of the problem was Secretary of War Newton D. Baker's failure to identify the ultimate responsible party for shaping the army's war program in 1917. Baker was not the most obvious choice for secretary of war. He had earned an excellent reputation among progressives as the highly successful city solicitor and later mayor of Cleveland. Little in his background or temperament made him a likely candidate for secretary of war. That did not stop Woodrow Wilson from nominating Baker when Secretary Lindley Garrison tendered his resignation in 1916 because he believed the president's belated and rather tepid support for the Preparedness Movement risked national security in an ill-considered pursuit of domestic political gain. The president nominated Baker in part because of his known antimilitarism and rumored pacifism. Wilson had long admired Baker, whose achievements in Cleveland had made him a rising star in the Democratic Party, and he had considered nominating the mayor for a cabinet position earlier in his administration. Given the political context of 1916, however, Wilson calculated that nominating Baker to serve as secretary of war would signal to domestic and international audiences alike that his late nod to the Preparedness Movement did not constitute a decision to enter the war. [63]

While Baker was an excellent choice for that purpose, he had much to learn before he would earn his reputation as a strong and effective secretary of war. In 1916 and 1917, however, Baker steered an ineffectively moderate course in the War Department. Accordingly, he supported the National Defense Act of 1916, which simultaneously ensured the continued existence of the General Staff and severely restricted its strength and authority to plan and prepare for war according to its original mandate. In the absence of a policy framework based on past experience or a close study of military problems, Baker's natural inclinations were to defer to perceived professional and technical expertise of senior and generally traditionalist officers, serve as an unquestioning conduit for President Wilson's opinions, and attempt to satisfy all interested parties in the event of disagreement or controversy. [64]

The secretary of war's relative passivity in managing the army during its first year in the war caused many of the most significant problems that plagued the war effort. Baker gave considerable latitude to Gen. John J. Pershing when he was appointed to command the American Expeditionary Forces in France, vesting him with "all necessary authority to carry on the war vigorously." Accordingly, Pershing believed that the War Department would answer to him, not the other way around. He believed he could dictate all of the terms and that the War Department would instantaneously comply. [65]

Pershing and nearly two hundred members of the AEF headquarters embarked for Europe on the SS *Baltic* on May 28, 1917. During the twelve-day transit, Pershing's staff convened a number of planning boards to consider all-important problems whose solutions would fundamentally shape the American war effort. Topics included the eventual size of the AEF, the theater of operations in which the AEF should be employed, when to commit troops to battle, and whether or not any amalgamation of US units with British and French units should be permitted. Pershing and his principal staff officers determined that the AEF should eventually grow to 1 million soldiers; that it would be employed along the southern portion of the Western Front in the Lombardy region; that it would remain a distinct national force rather than be deployed piecemeal as reinforcements for larger British and French units; and that it would be committed as soon as sufficient shipping could be arranged to transport divisions to France.[66]

Such questions, however, do not fall within the proper purview of a field commander. All dealt with problems of national policy, politics, national economics, and coalition warfare. The administration and the War Department should have provided Pershing with specific guidance for most of the questions his staff considered during its voyage to Europe. At the very least, AEF planners should have worked with staff officers in the War Department to verify that their plans were realistic and their requests were feasible. By planning while isolated in the hold of the *Baltic* for nearly two weeks, however, Pershing and his staff created their vision and expectations in a vacuum, without meaningful input from either the War Department that had to mobilize, train, and ship forces to Pershing or from the allied armies alongside whom the AEF would fight. Unsurprisingly, then, Pershing's plans and expectations were not entirely feasible.

The first and most significant obstacle was the lack of shipping. The tonnage required for the forces envisioned by AEF planners on board the SS *Baltic* did not exist. As Pershing's staff crafted its plans, the feud between Goethals and Denman was relegating the Emergency Fleet Corporation and the Shipping Board to a painfully ineffective and irrelevant existence from which it would not recover until 1918. With all appropriate ships available in the United States in the summer of 1917, the War Department estimated that it could only ship 650,000 soldiers to France prior to July 1918, assuming minimal losses at sea. That did not stop Pershing and his staff from drafting plans that called for more than 1.3 million soldiers in France by July 1918. With no significant tonnage of new American shipping forthcoming, the army had to rely on substantial British assistance to transport and sustain the AEF. But Pershing soon learned that German U-boats had sunk more than 1.5 million tons of British shipping in April and May 1917 alone. The

United Kingdom could not afford to dedicate any of its ships to support the AEF until it reduced its monthly losses. Because of this, the War Department's efforts resulted in shipping only 194,000 American soldiers to France by December 1917, despite the fact that the army by then had swelled to 1.1 million soldiers.[67]

Even before troops could be sent abroad, however, Pershing's plans made significant problems for mobilization efforts at home. The War Department was already hard-pressed to construct training camps in time to receive the first round of draftees. It contracted camp construction based on the assumption that the strength of American divisions would be approximately 21,000 soldiers, as outlined in existing army tables of organization. Pershing and his staff, however, decided that the AEF would deviate from established doctrine and field divisions that were each approximately 28,000 soldiers strong. This was no small administrative problem. Divisions that were more than 30 percent larger than anticipated necessarily required more than 30 percent more barracks, latrines, uniforms, food, and equipment than the War Department had anticipated. Because Baker had empowered Pershing with such authority, the War Department had to mobilize divisions at the strength that Pershing wanted. But it could not react in time to adjust the construction and supply contracts that had been drafted to build and sustain camps designed to mobilize smaller divisions. Although it was not the only factor, this contributed to chronic shortages of supplies at army training camps throughout 1917 and well into 1918.[68]

Exacerbating this situation was a fairly rapid succession of absentee and ineffective chiefs of staff of the army who proved unable to bring order from chaos. Hugh Scott held that post when the United States entered the war and officially held it until he retired on September 22, 1917. But he was absent for the vast majority of his wartime tenure because the Wilson administration elected to send him on a diplomatic mission to Russia from May through August of that year. Tasker Bliss filled the role in his absence and formally became the chief of staff upon Scott's retirement. Bliss was a dedicated and talented officer, yet too detail-oriented to be an effective chief of staff. Often lost in minutiae, Bliss's plodding pace in sorting through official business delayed action on urgent matters and did considerable harm to the war effort. Furthermore, he was ordered to France for six of the eight months that he served as chief of staff, leaving John Biddle to serve in his stead. Prior to the war, Biddle had been the superintendent of West Point. He had no business leading the War Department, and his own awareness of that fact defined his approach to the job. Biddle considered himself a caretaker waiting for his replacement to arrive, and therefore he hesitated to make decisions of any significant weight.[69]

Short of billets, supplies, ships, and strong leadership of the stateside arm of its war effort, the army mobilized and deployed to France at a painfully slow pace. Eight months after declaring war, fewer than 200,000 American soldiers were in France, and most of those were either rear-echelon troops or combat soldiers still in training and not yet committed to the front lines. Although elements of the First Division began serving "training" rotations in the trenches on October 21 and suffered their first combat losses on November 3, Pershing's staff reported on November 6 that none of the four American infantry divisions then in France were ready for frontline service for any purpose other than training. American and Allied officials alike wondered whether the army would be able to field forces of sufficient quality and quantity to play any role in stopping anticipated German offensives in 1918.[70]

Goethals was an unwilling spectator as the war effort sputtered and stalled. "I would give anything to go to France," he wrote to his son in July 1917, "but I see no hope of that." With the dust just then settling from his feud with Denman and subsequent resignation from the Shipping Board, Goethals observed, accurately for the time being, "The President isn't going to give me anything to do, that's certain." Disappointed but well aware of his place on the sidelines, Goethals returned to his engineering firm, resigned to a fate that demanded he "go to road work and whatever else may turn up."[71] Ever persistent, Goethals kept trying to convince anyone who would lend a sympathetic ear to an eager, if aged, soldier. In August, he met with Secretary of War Baker and cabled General Pershing in France requesting command of all American engineers overseas. Pershing neglected to respond, and Baker politely declined, arguing that such a move would be impolitic because Goethals had retired as a major general and would therefore outrank the chief of engineers, who was then still a brigadier general.

In October, Goethals reported somewhat despondently that a friend was "kind enough to say that he is going to try and influence Pershing to send for me, but I haven't any hopes."[72]

A few different motivations inspired these rejections. Politically, Goethals's name was tarnished. Given his links to Republican leaders, Wilson and Baker were already reluctant to place Goethals in any position where he could achieve prominence unless absolutely necessary. The public fiasco with the Emergency Fleet Corporation left Wilson feeling burned and exasperated. It would take much for him to allow Goethals to serve in any meaningful capacity again. Meanwhile, simultaneously convinced that modern war was a younger man's business and jealously mindful of his position and prerogatives as commander of the AEF, Pershing was reluctant to allow older, well-known generals to serve in the AEF.[73]

While in limbo, Goethals was the object of some suspicion rooted in the nativist sentiment pervasive in the United States during and after the First World War. For at least a century, American nativism had ebbed and flowed in cycles that generally corresponded with economic boom and bust cycles. During the Gilded Age and Progressive Era, however, nativism increased exponentially as mass industrialization and urbanization generated a significant increase in immigration. Tensions related to this increase intersected with ethnocentrism and a popular pseudoscientific eugenics movement to produce a phase in the history of American nativism in which Americans began to view Europeans in highly racialized terms.[74]

The outbreak of war in Europe in 1914 only made matters worse. Popular leaders like Theodore Roosevelt added fuel to the fire by declaring their hatred for all "hyphenated Americans" and demanding "100% Americanization" as a necessary precondition of wartime readiness. When the United States entered the war in 1917, nativist sentiment easily transitioned to anti-German sentiment. Paranoid about German spies and sabotage within the United States. Vigilante organizations popped up throughout the country to monitor their communities and enforce patriotism. One such organization, the American Protective League, boasted over 250,000 members nationwide. More than a grassroots organization, it gained official sanction to serve as a domestic espionage agency working closely with both the Justice De-

partment's Bureau of Investigation—predecessor to the modern FBI—
and the War Department's Military Information Division.[75]

In such an environment, Goethals fell under some suspicion. Although his ancestors were Flemish and Dutch, some assumed from his
last name that he was of German descent. Furthermore, in 1913 as the
Panama Canal neared completion, Goethals took a widely publicized
European tour during which he met with and was received warmly by
Kaiser Wilhelm II. In May 1917, an anonymous citizen referring to
himself only as "a true American" sent a memorandum to the *Providence Journal* alleging that Goethals had worked closely with a German
agent in the Canal Zone, surreptitiously communicating with German
naval officers by flashing lights out to sea from a room in the Tivoli
Hotel. The author of the memorandum also alleged that Goethals
had exaggerated the effect of the mud slides in 1915 and 1916 in order
to redirect ships carrying munitions bound for Russia around Cape
Horn, consequently denying the Russian army the timely arrival of
munitions needed to defend against German offensives on the eastern front. The editor of the *Providence Journal*, likely a member of the
American Protective League, passed these allegations to the Bureau of
Investigation. Its chief thought the accusations were likely false, but
forwarded them to the Military Information Division, which pursued
the accusations only so far as to determine whether the German agent
named in the memorandum was in the Panama Canal Zone. While it
does not appear that these accusations carried much weight in military
and political circles, they did plant seeds of doubt about Goethals
among the more paranoid.[76]

Regardless of how he came to be sidelined, Goethals stewed unhap-
pily as a passive observer of the war. In August, he noted that efforts
to resolve the shipping crisis were "getting nowhere." In September,
he was becoming more overtly critical of the war effort, telling his
family that he wished Elihu Root were back "in Washington at the
helm." Succinctly assessing the state of the war effort at home, Goethals commented acidly that "confusion still reigns here." By October,
he had entirely stopped pulling punches in his correspondence. Noting that the papers announced that Maj. Gen. John Biddle was likely
to succeed Tasker Bliss as acting chief of staff of the army, Goethals
remarked, "I am glad they are going to have brains and good judgment

there at last." November found Goethals no less critical, however, reporting that "everything is confusion in Washington" and that the mobilizing army was "seriously handicapped by lack of chow, clothing, rifles, and equipment of all kinds."[77]

Goethals's criticism of the War Department was consistent with the opinions and observations of many long-serving military officers early in the war. Col. Robert L. Bullard, a veteran officer of over three decades of service who would be promoted to command at the division, corps, and army level in 1918, jotted in his diary in June 1917, "Of my stay in Washington the great impression left is that if we really have a great war, the War Department will quickly break down." Peyton C. March, who would become the chief of staff in 1918, found that "the War Department, including the General Staff, had no conception of what we were entering upon" as the United States joined the war. Pershing himself described the War Department in 1917 as "suffering from a kind of inertia."[78]

These officers were justifiably critical of the war effort up to that point. With only some exaggeration, Oregon senator George E. Chamberlain claimed on January 19, 1918, that "the military establishment of America has fallen down."[79] Much went wrong in the first year of US involvement in the First World War. Cultural and political resistance to the Root reforms had ensured the survival and preeminence of the War Department's anachronistic supply bureaus. Meant to procure and distribute supplies for a small peacetime army dispersed throughout the continental United States, the bureaus could not possibly manage the demands of mobilizing and supplying millions of men. Although they tried their utmost, they could not keep pace with the enormous pace of modern industrialized warfare. They simply could not produce, procure, and distribute supplies at the same rate that the War Department was inducting soldiers drafted under the auspices of the Selective Service Act.[80]

Beyond failures of logistics, the American war effort in 1917 suffered from many other shortcomings. It lacked coherence and unity in communication and coordination between the AEF and the War Department. Pershing's rapidly changing plans and demands tended to upset or render the War Department's plans and initiatives totally irrelevant.[81] Moreover, in rushing to meet Pershing's demands, the

War Department dispatched severely undertrained units to France. And what little stateside training they did receive was based on faulty doctrine that failed to appreciate the extent to which modern artillery and machine guns had changed warfare. This was due to Pershing's abiding belief that stagnation on the western front was a product of European failures and that the war could be won with bayonets and the American spirit.[82] Officers like Goethals, Bullard, March, and Pershing, however, did not recognize all of these problems as they arose. Because those issues that were evident enough to be recognized by senior officers in the first year of the American war effort had been logistical in nature, officers focused specifically and somewhat exclusively on supply failures and the problems of mismanagement within the War Department.

Politicians and the public at large also focused on problems of logistics and management. As within the military, these problems stood out most clearly to the public because the army's experience of the war throughout 1917 was almost entirely limited to mobilization. Shortcomings in tactical doctrine would not reveal themselves until the AEF was more heavily engaged in combat in 1918. Similarly, many of the problems generated by Pershing's changing plans and demands would not be readily apparent until he later outlined a program that called for fielding one hundred American divisions in France by summer 1919, an expectation that defied any realistic appraisal of the country's ability to raise, equip, train, ship, and sustain a force of that strength.[83]

Conversely, mismanagement and supply shortages had become obvious to even the most casual observers. Reports of unacceptably high rates of illness at mobilization camps that were undersupplied for adverse weather shocked an American society that expected more from its government and military. Reports such as one coming out of Camp Custer, Michigan, that soldiers were splitting into two groups to alternate between their barracks and outdoor training sites because a shoe shortage forced them to share footwear, triggered troubling memories of the scandals surrounding the mobilization for war in 1898. Mismanagement of railroad shipments caused an energy crisis in the Northeast as coal cars stacked up beyond Philadelphia on the hopelessly congested rail lines leading to New York. And in France, the AEF received several newly arrived artillery batteries and machine gun companies that had gone through their mobilization training in the United States without ever having seen or used a howitzer or a machine gun. Such reports shocked and embarrassed soldiers and civilians alike. This was no way to win a war.[84]

Within military and civil spheres alike, the managerial revolution provided a conceptual framework to diagnose and attempt to repair the army's ills. Americans in and out of uniform believed that their war machine malfunctioned because of poor management and a faulty organization within the War Department. In his speech proclaiming that the war effort had "fallen down," Senator Chamberlain blamed "inefficiency in every bureau and department of the Government of the United States."[85] Facing congressional inquiries and a rising tide of negative press, Secretary Baker fell under increasing pressure to make a bold course correction. As the supply crisis became more severe, some politicians and newspaper editors began to call for his resignation. Baker needed to find a solution quickly. Seeking an officer of proven managerial expertise to solve the most readily apparent problems of a troubled mobilization, he advised President Wilson to recall Goethals from the retired list to serve as the acting quartermaster general of the army.[86]

Coinciding with changes in leadership within the Ordnance and Coast Artillery Departments, this first step in a thorough reorganization of the War Department met with widespread approval. As the agency responsible for supplying all of the basic items that an army needed to survive, the quartermaster general shouldered much of the blame for the mounting supply crisis. Installing Goethals comforted the army and the general public alike. It was widely believed that if anyone could successfully organize logistics on behalf of the army, the "Czar of Panama" could. Shortly after hearing the news, Pershing wrote a congratulatory letter to Goethals. "If anything in our army needs rehabilitation by a man of ability and affairs," he mused, "it is the Quartermaster's Department, and we all look for great improvement in its management." Not to be outdone, Theodore Roosevelt sent Goethals a characteristically direct and enthusiastic note: "I congratulate you, and thrice over I congratulate the Country!"[87]

Goethals maintained a modest, business-as-usual reaction to the news. "I notice by the morning paper," he wrote his son, "that the order is to issue placing me on active duty and assigning me as Acting Quartermaster General, so I am cleaning up here so as to be ready to go to Washington." Rather than dwell upon the news or the task ahead, he continued, "Among other things, I am sending out my Christmas remittances, so I am including yours, not knowing what my plans to be," making sure to give specific instructions for his daughter-in-law to receive half of the money. In his reply to Pershing, Goethals claimed to "need condolences more than congratulations," and went on to declare, "I am going to do the best I can and trust that we will succeed in keeping you supplied."[88]

Deep down, however, Goethals was elated to be free from what he considered to have been an exile to a state of helpless and useless obscurity. He looked forward to 1918, enthusiastic that he would no longer merely mark time as a passive observer of the war. And he hoped that he could give new energy and efficiency to the sputtering American war effort. From Washington, he wrote to Theodore Roosevelt with a determined air, "How long I am going to last here depends upon the support received and the lack of interference."[89] Bringing the same attitude and energy that sustained him through his years in Panama, Goethals would fundamentally reorganize army logistics in 1918. In doing so, he helped not only to build, deploy, and sustain the AEF through the end of the war but also to usher in a sea change in the army's institutional culture. Accepting that change was necessary on the near term conditioned the army to permanently abandon its anachronisms and adapt to meet twentieth-century challenges.

6

Resolution

Maj. Gen. George W. Goethals's appointment as acting quartermaster general in December 1917 was among the first of
Newton Baker's moves to shake up the War Department. It came with
a clear expectation that he would lead the troubled Quartermaster
Department in a new direction. When the United States entered the
war, the department was responsible for paying the soldiers, as well
as procuring and distributing their food, uniforms, and nontechni-
cal supplies and equipment. In wartime, its portfolio swelled to include the construction of cantonments and training camps, shipping
troops and supplies overseas, and also transporting supplies within the
United States—a responsibility it shared with several other bureaus. As
the months passed, however, it was apparent to even the most casual
observers that the Quartermaster Department was adrift and unable
to meet its many and varied responsibilities.

Civilian agencies and War Department bureaus alike assumed
responsibility for several quartermaster functions. Although the department retained a branch devoted to subsistence, purchasing food
became the purview of a wartime civilian agency—the Food Administration. Similarly, the Council of National Defense divested the
Quartermaster Department of much of the procurement of material
for uniforms and non-technical equipment. The General Staff then
carved the Transport Service out of the Quartermaster Department,
renamed it the Embarkation Service, and claimed ownership of it. In
combination, these changes further confused lines of authority and
responsibility, leading to considerable duplication of effort. Instead of
relieving the burden, they caused the Quartermaster Department to
flounder even more than it already had.[1]

A major part of the problem was that the traditional organization of the War Department was wholly inappropriate for modern industrialized warfare. While the industrial economy that produced supplies the army needed was organized by commodities, the War Department was organized strictly by military function, with several bureaus retaining independent responsibility for the procurement and distribution of supplies related to their army functions. Theoretically, this made perfect sense. Ordnance officers were ideally suited to purchase weapons and munitions; quartermaster officers were experts on clothing and subsistence; engineers were experts on their specialized equipment; and medical officers knew best how to supply field hospitals. In practice, however, the bureaus competed for the same resources. For example, ordnance officers purchasing shoulder straps and ammunition carriers, medical officers gathering supplies for hospital tents, and quartermasters procuring material to clothe the army all drew upon the same cloth and leather supplies and markets.

Such overlapping demand existed for all commodities and many finished goods. Upon his arrival at the War Department, Goethals found "that the Quartermaster General was buying clothing; that the Signal Corps was buying clothing; that the Medical Department was buying some clothing; that the Ordnance Department was furnishing blankets, so that we were all competing with each other." Continuing, he reported that the Quartermaster Department was "furnishing harness and saddles for mules, and also furnishing wagons; the Ordnance Department was furnishing saddles and harness for horses."[2] Similar competition existed for trucks. Although the Quartermaster Department had designed and started building "liberty Trucks"—warhorses for a modern age—the Ordnance Department and Signal Corps were purchasing other trucks and truck parts in bulk on the private market. Designed to operate independently, the supply bureaus' lack of coordination made for a horribly inefficient procurement process characterized by a lack of standardization, system-wide shortages, delays, and artificially high costs resulting from significant competition over increasingly scarce resources.[3]

Leadership was another part of the problem. Throughout 1917, Henry G. Sharpe served as quartermaster general. A member of the same West Point class as Goethals, Sharpe had spent more than three decades in the Commissary and Quartermaster Departments. In fairness, this dedicated officer notched up some notable achievements in 1917, especially establishing a Warehousing Division within the Quartermaster Department and developing a standard truck for army service. But his shortcomings far outweighed his successes. He contributed to confusion in the logistics system by allowing key duties to be stripped from his purview and was slow to reorganize his department to address more efficiently those missions for which he continued to be responsible. Most important, he failed to centralize control over his bureau's procurement efforts. Under Sharpe's lax style of management, individual department and depot quartermasters stationed throughout the United States held considerable purchasing prerogatives with no oversight from Washington. This exacerbated weaknesses inherent in the bureau system by fostering competition for resources within a bureau that already competed with other bureaus for the same resources.[4]

Sharpe had nothing to do with the final part of the problem. He had been seriously handicapped by personnel turnover among his headquarters staff. In the small peacetime army, most of the quartermaster general's headquarters staff were long-serving civilians, not uniformed officers. As the army began to expand in 1917, Sharpe "commissioned a great many of the more efficient men in the department, with the expectation that they would remain in the department and perform their former functions." Inexplicably, however, Chief of Staff Tasker Bliss "decided that they should be transferred elsewhere." This ill-considered decision stripped the department of its most knowledgeable and experienced personnel, leaving it, in Goethals's rather understated estimation, "in bad condition as far as its organization was concerned."[5]

From his first day at the War Department, Goethals approached his work with the same managerial philosophy that had served him so well in Panama. He endeavored to put the right organization, systems, and people in place to facilitate centralized authority and decentralized operations. He had considerable leeway to make whatever changes he deemed necessary. Despite his very public failure at the helm of the Emergency Fleet Corporation, Goethals was appointed acting quartermaster general with a clear mandate for change. "I went there with the understanding that I was to have a free hand," he later told a con-

Maj. Gen. George W. Goethals, photographed in 1918 or 1919. (Library of Congress, Prints and Photographs Division, LC-USZ62-106238)

gressional committee, adding that "it was accorded me throughout."[6] Although this characterization was not entirely true—conservative factions within the War Department frustrated several of Goethals's initiatives throughout 1918—he was considerably more empowered than his classmate and predecessor ever was. "When Goethals took over the work," Sharpe later recalled, "he could do a great many things that no one else could do."[7]

Taking advantage of this leverage, Goethals moved quickly to resolve the personnel problem in the Washington office. Absent a robust headquarters staff, he could not hope to effect positive change in the department at large—with its many depots, warehouses, officers, and agents spread throughout the country busily conducting the bureau's business. He leaned heavily on the private sector to furnish him with much-needed expertise and manpower. Understanding that he did not have the luxury of time to foster adequate expertise in expeditionary logistics and the industrial economy within the army, Goethals recruited successful civilian managers and executives to fill key positions within the department. He hired some in entirely civilian capacities. Robert J. Thorne—formerly the head of Montgomery, Ward, and Company, one of the two largest mail-order and merchandising corporations in the country—was a "dollar-a-year man" who served in the War Department as the assistant quartermaster general with neither a commission nor a salary. For others, Goethals arranged direct commissions for civilians to join his department as uniformed officers, reasoning that "there was something about the uniform which when a man puts it on seems to change his entire attitude."[8]

This tended to civilianize the Quartermaster Department, an outcome that Goethals fully intended. As an adherent to the principles and practices of the managerial revolution, he believed that civilian businessmen and executives possessed the most relevant and applicable experience and expertise that he needed to inject into the Quartermaster Department. More important, however, civilianizing the department was the opening gambit in a much more ambitious endeavor to consolidate War Department procurement under one responsible agency, later reasoning that he hired so many civilians because the Quartermaster Department was "a large purchasing organization." A product and adherent of the experiential model of officer development, Goethals believed that the army's utter lack of relevant experience in large-scale procurement within an industrial economy meant that there were few, if any, officers competent to handle the work. Instead, he "thought it could be handled better by civilians than by military men."[9]

Goethals's characterization of the Quartermaster Department as "a large purchasing organization" reflected a hope of what he wanted it to become, not a description of what it was when he inherited it. Goethals abhorred the inefficient multi-bureau approach to purchasing military supplies. As early as January 1918, he met with Maj. Gen. John Biddle—who served as the army's acting chief of staff after Bliss went to Europe to serve on the Supreme War Council—to propose consolidating under the Quartermaster Department procurement of all supplies other than major parts and end items related to ordnance and aircraft. Never a particularly forceful personality, Biddle agreed in principle but refused to order such a change. Instead, he encouraged Goethals to build a consensus among the bureau chiefs "so that it might be worked out satisfactorily with them."[10] As Goethals's proposal did not significantly affect the Ordnance Department, he received that bureau's acquiescence. Aghast at the prospect of losing their traditional prerogatives, the other bureaus mounted a stiff resistance.

Parochialism and traditionalism motivated their opposition, which was based upon specious arguments supporting the army's traditional multibureau procurement system. The Medical Corps argued that Goethals and the Quartermaster Department were "not competent to buy medicines." "Neither were the doctors," retorted Goethals, as "they would have to get chemists, and I could get chemists to buy medicines the same as the doctors would have to do." Absurdly, the Corps of Engineers rejected Goethals's proposal on the grounds that he, as acting quartermaster general, lacked the requisite expertise to "buy the various varieties of rope" that army engineers required. Having become the most renowned army engineer of his generation through more than three decades of exemplary service and the successful completion of the Panama Canal, Goethals must have been surprised to learn that the Corps of Engineers held such doubts.[11]

Stymied in his campaign for immediate and wholesale change, Goethals adopted an incremental approach. He began with a functional reorganization of the Quartermaster Department intended to maximize its purchasing capabilities. Between January and April

1918, he adjusted the department's organization no less than nineteen times. He endeavored to centralize and maintain control over all of the department's purchases within his office in Washington. At the same time, he decentralized operations related to the production and distribution of supplies, delegating those responsibilities to the various depot quartermasters stationed throughout the country and creating a much more effective organization in the process. His office assessed requirements, prioritized the allocation of finite resources, approved contracts, and scheduled distribution of military supplies to all of the army's camps and cantonments. Depot quartermasters coordinated with contracted suppliers in their respective areas and oversaw the storage and distribution of supplies within their assigned regions.[12]

Reorganizing the Quartermaster Department along these lines was an indirect means of attacking the traditional bureau system. Having failed to generate momentum for his proposal to consolidate procurement under a single responsible entity, Goethals sought to make the Quartermaster Department the dominant purchasing agency in the War Department. He was not giving up on his proposal at all; instead, he was attempting to position the Quartermaster Department as the nucleus of a future consolidated procurement agency.[13]

At the same time, Biddle had committed the War Department to an intermediate step. By agreeing in principle with Goethals's procurement proposal, Biddle acknowledged that the army's purchasing systems were inadequate tools for the ongoing war effort. Although he stopped short of creating an organization powerful enough to control and coordinate bureau activities, Biddle recognized and acknowledged that there were major problems in his supply operations. He also saw clearly that there were major problems in the movement of troops and supplies from divisional training camps to ports and ultimately overseas. To address these issues, Biddle created two new General Staff divisions: Purchase and Supply, and Storage and Traffic.[14]

The Storage and Traffic Division was born of a major supply crisis in the winter of 1917–1918. The Quartermaster, Ordnance, Signal Corps, Engineers, and Medical Departments were not only each purchasing their own supplies but also independently shipping supplies to ports on the Eastern Seaboard and attempting to arrange for shipment of those supplies overseas. Thoroughly uncoordinated, their efforts created massive problems along rail lines, in warehouses, and at the ports, particularly around New York and New Orleans. There, the Quartermaster Department discovered food meant for shipment overseas was beginning to spoil, having sat in the warehouse for too long because the War Department had lost track of where many of its Europe-bound supplies were while trying to clear the congestion on the railroads and at the ports.[15]

Reports of this failure of logistics hit a nerve in a War Department sensitive to anything reminiscent of the scandals surrounding its mobilization for the war with Spain in 1898. As it noted in a postwar report, "The lack of an effective system of traffic control resulted in such a competition for transportation and in such a congestion of railroad equipment . . . as to result in rendering inoperative a large part of the available railroad equipment of the country." The chief of staff reported that the massive congestion on the railroads contributed "to the fuel shortage which at one time threatened seriously to interfere with the sailing of our transports." Of equal significance, it caused the misuse of valuable "storage facilities at the ports and piers," which were filled to capacity "with unessential materials" by well-intended teams of workers trying to clear the congested railroads, preventing the timely "shipment of essential materials and supplies." This was a complex problem that appeared to demand "a central controlling agency to control every shipment of materials and supplies from its point of origin in the United States" to ports in France.[16]

Having spent part of the fall and winter of 1917 as a consulting engineer for commissions developing the harbor in New York and exploring a Hudson River tunnel project, Goethals was intimately familiar with the problems related to congestion at the seaboard. They were, in fact, the first issues he took up with Biddle as acting quartermaster general. Shortly after these discussions, Biddle organized the Division of Storage and Traffic and assigned Goethals to lead it, granting him additional authority by appointing him as an assistant chief of staff.[17]

The Storage and Traffic Division was meant to bring order to chaos on the railroads and at the ports. Goethals recalled that "all transportation matters in the United States for the Army were concentrated in my hands." The War Department quickly expanded that mandate "so that all shipments made to contractors and by contractors to the various bureaus" were also assigned to Goethals and the Storage and

Traffic Division. Going further, the chief of staff attached the Embarkation Service as a subdivision of the Storage and Traffic Division and
gave Goethals the authority to construct and purchase warehouses and
storage facilities at rail hubs and ports. In effect, these changes made
Goethals and the Storage and Traffic Division singularly responsible
for moving troops and supplies from their points of origin—production centers or training camps—to France as expeditiously as possible.[18]
This was no easy task, laden with complex problems compounded by
the fact that Goethals's appointment as director of Storage and Traffic
did not bring relief from his already significant duties as acting quartermaster general.

In that capacity, at the same time that he was organizing the Storage
and Traffic Division, Goethals was also working to resolve a critical
shortage of uniforms. By January 1, 1918, the army had swelled to
1,149,000 soldiers.[19] Clothing them adequately placed an enormous
strain on both the War Department and the nation's wool industry.
In one revealing statistic, the army alone purchased more wool socks in
1918 than the total of number of wool socks produced in the United
States in all of 1914.[20] The Council of National Defense had stripped
the struggling Quartermaster Department of responsibility for purchasing uniforms for the army in 1917, but had proven to be no more
effective in getting the job done.

Goethals succeeded in convincing the Council of National Defense
to give responsibility for uniforms back to the Quartermaster Department. He then worked through that council to fix prices for cloth
purchases and commandeer the nation's wool supply. The department
then arranged contracts for uniform production with various plants
throughout the country, moving to commandeer any plant that failed
to produce the number of items stipulated in its contract.[21] Going out
on a limb, Goethals ordered three times the amount of supplies that
he was authorized. Although the mobilization plan the army adopted
in 1917 called for raising 1.3 million soldiers, Goethals correctly anticipated that the program would expand dramatically in 1918, and
planned Quartermaster Department orders and contractors to support an army of 3 million.[22] The combined effect of these measures
resolved the army's clothing problem. Enough supplies made it to
France to supply the average AEF soldier with new blankets, shirts,
and trousers every two months; a new overcoat every five months; a

new underwear issue every month; and new socks every three weeks as long as the AEF's internal systems of transportation and distribution in France worked smoothly.[23]

Goethals could not have resolved the clothing supply issue without concurrent progress on the problem of congestion along rail lines and at the ports. If the materials and supplies could not move to the ports, they could not be shipped to France. Once again, Goethals approached this problem as he approached the Panama Canal—he centralized control and decentralized operations. He sought the right people to put in charge of functional subdivisions in the new organization and empowered them to take considerable initiative to meet his intent. He placed Col. Briant Wells in charge of the Storage Division, giving him the responsibility of building and running a storage system based on a series of warehousing recommendations provided by an executive of the Western Electric Company. To manage War Department railroad transportation, Goethals appointed Harry M. Adams, formerly a vice president of the Missouri Pacific Railroad, to serve as the director of inland transportation. Charged with moving troops and supplies by rail to the ports, Adams quickly resolved many of the problems that had previously hampered War Department efforts. Army officers and railroad officials alike respected his authority and expertise, for the most part giving him their full cooperation.

At the same time, Goethals placed the Embarkation Service in the capable hands of Maj. Frank T. Hines, who had begun the war as an obscure captain of coast artillery. Hines developed a much more efficient operation at the ports, accelerating the pace of troop shipments by minimizing the amount of time it took to prepare, load, and launch ships to France.

Synchronizing their efforts, Goethals had instituted a system by March 1918 that ensured that the chaos wrought by uncoordinated shipments arranged by independent bureaus in 1917 would not be repeated in 1918. This system established and ensured adherence to planned priorities for rail shipments to the ports by prohibiting the movement of any War Department freight by rail without coordination with and releases from both the Inland Transportation Service and the Embarkation Service. Further, he ensured that the Storage Division was tied into the process, storing goods and equipment by priority to more efficiently load and unload trains and ships.[24]

Despite these improvements, the Storage and Traffic Division faced considerable complications and obstacles. As an experimental organization conceived in the midst of crisis, its authority was unclear, and Goethals had a difficult time compelling the bureau chiefs to cooperate. In their eyes, he was just another bureau chief who did not merit any special deference. Their perception only became more negative when the secretary of war endorsed War Department General Order 14 on February 9, 1918, making Goethals an assistant chief of staff leading one of the General Staff's five divisions.[25] The bureau chiefs then saw him as part of an overactive General Staff encroaching upon their traditional prerogatives.

In the context of resistance from other bureau chiefs, Goethals's system of requiring releases from both the Inland Transportation Service and the Embarkation Service takes on a different light. It was not the product of consensus within the War Department on the best way forward but a last-resort measure meant to compel the cooperation of unwilling bureaus in his attempt to better coordinate the movement of troops and supplies to the seaboard. The bureaus had no choice but to cooperate. The Railway Administration, which had been administering the nation's railroads under the leadership of Treasury Secretary William G. McAdoo since President Wilson federalized the railroads on January 1, 1918, would not allow anything to move without the Storage and Traffic Division's documented approval.

Beyond resistance from the bureaus, the civil boards and agencies that helped administer the war effort sometimes delayed and disrupted Goethals's efforts to improve the efficiency and effectiveness of War Department logistics. A storage project that Goethals considered to be critically important was delayed for months by resistance from Bernard Baruch, first as a member of the Council of National Defense and later as chairman of the War Industries Board. Their first significant clash erupted over Goethals's proposal for the army to purchase land and build a terminal and storage facility in South Brooklyn. He considered the location ideal because New York harbor was the principal port of embarkation for troops and supplies bound for France. But Baruch objected strenuously, advocating instead for temporary storage facilities along New York's West Side. He assailed Goethals's proposal, questioning the size of the project, the materials needed to carry it out, the quality of the cement available to support the project, the impact on steel production, and the ability of the railroads to carry enough construction material into Brooklyn to complete the project. Baruch's determined resistance lasted from February to June 1918, when Secretary Baker decided in Goethals's favor. It was a hollow victory, however. Baruch's prolonged resistance delayed construction so much that the project was not completed before the war ended.[26]

Furthermore, persistent shipping shortages muted the effect of the Storage and Traffic Division's achievements. As early as January, Goethals "called attention to the fact that we were getting more men overseas than the available shipping at the disposal of the War Department would supply."[27] He raised the alarm again in February, this time persuading Secretary Baker to appoint a Shipping Control Committee to work with the War Department to maximize the capacity of available tonnage.[28] Even so, nothing could change the fact that the United States had entered the war with a fraction of the shipping it needed or that the Shipping Board's shipbuilding program was proceeding very slowly. As the War Department noted in its official postwar report, "The carrying capacity of the available ocean tonnage was at all times the neck of the bottle of supply."[29]

By the spring of 1918, then, the army had not yet found a solution to its logistics woes. From his position as acting quartermaster general and director of Storage and Traffic, though, Goethals's options for improving the situation were limited. He could not argue his way out of jurisdictional disputes with the civil boards and committees involved in managing the war effort. And he certainly could not influence the pace of American shipbuilding. He could, however, use his influence to push for further reform of War Department logistics systems and processes.

The Purchase and Supply Division's performance to that point lent weight to Goethals's argument for radical change. Organized at the same time as the Storage and Traffic Division, the Purchase and Supply Division was charged to "have cognizance and supervision of the purchase and production of all munitions and other supplies." It was also responsible for "the supervision and direction of all purchases, procurement and production activities of the several bureaus, corps, and other agencies of the War Department."[30] The division failed on both fronts. While the bureaus found the Storage and Traffic Division annoying, they saw the Purchase and Supply Division as an existential threat to their prerogatives. Viewing it with suspicion and hostility, they refused to cooperate and actively worked to undermine it.[31]

With considerably less fame and force of will than Goethals, Brig. Gen. Palmer Pierce was unable to create an organization strong enough to overcome resistance from the various bureau chiefs who remained wedded to the traditional model of independent production and procurement. According to one postwar analysis, the Purchase and Supply Division's authority was "supervisory," giving it only "overhead functions with the power to interfere but not to remodel." It concluded that the division "gave rise to a great deal of duplication and complication."[32] Unlike congestion on the railroads and at the ports, production and procurement were problems that were at least as acute in the spring as they had been in the winter.[33]

Once again, Goethals raised the issue of consolidating War Department logistics functions under one responsible agency in February and March 1918. Taking his supply apparatus in Panama as a model, Goethals argued that "there should be one central purchasing bureau which would get the supplies, and supplies would be shipped by that same agency to the seaboard, and then shipped from the seaboard overseas by the same agency." He reasoned that under such a system, "There could not be any friction; there could not be any interference." Getting to the heart of the matter in terms similar to his arguments for centralized control in the Canal Zone, Goethals opined, "If you have a job to do, you want to give it to one man and let him do it."[34] Reflecting the principles of the managerial revolution and the practices of some of the largest trusts and corporations that dominated the Gilded Age and Progressive Era, Goethals advocated for the vertical integration of War Department logistics. He firmly believed that the same organization should control army supply from the point of production to the point of delivery to the end user, in this case the AEF in France.[35]

Goethals had a receptive audience in the new chief of staff, Maj. Gen. Peyton C. March. Under pressure from Congress to revitalize a sluggish war effort, Baker cabled Pershing on January 26 to request March's service. March had gone to France the previous summer as the commander of the First Division's artillery brigade. In the meantime, he had been placed in command of all AEF artillery and had organized a rigorous training program for all American artillery units arriving in France. Pershing was reluctant to give up such an effective commander, but saw the value in having an officer with a reputation for ruthless efficiency serving as chief of staff of the army.[36]

March brought renewed focus and energy to the War Department. Some wrongly assumed that March and Goethals were too much alike and that their strong personalities would inevitably clash. That was not the case. Goethals and March knew each other not only from General Staff service more than a decade prior but also from West Point, where Goethals had been one of March's engineering instructors. The two were on friendly terms prior to serving together in 1918 and they became close friends during the war. March respected Goethals's abilities, considering him to be "one of the ablest officers of the Army." For his part, Goethals was thrilled to have a chief of staff who was attentive, decisive, and perfectly willing to upset old army traditions if he thought they were doing harm to the war effort.[37]

Intensely focused on improving the War Department's efficiency, March was keen to put an end to the several divisions of authority in army logistics. He spent much of his first month in the War Department observing it in action. In the process, March confirmed his high opinion of Goethals and concluded that Pierce "wasn't any good."[38] On April 9, he called Goethals into his office to discuss dismissing Pierce and merging the two supply divisions of the General Staff into one. Surprisingly, Goethals demurred, concerned that he was already too taxed to take on any more responsibility.

The previous month, March had also concluded that Goethals was overworked as both the director of the Storage and Traffic Division and the acting quartermaster general. He agreed to recall Robert E. Wood from service with the Forty-Second Division in France to relieve Goethals from his quartermaster duties. March had been deeply impressed with Wood while serving with the AEF, and Goethals was excited to work once again with Wood, who had rendered excellent service in Panama as the chief quartermaster of the Isthmian Canal Commission. Wood's return had been delayed, however, and Goethals felt overburdened and unable to absorb the Purchase and Supply Division until Wood could take over the Quartermaster Department. Ending the meeting, March assured Goethals that he understood and that the two would discuss the matter further at another time. Later that week, and without the promised second meeting, Goethals was surprised to learn that the chief of staff was pressing forward anyway.[39]

March acted with characteristic bluntness. He decided that Pierce would leave the War Department and devote "such abilities as he may have to the War Industries Board." Goethals was given the unpleasant task of breaking the news to Pierce and stayed up half the night "trying to paint a picture of gold, tinsel, and gold lace of his new duties with the War Industries Board." He "was just starting in to paint it to Pierce" when March walked by. Annoyed at seeing Pierce still in the building, the chief of staff snapped, "Pierce, I have cut your head off and ordered you out of the War Department."[40] In an order that took effect on April 16, March merged Pierce's Purchase and Supply Division with Goethals's Storage and Traffic Division, creating the new Division of Purchase, Storage, and Traffic. Appointing Goethals to lead it, his instructions were simple and direct. "You are given complete charge of all matters of supply," he told Goethals. "You can make any changes in personnel, methods, and general set-up necessary to get results, and don't bother me with details," he added. Pointedly, he added, "I hold you responsible for results, and I will take all the responsibility for anything you have to do to get them."[41]

Thus began one of the most effective partnerships in the army during the First World War. As March's actions and instructions show, he and Goethals not only agreed upon what the major problem of the American war effort to that point had been—but also shared both an impassioned if at times ruthless commitment to getting results and similar managerial philosophies and techniques in leading organizations to achieve those results. As March would recall years later, his instructions to Goethals in April 1918 served as the foundation for a relationship in which the two "worked together in utmost harmony."[42]

Notwithstanding March's heady instructions and excellent working relationship with Goethals, the creation of the Purchase, Storage, and Traffic Division (PS&T) did not constitute a sharp break from immediate precedent. Organizationally, the new agency looked more like the old Storage and Traffic Division with the formerly separate Purchase and Supply Division appended to it than as a separate and distinct division of the General Staff. Additionally, the nascent PS&T

was not empowered to control bureau procurement. As with Pierce's Purchase and Supply Division, Goethals held only supervisory and coordinating authority, while the bureaus maintained executive and operating control over their own functionally divided lines of procurement. The War Department did not permit wholesale reorganization in the spring of 1918 because it feared that drastic measures might interrupt the flow of troops and supplies to France.[43] Therefore, while the April 1918 reorganization of the War Department certainly sprang from a recognition that the existing system was inadequate, it did not directly resolve the defects of the bureau system.

Instead, the creation of PS&T in April 1918 was another intermediate step in the evolution of the War Department. Goethals found his new circumstances to be confusing and frustrating. Divided lines of authority meant that he answered to the chief of staff for all matters related specifically to the army, but reported to Assistant Secretary of War Benedict Crowell for commercial and industrial issues. More frustratingly, Goethals was surrounded by agencies and people—with March being the notable exception—who challenged his ability and authority to do anything. The bureaus jealously guarded their traditional prerogatives and resisted Goethals's attempts to coordinate stateside logistics. Crowell was a bureaucratic empire builder who believed that logistics and mobilization should be managed by civilian officials and businessmen, not military officers. Furthermore, the newly reorganized and empowered War Industries Board—now under the capable chairmanship of Bernard Baruch—aggressively asserted itself in PS&T business. By the end of May, Goethals admitted to former secretary of war Henry L. Stimson that although he had entered the job with a mental "picture of a smooth-running machine," he had "gotten to that pessimistic state" in which he doubted "if this ideal will be even approached, let alone realized." Fearing that Goethals was thinking of resigning, Stimson replied, "However that may be, you simply must hold yourself in and hold on, no matter what your discouragements."[44]

Although discouraged, Goethals certainly was hanging on. He had encountered similar organizational and bureaucratic challenges in Panama. Unsurprisingly, he turned to familiar practices and techniques to overcome them, endeavoring first to put his division on a sound organizational footing. He sought reliable subordinates and demanded that they rise to the occasion. Wood's assumption of duties as acting quartermaster general in early May helped considerably not only by re-lieving Goethals of a job he considered "the most vexatious one I have ever tackled" but also by giving him an energetic, capable, and loyal chief in the bureau most intricately connected to the PS&T.[45] Goeth-als retained the services of the energetic and effective heads of Storage, Inland Traffic, and Embarkation whom he had installed while leading the Storage and Traffic Division. He also brought in the very capable Brig. Gen. Hugh S. Johnson to rebuild and lead Pierce's old Purchase and Supply Division. Johnson admired and respected Goethals, and that sentiment quickly became mutual as Johnson became Goethals's most valuable uniformed subordinate.[46] Finally, Goethals appointed Gerard Swope—formerly an executive with Western Electric—to serve as a civilian assistant, upon whom he came to rely just as heavily as he relied upon Johnson.[47]

Next, arranging an effective working relationship with the War In-dustries Board was imperative. Goethals's efforts toward this end were uncharacteristically ambivalent. Partially because of his ongoing clash with Baruch over storage facilities in Brooklyn, and partially because of his profound mistrust of committees supervising large projects that he had nurtured since his first year in Panama, Goethals plainly did not trust the War Industries Board. Like March and many others in the War Department, Goethals believed the board inappropriately asserted itself in purely military matters.[48] While he recognized that the War Department must have representation on the War Industries Board, he did everything he could to avoid being that representative. He proposed that Second Assistant Secretary of War Edward R. Stet-tinius be sent to serve as both a liaison and a buffer between the War Industries Board and the army.[49] In early May, March informed Goeth-als that because Palmer Pierce had been assigned to lead a brigade bound for France, he had recommended that Goethals replace Pierce as the army's representative to the War Industries Board. "I didn't thank March for this because it's a duty which doesn't appeal to me, and I had expressed myself very strongly against it some days ago when he approached me on the subject," Goethals remarked. Fully aware that Baruch and Goethals had already clashed over facilities in Brook-lyn, and remembering the Goethals-Denman fiasco, the president rejected March's recommendation. Delighted, Goethals remarked sardonically, "So I have escaped a job for which I am even less fitted that the one which I have now."[50]

Instead, Hugh Johnson became the War Department's representative on the War Industries Board. This was entirely fitting, as Johnson's work as the director of purchase and supply necessarily brought him into the most contact with Baruch and the WIB. It was also in keeping with the recommendations of a General Staff study of problems associated with Purchase and Supply.[51] Johnson was an excellent choice; he quickly established a much closer and more effective relationship with Baruch than Goethals ever could, and he ensured that the WIB's work with industry aligned as closely as possible with the army's requirements and priorities. With a lingering memory of a more acrimonious relationship with Goethals, Baruch recalled, "When General Hugh Johnson began to sit in for Goethals, things improved considerably—as they always did where Johnson was involved."[52] Together, the two did much to synchronize army procurement with industrial production for the anticipated campaign of 1919. The relationship was so effective that it smoothed over some of the tensions between Goethals and Baruch, to the extent that the Wall Street financier occasionally attended postwar reunions of Goethals's PS&T.[53]

At the same time, Goethals focused on making the War Department's internal procurement processes more rational and efficient. To that end, the Overman Act allowed Goethals to begin to establish an interbureau procurement system in May 1918. Signed into law on May 21, the Overman Act gave the administration discretionary authority to reorganize executive agencies to better support the war effort without seeking congressional approval, with profound implications for Goethals and his vision for a consolidated supply agency within the War Department.[54] Fundamental changes were now possible if he could persuade March that a change needed to be made, and March could then persuade the secretary of war. Throughout the rest of the war and for months after its conclusion, the Overman Act denied the bureau chiefs redress to their most important patrons, negating the influence of congressional politics that had done so much to facilitate bureau resistance to the Root reforms since 1903. Only after the passage of the Overman Act could the PS&T take any concrete measures to consolidate War Department procurement.[55]

The first measures were necessarily cautious and incremental. Even with the Overman Act, Goethals could not change War Department logistics by fiat. He still had neither executive nor operating authority in procurement. He was empowered with only supervisory and coordinating authority—as before, the bureaus were still the operative agencies in War Department procurement. To minimize competition and inefficiency, Goethals and Johnson worked to consolidate procurement processes "article by article as a conscious and deliberate preparation for the more drastic unification which was later affected."[56] First, they established a clearance process in which no bureau supply request could go to the War Industries Board or to a private contractor without going through the PS&T. Then they set up an interbureau procurement system meant to eliminate unnecessary competition between bureaus for the same finite resources.[57]

The interbureau procurement system resolved some of the problems created by competitive bureau purchasing. In the new system, bureaus had to submit to Goethals's division their requirements for commodities or items that multiple bureaus needed. The PS&T staff then identified the bureau that required the greatest quantity of any given commodity or item and assigned it the responsibility of purchasing in sufficient bulk to account for all bureaus' needs. Goethals's division would then apportion to each bureau its share of the commodity or item. This took a gradual and relatively cautious approach to procurement reform that centralized procurement of individual articles within individual agencies while stopping short of centralizing procurement of all supplies within any one agency.[58] The Quartermaster Department became the dominant purchasing bureau, responsible for more than 80 percent of bureau purchases for commodities including cotton, wool, leather, and silk. To Ordnance, Goethals gave purchasing responsibility for cartridges, carriers, and flashlights. The Construction Division retained responsibility for cement, sand, gravel, and electrical equipment. The Corps of Engineers purchased steam shovels, cranes, and railroad equipment. The Signal Corps purchased telephones, electrical wire, and cable as well as various commodities needed for the army's new aviation units.[59]

Goethals adopted such a cautious course in an effort to avoid alienating the bureaus. He attempted to assuage bureau concerns by granting exceptions to the interbureau procurement system for items and commodities that the bureaus considered especially technical or specialized. For example, although he assigned procurement and distribution of cotton and cotton-based products to the Quartermaster Department, he allowed the Signal Corps to continue purchasing cloth for airplanes, balloons, and aviators' uniforms. He also consented to the Medical Department retaining responsibility for purchasing and distributing material for surgical dressings and gas masks.[60]

In the end, his proposals and actions alienated the bureaus anyway. As Hugh Johnson recalled well after the war, the interbureau procurement system generated "agonized writhings and enmities, some of which have never entirely disappeared."[61] Writing to his son in France at the end of May, Goethals noted that he was making progress in procurement reform, but he reported that "opposition crops out on the part of the bureaus at every attempt to consolidate purchases."[62] In his own postwar report, March accurately noted that "there were many complaints" and that "the inter-bureau procurement requisition [process] became a point of complaint around which could center the widespread opposition to the general process of supervision and centralization that was going on."[63] Nevertheless, in the wake of the Overman Act, this amounted to nothing more than sour grapes. As long as Goethals maintained March's support—which he did—the bureaus could complain but not effectively resist.

Although pleased with the progress he had made, Goethals was not satisfied with the state of army logistics. He still envisioned a single War Department agency responsible for all army procurement and all army logistics in general. Every measure he took was meant to serve as an incremental step toward that goal. He put it plainly in a letter to his son while in the midst of establishing the interbureau procurement system. "What I am arriving at," he wrote, "is what I believe should be brought about, a single purchasing agency for the War Dept."[64] The course of the war in France, however, interrupted his patient and persistent campaign for procurement reform and the consolidation of responsibility and authority for War Department logistics.

Although fully aware of the problems hindering the American war effort, the German high command rightly viewed the United States as a vast reservoir of manpower that would eventually tip the military balance on the western front in favor of the Allies. The German army therefore opted to launch a series of bold offensives against the French and British in 1918 in an attempt to conclude the war before the AEF grew and developed enough to make a significant impact on the battlefield. Using innovative new assault tactics, the Germans launched their first offensive on March 21, 1918, overrunning nearly one hundred square miles of territory that day alone. This was the first of five significant German offensives between March and July.

In these offensives, however, the German army did little more than impale itself on Allied defensive positions along the western front, expending critical manpower and resources that it could not do without later. But that fact was not immediately clear to any but a few of the participants. Germany perceived great opportunities ready for the taking, and the Allies saw in the German onslaughts a severe crisis that could threaten both Paris and critical rail lines needed to sustain their troops on the front lines. Scrambling to blunt and contain the offensives, the Allies rushed reserves forward to the front, including untried American divisions in the AEF's first experiences with major combat.[65] They also called for the United States to send more troops, specifically infantrymen and machine gunners. Given the perceived emergency, the secretary of war agreed to increase the pace of troop shipments and devote a disproportionally greater amount of shipping tonnage to infantrymen and machine gunners than to support personnel and supplies.[66]

In the late spring and early summer, then, troop shipments became the Purchase, Storage, and Traffic Division's main effort. Succinctly summarizing the War Department's priorities, Goethals declared in early May, "We must get men over as rapidly as possible and everything must give way to this." Accordingly, Goethals devoted more and more of his time to moving troops to the seaboard and shipping them to France. While he continued to give some attention to procurement reform, it necessarily took a back seat to ferrying troops to France.[67]

Procurement reform received less emphasis because increasing the rate of American soldiers to France consumed every subdivision of the PS&T except for Johnson's Purchase and Supply. Much of the burden rested on Brig. Gen. Frank T. Hines, Goethals's energetic and able chief of the Embarkation Service. Hines and his subordinates worked wonders. They ripped out the cabin walls from the interior of ships and placed tiered bunks in all berths, doubling passenger capacity in some ships. Going further, they refined dockside procedures and fashioned double-decker gangplanks to speed up the process of boarding transports, ultimately making the process so efficient that 10,000 soldiers could board their transports in less than two hours. The Embarkation Service became such a well-oiled machine that on August 31, 1918, its personnel at Hoboken embarked 51,356 soldiers—nearly two entire divisions—on seventeen ships in a single day.[68]

With the Embarkation Service operating at maximum capacity, an additional burden was placed on the Inland Traffic and Storage subdivisions. Coordinating the movement of supplies and entire divisions of troops to and from production centers, storage facilities, training camps, and mobilization centers all across the country effectively enough to avoid traffic jams on the rail lines and delays at the ports was an enormous undertaking. Goethals had to synchronize the disparate efforts of all of his subdivisions to prevent a replication of the confusion and congestion from the previous winter. Having done that on a large scale years earlier in Panama, Goethals was well prepared to handle the job.[69]

Goethals and the PS&T were astoundingly successful in revitalizing the American troop shipment program. In March 1918, some 85,000 troops sailed to France, most of whom departed prior to the opening of the German spring and summer offensives on March 21. In April, the Embarkation Service placed 118,642 soldiers on transports bound for France, a 40 percent increase. In May, 245,945 doughboys sailed across the Atlantic. The PS&T's greatest output came in August 1918, when it shipped 306,350 soldiers to Pershing and the AEF. Altogether, 1.5 million of the approximately 2 million American soldiers who served in France during the First World War made the journey across the Atlantic in the last six months of the war. This was not the outcome the Germans had intended for their spring and summer offensives. Ironically, operations designed to force an end to the war before the United States could field a sizable army in France only served to hasten the pace of American deployments to France. But the mere presence of an army does not necessarily attest to its effectiveness and capability. Ultimately, the rapid expansion of the AEF revealed major cracks in the foundation of the American war effort.[70]

Despite its considerable achievements, Goethals saw systemic weaknesses in the troop shipment program. He correctly surmised that the increased numbers of outbound troops correlated with a decrease in the amount of training those troops received prior to embarkation. "Manpower is needed, but untrained manpower is not desired, and just herein lies our weakness," he noted. Further, he accurately observed that the massive increase in troop shipments was largely dependent upon "British ships placed at our disposal for the purpose, and we're bragging about this to such an extent that there is bound to be disappointment later."[71] Critical shipping shortages continued to plague the American war effort. While PS&T more than tripled the War Department's troop shipment rates, approximately 48 percent of those troops sailed on British tonnage. Goethals knew that if the British saw cause to be less generous—which they did later that fall—the army's designs for an anticipated climactic campaign in 1919 would be at grave risk. Finally, the War Department's capacity to ship cargo to France remained comparatively stagnant while its capacity to ship troops increased exponentially, setting conditions for serious logistical problems in the AEF later in the year.[72]

Before he could address these issues, Goethals became mired in a controversy rooted in nagging and unanswered questions about the proper relationship between March as the chief of staff of the army and Pershing as a field army commander. March correctly believed that the chief of staff led the entire army and that a field army commander led only a part of it. Pershing, on the other hand, believed that everything and everyone in the army was subordinate to the commander in the field. Although he recognized that he was subordinate to the secretary of war, he viewed the War Department as an auxiliary organization that had no responsibility other than to adhere strictly to his requests and recommendations.[73] The tension inherent in these conflicting views came to a head in the summer of 1918 over issues related to army logistics and administration.

Goethals's successes in increasing the monthly totals of soldiers and supplies bound for Europe in response to Germany's offensives exposed a critical weakness in the AEF's logistics organization—the Services of Supply. Operating eleven ports, hundreds of miles of railroads, and dozens of depots and distribution centers throughout France, the Services of Supply had an enormous mission that was only getting larger as the revitalized troop shipment program swelled the ranks of

The mechanization and industrialization of warfare presented daunting challenges to the United States upon its entry into the First World War. The proliferation of rapid firing weapons, heavy artillery, tanks, airplanes, and other emerging technologies that became central characteristics of warfare in the twentieth century imposed a material burden that the United States had not experienced in past wars or adequately anticipated before entering the war. As a result of this and of German actions in the spring and summer of 1918, the United States had to focus on shipping soldiers overseas and purchase or borrow much of the equipment and supplies needed to sustain them. In this photograph, the soldiers' helmets were most likely British, and the tanks on which they rode were French, as were the artillery pieces and the vast majority of the artillery ammunition expended to prepare the battlefield for their advance. Other than the soldiers wearing the uniform and braving the enemy fire, few things captured in this particular photograph are actually American. (National Archives, 111-SC-22334)

the AEF. As spring turned to summer, the War Department had actually outpaced the AEF's ability to receive men and materiel. Ships arriving at AEF ports in France waited, on average, over two weeks to be unloaded and sent back across the Atlantic. Supplies piled up on French docks awaiting transportation to American depots in the

French interior. Units at the front and in training behind the lines began to experience supply shortages that were simply inexcusable given the amount of supplies that had already been shipped to France.[74]

As reports of such conditions made it back to Washington, there was a growing consensus among key decision makers that a rearrangement of leadership might be necessary. It had already occurred to some that Pershing was overburdened. This had influenced, in part, the decision to send Tasker Bliss to France that winter to represent the United States on the Supreme Allied War Council, thus relieving Pershing of some diplomatic responsibilities. Still, logistics problems in France suggested to some that Pershing's job was too big for one person. On June 3, the president's close friend and advisor Edward M. House proposed that Pershing "be relieved from all responsibility except the training and fighting of our troops."[75] March had come to the same conclusion and felt that the best possible solution was to separate the Services of Supply from the AEF and send Goethals to France to lead it, making Goethals an autonomous authority that would coordinate with Pershing but answer directly to the War Department rather than be a subordinate of Pershing's within the AEF.[76]

Increasingly confident in his position as chief of staff, March assumed this plan would be accepted, and he acted accordingly. He discussed the matter with Baker, who in turn briefed the president. Both agreed that it would be best to postpone a decision until Pershing could be consulted. March wrote Pershing on July 5, informing him that "the Administration is very much concerned about the responsibilities that have hitherto been put on your shoulders" and that it was "inevitable that a subdivision of your work must be made in the near future."[77]

Pershing, however, wanted nothing of it, justifiably disturbed by the notion of losing control over his own lines of communication and logistics enterprise. In fairness, it would have been difficult to find any good field army commander who would accept such a scheme. Moreover, urged on by James G. Harbord—a fiercely loyal subordinate who began the war as the AEF chief of staff and had since advanced to command the Second Division—Pershing interpreted the proposal as the opening gambit in what he assumed was a deliberate campaign by March to seize control of the AEF. In letters and cables to Baker, Pershing opposed Goethals's transfer to the AEF Services of Supply in the

The tension inherent in a collision between twentieth-century means and nineteenth-century modes of warfare complicated logistics, in particular the war effort in general for all belligerents, not least of all the Americans. This photograph captures the nature and fruit of that tension. Here, an American soldier struggles with a stubborn mule whose refusal to pull a cart any further holds up a lengthy supply convoy comprised not only of mule- and horse-drawn carts and wagons of old but also new trucks and other automobiles. (National Archives, 111-SC-20902)

strongest possible terms. To address problems that had invited scrutiny in the first place, Pershing relieved the commander of the Services of Supply and replaced him with Harbord, who promptly and energetically breathed new life into that organization. This satisfied Baker and Wilson and averted the divorce of the Services of Supply from the AEF. By the first week of August, the organization and command of the Services of Supply was a dead issue, Goethals would remain in Washington.[78]

But March and Goethals had been operating under the assumption that the War Department's chief logistician would soon sail for France. In a letter to his son on June 9, Goethals wrote, "March sent for me and said he thought he had arranged matters so that he could send me over, if the reorganization he has in mind could be put through." The prospect of service abroad excited Goethals. "I do hope that there is going to be no slip up," he mused, "for a desk job isn't to my liking when I know I can do useful work over there along lines which I feel competent to handle."[79] March was so certain that the transfer and reorganization of the Services of Supply would be approved that he designated a successor to lead PS&T and ordered him to shadow Goethals in his remaining days in the War Department to ensure the transition went smoothly.

By the end of June, however, Goethals found his uncertain prospects for service in France to be painfully distracting. "Another week has gone by with no new developments, my matters resting in status quo, much to my disgust and to the detriment of my patience and nervous system," Goethals wrote. He reported that he had been "advised that it's coming out all right though this gives no relief from the strain that uncertainty always imposes on me." While he kept working to hasten troop shipments, proudly noting that the rapid expansion of the troop shipment program had swelled the AEF ranks to more than 900,000 soldiers, Goethals delayed any further actions related to procurement reform, focusing instead on morale issues in the Services of Supply that he assumed he would soon have to address. "I gather that there is considerable discontent among the Q.M.'s [quartermasters] over there due to a feeling that they haven't received the recognition in the way of promotion they feel they merit," he reported. Echoing ideas he put into practice in Panama, he remarked, "I am sorry to hear it, for a disgruntled force isn't an efficient one," and he resolved that "there will have to be a change in this respect."[80]

Although March considered the matter an open question until its definitive resolution in early August, Goethals had given up all hope of service in France by mid-July. Told that his orders to sail for France were imminent, Goethals packed his field equipment and let Hugh Johnson know that he expected to be gone any day. Shortly afterwards, however, he was told to wait until the president and the secretary of war heard from Pershing. At this point, Goethals knew it would not happen. As Pershing had turned down his requests for service in the AEF in 1917, he saw no reason to expect a different response in 1918, especially since the proposal involved making Goethals and the Services of Supply independent of Pershing's control. He attempted once again to focus completely on PS&T, but was hampered by the constant and awkwardly distracting presence of his replacement. "Now I have lapsed back and am trying to take up my work," he wrote, "but it's a difficult thing to do with a successor at my elbow ready to take it up, but who may not care to follow along the lines I am laying down."[81]

Goethals felt dejected. He described the whole affair as "a great and bitter disappointment." Venting to his son about the way the matter was handled, he wrote, "I had not been looking forward to anything of the kind, it came out of a clear sky, and I wish now that March hadn't mentioned the subject at all until it was consummated."[82] While he certainly grasped the importance of his work in the War Department, Goethals believed that he could render more important service abroad. Although this was a somewhat natural reaction for a long-serving military professional, Goethals's disappointment also reflected his generation's broader struggle to grasp the realities, demands, and implications of modern industrialized warfare. Old and deeply ingrained values proved remarkably resilient; throughout the war, he remained partially blind to the importance of his work, denigrating it because it took place in the United States, not in France.[83]

Nevertheless, Goethals saw that there was "nothing to do but grin and bear it," and he resolved to focus solely on PS&T.[84] The War Department had kicked into high gear after the German offensives in the spring, but it still did not run smoothly. Lingering questions over the proper relationship between the General Staff and the bureaus continued to slow and even threaten the American war effort. On July 18, Goethals submitted a lengthy memorandum to the chief of staff urging another reorganization of army logistics.[85] Summarizing his principal justification for reorganization, Goethals argued, "The present system is organically unsound in sufficient degree to render it doubtful, or at least uncertain, whether it can carry the load a year hence." His long and detailed memo contained a strong indictment of the organization and operation of War Department logistics and a well-considered proposal for a new supply organization intended to place the army on a better footing for an anticipated climactic campaign in 1919.[86]

Although the establishment of the Purchase, Storage, and Traffic Division was a step in the right direction, Goethals believed the weaknesses remaining within the army supply system were so significant that they threatened the system itself. His memo offered a twelve-point critique of the existing system. Even after the limited consolidation of supply as PS&T was established, Goethals argued that the War Department still treated logistics as "divided and subsidiary functions" of the bureaus rather than as a major task requiring the attention of a single "grand division" of the War Department. More problematically, the War Department continued to organize its logistics operations by end-user function, despite the fact that the industrial base upon which it relied was organized by commodity. This led to similar duplication of effort, competition between the several purchasing and procurement agencies within the War Department, and artificially high prices due to competitive nonbulk orders by these agencies that had plagued the department earlier.[87]

Furthermore, Goethals argued that although the PS&T had been granted supervisory and coordinating authority, the existing system could not be supervised or coordinated effectively. Even at this late point in the war, he counted nine agencies with some degree of responsibility for supplying the army and pointed out that this had generated nine distinct systems for generating requirements, procurement, distribution, and accounting for both finances and property. Additionally, Goethals assessed that there were "at least five independent conduits of supply reaching from primary sources to ultimate points of use, so completely segregated that there can be no certainty of synchronization although they furnish articles of *related use*." Anticipating bureaus' objections, Goethals wrote, "The theory on which the technical supply bureaus were built (to supply highly technical material for technical troops) is lost in practice since we find each of them procuring *some* supplies for the Army as a whole" and that even a small unit "must look to each of the bureaus for some necessary part of its equipment." Finally, Goethals argued that granting the PS&T supervisory authority over a system with such pronounced divisions of responsibility "duplicate[d] executive control" and caused "conflicts of authority" between himself and the bureau chiefs.[88]

To remedy these problems, Goethals proposed that the chief of staff grant the director of PS&T "executive—not supervisory" authority over army supply. He argued that the War Department had two chief functions, operations and supply, and that all other War Department tasks were subsidiary to one of these two primary functions. According to Goethals, those managing operations should generate requirements. Except for purchasing and inspecting ordnance systems and aircraft, the consolidated supply division would take it from there. In practical terms, this proposal required no major reorganization of PS&T beyond adding a Facilities Division to manage all army real estate and a more robust Accounts Division to manage War Department finances. Goethals believed he could accomplish the reorganization by October 1, 1918, if March expeditiously reviewed and approved the proposal. But approving his proposal required a paradigm shift that entirely removed most bureaus—all except the Quartermaster, Ordnance, and Aircraft Departments—from the army supply system.[89]

To Goethals's mounting frustration, March's decision on the recommendation came excruciatingly slowly. Just over a week after submitting the memo, Goethals complained that "the wills of the Gods certainly grind exceeding slow" and that he was growing "impatient over the delays in getting action." One month later, he was still waiting. On August 18, he reported to his son, "March said he would let me go ahead and would write me a letter 'tomorrow' but as it hasn't yet come, I presume 'tomorrow' is still in the future." Exasperated, he vented that he felt he was "just sawing wood." In another letter written one week later, Goethals was hopeful that a cable from Pershing sounding the alarm over urgent supply requests going unfilled would spur action on his recommended reorganization.[90]

It is difficult to explain March's uncharacteristic indecisiveness on Goethals's proposed reorganization of War Department logistics. Possibly he did not agree with the proposal in the first place. This may have been the issue to which March referred when he wrote in his memoir, "I could not see my way clear to approve certain of his [Goethals's] proposed schemes, but we thrashed them out amicably, and my disapproval made no difference in our relations."[91] In August, March sent the proposal to the bureau chiefs for their recommendations, knowing full well that they would recommend disapproval. Unsurprisingly, the bureau chiefs' reactions "were, in the main, strongly adverse," with the chief of engineers "being particularly vigorous in opposition."[92] March had a reputation for decisiveness, and he was not afraid to make major decisions without first building consensus. He was, according to one of his subordinates in the War Department, "a twentieth-century

Richelieu."⁹³ By sending the proposal to the bureau chiefs, March may have hoped to kill it.

It is also entirely possible that March was too overburdened to give the proposal due attention. In June, Pershing radically revised his projections for the ultimate size of the AEF, upending all assumptions that had informed the War Department's mobilization program. Since the spring of 1918, the War Department had planned on sending fifty-four divisions to France by the end of 1919. On June 19, Pershing cabled the War Department that his minimum requirement would be sixty-six divisions in France by May 1919. Four days later, he cabled the War Department to revise those numbers, calling for one hundred divisions by July 1919. To those managing mobilization in the War Department, the resources required to raise and sustain an army of that strength were mind-boggling. March needed time to assess whether or not the program was possible.⁹⁴

Goethals and Swope studied Pershing's proposal and found it to be completely unrealistic. They believed the War Department could definitely raise and sustain sixty divisions, and possibly eighty, but shipping remained the critical limiting factor. Even at eighty divisions, Goethals and Swope forecasted serious deficiencies in cargo tonnage needed to sustain an army that size in France. They could move the soldiers that the program demanded, but not the supplies the soldiers needed.⁹⁵ March and Baker weighed these concerns and adopted the eighty-division plan as the army's new program. Understanding that there would be cargo deficiencies, March revised sustainment requirements so that PS&T would ship an average of thirty pounds of supplies per day for each AEF soldier, down from the earlier planning factor of approximately fifty pounds per soldier per day.⁹⁶

The process by which the army adopted the eighty-division program showed that the General Staff was just beginning to function properly, fifteen years after its creation. Despite resistance from the bureaus and from Pershing himself, the chief of staff and parts of the General Staff had received a plan from a field army commander, performed a fairly complete analysis, revised the plan to a more reasonable—if still overly optimistic—assessment of resources and infrastructure available to carry out the plan, and made it the army's official program. Nevertheless, resistance to the General Staff was still significant. The bureaus continued to obstruct any perceived encroachment onto their traditional prerogatives, seeing Goethals's proposed reorganization of army supply not as a serious program for improving a struggling war effort but as the latest threat to their power and authority. Furthermore, Pershing refused to accept that March could reject or revise his hundred-division program, and he continued to develop operational plans for an AEF that would be one hundred divisions strong in 1919, even as the War Department developed plans to raise, equip, train, and ship eighty divisions.[97]

As time passed, March saw a connection between such resistance and lingering problems in the American war effort. By producing plans based on an anticipated one hundred divisions, Pershing generated requirements that did not match the official army program, disrupting plans developed according to priorities set by the War Department based on the eighty-division program. Furthermore, the inefficient bureau system struggled, and failed in some areas, to meet even those requirements generated by the more limited fifty-four-division program that informed the War Department's efforts earlier in the summer. Hearing reports in August that the AEF's supply situation was gradually getting worse, not better, March assessed that the traditional bureau system was not up to the task of sustaining a seemingly ever-increasing war effort. He concluded that the chief of staff and the General Staff required more explicit authority to frame, formulate, and execute army programs and missions.[98]

On August 26, 1918, March acted. With Baker's approval, he issued War Department General Order 80, which stated, in part, "The chief of the General Staff is the immediate advisor of the Secretary of War on all matters relating to the Military Establishment, and is charged by the Secretary of War with the planning, development, and execution of the Army program." Going a step further, the order stipulated that the chief of staff "takes rank and precedence over all officers of the Army" and is charged with ensuring "that the policies of the War Department are harmoniously executed by the several corps, bureaus, and other agencies of the Military Establishment and that the army program is carried out speedily and efficiently."[99] This clarification of authority was the change necessary for Goethals's proposed reorganization to be approved. It is no coincidence that on the same day that March issued General Order 80, he also officially approved the reorganization of army supply proposed by Goethals nearly six weeks earlier.[100]

Goethals dedicated himself completely to the reorganization. His weekly letters to his eldest son lapsed for an entire month after March finally gave his approval.[101] He focused on little else, perhaps because it seemed to be the only part of the war effort he could definitively control and influence. By the fall, Goethals no longer believed he could fix what he perceived to be critical and potentially fatal flaws in the war effort. Compounded by Allied calls in the spring and summer to send only infantrymen and machine gunners to France and the upward revision of the army program to eighty divisions, there was a gross imbalance between troops and supplies shipped overseas in the last months of the war. As the British withdrew some of the tonnage they had dedicated to American troop and supply shipments during the German offensives in the spring and summer, Goethals scrambled to find enough shipping to sustain the war effort into 1919, but found that the Shipping Board was nowhere close to meeting the lofty levels of ship production it had promised. By late October, Goethals felt as though he was minding a dam that would burst if the war continued. In a strikingly pessimistic letter to his son on October 27, he admitted, "We are hustling men over while the cargo end gets worse and worse . . . I shouldn't be surprised to see the whole shipping situation collapse." To his discerning eye, all signs suggested that a crippling supply crisis loomed in 1919.[102]

Unable to do anything about shipping shortages, Goethals set about refashioning the Purchase, Storage, and Traffic Division as the War Department's central supply agency. He moved deliberately, first addressing organizational adjustments to prepare the division for its expanded scope and responsibilities, including creating a new subdivision for finances. Next, he consolidated the storage activities of those bureaus that had retained independent storage authority under the old system. He then ordered the transfer of procurement functions from the Corps of Engineers, Signal Corps, and Medical Department to the PS&T, effective November 1, 5, and 15, respectively. Concurrently, Goethals issued a directive on November 7 formally announcing that "the function of the Director of Purchase, Storage, and Traffic is executive and not supervisory only" and that "the Director is in command of the supply organizations of the Army."[103]

The armistice of November 11, 1918, halted his efforts. With the war over, Secretary of War Baker suspended any further reorganization of the War Department. Acknowledging that the Overman Act gave blanket authority to reorganize executive agencies during the war, Baker thought it best to delay any further reorganization until Congress passed legislation on the size and structure of the postwar army. Thus interrupted, Goethals was unable to complete his campaign to place army logistics on a permanently more rational and efficient footing.

Despite this lack of clear resolution at the war's end, Goethals's work was resoundingly successful. The major shortcomings he had correctly identified at various points in 1918 were not his own. Instead, they were related to shortages in shipping that he could not resolve and to an obsolete War Department organization that he ultimately helped to overturn, although too late to have any practical impact on the war. While those who went abroad received considerably more publicity for their service, many of those who were in a position to have observed what Goethals had achieved strongly praised his performance. Several argued that the significance of Goethals's contributions to the American war effort were equal to or greater than his accomplishments at the Panama Canal.[104] Peyton March was particularly in awe of what Goethals had done with PS&T, writing in a letter to Goethals five years after the war ended, "I was asked by some responsible people what my solution would be of the problem of putting Austria on its feet, and I replied that I would make you the General Manager of Austria, under whatever title they pleased, at your own price, and give you carte blanche."[105]

In the context of the war, the most important achievement of Goethals's PS&T was its impressive troop shipment program in the summer and fall of 1918. The rapid buildup of American troops on the continent affected German decisions at both the operational and strategic levels of war. Ultimately, estimates of American troop shipments influenced the German decision to seek an armistice in 1918 rather than remain on the defensive into 1919.[106] Although Goethals had not succeeded in setting up a logistics system that could sustain the anticipated war-ending campaign of 1919, he had done much to help end the war in 1918 before the system could actually fail. Ultimately, Goethals's greatest contribution to the war effort was not in the final realization of his forward-thinking plans and recommendations but in finding enough short-term solutions to allow the army to transport enough soldiers and supplies to France in 1918 to influence Germany's strategic calculus on how to wage the war and when to seek peace.

Going beyond the war, Goethals's service helped the forces of cultural change within the army achieve critical mass. The adaptations the army embraced in 1918 constituted a tacit acknowledgment that traditional systems and practices were antiquated and inadequate for the challenges inherent in modern industrialized warfare. Recognition of that point was far from universal, and there was certainly a fair amount of reactionary resistance to even the most sensible ideas and corrective actions. Nevertheless, lessons learned and measures adopted in 1918 fueled a spirit of adaptation and innovation during the army's interwar years that ultimately closed the gap between the institution's culture and its structures that had been created by the Root reforms. Through his considerable efforts in 1918, Goethals played a prominent if somewhat inadvertent role in bringing to an end the long and somewhat tortured process of army reform that had begun in the late nineteenth century.

But such change was not immediate. Although Goethals and March agreed that the reorganized PS&T should be a permanent feature of an army led by a powerful chief of staff and a robust General Staff, theirs was a minority opinion within the War Department. The prevailing sense of crisis vanished when the war ended, taking with it the immediate impetus for change. In general, Goethals's generation of officers succumbed once again to the appeal of comfortable tradition although with less consensus and more contention. When Goethals retired on March 1, 1919, his replacement—a career quartermaster officer—immediately rolled back the most important features of the fall 1918 reorganization of army logistics by resurrecting bureau autonomy and restoring the division's earlier status as a relatively weak coordinating agency rather than a powerful executive arm of the War Department.

With the Overman Act set to expire six months after the end of the war, bureau chiefs attacked Goethals's methods in postwar congressional hearings. Maj. Gen. Clarence C. Williams of the Ordnance Department testified that "not one single constructive thing has come out of the Purchase, Storage, and Traffic Division." The chief of engineers reported to Congress that it was "providential" that Goethals's reorganization had not fully matured until the first week of November and therefore was "not actually tested by war," and he insisted that such a test would have revealed that the reorganization had merely broken a well-functioning system. Other bureau chiefs echoed similar sentiments, arguing that Goethals and the PS&T were unwanted interlopers in their domains, and that the reorganized postwar army should confine the PS&T—and any division of the General Staff, for that matter—to a purely supervisory and coordinating role.[107]

Such pushback was a function of the larger debate over the role of the chief of staff and General Staff. There were two prevalent points of view among career officers. One school of thought held that the chief of staff and the General Staff had assumed too much power in the summer and fall of 1918. Another argued that a strong chief of staff and empowered General Staff divisions like Goethals's were far superior to old methods and were the way of the future. Those most publicly and vociferously participating in the debate were the army's senior leaders—the long-serving stalwarts of Goethals's generation. In effect, then, this aged generation of officers was at war with itself over the future of the army. Its failure to achieve consensus, budgetary shortfalls, and a sharp postwar reduction of forces tipped the scales in favor of the more traditionalist view. The National Defense Act of 1920 limited the General Staff to a chief of staff, four assistants, and eighty-eight other officers—less than a third of what March and other advocates for a robust General Staff had called for—and defined its role as a planning and coordinating agency with extremely limited executive authority.[108]

That regressive turn, however, proved temporary. The fact that it was contested at all within a generation of officers that for decades had instinctively embraced nineteenth-century norms and traditions signaled that the force and appeal of traditionalism was finally waning. As the last holdouts of Goethals's generation left the ranks and officers from the next generation who experienced the First World War at more middling grades were promoted to positions of significant responsibility, traditional forms and practices began to hold a considerably less robust appeal. The next generation accepted that their experiences in the war had confirmed not only the value of formal training and education but also the need for a powerful and active chief of staff and General Staff—finally realigning the army's institutional culture with its structures.[109]

Epilogue

Despite traditionalism's resurgence in the wake of the war, it was actually withering on the vine. Once again, a significant crisis had shifted the parameters of what officers considered desirable and feasible, setting conditions for major changes to the very fabric of their institution. The First World War indelibly affected and altered the army, allowing for incremental changes that ultimately closed the gap between its institutional structures and culture. Though not on a consistent trajectory, the interwar army was defined by adaptation and innovation, even when constrained by necessarily limited budgets and resources during the Great Depression.

Among the First World War's many casualties was the army's traditional rejection of formal education and training in favor of experiential learning. In the wake of the war, formal training and education became a vital part of officers' careers, to such an extent that Omar Bradley later recalled that the biggest difference between service in the army before and after the First World War "was the school system." The officer corps embraced postgraduate military education as a means of producing competent leaders and staff officers during the interwar years. Successful completion of the Command and General Staff School at Ft. Leavenworth came to be a prerequisite of continued promotion just as attendance at the Army War College became the last necessary waypoint along the path to high command.[1]

Senior army leaders increasingly linked military education to continued promotion and steered promising subordinates toward army schools. By 1924, Maj. Dwight D. Eisenhower believed attendance at Ft. Leavenworth's Command and General Staff School was absolutely necessary to remain competitive for promotion. When it seemed that the chief of infantry would deny him one of the seats in the course reserved for infantry officers, Brig. Gen. Fox Conner, who had risen to prominence as Pershing's chief of operations in 1917–1918, arranged for Eisenhower's temporary transfer into the Adjutant General Corps in order to secure one of that branch's seats in the course. Eisenhower did not let his mentor down; through dogged dedication, he finished first in his class. The future Supreme Allied Commander considered his educational experience at Ft. Leavenworth a watershed moment in his career, and he continued to pursue formal education whenever he had the opportunity, graduating in 1928 from the Army War College and in 1931 from the Army Industrial College, established in 1924 and developed throughout the next decade to train officers in mobilization and logistics in order to avoid a repeat of the problematic mobilization in 1917–1918.[2]

The General Staff had a more circuitous and delayed path to true acceptance within the army. Because of the inertia encouraged by both habit and bureaucracy, the General Staff's regression immediately after the First World War defined its role throughout the interwar years, and that relatively limited role similarly defined officers' perceptions of the General Staff, particularly among the most senior ranks. Although the chief of staff became increasingly powerful—far beyond Pershing's vision for that office even when he held it from 1921 through 1924—the bureau chiefs remained, collectively, the most significant institutional forces shaping army force structure, procurement, and doctrine.[3] Change on this point demanded the ascension of a new generation to the top of the army's hierarchy and a renewed sense of urgency brought on by new crises in a new world war.

To meet the challenges of the Second World War, Chief of Staff George C. Marshall recognized the imperative to change. Early in his tenure, he had argued that the old "flag-waving days of warfare are gone" and that the modern army needed to be "composed of specialists, thoroughly trained in every aspect of military science and, above all, organized into a perfect team." Marshall turned those words into action, overhauling the War Department in early 1942 to build a more robust and active General Staff bolstered by new service organizations imbued with nearly total authority over all parts of the army. Bureau chiefs filled important roles, but were clearly subordinate to the Army Service Forces, whose chief enjoyed not only executive authority but also command authority. Revealing that the pendulum had swung largely because of his generation's experiences in the First World War, Marshall created the Army Service Forces in the image of Goethals's Purchase, Storage, and Traffic Division, organizing it to serve as the single executive agency responsible for managing army logistics. With some modifications that expanded the scope of its mission, the Army Service Forces functioned almost exactly as Goethals had envisioned the Purchase, Storage, and Traffic Division, providing invaluable service throughout the Second World War.[4] It had taken nearly forty years, but the army's institutional culture had finally and completely caught up to its structures.

In the end, George W. Goethals saw neither the true completion of military reform nor the full impact he had on the army. After retiring from the service in March 1919, he returned to private life, once again opening an engineering firm of his own. Because he was reluctant to use his name and fame for profit, however, Goethals's firm was never very successful. As his military career suggested, Goethals was at his best when pulled into public service. Although he served quite effectively as New York's coal administrator and helped the state manage its shortage of coal caused by a massive coal miners' strike in 1922, his firm foundered, ultimately dissolving in 1923. Afterward, Goethals worked alone as a consulting engineer, providing particularly useful service to the Port of New York Authority in several bridge, tunnel, and harbor improvement projects. With a variable work schedule, Goethals kept an apartment in New York at which he lived when working out of his office in Lower Manhattan. When not working, he went to the house he had built decades earlier on Martha's Vineyard, where he spent much of his leisure time gardening, admiring the ocean views from his front porch, or taking long walks around the island, frequently joined by a growing brood of grandchildren.[5]

But Goethals became ill in 1927. He had developed a powerful addiction to cigarettes as a way of dealing with the stress of his work in Panama. Unaware of its health risks, he maintained a chain-smoking habit for the rest of his life. In the summer of 1917, he went so far as to give his public endorsement to a campaign to raise funds to ship tobacco and cigarettes to American soldiers in France, declaring that "tobacco will be the greatest solace during the long vigils of trench warfare, and it is almost as essential, in many cases, as food itself."[6] A year later, a journalist observed Goethals at work in the War Department making "such short shift of obstacles, callers, cigarettes, lunch, and other incidentals" while intensely focused on his work in supplying and sustaining an unprecedentedly large American army at war. After nagging illnesses kept him inactive for most of the year, Goethals finally followed his son Tom's advice and submitted to a full medical examination in September 1927, which revealed that he was suffering from terminal lung cancer. Nevertheless, Goethals decided to fight the illness. He moved into his New York apartment, where he had access to more specialized care, undergoing experimental treatment when opportunities were presented to him. Nothing worked. Goethals died in his apartment on January 21, 1928, surrounded by his wife and two sons.[7]

Obituaries understandably focused on and celebrated his achievements at the Panama Canal.[8] Some officers, however, suggested that his service during the First World War was of equal or greater significance. Maj. Gen. Charles P. Summerall, then serving as the chief of staff of the army, remarked that Goethals's "epochal achievement in completing the waterways which unite the Atlantic and Pacific Oceans at the Isthmus of Panama has obscured the brilliance of many similar accomplishments throughout a period of over forty years as a military engineer, military supply officer, and military administrator."[9] One of the honorary pallbearers at Goethals's funeral, Gen. Peyton C. March, went even further. In his memoir, March wrote, "The work that he did as the virtual Chief of Supply of the Army far transcended in magnitude, and certainly equaled in importance in its effect on world history, the construction of the Panama Canal."[10]

In weighing Goethals's influence on the nation and even the world, such sentiments seem hyperbolic. But in assessing Goethals's lasting impact upon the army, Summerall and March were correct. Goethals's work in Panama was a feather in the army's cap, but it did little to influence the institution. Through his service during the First World War, however, Goethals played a substantial though not necessarily planned role in bringing to a conclusion a decades-long process of military reform that stretched from late nineteenth-century experiments with postgraduate military education, through the Root reforms, and to the ultimate realization of the potential of those reforms immediately before and during World War II. It is because of his interactions with and influence upon the army that Goethals's story is more than just an individual narrative.

His experiences in the army closely reflect, in a general sense, the collective experiences of his generation of officers. Attending West Point when it was stagnant as an educational institution, he gained more of an introduction to the military profession than a robust education. Deliberately designed to reflect traditional modes of education and interpretations of professionalism, West Point sparked his ambition and inspired a deep, personal commitment to the army. Due to its small size and frontier disposition, the army was inclined to ignore the emerging consensus that favored formal training and education as an important component of occupational and professional specialization. Accordingly, his years at West Point constituted one of the last periods of time the army took pains to deliberately train and educate him.

Thereafter, he served in an army that expected him to learn and develop through experience. At the same time, the army took few measures to standardize its assignments process to ensure that it systematically exposed him to jobs that offered enriching experiences. Meandering through an unsystematic process of assignments and officer development, he took advantage of several excellent opportunities to learn and excel as he advanced through the ranks. In the process, he earned a reputation as one of his generation's best and brightest officers. Although he was well attuned and willing to subscribe to some of the changes taking place in society at large, especially modern theories and practices of management, he generally perceived his own success to be a validation of traditional systems of thought and practice in the army, even long after the conditions that made them necessary ceased to exist. Because of the problems he observed and experienced during the war with Spain in 1898, he tolerated the new institutional structures imposed by the Root reforms, but continued to cling and adhere to comfortably traditional norms, values, and behaviors.

In the crucible of the First World War, however, severe crises in the American war effort shook his faith in tradition. By then a senior army leader, he responded to these crises by deviating from tradition to create and implement short-term solutions for immediately pressing problems. In the end, his efforts worked, but probably only because the war ended in 1918. From his vantage point, he knew that the

American war effort would be in jeopardy in 1919, and in that knowledge lay at last a tacit recognition of the inadequacy and obsolescence of nineteenth-century systems and practices.

This general and deliberately impersonal description of Goethals's career also summarizes the careers of Tasker H. Bliss, John J. Pershing, Hunter Liggett, Peyton C. March, and many others from that generation. The only significant points of variance among different members of that generation are in the conclusions they drew from the experience of the First World War. On this point, Goethals's generation was deeply divided, and its inability to achieve consensus caused a relatively brief period of institutional stagnation. Ultimately, the driving force behind postwar changes to the army's institutional culture was the next generation's consensus about the war and its implications.

This reveals a long-neglected aspect of military reform in the late nineteenth and early twentieth centuries: the slow shift in the army's institutional culture. Turn-of-the-century military reform is too often treated solely as the story of Elihu Root's program of reforms and the efforts of a few exceptionally dedicated, impassioned, and progressive military thinkers. Such a narrative oversimplifies and artificially shortens the process of institutional change, which was then and is now a process that is structural and cultural in equal parts. In the case of army reform as the nineteenth century gave way to the twentieth, structural changes wrought by the Root reforms happened relatively quickly, from 1899 to 1903. But structural change was the hare to cultural change's tortoise. It took more than three decades and a world war to change the army's institutional culture to such an extent that it fully realigned with the army's institutional structures.

The dynamics of cultural change in the army during the late nineteenth and early twentieth centuries are instructive. They reveal four general and interconnected implications about cultural change in any major organization or institution, military or civil. First, the army's experience of cultural change suggests that it happens slowly within large institutions because the conditions that shape institutions change faster than the institutions themselves can change. Practices born of necessity become enshrined as tradition and outlive the conditions that made them necessary. The realization that a given value, belief, or practice is outdated almost inevitably comes long after the point at which it has passed into irrelevance. The army's passive reliance upon experiential learning was rooted in its traditionally small size, mission, and frontier disposition. When the frontier vanished, the need for the army to be dispersed in small-unit outposts scattered throughout the American West likewise disappeared. As larger units consolidated on larger posts, the army fell into a true peacetime routine during which it was not in constant operational use. This held enormous possibilities for the emergence of more robust systems of training and education. Despite the occurrence of some large-unit maneuvers, those possibilities were largely unrealized as officers clung to traditional but newly outmoded beliefs about training and education. That perception and the practices derived from it had long outlived the conditions that made them necessary.

Stemming from this, the second implication is that cultural change happens slowly in large institutions because people have a tendency to resist change. Goethals's story shows that even an agent of change can still resist change. The gap between the army's institutional culture and its structures closed when the army and its officer corps fully embraced both a rigorous military education system and an active general staff. Goethals resisted both until the last year of his career, and ultimately he only supported the latter half of that equation. Even as late as 1922, he was publicly expounding upon the virtues of experiential learning as superior to formal, classroom-oriented education. Goethals's partial embrace of change was the mirror image of Pershing's. During his tenure as chief of staff of the army (1921–1924), Pershing did much to foster the growth of the army's educational system. At the same time, he confined the General Staff to administration, allowed the bureau chiefs to reign supreme in logistics, and attempted to redefine the role of the chief of staff in the image of the nineteenth-century commanding general. In their belated and incomplete endorsements of change, Goethals and Pershing were closely aligned with their generation's response to the Root reforms. Uncomfortably new structures that departed from tradition inspired resistance through the First World War. Although the war provided ample evidence that traditional systems and practices were inadequate for modern warfare, this generation of officers collectively moved from resistance only to ambivalence. After decades of service, the force of tradition was too powerful to overcome completely.[11]

Third, changes in organizational and institutional culture are not simply generational. The mere existence of generations and transitions between generations does not necessarily mean that cultural change will occur. Goethals's peers and colleagues idealized and idolized the Civil War generation that came before them. Far from repudiating their predecessors, they borrowed much and deviated little from the values and practices bequeathed to them. Furthermore, those officers in the generation that succeeded Goethals's did not complete the army's slow process of cultural change just because they were a new generation. They did so because the experience of the First World War had fundamentally altered their perceptions at a point in time when they were newcomers to the institution, and therefore less deeply attached to its traditional norms, values, and behaviors.

Finally, and related to the point above, crisis is the most important and reliable stimulus for change in organizational and institutional culture. The force and effect of crisis far outweighs possibilities presented by generational transition alone. Absent the troubled mobilization for the war with Spain in 1898, it is unlikely that Goethals's generation would have tolerated the new institutional structures imposed by the Root reforms. They may not have had to, as it is equally unlikely that the legislation that enacted the reforms would have passed through Congress without the scandals surrounding mobilization in 1898. Two decades later, it was the crisis of a stalled and strained war effort in 1917–1918 that broke the traditional consensus for Goethals's generation and set the necessary conditions for real change in the army's institutional culture during the interwar years. And it was another crisis in 1941–1942 that prompted the army to take its final step on the long road to reform.

George W. Goethals dedicated his entire adult life to the army and the improvement and efficiency of vast organizations. It is entirely fitting, then, that the story of his life reveals so much about both the army he served and the dynamics of organizational and institutional change.

Notes

List of Abbreviations

ADAH   Alabama Department of Archives and History, Montgomery
CCNY   City College of New York Archives and Special Collections,
          New York
LC   Manuscript Division, Library of Congress, Washington, DC
NARA I   National Archives and Records Administration I,
          Washington, DC
NARA II   National Archives and Records Administration II,
          College Park, MD
RG   Record Group
USACE   Office of History, US Army Corps of Engineers, Alexandria, VA
USAWW   US Army Center for Military History. *The United States Army in
          the World War, 1917–1919,* 17 vols. Washington, DC: Center for
          Military History, 1988
USMA   US Military Academy Special Collections and Archives,
          West Point, NY
VMI   Virginia Military Institute Archives, Lexington

Prologue

1. "West Point Cadets Cheer War Veterans," *New York Times,* June 13, 1912, 22.

2. US Congress, House of Representatives, *Address of Col. George W. Goethals, United States Army, at the Graduation Exercises of the Class of Nineteen Twelve, United States Military Academy, West Point, N.Y., Wednesday, June 12, 1912,* 62nd Cong., 2nd sess., 1912, H.Doc 904 (Washington, DC: Government Printing Office, 1912), 5–8. The quotations are on pages 5 and 6, respectively, and Goethals mentions being only the second graduation speaker to not be a general on 5. For Goethals's aversion to public speaking, see George W. Goethals

to Lewis Sayre Buchard, June 11, 1927, folder 6, Goethals File, City College of New York Archives and Special Collections, New York.

3. The organization, function, and culture of the US Army that Goethals entered in 1876 is thoroughly examined in Edward M. Coffman, *The Old Army: A Portrait of the American Army in Peacetime, 1784–1898* (New York: Oxford University Press, 1986).

4. For overviews of Root's reforms, see Otto Nelson Jr., *National Security and the General Staff* (Washington, DC: Infantry Journal Press, 1946), 39–72, and James E. Hewes Jr., *From Root to McNamara, Army Organization and Administration, 1900–1963* (Washington, DC: US Army Center of Military History, 1975), 6–12.

5. A succinct historiography of field of military history and analysis of military historians' adoption of social and cultural historical methods can be found in Wayne E. Lee, "Mind and Matter: Cultural Analysis in American Military History: A Look at the State of the Field," *Journal of American History* 93 (2007): 1116–1162. He introduces "new" military history on 1117.

6. Frederick Jackson Turner, *The Frontier in American History* (New York: Henry Holt, 1920), chap. 1.

7. Robert Hine and John Faragher have been at the forefront of this interpretation. See Robert V. Hine and John M. Faragher, *The American West: A New Interpretive History* (New Haven, CT: Yale University Press, 2000), and Robert V. Hine and John M. Faragher, *Frontiers: A Short History of the American West* (New Haven, CT: Yale University Press, 2008).

8. See William Appleman Williams, *The Tragedy of American Diplomacy* (Cleveland, OH: World, 1959); Walter LaFeber, *The New Empire: An Interpretation of American Expansion, 1860–1898* (Ithaca, NY: Cornell University Press, 1963); Andrew J. Bacevich, *American Empire: The Realities and Consequences of U.S. Diplomacy* (Cambridge, MA: Harvard University Press, 2002); Paul A. Kramer, *The Blood of Government: Race, Empire, the United States, and the Philippines* (Chapel Hill: University of North Carolina Press, 2006). Eric Hobsbawm, *The Age of Empire: 1875–1914*, reprint (New York: Vintage, 1989) provides an analysis that places economic motivations for imperialism within the context of multipolar efforts to export corporate capitalism on a global scale.

9. On Wilson's decision for war, see David F. Trask, *The AEF and Coalition Warmaking, 1917–1918* (Lawrence: University Press of Kansas, 1993), 1–4; John Milton Cooper, *Woodrow Wilson: A Biography* (New York: Vintage, 2009), 374–385; and Justus D. Doenecke, *Nothing Less than War: A New History of America's Entry into World War I* (Lexington: University Press of Kentucky, 2011). For a new and compelling examination of the American public's perception of its role in the world and in the war, see Michael S. Neiberg, *The Path to War: How the First World War Created Modern America* (New York: Oxford University Press, 2016).

10. Ronald J. Barr, *The Progressive Army: U.S. Army Command and Administration, 1870–1914* (New York: St. Martin's Press, 1998).

11. James L. Abrahamson, *America Arms for a New Century: The Making of a Great Military Power* (New York: Free Press, 1981).

12. The classic articulation of the unitary interpretation is Richard Hofstadter, *The Age of Reform: From Bryan to F.D.R.* (New York: Vintage, 1955), which contended that progressivism was a singular movement driven by a middle class that felt threatened by a perceived loss of social status. Pluralists began to push back against the unitary interpretation in Peter G. Filene, "An Obituary for 'The Progressive Movement,'" *American Quarterly* 22 (Spring 1970): 20–34, and Daniel T. Rodgers, "In Search of Progressivism," *Reviews in American History* 10, no. 4 (December 1982), 113–132, questioning the value of progressivism as a concept when there were so many progressive movements. While Filene questioned the utility of the term "progressive," Rodgers categorized three distinct strains of progressivism: antimonopolism, the rise of social cohesion over individualism, and social efficiency.

The pluralist interpretation gained significant traction, receiving articulate support in Arthur S. Link and Richard L. McCormick, *Progressivism* (Wheeling, IL: Harlan Davidson, 1983), and John Whiteclay Chambers II, *The Tyranny of Change: America in the Progressive Era, 1890–1920*, 2nd ed. (New Brunswick, NJ: Rutgers University Press, 2000). The first edition of the latter appeared in 1980 as *The Tyranny of Change: America in the Progressive Era, 1900–1917*. Chambers argues that "new interventionism" may be a more useful construct than progressivism because "'modernization' resulted not only from the actions of people who called themselves progressives but also from initiatives taken by other groups, including many radicals, nonprogressive reformers, and advocates of conservative reforms." Continuing, he states that "all were willing to intervene in the economy and society, and sometimes world affairs, on an unprecedented scale." See Chambers, 136.

The pluralist challenge advanced but did not completely resolve the debate. Michael McGerr recently offered a strong case for the unitary interpretation of a middle-class-based progressivism, but his interpretation allows for a more idealistic and humanistic middle class than Hofstadter's and identifies "four quintessential progressive battles: to change other people; to end class conflict; to control big business; and to segregate society." See Michael McGerr, *A Fierce Discontent: The Rise and Fall of the Progressive Movement in America, 1870–1920* (New York: Oxford University Press, 2003), xv.

In contrast, a strongly articulated recent argument for the pluralist interpretation asserts that McGerr's concept of "progressive battles" is incorrect. Instead, it contends that there were four main progressivisms—political, economic, social justice, and foreign policy—and that these progressivisms occasionally contradicted each other but did not necessarily operate to the exclusion of one another. See Maureen A. Flanagan, *America Reformed: Pro-*

gressives and Progressivisms, 1890s–1920s (New York: Oxford University Press, 2007).

13. Compare Barr, *The Progressive Army* against Abrahamson, *America Arms for a New Century.*

14. This is known as the "organizational synthesis." See Louis Galambos, "The Emerging Organizational Synthesis in Modern American History," *Business History Review* 44, no. 3 (Autumn 1970): 279–290. See also Stephen Skowronek, *Building a New American State: The Expansion of National Administrative Capacities, 1877–1920* (New York: Cambridge University Press, 1982).

A landmark work of this school of thought is Alfred D. Chandler's *The Visible Hand: The Managerial Revolution in American Business,* published in 1977. Chandler traces the evolution of small, local firms to large national corporations throughout the nineteenth century and into the twentieth. He focuses especially on the railroads, which made the transition the earliest and affected developments in industries that produced or traded in goods related to the railroads by the last few decades of the nineteenth century. These organizations ballooned so rapidly that they were forced to become pioneers in finding new ways to manage their operations efficiently. Through trial and error, these corporations reorganized, creating a distinct and conscious class of managers—technical experts in their own fields with their own hierarchies, whose motivations and methods differentiated them from both owners and workers. The managers grew more powerful, eventually becoming "the most influential group of economic decision makers" within firms constituting a managerial enterprise that was in turn becoming "the most powerful institution in the American economy." See Alfred D. Chandler Jr. *The Visible Hand: The Managerial Revolution in American Business* (Cambridge, MA: Belknap Press, 1977), 1.

15. McGerr, *A Fierce Discontent,* 128–129; Wiebe, *The Search for Order,* 113–127; Martin J. Sklar, *The Corporate Reconstruction of American Capitalism, 1890–1916* (New York: Cambridge University Press, 1988), 431–432; Paul Starr, *The Social Transformation of American Medicine: The Rise of a Sovereign Profession and the Making of a Vast Industry* (New York: Basic Books, 1982), chap. 3.

16. David B. Tyack, *Turning Points in American Educational History* (Waltham, MA: Blaisdell, 1967), 121–180; Laurence Veysey, *The Emergence of the American University* (Chicago: University of Chicago Press, 1982), chaps. 1–4.

17. For the business interest interpretation, see W. Norton Grubb and Marvin Lazerson, "Education and the Labor Market: Recycling the Youth Problem," in *Work, Youth, and Schooling: Historical Perspectives on Vocationalism in American Education,* ed. Harvey Kantor and David Tyack (Stanford, CA: Stanford University Press, 1982), 110–141. For the social justice interpretation, see Lawrence Cremin, *The Transformation of the School: Progressivism in American Education, 1876–1951* (New York: Alfred A. Knopf, 1961). For the Americanization interpretation, see Tyack, *Turning Point,* as well as Patricia

Albjerg Graham, *Schooling in America: How the Public Schools Meet the Nation's Changing Needs* (New York: Oxford University Press, 2005), chap. 1.

18. The career officer and sometime historian William A. Ganoe first formulated this thesis in *The History of the United States Army* (1924). Ganoe's interpretation was subsequently ratified three decades later by historian Walter Millis in his examination of the evolution of US military policy since the American Revolution, *Arms and Men: A Study in American Military History* (1956). See William A. Ganoe, *The History of the United States Army* (New York: Appleton, 1924), 355–418, and Walter Millis, *Arms and Men: a Study in American Military History* (New Brunswick, NJ: Rutgers University Press, 1986), 131–210. *Arms and Men* was originally published in 1956.

One year after Millis's work was published, Samuel Huntington's widely influential *Soldier and the State* (1957) codified the military renaissance thesis as accepted wisdom. Huntington, a political scientist, theorizes that the essential elements of professionalism are a corporate identity, a sense of responsibility, and expertise—and that expertise is best developed, refined, and exercised in a distinct military sphere that is relatively isolated from society and subject to minimal interference from civil government. He places the beginning of the army's professionalization in the late nineteenth century. Huntington believed the army's frontier mission provided the physical and psychological isolation necessary to allow officers to construct a distinct body of expertise and a military sphere with which they personally identified at a time when American society was becoming increasingly conditioned to accept occupational specialization and expertise. This set off a period of change culminating with the Root reforms, which Huntington interprets as "the creation of the American military profession." See Samuel P. Huntington, *The Soldier and the State: The Theory and Politics of Civil-Military Relations* (Cambridge, MA: Belknap Press, 1957), 7–18, 222–269.

19. In 1967, Russell F. Weigley offered a competing interpretation that supports the notion that reforms of the late nineteenth and early twentieth centuries represented a military renaissance of sorts, but places the origins of American military professionalism between the years 1820 and 1840. Defining military professionalism rather narrowly as expertise derived from the study of history, strategy, and certain fundamental principles of warfare, this interpretation holds that it originated in Europe in response to the increasing complexity of warfare wrought by the development of massive citizen armies during the Napoleonic Wars. The nascent military professionalism was then transmitted to the army when officials at the Military Academy imported Prussian theories and French practices to reform the curriculum at West Point. Although this military professionalism spread throughout the antebellum army in the form of professional journals and the periodic formation of short-lived technical schools, the immediate effect of military professionalism was blunted by social trends in Jacksonian America that resisted occupational

specialty, mistrusted professional autonomy, and restrained professional consolidation.

According to Weigley, professionalization of the military therefore served
to further isolate it from society, providing a psychological isolation that he
perceives to be a condition that helped spawn a late nineteenth-century military renaissance. By portraying professional reform as something that can
only take place in isolation, Weigley sustains a significant and highly problematic component of Huntington's argument.

In a more significant challenge to the military renaissance thesis, Weigley
argues that the Root reforms were incomplete and that their only unqualified
success was the establishment of an effective institutional system of military
education for its officers. According to Weigley, the other major development of Root's tenure, the General Staff, was hampered by internal resistance
within some quarters of the army, congressional resistance, and an improvisational nature rooted in the fact that none of the officers appointed to the new
body had any experience in or knowledge of general staff functions and operations. He suggests that this resistance prolonged the processes of change.
Unfortunately, Weigley was satisfied with having blurred to some extent the
bold line that his predecessors had drawn to categorically separate the old
and the new armies. He did not probe the nature of resistance to the General
Staff. See Russell F. Weigley, *History of the United States Army*, enlarged ed.
(Bloomington: Indiana University Press, 1984), 144–172, 265–341.

This interpretation was initially an unwelcome departure from what at that
time was generally accepted wisdom. Most scholars continued to interpret reform in the late nineteenth and early twentieth centuries as the beginning of
military professionalism in the army. Timothy K. Nenninger's groundbreak-
ing examination of military education in the turn-of-the-century army ac-
knowledges that the roots of military professionalism took hold between the
War of 1812 and the Civil War, but he argues that "with the exception of the
service academies, all the permanent characteristics that identify the American military as a profession originated in the years between the Civil War and
the First World War." Around the same time, Edward M. Coffman began
work on his seminal two-volume social history of the army, tellingly titled *The
Old Army: A Portrait of the American Army in Peacetime, 1784–1898* (1986) and
The Regulars: The American Army, 1898–1941 (2004). In these works, Coffman
stakes out the position that while its seeds were planted early in the nineteenth century, American military professionalism truly began to develop in
the late nineteenth century. He argues that Elihu Root harnessed the ideas
and initiatives of late nineteenth-century reformers and lessons learned from
the war with Spain, and packaged them into an effective program of reform
that fundamentally transformed the army. "Elihu Root," he concludes, "fixed
the course for the twentieth century."

Much of the debate then shifted away from questions about timing and toward questions about motivations for professionalization, with strikingly different motivational interpretations all springing from a common assumption that military reform in the late nineteenth and early twentieth centuries in general, and the Root reforms specifically, were transformational, bringing the army into a new professional age. Peter Karsten argued that professional reform in the army, like reform in the navy, sprang from self-interested and ambitious junior officers rebelling against the lack of opportunity and upward mobility in the peacetime military. See Peter Karsten, "Armed Progressives: The Military Reorganizes for the American Century," in *Building the Organizational Society: Essays on Associational Activities in Modern America*, ed. Jerry Israel (New York: Free Press, 1972), 197–232.

Unconvinced, James Abrahamson pointed instead to military threats perceived by the officer corps. He argued that army officers shaped their agendas of reform in order to more effectively balance against the military capabilities of potentially hostile foreign powers. See Abrahamson, *America Arms for a New Century*.

Later, Ronald J. Barr posited that professionalization was a tool of expansionist-minded officers and politicians eager to build a military better suited for an imperialist agenda. See Barr, *The Progressive Army*.

20. Those who have recently questioned the significance of turn-of-the-century reform have based their conclusions on an apparent consistency and continuity in military thought and practice within the army in the decades preceding the First World War. Daniel Beaver argues that despite radical changes in structures and technology, there was more continuity than change in the functional behavior of the various parts of the War Department throughout the period of reform. In defense of the conduct of the administrative bureaus of the War Department during the war with Spain and prior to 1917, he suggests that human nature is inclined to resist change and that altering ingrained behavior would naturally be more gradual and incremental than adopting new technology and reshaping organizational structures. See Daniel R. Beaver, *Modernizing the American War Department: Change and Continuity in a Turbulent Era, 1885–1920* (Kent, OH: Kent State University Press, 2006).

One year later, Brian Linn argued that there has been a significant degree of continuity in military thought throughout US history and that it has always been defined by the interplay of three dominant schools of strategic thought: "Heroes," who typically form aggressive, offensive strategies and emphasize the human element in war; "Guardians," who prefer defensive strategies that rely upon the effective use of technology; and "Managers," who perceive efficient organization and utilization of resources to be the key to victory. With this framework, Linn interprets reform in the late nineteenth and early twentieth centuries not as a function of professionalization but as the result of a temporary rise of the "Managers" to institutional preeminence in the continuous ebb and flow of competition and collaboration between the three archetypes. See Brian M. Linn, *The Echo of Battle: The Army's Way of War* (Cambridge, MA: Harvard University Press, 2007), 93–115.

21. Another notable recent challenge to the military renaissance thesis comes from three authors who argue persuasively that American military professionalism originated in the antebellum period. William Skelton stakes the claim that although it lacked robust educational and developmental systems and institutions beyond the Military Academy at West Point, the army of the nineteenth century had professional features. The most important of these, which Skelton regards as the key to military professionalism at that time, was a stable officer corps that deeply identified with the army and was committed to lengthy careers of military service. See William B. Skelton, *An American Profession of Arms: The Army Officer Corps, 1784–1861* (Lawrence: University Press of Kansas, 1992).

Mark Grandstaff agrees that professionalism had been fully established in the antebellum army, but he makes the important observation that the Civil War had so completely altered the demographics of the officer corps that subsequent professional reform had different stimuli, motivations, and characteristics and should therefore be regarded as a second phase in professionalization. See Mark R. Grandstaff, "Preserving the 'Habits and Usages of War': William Tecumseh Sherman, Professional Reform, and the U.S. Army Officer Corps, 1865–1881, Revisited," *Journal of Military History* 62 (July 1998): 521–545.

More recently, Samuel Watson's sweeping two-volume study of the army's officer corps between the War of 1812 and the Mexican War reaffirms the origins of the American military profession in the antebellum period after 1820, but differs from Skelton by centering it on the development of a collective sense of responsibility and subordination to civil government among a stable, cohesive, and expert officer corps. See Samuel J. Watson, *Jackson's Sword: The Army Officer Corps on the American Frontier, 1810–1821* (Lawrence: University Press of Kansas, 2012), and Samuel J. Watson, *Peacekeepers and Conquerors: The Army Officer Corps on the American Frontier, 1821–1846* (Lawrence: University Press of Kansas, 2013).

22. Watson, *Jackson's Sword*, 11.

23. See Ira D. Gruber, *Books and the British Army in the Age of the American Revolution* (Chapel Hill: University of North Carolina Press, 2010), 3–64; Don Higginbotham, *George Washington and the American Military Tradition* (Athens: University of Georgia Press, 1984); and Starr, *Social Transformation of American Medicine*, 30–78.

24. Most recently, J. P. Clark has made an invaluable contribution to this debate with *Preparing for War: The Emergence of the Modern U.S. Army, 1815–1917* (2017). He examines shifting concepts of purpose, practice, and professionalism in the army by tracing a century's worth of arguments about how best to prepare for war within four successive generations of officers.

He labels these as the foundational, Civil War, composite, and progressive generations and defines them by the consensus they each arrive at about war preparation and military professionalism. There is much to be commended in this approach. Clark's generational model moves beyond demonstrating that military professionalism is a social and cultural construction and shows how the construction itself changed incrementally from one generation to the next. See J. P. Clark, *Preparing for War: The Emergence of the Modern U.S. Army, 1815–1917* (Cambridge, MA: Harvard University Press, 2017).

At the same time, such a model risks placing too much emphasis on generational transition as the most important impetus for institutional change. Generational transition alone does not guarantee institutional change; other factors must be considered as well. As will be shown in this study, external shock is at least as significant an impetus for change as generational transition.

25. Surprisingly little has been written about Goethals. Joseph Bucklin Bishop and his son Farnham published the only book-length biography of George W. Goethals in 1930. The elder Bishop, a journalist by trade, served under Goethals in Panama as the secretary to the Isthmian Canal Commission. Originally placed on the commission as President Theodore Roosevelt's personal spy in the Canal Zone, he quickly came to respect Goethals, becoming one of his most steadfast and vocal supporters. Bishop began working on this biography when Goethals passed away in 1928, but he died soon thereafter. His son, also a journalist, managed to complete the manuscript and send it to his publisher only weeks before his own death. While a monument to loyal friendship, this work is far from an impartial scholarly appraisal of a significant life. Intended to praise a recently departed friend, it is at times polemical and hagiographical. Written so soon after its subject's passing, *Goethals: Genius of the Panama Canal* is in many instances inaccurate. It records as fact the hearsay and legend that surrounded a famous figure. As its title suggests, the Bishops' book is most concerned with Goethals at Panama and generally pays only cursory attention to other periods in Goethals's life. See Joseph Bucklin Bishop and Farnham Bishop, *Goethals: Genius of the Panama Canal* (New York: Harper & Brothers, 1930).

Whether out of fear of meeting the same sad fate as the Bishops or not, no scholar has attempted a full biographical study of Goethals. Walt Griffin came the closest in a PhD dissertation completed in 1988. This is a work of admirable scholarship in which Griffin interprets Goethals's managerial philosophy as being founded upon a generally constant effort to centralize executive power under one responsible person at the top of a rationalized organizational hierarchy. As its title implies, however, Griffin's dissertation analyzes Goethals almost entirely in the context of the Panama Canal. Other parts of Goethals's life appear briefly, only as a factual prelude and postscript to his years leading the effort to construct the Panama Canal. Griffin makes little effort to discern how Goethals developed this managerial ethic or to examine the broader implications of Goethals's career beyond the years he spent at the Panama Canal. See Walt Griffin, "George W. Goethals and the Panama Canal," (PhD diss., University of Cincinnati, 1988).

Phyllis Zimmerman also produced a monograph on George W. Goethals's service during the First World War. While her research is notable, her conclusions demand modification as she misinterprets and undervalues the long-term impact of Goethals's work within the War Department. See Phyllis A. Zimmerman, *The Neck of the Bottle: George W. Goethals and the Reorganization of the U.S. Army Supply System, 1917–1918* (College Station: Texas A&M University Press, 1992).

26. Such an approach follows the example of Drew Gilpin Faust, whose *James Henry Hammond and the Old South: A Design for Mastery* (1982) reveals the utility of using an individual biography to learn more about a larger social group. Although specific events and biographical details are unique to Hammond's life experience, Faust demonstrates that his general patterns of behavior, relationship with his slaves, and political philosophies reveal as much about South Carolina's antebellum planter class as they do about Hammond himself. See Drew Gilpin Faust, *James Henry Hammond and the Old South: A Design for Mastery* (Baton Rouge: Louisiana University Press, 1982). For a similarly exemplary work, see Thomas Alexander Hughes, *Over Lord: General Pete Quesada and the Triumph of Tactical Air Power in World War II* (New York: Free Press, 1995), which effectively uses Quesada's biography to trace the evolution of close air support and air to ground integration tactics and doctrine in World War II and the cultural struggle within the Army Air Corps, and later within the Air Force, between advocates of strategic air power and advocates of tactical air power.

27. This definition is derived from Wayne E. Lee, "Warfare and Culture," in *Warfare and Culture in World History*, ed. Wayne E. Lee (New York: New York University Press, 2011), 3, and Isabel V. Hull, *Absolute Destruction: Military Culture and the Practices of War in Imperial Germany* (Ithaca, NY: Cornell University Press, 2005), 2.

28. This is drawn from Mark Grimsley, "Success and Failure in Civil War Armies: Clues from Organizational Culture," in *Warfare and Culture in World History*, ed. Wayne E. Lee (New York: New York University Press, 2011), 115–141. Grimsley suggests that the habits and traditions of organizational culture prevented commanders who inherited previously existing field armies but were consistently unable to influence their commands' character and culture as fully and as quickly as they intended. See especially pages 122–134. Although Grimsley deals with organizational culture of field armies, his ideas are equally valid at the institutional level.

29. This view of Goethals's generation complements J. P. Clark's interpre-

tation of what he labels the "composite generation." See Clark, *Preparing for War*, 7–8.

Analyzing institutional culture and the course of reform from the perspective of Goethals and his generation of officers is an adaptation of the "history from the middle" as advocated by Paul Kennedy. Kennedy argues that the traditional practice of writing military history from the top-level perspective of commanding generals and statesmen and more recent trends of analyzing military history from the bottom, focusing on the experience of soldiering and combat, are valuable but provide incomplete perspectives. He holds that analyses of causality and change must account for the existence and identification of a problem, the creation or discovery of a solution, and the application of the solution. The latter two, according to Kennedy, are the most critical aspects to narratives of causality and change. Because the creation or discovery of a solution and its subsequent application usually fall within the purview of individuals at neither the highest nor the lowest ends of military hierarchies, they often cannot be adequately addressed in top-down or bottom-up analyses. Kennedy urges historians who encounter problems with noticeable gaps when analyzed from the top and from the bottom to change course and approach from the middle. See Paul Kennedy, "History from the Middle: The Case of the Second World War," *Journal of Military History* 74 (January 2010): 35–51. This article provides the theoretical model and a single demonstrative case study. The full use of the model is better demonstrated in Paul Kennedy, *Engineers of Victory: The Problem Solvers Who Turned the Tide in the Second World War* (New York: Random House, 2013).

Kennedy's model has its share of limitations. The most glaring is that its applicability depends on the existence of an empowered "middle." Typically, military historians consider general officers to constitute the top and everyone else to constitute the bottom. This is the case because traditionally, general officers make the plans and policies while everyone else executes the plans and adheres to the policies. This began to shift in the late nineteenth century when industrialized warfare became complex enough to require planning and coordinating bodies within military organizations. As militaries recognized this need and adapted accordingly, they created bodies of mid-level officers responsible for developing and shaping plans and policies to a significant degree. Thus was born an empowered "middle," defined not only by rank but also by function. Consequently, Kennedy's model appears to be suitable only for problems in military history situated during and after this development.

Army reform in the late nineteenth and early twentieth centuries is a problem whose chronological and analytical difficulties point to the utility of a from-the-middle approach. Scholarship calling attention to functional continuity within the War Department in spite of reformist policies suggests that there are unresolved analytical gaps in top-down histories from the perspectives of both leading reformers and leading sources of resistance to reform. The view from the bottom in this case is irrelevant. Enlisted soldiers had no voice in how the army was organized and run, and they had no part in the most significant reforms of the period.

To advance the debate on turn-of-the-century army reform, the problem must be approached from the middle as it existed at that time—from the perspective of officers who did not decide on creating the General Staff or formal systems of education and development but who were nevertheless ordered to help design and implement such reforms. The appropriate focus of a from-the-middle analysis of army reform is Goethals's generation of officers, who entered the army between 1870 and 1890.

30. On tensions between the General Staff and the administrative bureaus, see James E. Hewes Jr., *From Root to McNamara, Army Organization and Administration, 1900–1963* (Washington, DC: US Army Center of Military History, 1975), 10–50; and Otto Nelson Jr., *National Security and the General Staff* (Washington, DC: Infantry Journal Press, 1946), 73–273.

31. Examples of the former include Ronald G. Machoian, *William Harding Carter and the American Army: A Soldier's Story* (Norman: University of Oklahoma Press, 2006), and T. R. Brereton, *Educating the U.S. Army: Arthur L. Wagner and Reform, 1875–1905* (Lincoln: University of Nebraska Press, 2000). The best example of the latter is Daniel R. Beaver, *Modernizing the American War Department: Change and Continuity in a Turbulent Era, 1885–1920* (Kent, OH: Kent State University Press, 2006).

32. US Department of War, *Annual Reports of the War Department*, 46th Cong., 2nd sess., 1880, H. Ex. Doc. 2, vol. 2, pt. 1 (Washington, DC: Government Printing Office, 1880), 1.

33. Goethals to George H. Morgan, February 6, 1925, folder 40, Goethals Papers, LC.

34. This is a point that will receive significant elaboration in chaps. 1–3. For a good example of the development of a highly successful line officer of Goethals's generation, see Edward M. Coffman, *The Hilt of the Sword: The Career of Peyton C. March* (Madison: University of Wisconsin Press, 1966), 1–51.

35. Gustav J. Fiebeger, "George Washington Goethals," *Fifty-Ninth Annual Report of the Association of Graduates of the United States Military Academy at West Point, New York, June 8, 1928* (Saginaw, MI: Seeman & Peters, 1929), 127.

36. "Army Men Pay Tribute," *New York Times*, January 22, 1928, 30.

1. Education

1. "Goethals, Canal Builder, a Brooklyn Boy," *Brooklyn Daily Eagle*, October 12, 1913, 1; Joseph Bucklin Bishop and Farnham Bishop, *Goethals: Genius of the Panama Canal* (New York: Harper & Brothers, 1930), 27. Very little is known about Goethals's early family life. No correspondence between Goethals and his parents or siblings survives today. It seems that the relationship

became estranged at some point in his early adulthood—possibly shortly after George entered the army—when John and Marie moved with Annie to California. In later years, George refused to speak to interviewers about his family and childhood, and Annie refused to speak to interviewers about George. George's brother, John, granted one lengthy interview to the *Brooklyn Daily Eagle*, in which he remembers their childhood fondly and displays no hostility or ill-will toward his brother.

2. "Goethals, Canal Builder," 1.

3. Barbara Finkelstein, "Perfecting Childhood: Horace Mann and the Origins of Public Education in the United States," *Biography* 13, no. 1 (Winter 1990): 6–20.

4. "Goethals, Canal Builder," 1.

5. "Goethals, Canal Builder," 2.

6. "Goethals, Canal Builder," 2.

7. Bishop and Bishop, *Goethals*, 28.

8. Thomas Goethals interview by author, Vineyard Haven, MA, December 21, 2012.

9. "Goethals, Canal Builder," 2. For City College's requirements, see "Twenty-Fourth Annual Register of the College of the City of New York, 1872–1873," CCNY, 20–21.

10. For the initial mistake, see Applicant #118, "Applicants for Admission to the College, June 1872," in Admission 1867–1873 book, box 9, NYCC Office of the Registrar, CCNY. For Goethals's subsequent explanation, see Goethals to E. B. Barnes, November 13, 1912, container 17, Goethals Papers, LC.

11. Applicant #118, "Applicants for Admission to the College."

12. David B. Tyack, *Turning Points in American Educational History* (Waltham, MA: Blaisdell, 1967), 121–180; Laurence Veysey, *The Emergence of the American University* (Chicago: University of Chicago Press, 1982), chaps. 2–3.

13. Frederick Rudolph, *The American College and University: A History*, 2nd ed. (Athens: University of Georgia Press, 1990), 241–372. See also John R. Thelin, *A History of American Higher Education*, 2nd ed. (Baltimore: Johns Hopkins University Press), 74–204; Daniel T. Rodgers, *Atlantic Crossings: Social Politics in a Progressive Age* (Cambridge, MA: Belknap Press, 1998), 97–98, 108–110. The quotation is from Rudolph, 329.

14. At that time, City College followed a five-year curriculum. See "Twenty-Fourth Annual Register of the College of the City of New York, 1872–1873," Annual Registers, CCNY, 11–15.

15. Goethals's changing ambitions are outlined in "Goethals, Canal Builder," 2; his academic standing can be found in the June 1873, July 1874, and June 1875 Merit Rolls in box 3, 1870–1876, Merit Rolls, CCNY.

16. "Statement of Leigh H. Hunt, '77," undated, George W. Goethals file, CCNY.

17. Frank H. Gilbert to Donald A. Roberts, March 3, 1912, Goethals file, CCNY.

18. A. H. Man to Roberts, March 31, 1928, Goethals file, CCNY.

19. "Goethals, Canal Builder," 2. Beers's critical role in obtaining the nomination for Goethals is also indicated in Goethals to Beers, May 1, 1876, and O. B. Ackerly to Goethals, December 17, 1912; both found in container 18, Goethals Papers, LC.

20. "Goethals, Canal Builder," 2.

21. Goethals to N. P. Beers, May 1, 1876, container 18, Goethals Papers, LC, and "Official Register of the Officers and Cadets of the US Military Academy, West Point, NY, June, 1877," 23–35, Official Registers of Officers and Cadets, USMA. Goethals did not complete his studies at CCNY, but was designated a graduate of the CCNY class of 1877 and granted a bachelor of science degree by a special vote of the college faculty in 1922. See S. W. Rudy, *The College of the City of New York: A History, 1847–1947* (New York: City College Press, 1949), 200.

22. William B. Skelton, *An American Profession of Arms: The Army Officer Corps, 1784–1861* (Lawrence: University Press of Kansas, 1992), 167–180; William B. Skelton, "West Point and Officer Professionalism, 1817–1877," in *West Point: Two Centuries and Beyond*, ed. Lance Betros (Abilene, TX: McWhiney Foundation Press, 2004), 26–35; Edward M. Coffman, *The Old Army: A Portrait of the American Army in Peacetime, 1784–1898* (New York: Oxford University Press, 1986), 96–103.

23. See, for example, George W. Goethals, "Officer's Individual Report," May 24, 1890, file # 3644-ACP-1880, box 667, entry 297, RG 94, NARA I. Self-study as a measure of professionalism in earlier periods is well documented in Ira D. Gruber, *Books and the British Army in the Age of the American Revolution* (Chapel Hill: University of North Carolina Press, 2010), 23–34; Paul Starr, *The Social Transformation of American Medicine: The Rise of a Sovereign Profession and the Making of a Vast Industry* (New York: Basic Books, 1982), 18, 30–112; and Don Higginbotham, *George Washington and the American Military Tradition* (Athens: University of Georgia Press, 1984), 118–124.

24. Stephen A. Ambrose, *Duty, Honor, Country: A History of West Point* (Baltimore: Johns Hopkins University Press, 1966), 191–198; Lance Betros, *Carved from Granite: West Point since 1902* (College Station: Texas A&M University Press, 2012), 2–3, 18–21; Theodore J. Crackel, *West Point: A Bicentennial History* (Lawrence: University Press of Kansas, 2002), 137, 159–160; and Bishop and Bishop, *Goethals*, 42.

25. Ambrose, *Duty, Honor, Country*; Crackel, *West Point*, 141–145; Betros, *Carved from Granite*; and Donald B. Connelly, "The Rocky Road to Reform: John M. Schofield at West Point, 1876–1881," in *West Point: Two Centuries and Beyond* (Abilene, TX: McWhiney Foundation Press, 2004), 175–178.

26. "Goethals, Canal Builder," 2; "Statement of Leigh H. Hunt, '77," undated, Goethals file, CCNY.

27. "Goethals, Canal Builder," 2.

28. "Official Register of the Officers and Cadets of the US Military Academy, West Point, NY, June, 1877," 20; "Official Register of the Officers and Cadets of the US Military Academy, West Point, NY, June, 1878," 16; "Official Register of the Officers and Cadets of the US Military Academy, West Point, NY, June, 1879," 14; "Official Register of the Officers and Cadets of the US Military Academy, West Point, NY, June, 1880," 12, 28.

29. Goethals to Lewis Sayre Burchard, June 11, 1927, Goethals file, CCNY.

30. Gustav J. Fiebeger, "George Washington Goethals," *Fifty-Ninth Annual Report of the Association of Graduates of the United States Military Academy at West Point, New York, June 8, 1928* (Saginaw, MI: Seeman & Peters, 1929), 127.

31. Quotation from Fiebeger, "George Washington Goethals," 127. See also Bishop and Bishop, *Goethals*, 40–51. For Goethals's nickname of "Goat," see George H. Morgan to Goethals, August 22, 1911, container 14, Goethals Papers, LC.

32. US Congress, House of Representatives, *Address of Col. George W. Goethals, United States Army, at the Graduation Exercises of the Class of Nineteen Twelve, United States Military Academy, West Point, N.Y., Wednesday, June 12, 1912*, 62nd Cong., 2nd sess., 1912, H.Doc 904 (Washington, DC: Government Printing Office, 1912), 5–8. The quotation is on page 6.

33. Ambrose, *Duty, Honor, Country*, 199; *Annual Reports of the War Department*, 46th Cong., 2nd sess., 1880, pt. 1, 2:1.

34. See Thelin, *American Higher Education*, 129–154; Starr, *Social Transformation*, 17–21, 79–179; Michael McGerr, *A Fierce Discontent: The Rise and Fall of the Progressive Movement in America, 1870–1920* (New York: Oxford University Press, 2003), 128–129; Robert H. Wiebe, *The Search for Order, 1877–1920* (New York: Hill and Wang, 1967), 113–127; Alfred D. Chandler Jr., *The Visible Hand: The Managerial Revolution in American Business* (Cambridge, MA: Belknap Press, 1977), 130–133, 466–468.

35. This point is expanded upon in chaps. 2 and 3.

36. Coffman, *The Old Army*, 96–97, 274; Skelton, *American Profession*, 248–254; James L. Abrahamson, *America Arms for a New Century: The Making of a Great Military Power* (New York: Free Press, 1981), 33.

37. Timothy K. Nenninger, *The Leavenworth Schools and the Old Army* (Westport, CT: Greenwood Press, 1978), 1–33.

38. Bishop and Bishop, *Goethals*, 53; Gustav J. Person, "The Engineer School of Application at Willets Point," *Engineer* 42 (May–August 2012): 49–50; quotation from Henry L. Abbot, "Early Days of the Engineer School of Application," *United States Army Engineer School of Application Occasional Papers*, No. 14. (Washington, DC: Engineer School of Application, 1904), 4.

39. US Army Corps of Engineers, *Annual Report of the Chief of Engineers to the Secretary of War for the Year 1881*, 47th Cong., 1st sess., H. Ex. Doc. 1, pt. 2 (Washington, DC: Government Printing Office, 1881), 2:419–425.

40. Abbot, "Early Days of the Engineer School of Application," 35–37.

41. Nenninger, *Leavenworth Schools*, 34–50. See also T. R. Brereton, *Educating the US Army: Arthur L. Wagner and Reform, 1875–1905* (Lincoln: University of Nebraska Press, 2000), 47–66. The Marshall quotation can be found in Larry I. Bland and Joellen K. Bland, eds., *George C. Marshall Interviews and Reminiscences for Forrest C. Pogue*, rev. ed. (Lexington, VA: George C. Marshall Research Foundation, 1991), 152.

42. See J. P. Clark, "The Many Faces of Reform: Military Progressivism in the US Army, 1866–1916" (PhD diss., Duke University, 2009), 160; and Donald B. Connelly, *John M. Schofield and the Politics of Generalship* (Chapel Hill: University of North Carolina Press, 2006), 318–321. Also, as will be explained in chapter 3, we may accurately describe Goethals's time at Willet's Point as the last formal training and education in his career despite the fact that he was a member of the inaugural Army War College class of 1905.

43. Samuel Crowther, "Don't Fear to Attempt a Thing Just Because It Looks Big," *American Magazine*, January 1922, 16.

2. The School of Experience

1. Throughout the nineteenth century, the population of the United States increased by a third in each decade prior to the Civil War and by a quarter every decade after it. See Walter Nugent, *Habits of Empire: A History of American Expansion* (New York: Vintage Books, 2009), 234.

2. Frederick Jackson Turner provided one of the more famed articulations of this view. See Turner, "The Significance of the Frontier in American History," in *The Frontier in American History* (New York: Henry Holt, 1920), 1–38. But this view reflects what one historian equates to a "continuous narrative" that had been articulated well before by Thomas Jefferson in his "empire of liberty" speech. See Nugent, *Habits of Empire*, xiii.

3. Richard White, *Railroaded: The Transcontinentals and the Making of Modern America* (New York: Norton, 2011), 458. On perceptions of the frontier being "closed," see Bruce Cumings, *Dominion from Sea to Sea: Pacific Ascendancy and American Power* (New Haven, CT: Yale University Press, 2009), 35–38.

4. This chapter examines Goethals's experiences in Washington Territory, as well as on the Ohio and Tennessee Rivers. While neither river was located on the frontier, river improvement and canal construction were certainly missions of the frontier army, in that they were means of facilitating communications and trade throughout an expanding nation. It is in that light that I categorize them as part of Goethals's experiences with the frontier army and use them as examples of the theory and practice of experiential officer development within the frontier army.

5. George W. Goethals, "Annual Report for the Fiscal Year Ending June 30, 1883," October 1, 1883, file 3570, box 42, entry 52, RG 77, NARA I, 1.

6. For a general summary of army campaigns against Native Americans, see Robert M. Utley and Wilcomb E. Washburn, *Indian Wars* (Boston: Mariner Books, 2002), chaps. 4–11. For a study more focused on campaigns after the Civil War, see Robert M. Utley, *Frontier Regulars: The United States Army and the Indian, 1866–1891* (Lincoln, NE: Bison Books, 1973), chaps. 7–20.

7. A thorough analysis of the breadth of the army's frontier mission can be found in Michael L. Tate, *The Frontier Army and the Settlement of the West* (Norman: University of Oklahoma Press, 1999). See also Robert Wooster, *The American Military Frontiers: The United States Army in the West, 1783–1900* (Albuquerque: University of New Mexico Press, 2009), especially chaps. 6–7, 10–12.

8. Wooster, *American Military Frontiers*, xii.

9. Russell F. Weigley, *History of the United States Army* (Bloomington: Indiana University Press, 1984), 267, 598; Coffman, *The Old Army*, 215–216, 282–283; Harry P. Ball, *Of Responsible Command: A History of the U.S. Army War College* (Carlisle Barracks, PA: Alumni Association of the US Army War College, 1983), 7; and J. P. Clark, "The Many Faces of Reform: Military Progressivism in the U.S. Army, 1866–1916" (PhD diss., Duke University, 2009), 61–62.

10. It is worth noting too that the old army promoted at a glacial rate, and officers could be lieutenants and captains for decades. On life for junior officers in the late nineteenth century, see Coffman, *The Old Army*, 215–286. Commanding Generals William T. Sherman and John Schofield saw the need to insert more classroom education into officers' careers and experimented with limited programs of reform, most notably Schofield's lyceum program. But their efforts depended on a broad willingness to change routines and habits that had become ingrained in the army's institutional culture. Such willingness proved to be largely absent, dulling the effect of Sherman's and Schofield's efforts. See Coffman, *The Old Army*, 271–278; Donald B. Connelly, *John M. Schofield and the Politics of Generalship* (Chapel Hill: University of North Carolina Press, 2006), 301–322; and Clark, "The Many Faces of Reform," 160–161.

11. Robert Wooster, *Nelson A. Miles and the Twilight of the Frontier Army* (Lincoln: University of Nebraska Press, 1993), 133. For general information about the Department of the Columbia, see Walter R. Griffin, "George W. Goethals, Explorer of the Pacific Northwest, 1882–1884," *Pacific Northwest Quarterly* 62, no. 4 (October 1971): 130–133, and Wooster, *Nelson A. Miles*, chap. 8.

12. For strength and disposition of Corps of Engineers officers, see *Report of the Secretary of War*, 48th Cong., 1st sess., 1883, H. Ex. Doc. 1, pt. 2 (Washington, DC: Government Printing Office, 1883), 2:3–4.

13. Wooster, *Nelson A. Miles*, 269.

14. Wooster, *Nelson A. Miles,* 134–135.

15. See Goethals to Chief of Engineers, May 24, 1883, file 2172; Goethals to Chief of Engineers, May 31, 1883, file 2176; Goethals to Chief of Engineers, May 15, 1883, file 2181; and Goethals to Chief of Engineers, April 1, 1884, file 1450–all in box 44, entry 52, RG 77, NARA I. See also Goethals, "Annual Report for the fiscal year ending June 30, 1883," October 1, 1883, file 3570, box 42, NARA I.

16. William T. Sherman to Robert T. Lincoln, August 30, 1883, reel 47, Sherman Papers, LC. I am indebted to J. P. Clark for sharing this source with me.

17. Nelson A. Miles to Goethals, March 11, 1908, container 7, Goethals Papers, LC; Sherman to Lincoln, August 30, 1883, reel 47, Sherman Papers, LC.

18. See Griffin, "Goethals, Explorer," 133–139 for an excellent account of this expedition.

19. Goethals to Chief of Engineers, May 15, 1883, file 2181, box 41, entry 52, RG 77, NARA I; Goethals, "Annual Report for the Fiscal Year Ending June 30, 1883," October 1, 1883, file 3570, box 43, entry 52, RG 77, NARA I, 20–21; Goethals to Chief of Engineers, April 1, 1884, file 1450, box 44, entry 52, RG 77, NARA I; Goethals to Chief of Engineers, July 1, 1884, file 2482, box 45, entry 52, RG 77, NARA I.

20. Crowther, "Don't Fear to Attempt a Thing Just Because It Looks Big," *American Magazine,* January 1922, 93. See also Griffin, "George W. Goethals, Explorer of the Pacific Northwest, 1882–1884," 139.

21. Crowther, "Don't Fear," 93.

22. Wooster, *Nelson A. Miles,* 135–136; and Goethals to Chief of Engineers, May 31, 1883, file 2182, box 41, entry 52, RG 77, NARA I.

23. This incident is outlined in Joseph Bucklin Bishop and Farnham Bishop, *Goethals: Genius of the Panama Canal* (New York: Harper & Brothers, 1930), 56–58. Although the accompanying letters do not survive in the archives, the Office of the Chief of Engineers recorded receiving a letter from the adjutant general in March 1884, noting that "Commanding General wants Carter in place of Goethals," and "Comdg Genl Columbia wants Carter in place of G- as Engr. Officer," on pages 73 and 144 in vol. 6, entry 48, RG 77, NARA I. The recommendation by the chief of engineers to transfer Goethals to Cincinnati is found in John Newton to Adjutant General, August 8, 1884, file 3644-ACP-1880, box 667, entry 297, RG 94, NARA I. On Miles's personality, see Wooster, *Nelson A. Miles,* 269.

24. *Report of the Secretary of War,* 48th Cong., 1st sess., 1883, 2:3–4. River and harbor improvements were far and away the highest priority for the Corps of Engineers at the time. Out of 103 officers within the Corps of Engineers, 55 were assigned to duties related to such works.

25. Goethals to Lieut. Col. W. E. Merrill, October 11, 1884, quoted in

Report of the Secretary of War, 49th Cong., 1st sess., 1885, H. Ex. Doc. 1, pt. 2 (Washington, DC: Government Printing Office, 1885), 2:1829–1830.

26. Merrill to Brig. Gen. John Newton, October 14, 1884, quoted in *Report of the Secretary of War*, 49th Cong., 1st sess., 2:1885, 1829–1830.

27. Leland R. Johnson, *The Ohio River Division, U.S. Army Corps of Engineers: The History of a Central Command*, (Cincinnati: US Army Corps of Engineers Ohio River Division, 1992), 18–21; and Leland R. Johnson, *The Davis Island Lock and Dam, 1870–1922* (Pittsburgh: US Army Engineer District, 1985), 5–8.

28. Johnson, *Ohio River Division*, 21–26; and Johnson, *Davis Island Lock and Dam*, 8–12.

29. Johnson, *Ohio River Division*, 26–27; and Johnson, *Davis Island Lock and Dam*, 12.

30. Johnson, *Davis Island Lock and Dam*, 17–18; and *Report of the Secretary of War*, 49th Cong., 1st sess., 1885, 2:1784–1785.

31. Johnson, *Davis Island Lock and Dam*, 2.

32. Johnson, *Ohio River Division*, 26–27; and Johnson, *Davis Island Lock and Dam*, 2.

33. Johnson, *Davis Island Lock and Dam*, 21; and Johnson, *Ohio River Division*, 26.

34. Johnson, *Davis Island Lock and Dam*, 21–22.

35. Johnson, *Davis Island Lock and Dam*, 2–3, 22.

36. Johnson, *Davis Island Lock and Dam*, 3, 108, and 133; and Johnson, *Ohio River Division*, 28.

37. *Report of the Secretary of War*, 49th Cong., 1st sess., 1885, 2:1799.

38. Johnson, *Davis Island Lock and Dam*, 17.

39. Johnson, *Davis Island Lock and Dam*, 34–45.

40. Johnson, *Davis Island Lock and Dam*, 45, 56–59.

41. Johnson, *Davis Island Lock and Dam*, 87–88; Bishop and Bishop, *Goethals*, 58–60.

42. Johnson, *Davis Island Lock and Dam*, 88; Bishop and Bishop, *Goethals*, 58–61; *Report of the Secretary of War*, 49th Cong., 1st sess., 1885, 2:1785–1833.

43. Johnson, *Davis Island Lock and Dam*, 91–92; Bishop and Bishop, *Goethals*, 61; and "Official Register of the Officers and Cadets of the U.S. Military Academy, West Point, NY, June 1886," 6, USMA.

44. *Report of the Secretary of War*, 49th Cong., 2nd sess., 1886, H. Ex. Doc. 1, pt. 2 (Washington, DC: Government Printing Office, 1886), 2:4; "Official Register of the Officers and Cadets of the U.S. Military Academy, West Point, N.Y., June 1886," Official Registers of Officers and Cadets, USMA, 6; and Lance Betros, *Carved from Granite: West Point since 1902* (College Station: Texas A&M University Press, 2012), 21.

45. Stephen A. Ambrose, *Duty, Honor, Country: A History of West Point* (Baltimore: Johns Hopkins University Press, 1966), 202.

46. "Official Register of the Officers and Cadets of the U.S. Military Academy, West Point, NY, June, 1880," 6, 12, and 28; Richard C. Drum to Chief of Engineers, June 19, 1885, file 2413, box 49, entry 52, RG 77, NARA I; and Chief of Engineers to Adjutant General, June 22, 1885, file 2413, box 49, entry 52, RG 77, NARA I.

47. Betros, *Carved from Granite*, 20.

48. Theodore J. Crackel, *West Point: A Bicentennial History* (Lawrence: University Press of Kansas, 2002), 162.

49. *Report of the Secretary of War*, 49th Cong., 2nd sess., H. Ex. Doc. 1, pt. 2 (Washington, DC: Government Printing Office, 1886), 2:4.

50. Maj. H. M. Adams to Redfield Proctor, August 14, 1889, 564, vol. 10, entry 73, RG 77, NARA I.

51. Capt. Thomas Turtle to Redfield Proctor, September 4, 1889, 649, vol. 10, entry 73, RG 77, NARA I; and John C. Kelton to Surgeon General, September 28, 1889, and Special Orders No. 238, AGO, October 12, 1889, file # 3644-ACP-1880, box 667, entry 297, RG 94, NARA I.

52. Donald Davidson, *The Tennessee*, vol. 1, *The Old River: From Frontier to Secession* (Nashville: J. S. Sanders, 1991), 230–231; US War Department, *Letter from the Secretary of War, Transmitting Report of the Surveys on the Tennessee River, Made in Compliance with the Act of March 2, 1867*, 40th Cong., 2nd sess., 1868, H. Ex. Doc. 271, 4–7; and "The Mussel Shoals Canal," *Harper's Weekly*, October 18, 1890. Nineteenth-century sources are inconsistent in their spelling of the area, usually choosing between "Mussel Shoals" and "Muscle Shoals." The latter appears relatively consistently in government documents and in sources from the twentieth century. I have chosen to use "Muscle Shoals" in the text and have changed "Mussel Shoals" to "Muscle Shoals" in some quotations for the sake of consistency. Original spelling will be maintained in the footnotes where appropriate, such as in titles of articles.

53. *Letter from the Secretary of War, Transmitting the Information Required by a Resolution of the House of Representatives of the 16th January Last, in Relation to an Examination of the Muscle Shoals in Tennessee River, with a View to Removing the Obstructions to the Navigation Thereof and the Construction of a Canal Around the Same*, 20th Cong., 1st sess., 1828, H.Doc 284, 5–9; *Letter from the Secretary of War*, 40th Cong., 2nd sess., 1868, 13–19, 25; and Davidson, *The Tennessee*, 1:284–286.

54. *Letter from the Secretary of War*, 40th Cong., 2nd sess., 1868, 25–26; and Davidson, *The Tennessee*, 1:284.

55. Davidson, *The Tennessee*, 1:231–245.

56. "Tennessee River Improvements," *Harper's Weekly*, April 27, 1895; Davidson, *The Tennessee*, 1:286–289; and Leland R. Johnson, *Engineers on the Twin Rivers: A History of the U.S. Army Engineers Nashville District, 1769–1978* (Nashville: US Army Engineer District, 1978), 52–59.

57. *Letter from the Secretary of War*, 40th Cong., 2nd sess., 1868, 4.

58. Donald Davidson, *The Tennessee*, vol. 2, *The New River: Civil War to TVA* (Nashville: J. S. Sanders, 1992), 156–166; Johnson, *Engineers on the Twin Rivers*, 124; *Letter from the Secretary of War*, 40th Cong., 2nd sess., 1868, 2–3.

59. Davidson, *The Tennessee*, 2:167; Johnson, *Engineers on the Twin Rivers*, 124; and *Report of the Secretary of War*, 51st Cong., 2nd sess., 1890, H. Ex. Doc. 1, pt. 2 (Washington, DC: Government Printing Office, 1890), 2:217.

60. Johnson, *Engineers on the Twin Rivers*, 126–132. Interestingly, the Muscle Shoals robbery contributed to the downfall of both the gang and Jesse James himself. Not long after the robbery, gang member William Ryan was apprehended in Nashville using money stolen from the Muscle Shoals engineers. Officials recovered the money and returned to Florence. Frank and Jesse James had been hiding in Nashville at the time, living under aliases. Fearing discovery, they were forced to uproot and move to Missouri, where Jesse James was assassinated in 1882.

61. Johnson, *Engineers on the Twin Rivers*, 141–145.

62. *Report of the Secretary of War*, 51st Cong., 2nd sess., 1890, 2:216, 222, and 2136–2148; and Johnson, *Engineers on the Twin Rivers*, 145–147.

63. See John W. Barlow, "Efficiency Report of 1st Lieut. Geo. W. Goethals," May 11, 1890 and George W. Goethals, "Officer's Individual Report," May 24, 1890, file # 3644-ACP-1880, box 667, entry 297, RG 94, NARA I. Although Goethals's report postdates Barlow's, the fact that most of the extracurricular study happened prior to Goethals's assignment to Barlow's command makes it almost certain that Barlow had a draft or advance copy of Goethals's report at the time he wrote his own. The quotation is from Barlow's report.

64. See *Report of the Secretary of War*, 51st Cong., 2nd sess., 1890, 2:216–224, 2111–2161. Aside from a mandatory entry of officers assigned to the district on page 216, subordinates only figure in Barlow's description of a congressionally mandated survey of the lower Cumberland River on pp 2153–2160, and it is distinctly possible that they are only included because he had to append their reports to his.

65. *Report of the Secretary of War*, 51st Cong., 2nd sess., 1890, 2:217, 2118–2120, and 2122; and "On a Trip of Inspection," *Florence Herald*, January 11, 1890.

66. See "The Grand Opening," *Florence Herald*, June 26, 1889; "Florence," *Florence Herald*, August 7, 1889; "Completion of the Mussel Shoals Canal," *Florence Herald*, August 7, 1889; "Mussel Shoals Canal," *Florence Herald*, April 19, 1890; and "Mussel Shoals Canal," *Florence Herald*, May 10, 1890, respectively.

67. W. O. Skelton to Joseph Wheeler, June 30, 1890, box 62, Joseph Wheeler Family Papers 1809–1943, ADAH.

68. "The Mussel Shoals," *Florence Herald*, March 15, 1890.

69. "Mussel Shoals Canal," *Florence Herald*, July 9, 1890.

70. Maj. H. M. Adams to J. W. Barlow, November 11, 1889, 136, vol. 11, entry 73, RG 77, NARA I. See also Maj. H. M. Adams to J. W. Barlow, November 30, 1889, 21, vol. 12, entry 73, RG 77, NARA I.

71. J. W. Barlow to Joseph Wheeler, July 2, 1890, box 62, Joseph Wheeler Family Papers 1809–1943, ADAH.

72. J. W. Barlow to Chief of Engineers, July 10, 1890, file 4531, box 27, entry 96, RG 77, NARA I.

73. Quotation from "Orders," July 10, 1890, file 4531, box 27, entry 96, RG 77, NARA I. See also George W. Goethals to Chief of Engineers, August 12, 1890, file 4924, box 31, entry 96, RG 77, NARA I; Johnson, *Engineers on the Twin Rivers*, 134; Bishop and Bishop, *Goethals*, 63; and "Opened in the Fall," *Florence Herald*, September 6, 1890, which is the first mention of Goethals in the *Herald*, and which identifies Goethals as "of this city."

74. *Report of the Secretary of War*, 51st Cong., 2nd sess., 1890, 2:217 and 2122; *Report of the Secretary of War*, 52nd Cong., 1st sess., 1891, H. Ex. Doc. 1, pt. 2, vol. 2 (Washington, DC: Government Printing Office, 1891), 2305–2310.

75. "The Mussel Shoals Canal," *Harper's Weekly*, October 18, 1890; "Pushing the Work," *Florence Herald*, October 15, 1890; "A Day's Outing," *Florence Herald*, October 18, 1890; "Through Mussel Shoals," *Florence Herald*, October 29, 1890; "Unobstructed Navigation," *Florence Herald*, November 12, 1890; J. W. Barlow to Chief of Engineers, November 11, 1890, and November 18, 1890, file 6370, box 43, entry 96, RG 77, NARA I; Johnson, *Engineers on the Twin Rivers*, 134; and Davidson, *The Tennessee*, 2:168.

76. Board of Promotion to Adjutant General, February 26, 1891, file 1443, box 59, entry 96, RG 77, NARA I; and "Oath of Office," January 22, 1892, File # 3644-ACP-1880, box 667, entry 297, RG 94, NARA I.

77. *Report of the Secretary of War*, 52nd Cong., 1st sess., 1891, 2:286; and Thomas S. Casey to Redfield Proctor, March 5, 1891, J. W. Barlow to Chief of Engineers, March 18, 1891, and George W. Goethals to Chief of Engineers, March 18, 1891, file 1634, box 60, entry 96, RG 77, NARA I.

78. *Report of the Secretary of War*, 52nd Cong., 1st sess., 1891, H. Ex. Doc. 1, pt. 2, 2:278; and Bishop and Bishop, *Goethals*, 63.

79. *Report of the Secretary of War*, 52nd Cong., 1st sess., 1891, H. Ex. Doc. 1, pt. 2, 2:ii–viii; and *Report of the Secretary of War*, 52nd Cong., 2nd sess., 1892, H. Ex. Doc. 1, pt. 2 (Washington, DC: Government Printing Office, 1892), 2:ii–vii.

80. *Report of the Secretary of War*, 52nd Cong., 1st sess., 1891, H. Ex. Doc. 1, pt. 2, 2:286, 2303–2311; *Report of the Secretary of War*, 52nd Cong., 2nd sess., 1892, 2:274–275 and 1945–1950; *Report of the Secretary of War*, 53rd Cong., 2nd sess., 1893, H. Ex. Doc. 1, pt. 2 (Washington, DC: Government Printing Office, 1893), 2:308–309, 2420–2433; and *Report of the Secretary of War*, 53rd Cong., 3rd sess., 1894, H. Ex. Doc. 1, pt. 2 (Washington, DC: Government Printing Office, 1894), 2:282–284, 1821–1831.

81. Sydney B. Williamson, untitled manuscript, January 16, 1934, Sydney B. Williamson Papers, 27–36. The quote is on pp. 35–36 of the manuscript. For further evidence of the burgeoning friendship, see "Little Jots and Dots," *Florence Herald*, June 21, 1894, which indicates that Williamson, his wife, and his sister-in-law lived with Goethals in the summer of 1894 while the rest of the Goethals family made their annual summer trek to Massachusetts.

82. The administrative and logistical overhead of the Florence District are outlined in *Report of the Secretary of War*, 52nd Cong., 2nd sess., 1892, 2:1951, 1956–1958; *Report of the Secretary of War*, 53rd Cong., 2nd sess., 1893, 2:2428–2421, 2433–2435; *Report of the Secretary of War*, 53rd Cong., 3rd sess., 1894, 2:1827, 1831–1833; see also George W. Goethals to Chief of Engineers, April 16, 1891, file 2514, box 67, entry 96, RG 77, NARA I. Goethals was never trained in administration or logistics, and would have no further experience in administrative or logistical matters prior to his appointment as chairman and chief engineer of the Isthmian Canal Commission.

83. *Report of the Secretary of War*, 52nd Cong., 1st sess., 1891, 2:2310–2311.

84. *Report of the Secretary of War*, 52nd Cong., 2nd sess., 1892, 2:1950; *Report of the Secretary of War*, 53rd Cong., 2nd sess., 1893, 2:2426–2427; and Williamson, manuscript, 28–29.

85. *Report of the Secretary of War*, 53rd Cong., 3rd sess., 1894, 2:1826; *Report of the Secretary of War*, 54th Cong., 1st sess., 1895, H. Ex. Doc. 2 (Washington, DC: Government Printing Office, 1895), 2:2294; George W. Goethals to Thomas L. Casey, June 24, 1893, file 2657/23, box 41, entry 98, RG 77, NARA I; Johnson, *Engineers on the Twin Rivers*, 138; and Williamson, manuscript, 29–30. The quotation is on page 30 of Williamson's manuscript.

86. Thomas L. Casey to Daniel S. Lamont, September 27, 1894, file 7329, box 32, entry 103, RG 77, NARA I; Thomas L. Casey to Joseph Wheeler, October 4, 1894, file 8453/4, box 160, entry 103, RG 77, NARA I, Washington, DC; and *Report of the Secretary of War*, 54th Cong., 1st sess., 1895, 2:3–4, 310, and 2277. At the time, of 118 officers in the Corps of Engineers, only 4 were detailed to the Office of the Chief of Engineers, including the Chief of Engineers. The Corps of Engineers maintained an office in Florence to oversee the region's canals—that office reported first to the Nashville District as of October 4, 1894, and subsequently to a reinstated Chattanooga District. "Goes to Washington" and "May Not Go," *Florence Herald*, October 4, 1894; and "No Change," *Florence Herald*, October 11, 1894.

87. Crowther, "Don't Fear to Attempt a Thing Just Because It Looks Big," 16.

88. Quoted in J. P. Clark, *Preparing for War: The Emergence of the Modern U.S. Army, 1815–1917* (Cambridge, MA: Harvard University Press, 2017), 136.

89. Captain James Chester, "Military Misconceptions and Absurdities," *Journal of the Military Service Institution of the United States* 14 (July–December 1893): 502–518. Quotations from pages 506 and 510.

90. Weigley, *United States Army*, 265.

91. See James L. Abrahamson, *America Arms for a New Century: The Making of a Great Military Power* (New York: Free Press, 1981); Timothy K. Nenninger, *The Leavenworth Schools and the Old Army* (Westport, CT: Greenwood Press, 1978), 21–50; and T. R. Brereton, *Educating the U.S. Army: Arthur L. Wagner and Reform, 1875–1905* (Lincoln: University of Nebraska Press, 2000), 13–66. For Leavenworth's continued rise and important contribution to victory in World War II, see Peter J. Schifferle, *America's School for War: Fort Leavenworth, Officer Education, and Victory in World War II* (Lawrence: University Press of Kansas, 2010).

92. Nenninger, *Leavenworth Schools*, 68–107.

3. War, Reform, and Resistance

1. This description of progressivism is derived primarily from pluralist interpretations advanced in Daniel T. Rodgers, "In Search of Progressivism," *Reviews in American History* 10, no. 4 (December 1982): 113–132; John Whiteclay Chambers II, *The Tyranny of Change: America in the Progressive Era, 1890–1920*, 2nd ed. (New Brunswick, NJ: Rutgers University Press, 2000); and Maureen A. Flanagan, *America Reformed: Progressives and Progressivisms, 1890s–1920s* (New York: Oxford University Press, 2007).

2. See Chambers, *Tyranny of Change*, chap. 5. Chambers provides an excellent definition of his concept of interventionism on pp. 136–137. On the impact of a transatlantic exchange of ideas, see Daniel T. Rodgers, *Atlantic Crossings: Social Politics in a Progressive Age* (Cambridge, MA: Belknap Press, 2000).

3. US Department of War, *Report of the Secretary of War*, 54th Cong., 1st sess., 1895, H. Ex. Doc. 2 (Washington, DC: Government Printing Office, 1895), 2:1–22.

4. *Report of the Secretary of War*, 54th Cong., 1st sess., 1895, 2:3; William J. Sewell to Daniel S. Lamont, file 10828/7, box 233; untitled memorandum, file 11572/4, box 248; memorandum, December 3, 1895, file 13340, box 283; George W. Goethals to Major Charles Allen, file 15632/37 box 337; and Goethals to W. P. Craighill, January 28, 1897, file 19019/15, box 431, all in entry 103, RG 77, NARA I.

5. US Department of War, *Report of the Secretary of War*, 54th Cong., 2nd sess., 1896, H. Ex. Doc. 2 (Washington, DC: Government Printing Office, 1896), 2:4.

6. Goethals to Allen, September 12, 1896, file 15632/337, box 337; memorandum, December 3, 1895, file 13340, box 283; and memorandum, file 15632/337, box 337, all in entry 103, RG 77, NARA I. See also "Individual Service Report of Geo. W. Goethals, Captain, Corps of Engineers, for the fiscal year ended June 30, 1896," July 11, 1896, file # 3644-ACP-1880, box 667, entry 297, RG 94; memorandum, file 11572/4, box 248, entry 103, RG

77; and A. Mackenzie to Inspector General, July 25, 1898, file 27681, box 580, entry 103, RG 77, all in NARA I.

7. William J. Sewell to Daniel S. Lamont, January 24, 1896, file 10828, box 233, entry 103, RG 77, NARA I; "Individual Service Report of Geo. W. Goethals, Capt. Corps of Engineers, for the fiscal year ended June 30, 1897," file # 3644-ACP-1880, box 667, entry 297, RG 94, NARA I; and John M. Wilson to Secretary of War, April 28, 1898, file 216151, box 557, entry 103, RG 77, NARA I.

8. This can be seen in Goethals's description of Maj. Gen. John R. Brooke preparing for battle during the war with Spain in 1898. Transcription of Goethals to "My Darling" [Effie R. Goethals], August 14, 1898, Thomas Goethals Private Collection, Vineyard Haven, MA.

9. George W. Goethals to William M. Black, December 19, 1912, box 17, Goethals Papers, LC.

10. John M. Wilson to Secretary of War, file 22967, box 492, entry 103, RG 77, NARA I.

11. Donald F. Trask, *The War with Spain in 1898* (Lincoln, NE: Bison Books, 1981), 1–59.

12. John R. Brooke to Adjutant General, May 1, 1898, file # 3644-ACP-1880, box 667, entry 297, RG 94, NARA I.

13. Adjutant General's Office Special Orders No. 118, May 20, 1898, and Oath of Office, May 26 1898, both in file # 3644-ACP-1880, box 667, entry 297, RG 94, NARA I; John M. Wilson to R. A. Alger, June 1, 1898, file 26640, box 562, entry 103, RG 77, NARA I.

14. General Ludlow, "Memorandum for General Corbin," May 23, 1898, file # 3644-ACP-1880, box 667, entry 297, RG 94, NARA I.

15. John M. Wilson to Alger, May 14 and June 1, 1898, file 26640, box 562, entry 103, RG 77, NARA I.

16. H. C. Corbin to General Ludlow, May 24, 1898, file # 3644-ACP-1880, box 667, entry 297, RG 94, NARA I

17. General Orders No. 22, HQ, First Army Corps and Department of the Gulf, Camp George H. Thomas, May 30, 1898, vol. 1, entry 33, RG 395, NARA I; John M. Wilson cablegram to Goethals, June 9, 1898, and Goethals cablegram to Wilson, June 9, 1898, file 26945, box 564, entry 103, RG 77, NARA I. Quotation from Goethals to "Toodles" [George R. Goethals], June 1, 1898.

18. *Report of the Commission Appointed by the President to Investigate the Conduct of the War Department in the War with Spain*, 56th Cong., 1st sess., S. Doc. 221 (Washington: Government Printing Office, 1900), 6:2683.

19. An excellent overview of sanitation and related supply problems at mobilization centers during the Spanish-American War can be found in Graham A. Cosmas, *An Army for Empire: The United States Army in the Spanish-American War* (College Station: Texas A&M University Press, 1994), 266–278.

20. George W. Goethals to "Dody" [George R. Goethals], June 10, 1898, Goethals Papers, LC.

21. *Report of the Commission Appointed by the President to Investigate the Conduct of the War Department in the War with Spain*, 56th Cong., 1st sess., 1900, 6:2683.

22. *Report of the Commission Appointed by the President to Investigate the Conduct of the War Department in the War with Spain*, 56th Cong., 1st sess., 1900, 6:2683–2686.

23. Goethals to "Toodles," June 17, 1898; and *Report of the Commission Appointed by the President to Investigate the Conduct of the War Department in the War with Spain*, 56th Cong., 1st sess., 1900, 6:2684.

24. Goethals to "Toodles," June 21, 1898; and *Report of the Commission Appointed by the President to Investigate the Conduct of the War Department in the War with Spain*, 56th Cong., 1st sess., 1900, 6:2687.

25. Goethals to "Toodles," July 3, 1898; Sydney B. Williamson, untitled manuscript, January 16, 1934, box 1, folder 2, Sydney B. Williamson Papers, VMI, 28; Special Orders No. 37, Headquarters, 1st Army Corps, Arroyo, Puerto Rico, August 11, 1898, volume 1, entry 34, RG 395, NARA I.

26. Goethals to "Toodles," July 3, 1898, and July 12, 1898.

27. Goethals to John M. Wilson, July 18, 1898, file 26289, box 563, entry 103, RG 77, NARA I.

28. See Goethals to "Toodles," July 3, 1898, July 12, 1898, and July 22, 1898. Goethals clearly regards Puerto Rico as only a possibility or mere "newspaper talk" in the earlier two letters. Only in the July 22 letter does he discuss Puerto Rico in certain terms that are also surprisingly specific and uncensored: "We are to go to Porto [sic] Rico and leave tomorrow at 2:30 P.M. for Newport News where we will be for a few days before going to our destination on board the *St. Louis*."

29. Cosmas, *An Army for Empire*, 232–234; Trask, *War with Spain*, 336–356.

30. Cosmas, *An Army for Empire*, 272. Approximately 2,200 soldiers at Camp Thomas were ill with typhoid fever on June 25, 1898. That number climbed to approximately 4,400 by August 15.

31. *Report of the Commission Appointed by the President to Investigate the Conduct of the War Department in the War with Spain*, 56th Cong., 1st sess., 1900, 6:2688.

32. Goethals to John M. Wilson, April 13, 1901, file 39037, box 915, entry 103, RG 77, NARA I.

33. Cosmas, *An Army for Empire*, 234–236; Trask, *War with Spain*, 357–362; Robert Wooster, *Nelson A. Miles and the Twilight of the Frontier Army* (Lincoln: University of Nebraska Press, 1993), 225–229; *Report of the Commission Appointed by the President to Investigate the Conduct of the War Department in the War with Spain*, 56th Cong., 1st sess., 1900, 6:2688.

34. Goethals to Wilson, April 13, 1901, file 39037, box 915, entry 103, RG 77, NARA I; Goethals to "Toodles," August 28, 1898.

35. Goethals to Wilson, April 13, 1901, file 39037, box 915, entry 103, RG 77, NARA I. Also noted in Williamson, manuscript, 34.

36. Cosmas, *An Army for Empire*, 234; and Wooster, *Nelson A. Miles*, 228.

37. Both quotations from Williamson, manuscript, 34.

38. Cosmas, *An Army for Empire*, 236; Trask, *War with Spain*, 362–363.

39. Cosmas, *An Army for Empire*, 236–237.

40. Trask, *War with Spain*, 362–363.

41. Transcription of George W. Goethals to "My Darling" [Effie R. Goethals], August 14, 1898, Thomas Goethals Private Collection, Vineyard Haven, MA. I am deeply indebted to Mr. Goethals, the grandson of George W. Goethals, for a most pleasant meeting in December 2012, during which time he showed me a transcribed copy of the original letter. This is the only surviving letter between Goethals and his wife, who burned her letters from him later in life out of a deeply valued sense of privacy. According to Mr. Goethals, she saved this one letter because she believed it to have historical value.

42. Transcription of Goethals to "My Darling" [Effie R. Goethals], August 14, 1898, Thomas Goethals Private Collection, Vineyard Haven, MA.

43. Transcription of Goethals to "My Darling" [Effie R. Goethals].

44. See David W. Blight, *Race and Reunion: The Civil War in American Memory* (Cambridge, MA: Belknap Press, 2001), 140–170 and 255–299.

45. Transcription of Goethals to "My Darling."

46. J. P. Clark, *Preparing for War: The Emergence of the Modern US Army* (Cambridge, MA: Harvard University Press, 2017), 175–176.

47. Goethals to "Toodles," August 22 and August 28, 1898. The quotation is from the August 22 letter.

48. Goethals to "Toodles," August 28, 1898.

49. Goethals to "Toodles" September 15, 1898.

50. Lance Betros, *Carved from Granite: West Point since 1902* (College Station: Texas A&M University Press, 2012), 214; US Department of War, *Annual Reports of the War Department*, 56th Cong., 1st sess., 1899, H. Ex. Doc. 2, vol. 1, part 1 (Washington, DC: Government Printing Office, 1899), 675; US Department of War, *Annual Reports of the War Department*, 56th Cong., 2nd sess., 1900, H. Ex. Doc. 2, vol. 1, part 1 (Washington, DC: Government Printing Office, 1900), 290.

51. John M. Wilson to Secretary of War, September 9, 1898, file # 3644-ACP-1880, box 667, entry 297, RG 94, NARA I; John R. Brooke telegram to Adjutant General, October 10, 1898 and October 18, 1898, and Henry C. Corbin telegram to John R. Brooke, October 19, 1898, file # 3644-ACP-1880, box 667, entry 297, RG 94, NARA I; US Department of War, "Report of the Chief of Engineers," Part 1, *Annual Reports of the War Department*, 57th Cong.,

1st sess., 1901, H. Ex. Doc. 2 (Washington, DC: Government Printing Office, 1901), 58.

52. *Annual Reports of the War Department*, 56th Cong., 1st sess., 1899, 1:675–677; *Annual Reports of the War Department*, 56th Cong., 2nd sess., 1900, 1:290–291.

53. John M. Wilson to Elihu Root, October 4, 1899, file 32857, box 722, entry 103, RG 77, NARA I; "Examination for Promotion," December 6, 1899, file # 3644-ACP-1880, box 667, entry 297, RG 94, NARA I.

54. Wilson to Root, May 10, 1900, file 35155, box 837, entry 103, RG 77, NARA I.

55. Leonard Wood to Wilson, April 1, 1901, and Wilson to Wood, April 7, 1901, file 32481/9, box 715A, entry 103, RG 77, NARA I.

56. Goethals to Wilson, August 31, 1900, file 36555, box 839, entry 103, RG 77, NARA I.

57. On river and harbor improvement projects in the district, see Department of War, "Report of the Chief of Engineers," pt. 1, *Annual Reports of the War Department*, 57th Cong., 2nd sess., 1902, H. Ex. Doc. 2 (Washington, DC: Government Printing Office, 1902), 2:108–124, 889–919. For Goethals's staff, see Goethals to Wilson, December 6, 1900, file 36791/5, box 845, entry 103, RG 77, NARA I. For Sydney B. Williamson's time in Newport, see Williamson, manuscript, 35–38.

58. See Robert S. Browning III., *Two if by Sea: The Development of American Coastal Defense Policy* (Westport, CT: Greenwood Press, 1983), 73–75, 150–167; David A. Clary, *Fortress America: The Corps of Engineers, Hampton Roads, and United States Coastal Defense* (Charlottesville: University of Virginia Press, 1990), 45–47, 124–130; and Brian M. Linn, *The Echo of Battle: The Army's Way of War* (Cambridge, MA: Harvard University Press, 2007), 22–26 and 32–36.

59. H. C. Hasbrouck to Adjutant General, Department of the East, August 14, 1900, file 36467 and "Proposed Operations in Newport Harbor," file 36467/1, box 837, entry 103, RG 77, NARA I.

60. Goethals to Wilson, October 1, 1900, file 36467/14, box 837, entry 103, RG 77, NARA I, 5. The section on searchlights is on pages 3–7.

61. Goethals to Wilson, October 1, 1900, file 36467/14, box 837, entry 103, RG 77, NARA I, 4–5.

62. Wilson to Goethals, October 8, 1900, and John M. Wilson to H.M. Robert, October 8, 1900, file 36467/14, box 837, entry 103, RG 77, NARA I.

63. Goethals, "Electricity in Permanent Seacoast Defenses," *Transactions of the American Institute of Electrical Engineers* 19 (October 1902): 665–683.

64. Department of War, "Report of the Chief of Engineers," Part 1, *Annual Reports of the War Department*, 57th Cong., 2nd sess., 1902, H. Ex. Doc. 2 (Washington, DC: Government Printing Office, 1902), 2:18; George W. Goethals, "Electricity in Permanent Seacoast Defenses," *Transactions of the American Institute of Electrical Engineers* 19 (October 1902): 665–683; and

George W. Goethals, "Electricity in Permanent Seacoast Defenses," *Journal of the United States Artillery* 19 (1903): 47–65.

65. Congress, Senate, William H. Carter, *Creation of the American General Staff*, 68th Cong., 1st sess., 1924, S. Doc 119 (Washington, DC: Government Printing Office, 1924), 54–55; and Department of War, "Report of the Secretary of War," *Annual Reports of the War Department*, 58th Cong., 1st sess., 1903, H. Ex. Doc. 2 (Washington, DC: Government Printing Office, 1903), 3–4.

66. Otto Nelson, *National Security and the General Staff* (Washington, DC: Infantry Journal Press, 1946), 14–22; Beaver, *Modernizing the War Department*, 21–26; Russell F. Weigley, *History of the United States Army* (Bloomington: Indiana University Press, 1984), 193–194, 286–287; and Robert L. O'Connell, *Fierce Patriot: The Tangled Lives of William Tecumseh Sherman* (New York: Random House, 2014), 204–205. Winfield Scott insisted on commanding the army from New York when he failed to set aside his own personal jealousies of President Zachary Taylor, whose Mexican war record Scott viewed as inferior to his own. Scott once again his headquarters to New York due to friction with a particularly active secretary of war, Jefferson Davis, during Franklin Pierce's administration, and almost certainly due to the awkwardness inherent in residing in Washington after losing the presidential election of 1852. And William T. Sherman went on an extended tour of Europe and then moved his headquarters to St. Louis when antagonized.

67. Daniel R. Beaver, *Modernizing the American War Department: Change and Continuity in a Turbulent Era, 1885–1920* (Kent, OH: Kent State University Press, 2006), 13–15; James E. Hewes Jr., *From Root to McNamara, Army Organization and Administration, 1900–1963* (Washington, DC: US Army Center of Military History, 1975), 5–9.

68. Edward M. Coffman, *The Old Army: A Portrait of the American Army in Peacetime, 1784–1898* (New York: Oxford University Press, 1986), 215–286; Timothy K. Nenninger, *The Leavenworth Schools and the Old Army* (Westport, CT: Greenwood Press, 1978), 3–7 and 21–31; Weigley, *United States Army*, 273–281; James L. Abrahamson, *America Arms for a New Century: The Making of a Great Military Power* (New York: Free Press, 1981), 19–62.

69. David J. Fitzpatrick, *Emory Upton: Misunderstood Reformer* (Norman: University of Oklahoma Press, 2017), 182–231; Coffman, *Old Army*, 271–274; Jörg Muth, *Command Culture: Officer Education in the US Army and the German Armed Forces, 1901–1940, and the Consequences for World War II* (Denton: University of North Texas Press, 2011), 23–25; J. P. Clark, "The Many Faces of Reform: Military Progressivism in the US Army, 1866–1916" (PhD diss., Duke University, 2009), 160; and Donald B. Connelly, *John M. Schofield and the Politics of Generalship* (Chapel Hill: University of North Carolina Press, 2006), 14–60.

70. Coffman, *Old Army*, 273; Weigley, *United States Army*, 276–281. On the link between successful innovation and the parameters of what is considered

acceptable and possible, see Elting E. Morrison, *Men, Machines, and Modern Times* (Cambridge, MA: M.I.T. Press, 1966). On changing social attitudes toward professional authority, see Paul Starr, *The Social Transformation of American Medicine: The Rise of a Sovereign Profession and the Making of a Vast Industry* (New York: Basic Books, 1982), 79–144; Michael McGerr, *A Fierce Discontent: The Rise and Fall of the Progressive Movement in America, 1870–1920* (New York: Oxford University Press, 2003), 128–129; and Robert H. Wiebe, *The Search for Order, 1877–1920* (New York: Hill and Wang, 1967), 113–127. The patronage dimension is covered excellently in Clark, *Preparing for War*, 118–119. That crisis is an essential ingredient to prompting reform and adaptation is suggested in Williamson Murray, *Military Adaptation in War, with Fear of Change* (New York: Cambridge University Press, 2011), 37–73.

71. Cosmas, *An Army for Empire*, 103–296; Trask, *War with Spain*, 145–422; Weigley, *United States Army*, 305–309; and Edward M. Coffman, *The Regulars: The American Army, 1898–1941* (Cambridge, MA: Belknap Press, 2004), 12–13.

72. Clark, *Preparing for War*, 183–187; Beaver, *Modernizing the American War Department*, 29–30; Weigley, *United States Army*, 309–312; Coffman, *The Regulars*, 26; and Cosmas, *An Army for Empire*, 278–298, 316–319.

73. Weigley, *United States Army*, 313–316; L. Michael Allsep Jr., "New Forms for Dominance: How a Corporate Lawyer Created the American Military Establishment" (PhD diss., University of North Carolina, 2008) 197–227 and 242–243. For a somewhat different view, see Clark, *Preparing for War*, 183–184. Clark suggests that McKinley may have had reform in mind when he selected Root for the post, trusting in the new Secretary of War's well-known political acumen. If McKinley had acted so boldly and deliberately, he kept his thoughts and motivations private. It is still true that many were surprised to see Root leading the charge of military reform—then-governor Theodore Roosevelt, influential in Republican circles and soon to be nominated as vice president in 1900, labeled the appointment as "foolish" and believed it indicated a lack of commitment to significant military reform on the part of the McKinley administration.

74. Walter Millis, *Arms and Men: A Study in American Military History* (New Brunswick, NJ: Rutgers University Press, 1986), 179–180; Weigley, *United States Army*, 320–322; and Clark, "The Many Faces of Reform," 136–137.

75. Nelson, *National Security and the General Staff*, 44–60; Hewes, *From Root to McNamara*, 6–12; Weigley, *United States Army*, 319–320; Clark, "The Many Faces of Reform," 141–145.

76. Goethals to C. L. Gillespie, May 22, 1903, file 46996/1, box 1122, entry 103, RG 77, NARA I; Carter, 50–54. The quotation is from "Report of the War College Board," March 9, 1903, quoted in Carter, *Creation of the American General Staff*, 53. On Root's intentions for the General Staff and

the education system to serve as a springboard, see Clark, *Preparing for War*, 199–200.

77. "Report of the Secretary of War," *Annual Reports of the War Department*, 1903, 4.

78. Hewes, *From Root to McNamara*, 10–50; Nelson, *National Security and the General Staff*, 73–273.

79. Quotation from Carter, *Creation of the American General Staff*, 55. See also Weigley, *United States Army*, 322–323.

80. "Report of the Secretary of War," *Annual Reports of the War Department*, 1903, 5.

81. "Report of the Secretary of War," *Annual Reports of the War Department*, 1903, insert facing page 68.

82. US Department of War, "Report of the Secretary of War," *Annual Reports of the War Department*, 56th Cong., 1st sess., 1899, H. Ex. Doc. 2 (Washington, DC: Government Printing Office, 1899), 49 and 50.

83. Harry P. Ball, *Of Responsible Command: A History of the US Army War College* (Carlisle Barracks, PA: Alumni Association of the US Army War College, 1983), 79–86.

84. Clark, *Preparing for War*, 202.

85. See John D. Wainwright, "Root versus Bliss: The Shaping of the Army War College," *Parameters* 4 (March 1974): 52–65; Clark, *Preparing for War*, 203–204.

86. Tasker H. Bliss, "Memorandum," August 3, 1903, file AWC 1147, box 1, entry 294, RG 165, NARA II, 15–16. Emphases are in the original.

87. Tasker H. Bliss, "Memorandum Report for the Chief of Staff," January 15, 1904, AWC 84, box 1, entry 294, RG 165, NARA II, 2–8. Quotations from pages 3, 4, and 8.

88. General Orders No. 155, War Department, September 17, 1904, file AWC 275 and Chief of the Third Division, "Memorandum for All Officers of the Third Division, General Staff," September 15, 1904, file AWC 276, box 2, entry 294, RG 165, NARA II.

89. Samuel Reber, "Memorandum of the Work of the Army War College for the Session Ending May 31, 1905," file AWC 488, box 2, entry 294, RG 165, NARA II; Ball, *Of Responsible Command*, 92–96.

90. Tasker H. Bliss, memorandum, September 26, 1904, file AWC 290, box 2, entry 294, RG 165, NARA II; J. D. Leitch to Goethals, April 28, 1911, box 12, Goethals Papers, LC.

91. Files AWC 506, AWC 694, AWC 197, AWC 502, and AWC 858, box 1, entry 294, RG 165, NARA II are the lease documents for 22 Jackson Place. Cramped conditions are reported in Bliss to Secretary of the General Staff, February 2, 1905, file AWC 395, box 1, entry 294, RG 165, NARA II. The building still stands today, but the address is now 736 Jackson Place.

92. William H. Carter, *Creation of the American General Staff*, 68th Cong., 1st sess., 1924, S.Doc 119 (Washington, DC: Government Printing Office, 1924), 55.

93. Thirty of the forty-two company and field grade officers detailed to the first General Staff came from the line, in addition to all of its general officers. See "Report of the War College Board," March 9, 1903, printed in Carter, *Creation of an American General Staff*, 52–54. A listing of all officers on the first General Staff may be found in "Report of the Secretary of War," *Annual Reports of the War Department*, 1903, insert facing page 68.

94. "Individual Service Report of Major Geo. W. Goethals," July 1, 1903, file # 3644-ACP-1880, box 667, entry 297, RG 94, NARA I.

95. "Efficiency Report of Major George W. Goethals," June 30, 1903, file # 3644-ACP-1880, box 667, entry 297, RG 94, NARA I.

96. "Efficiency Report of Major George W. Goethals," June 30, 1905, file # 3644-ACP-1880, box 667, entry 297, RG 94, NARA I.

97. James F. Bell to Adna R. Chaffee, March 25, 1904, file # 2145, box 252, RG 393, NARA I.

98. Ball, *Of Responsible Command*, 98.

99. "Efficiency Report of Major George W. Goethals," July 14, 1906, file # 3644-ACP-1880, box 667, entry 297, RG 94, NARA I.

100. "Report of the Secretary of War," *Annual Reports of the War Department*, 1903, insert facing page 68; Tasker H. Bliss, Memorandum No. 3, file # AWC 391, box 2, entry 292, RG 165, NARA II; Browning, *Two If by Sea*, 183; Clary, *Fortress America*, 150–151; "Individual Service Report of Geo. W. Goethals, Major, Corps of Engineers," September 18, 1906, file # 3644-ACP-1880, box 667, entry 297, RG 94, NARA I.

101. Goethals to Brigadier General Marshall, April 19, 1909, container 8, George W. Goethals Papers, LC.

102. Containers 5–18, Goethals Papers, LC contain Goethals's nonfamilial correspondence from his appointment in 1907 until the canal was nearing completion in 1913. In these containers, Goethals's correspondence with chiefs of staff or General Staff division chiefs is extremely sparing. He has a much livelier correspondence with Secretaries of War Taft, Stimson, and Garrison; successive chiefs of engineers; and the chief of the Bureau of Insular Affairs, Clarence R. Edwards.

103. John J. Pershing, *My Experiences in the World War* (New York: Frederick A. Stokes, 1931), 1:17.

4. Making the Dirt Fly

1. The course of the managerial revolution in private institutions is well covered in Alfred D. Chandler Jr., *The Visible Hand: The Managerial Revolution in American Business* (Cambridge, MA: Belknap, 1977), and Charles Perrow, *Organizing America: Wealth, Power, and the Origins of Corporate Capitalism*

(Princeton, NJ: Princeton University Press, 2002). For its impact in the public institutions, see especially Stephen Skowronek, *Building a New American State: The Expansion of National Administrative Capacities, 1877–1920* (New York: Cambridge University Press, 1982).

2. Tensions over the form and function of the General Staff will be discussed in the next two chapters.

3. Noel Maurer and Carlos Yu, *The Big Ditch: How America Took, Built, Ran, and Ultimately Gave Away the Panama Canal* (Princeton, NJ: Princeton University Press, 2011), 14–30. See also Walter LaFeber, *The Panama Canal: The Crisis in Historical Perspective*, rev. ed. (New York: Oxford, 1989), 3–10.

4. LaFeber, *Panama Canal*, 3–10; see also Maurer and Yu, *Big Ditch*, 21–30.

5. Matthew Parker, *Panama Fever: The Epic Story of the Building of the Panama Canal* (New York: Anchor Books, 2007), 21–27; Maurer and Yu, *Big Ditch*, 41–44.

6. Quotation from Ulysses S. Grant, *Memoirs and Selected Letters*, ed. Mary Drake McFeely and William S. McFeely (New York: Library of America, 1990), 133. "Flamingo Island" is Flamenco Island. On fatalities among the Panama Railroad Company workforce, see Maurer and Yu, *Big Ditch*, 43.

7. Parker, *Panama Fever*, 40–59. Panama was a Columbian province until November 1903.

8. The most detailed accounts of the French construction period are in David McCullough, *The Path between the Seas: The Creation of the Panama Canal, 1870–1914* (New York: Simon & Schuster, 1977), chaps. 1–8, and Parker, *Panama Fever*, chaps. 6–13. An effective and much more concise analysis appears in Maurer and Yu, *Big Ditch*, 57–66. The French mortality rate is based on estimates cited by McCullough on page 235 and by Maurer and Yu on page 61. William C. Gorgas estimated that the French lost one-third of their white workforce (he fails to mention the nonwhite workforce) to yellow fever alone on an annual basis throughout the French construction period. See Gorgas, *Sanitation in Panama* (New York: D. Appleton, 1915), 149.

9. Maurer and Yu, *Big Ditch*, 66–70.

10. "The Oregon Taking War Stores," *New York Times*, March 15, 1898, 1; "The Oregon Expected at Callao," *New York Times*, April 1, 1898, 1; "No News of the Oregon: Spanish Torpedo Boat Supposed to Be Looking Out for the Battleship," *New York Times*, April 22, 1898, 4; "The Oregon in Danger: Commodore Schley's Squadron May Sail South To-day to Protect Her from Spanish Attack," *New York Times*, April 23, 1898, 1; "The Oregon at Rio De Janeiro," May 1, 1898, 1; "Admiral Walker's Views: He Is Joyful over Dewey's Victory, but Shows Anxiety as to the Battleship Oregon," *New York Times*, May 4, 1898, 3; "The Oregon at Barbados," *New York Times*, May 22, 1898, 1; "The Oregon at Key West: All on Board Are Well and the Ship Is Reported Ready to Take Part in the War," *New York Times*, May 26, 1898, 3; McCullough, *Path between the Seas*, 254–255; and Maurer and Yu, *Big Ditch*, 71–72.

11. William J. Sewell to Daniel S. Lamont, January 24, 1896, file 10828, box 233, entry 103, RG 77, NARA I.

12. LaFeber, *Panama Canal*, 23–30; John Major, *Prize Possession: The United States and the Panama Canal, 1903–1979* (New York: Cambridge University Press, 1993), 34–49; Parker, *Panama Fever*, 220–246.

13. The first quotation is from Theodore Roosevelt, *Theodore Roosevelt: An Autobiography* (New York: Charles Scribner's Sons, 1913), 522–523. The second is from Theodore Roosevelt to George Otto Trevelyan, November 30, 1903, quoted in John Milton Cooper Jr., *The Warrior and the Priest: Woodrow Wilson and Theodore Roosevelt* (Cambridge, MA: Belknap Press, 1983), 71.

14. LaFeber, *Panama Canal*, 31–33.

15. Parker, *Panama Fever*, 280–303; McCullough, *Path between the Seas*, 438–458.

16. Gorgas, *Sanitation in Panama*, 155–156; John M. Gibson, *Physician to the World: The Life of General William C. Gorgas* (Durham, NC: Duke University Press, 1950), 138–152; Parker, *Panama Fever*, 300–301, 328–331.

17. John F. Stevens, *An Engineer's Recollections* (New York: McGraw-Hill, 1936), 1–53. Quotation from page 52. See also McCullough, *Path between the Seas*, 459–508, and Parker, *Panama Fever*, 304–342.

18. McCullough, *Path between the Seas*, 510, 647.

19. Joseph Bucklin Bishop and Farnham Bishop, *Goethals: Genius of the Panama Canal* (New York: Harper & Brothers, 1930), 92–93. Goethals accompanied Taft on several tours of inspection of fortifications on both coasts and in Panama. See "Correspondence of the Board to Revise the Report of the Endicott Board, 1905–6," entry 519, RG 165, NARA II, 1:26–100, and George W. Goethals to Toodles [George R. Goethals], October 22, 1905, and December 14, 1905, box 3, LC.

20. "Individual Service Report of Geo. W. Goethals, Major, Corps of Engineers," September 18, 1906, file # 3644-ACP-1880, box 667, entry 297, RG 94, NARA I; George W. Goethals, "Fortifications," *Transactions of the American Society of Engineers* 54 (March 1905): 57–76.

21. W. H. Taft, "Memorandum for the Chief of Staff and for the Chief of Engineers," June 30, 1905, file # 3644-ACP-1880, box 667, entry 297, RG 94, NARA I.

22. Taft to T. Roosevelt, August 21, 1906, reel 320, series 4, William Howard Taft Papers, LC.

23. McCullough, *Path between the Seas*, 503.

24. John F. Stevens to Theodore Roosevelt, January 30, 1907, reel 320, series 4, William Howard Taft Papers, LC. Quotations are from pages 2, 3, 4, and 6, respectively.

25. Stevens to Roosevelt, January 30, 1907, 1.

26. Roosevelt to Taft, February 12, 1907, reel 320, series 4, Taft Papers, LC.

27. McCullough, *Path between the Seas*, 504–505.

28. Mauer and Yu, *Big Ditch,* 100.

29. On Roosevelt's perception that the problem was more managerial than technical, see Alfred D. Chandler, "Theodore Roosevelt and the Panama Canal: A Study in Administration," in *The Letters of Theodore Roosevelt,* ed. Elting E. Morison, John M. Blum, and Alfred D. Chandler Jr. (Cambridge, MA: Harvard University Press, 1952), 6:1547–1557.

30. Roosevelt to Taft, August 14, 1906, reel 320, Taft Papers, LC.

31. William Loeb Jr. to William Howard Taft, February 27, 1906, reel 320, Taft Papers, LC.

32. Roosevelt, *Autobiography,* 528.

33. Much of this discussion refutes the conclusions in Walt Griffin, "George W. Goethals and the Panama Canal," PhD diss., University of Cincinnati, 1988, in which Griffin interprets Goethals's tenure at the Panama Canal as a long and ultimately successful quest for power and asserts such reorganizations of the ICC were the fruits of a deliberate campaign to gain more power. On Roosevelt's perception of the relationship between the canal and his personal legacy, it is worth noting that among the six chapters of his autobiography that examine aspects of the Roosevelt presidency, the Panama Canal gets a full chapter to itself. See Roosevelt, *Autobiography,* 502–531.

34. Quotations from George W. Goethals, "The Building of the Panama Canal: Success of Government Methods," *Scribner's Magazine* 57, no. 3 (March 1915): 265. See also William Loeb Jr. to Goethals, February 18, 1907, box 5, Goethals Papers, LC. "Individual Service Report of Geo. W. Goethals, Major, Corps of Engineers," September 18, 1906, file # 3644-ACP-1880, box 667, entry 297, RG 94, NARA I lists Goethals's address as 1903 S St., NW, Washington, DC. The home still stands today at the same address.

35. William Loeb Jr. to George W. Goethals, February 18, 1907, box 5, Goethals Papers, LC; "Individual Service Report of Geo. W. Goethals, Major, Corps of Engineers," September 18, 1906, file # 3644-ACP-1880, box 667, entry 297, RG 94, NARA I lists Goethals's address as 1903 S St., NW, Washington, DC. The home still stands today at the same address.

36. Bishop and Bishop, *Goethals,* 140–142.

37. Goethals to Toodles, March 10, 1907, container 3, Goethals Papers, LC.

38. George W. Goethals, "The Building of the Panama Canal: Organization of the Force," *Scribner's Magazine* 57 (May 1915): 533.

39. Goethals to Toodles, March 17, 1907, container 3, Goethals Papers, LC.

40. Goethals to Toodles, March 22, 1907, container 3, Goethals Papers, LC.

41. George W. Goethals, *Government of the Canal Zone* (Princeton, NJ: Princeton University Press, 1915), 2.

42. George W. Goethals, "The Building of the Panama Canal: The Human Element in Administration," *Scribner's Magazine* 57 (June 1915): 721.

43. Samuel Crowther, "Don't Fear to Attempt a Thing Just Because It Looks Big," *American Magazine,* January 1922, 92.

44. Isthmian Canal Commission, *Annual Report of the Isthmian Canal Commission for the Fiscal Year Ended June 30, 1907*, 60th Cong., 1st sess., 1907, S. Doc. 55 (Washington, DC: Government Printing Office, 1907), 34–37, 139.

45. US Department of War, "Report of the Secretary of War," *War Department, USA Annual Reports, 1907*, 60th Cong., 1st sess., H. Doc. 2, 1:7, 44–54.

46. See *Annual Report of the Isthmian Canal Commission for the Fiscal Year Ended June 30, 1907*, 26, 193; and Isthmian Canal Commission, *Annual Report of the Isthmian Canal Commission for the Fiscal Year Ended June 30, 1913*, 63rd Cong., 2nd sess., 1913, H. Doc. 426 (Washington, DC: Government Printing Office, 1913), 53, which noted a workforce of 44,733 in March 1913.

47. At the time, the Leavenworth Schools were organized to produce competent staff officers for echelons at division and above, and as we have seen, the Army War College was used more as a planning agency that supplemented the General Staff than as a truly educational institution. See Timothy K. Nenninger, *The Leavenworth Schools and the Old Army: Education, Professionalism, and the Officer Corps of the United States Army, 1881–1918* (Westport, CT: Greenwood Press, 1978), 68–111; and chapter 3, above.

48. Chandler, *Visible Hand*, 3–12.

49. Chandler, *Visible Hand*, 337–454; Robert H. Wiebe, *The Search for Order, 1877–1920* (New York: Hill and Wang, 1967), 151–155.

50. See Wiebe, *Search for Order*, chaps. 5–7; Michael McGerr, *A Fierce Discontent: The Rise and Fall of the Progressive Movement in America, 1870–1920* (New York: Oxford University Press, 2003), chap. 4; and Stephen Skowronek, *Building a New American State*, part 3.

51. Army historians have long emphasized the impact of the managerial revolution on the army. The traditional view, which focuses strongly on the Root reforms as a military manifestation of the managerial revolution, appears most directly in chapters titled "The Managerial Revolution" in both Walter Millis, *Arms and Men: A Study in American Military History* (New Brunswick, NJ: Rutgers University Press, 1986), 131–210, and Edward M. Coffman, *The Regulars: The American Army, 1898–1941* (Cambridge, MA: Belknap, 2004), 142–201. Brian Linn points, somewhat indirectly, to the influences of the managerial revolution in not only informing the perceptions and policies of the "managers" group in his guardians-heroes-managers construct of the army officer corps but also enabling the managers' rise to prominence in the late nineteenth and early twentieth centuries. See Brian McAllister Linn, *The Echo of Battle: The Army's Way of War* (Cambridge, MA: Harvard University Press, 2007), 7, 40–67, and 93–115.

52. The most extensive treatment of railroads in this context is Chandler, *Visible Hand*, 79–205. See also Perrow, *Organizing America*, 111–113; Richard Franklin Bensel, *The Political Economy of American Industrialization, 1877–1900* (New York: Cambridge University Press, 2000), 55, 290–291.

53. The wartime careers of key railroad engineers, managers, and execu-

tives—as well as the transition of wartime organizations, systems, and practices to private companies in peacetime—are succinctly but effectively explored in Richard White, *Railroaded: The Transcontinentals and the Making of Modern America* (New York: Norton, 2011), 3–36. There is an excellent discussion on the Union's war finance programs and their lasting postwar impact in Richard F. Bensel, *Yankee Leviathan: The Origins of Central State Authority in America, 1859–1877* (New York: Cambridge University Press, 1990), 239–302.

54. See Chandler, *Visible Hand*, 122–500. Although Chandler's work focuses on the managerial revolution in civil society, his principles are applicable to the atrophy of managerial concepts and practices in the military. Chandler points out that the rise of managers and managerial practices depended on the growth of corporate organizations and that the professionalization of managers depended upon the continuing growth of multiunit businesses in both size and diversity, as he points out in *The Visible Hand* on pages 6–9. After the Civil War, the army downsized sharply. With 1,000,692 soldiers in 1865, the army reported an end strength of 57,072 in 1866 and only 25,513 in 1875. See Russell F. Weigley, *History of the United States Army* (Bloomington: Indiana University Press, 1984), 598. An army that reduced its forces by approximately 97.5 percent over the course of nine years was not, by Chandler's model, an organization in which modern managerial practices could be expected to thrive.

55. Army historians have long made a convincing case for middle-class officers as a natural conduit of popular managerial theories and techniques in the late nineteenth and early twentieth centuries. Walter Millis described the period between the Civil War and World War I as the army's very own managerial revolution, an idea he considered so important that it became the title of chapter 3 in his work *Arms and Men*. The same can be said of Mac Coffman's *The Regulars*, although Coffman perceived the army's embrace of the managerial revolution to be limited to Root's tenure in office and the subsequent decade. See Coffman, *The Regulars*, chap. 5. See also James L. Abrahamson, *America Arms for a New Century: The Making of a Great Military Power* (New York: Free Press, 1981), chaps. 6–7.

56. Chandler, *Visible Hand*, 381–450.

57. Refer to chapter 2 for Goethals's stewardship of the Florence District.

58. Goethals to Toodles, March 22, 1907.

59. Goethals to Toodles, March 17, 1907.

60. Goethals, "Organization of the Force," 534.

61. Goethals to David D. Gaillard, June 1, 1908, folder 91, box 6, Gaillard Papers, USACE; Sydney B. Williamson, manuscript, January 16, 1934, box 1, folder 2, Williamson Papers, VMI, 41, 52.

62. Isthmian Canal Commission, *Annual Report of the Isthmian Canal Commission for the Fiscal Year Ended June 30, 1909*, 61st Cong., 2nd sess., 1909, H. Doc. 263 (Washington, DC: Government Printing Office, 1909), 3–4;

Williamson, manuscript, 41; Goethals, "Organization of the Force," 544; Mc-Cullough, *Path between the Seas,* 540–541; and Parker, *Panama Fever,* 402–403, 440–446.

63. *Annual Report of the Isthmian Canal Commission for the Fiscal Year Ended June 30, 1909,* 10; Williamson, manuscript, 41; Goethals, "Organization of the Force," 544; D. D. Gailliard, "Culebra Cut and the Problem of the Slides," *Scientific American,* November 9, 1912, 388–390, located in folder 52, box 6, Gaillard Papers, USACE; McCullough, *Path between the Seas,* 541, 543–554, and 611; Parker, *Panama Fever,* 402–403, 420–429.

64. *Annual Report of the Isthmian Canal Commission for the Fiscal Year Ended June 30, 1909,* 15; Williamson, manuscript, 41–42; Goethals, "Organization of the Force," 544; McCullough, *Path between the Seas,* 541–542; Parker, *Panama Fever,* 403.

65. Goethals to Taft, February 20, 1908, container 5, Goethals Papers, LC; *Annual Report of the Isthmian Canal Commission for the Fiscal Year Ended June 30, 1910,* 61st Cong., 3rd sess., 1910, H. Doc. 1030 (Washington, DC: Government Printing Office, 1910), 2–5. See also Goethals, "Organization of the Force," 542–543; Williamson, manuscript, 40–41; McCullough, *Path between the Seas,* 542–543; Parker, *Panama Fever,* 446–451.

66. Gorgas, *Sanitation in Panama,* 156.

67. Gorgas, *Sanitation in Panama,* 159–167, 182–205, and 219–222. Statistics on quinine are found on page 221. See also Parker, *Panama Fever,* 364–366.

68. *Annual Report of the Isthmian Canal Commission for the Fiscal Year Ended June 30, 1907,* 32, 193; *Annual Report of the Isthmian Canal Commission for the Fiscal Year Ended June 30, 1912,* 62nd Cong., 3rd sess., 1912, H. Doc. 967 (Washington, DC: Government Printing Office, 1912), 65, 533.

69. *Annual Report of the Isthmian Canal Commission for the Fiscal Year Ended June 30, 1909,* 61st Cong., 2nd sess., 1909, H. Doc. 263 (Washington, DC: Government Printing Office, 1909), 22–29.

70. Goethals to Toodles, April 9, 1907, container 3, George W. Goethals Papers, LC.

71. Goethals to Toodles, April 12, 1907, container 3, George W. Goethals Papers, LC.

72. An extensive account of Goethals's work habits can be found in Albert Edwards, "The Boss of the Job," *Outlook,* June 24, 1911, 391–411.

73. Goethals to Gaillard, June 1, 1908, folder 91, box 6, Gaillard Papers, USACE.

74. Goethals, "Organization of the Force," 544. Italics are in the original.

75. In his dissertation, Walt Griffin interprets Goethals's tenure in Panama as a somewhat contentious quest for consolidated executive power. See Griffin, "George W. Goethals and the Panama Canal." Julie Greene presents Goethals as a benevolent but also patriarchal and racist despot in Julie

Greene, *The Canal Builders: Making America's Empire at the Panama Canal* (New York: Penguin Books, 2009), 53–62.

76. Goethals to Toodles, March 22, 1907; Edwards, "The Boss of the Job," 400.

77. Goethals, *Government of the Canal Zone*, 50.

78. Goethals to Toodles, March 22, 1907.

79. Albert Edwards, "The Boss of the Job," 400.

80. Williamson, manuscript, 42.

81. Williamson, manuscript, 41.

82. Williamson, manuscript, 44; William L. Sibert to Goethals, February 2, 1908, Gaillard to Goethals, February 1, 1908, and Sibert to Gaillard, February 1, 1908, container 5, Goethals Papers, LC.

83. Robert E. Wood, *Monument for the World* (Chicago: Encyclopaedia Britannica, 1963), 34.

84. Williamson, manuscript, 42.

85. Goethals, "Organization of the Force," 541.

86. Marie D. Gorgas and Burton J. Hendrick, *William Crawford Gorgas: His Life and Work* (Garden City, NY: Doubleday, Page, 1924), 216–19

87. Goethals to Toodles, March 10, 17, and March 22, 1907.

88. Williamson, manuscript, 43; Goethals, "Organization of the Force," 546.

89. Williamson, manuscript, 43; Goethals, "Organization of the Force," 546; Griffin, "George W. Goethals and the Panama Canal," 332–361.

90. "Reasons Why the Isthmian Canal Commission Should Not Be Abolished prior to the Completion and the Official Opening of the Panama Canal," undated, folder 11, Gaillard Papers, USACE; William C. Adamson to Katherine Gaillard, October 29, 1912, Adamson to Gaillard, March 22, 1912, and Gaillard to "Brother Jim," undated, folder 90, Gaillard Papers, USACE, suggest that Sibert and Gaillard (and their wives) were lobbying over Goethals's head on matters related to the organization of the ICC, especially about the relative power of Goethals over other commissioners, even going so far as to write directly to William C. Adamson, the chairman of the House Committee on Interstate and Foreign Commerce and considering an attempt to orchestrate a wider circulation of their position in the press. Katherine Gaillard to Pierre Gaillard, September 19, [1912], folder 90, David D. Gaillard Papers, USACE, shows that Sibert, Gaillard, and Gorgas sent direct and indirect appeals all the way to the secretary of war.

91. Goethals to Toodles, June 13, 1907, container 3, Goethals Papers, LC. Goethals explained the seniority issue more completely in "Organization of the Force," 540.

92. Goethals to Albert Todd, August 12, 1911, container 13, Goethals Papers, LC.

93. Goethals to Toodles, April 22, 1907, container 3, Goethals Papers, LC.

94. First quotation from McCullough, *Path between the Seas,* 574. Second quotation from Katherine Gaillard to Frederic J. Esskin, August 21, 1935, folder 90, Gaillard Papers, USACE.

95. Goethals to Jacob M. Dickinson, April 2, 1910, container 10, Goethals Papers, LC; Goethals to Lindley M. Garrison, May 15, 1913, container 20, Goethals Papers, LC; Katherine Gaillaird to Pierre Gaillard, September 19, [1912], folder 90, Gaillard Papers, USACE.

96. Goethals, "Organization of the Force," 543.

97. Williamson, manuscript, 43.

98. "Goethals Buried beside the Hudson," *New York Times,* January 25, 1928.

99. Wood, *Monument for the World,* 34.

100. An excellent, though brief, overview of the general state of labor management during the managerial revolution can be found in Perrow, *Organizing America,* 173–175. Perrow characterizes labor policies at that time to have been "in most respects inadvertent." His conclusions are largely based on and well supported by Walter Licht, *Working for the Railroad: The Organization of Work in the Nineteenth Century* (Princeton, NJ: Princeton University Press, 1983).

101. Goethals, "Human Element," 724, 734.

102. Quoted in Goethals, *Government of the Canal Zone,* 46. Unquestionably, Julie Greene has done the best work on labor in the Canal Zone. See especially Greene, *The Canal Builders;* Julie Greene, "Spaniards on the Silver Roll: Liminality and Labor Troubles in the Panama Canal Zone, 1904–1914," *International Labor and Working-Class History* 66 (Fall 2004): 78–98; and Julie Greene, "Movable Empire: Labor, Migration, and US Global Power," *Journal of the Gilded Age and Progressive Era* 15, no. 1 (January 2016): 4–20. Greene, however, views racism, patriarchy, and imperialism as the major elements that influenced Goethals's management of labor. I disagree. While Goethals's views on race and the imperial context of the Panama Canal certainly influenced his thinking and actions to some degree, these factors bore considerably less influence on his approach to labor than his overriding concern for completing the canal.

103. *Annual Report of the Isthmian Canal Commission for the Fiscal Year Ended June 30, 1907,* 139. All figures taken from the June 30, 1907 data.

104. *Annual Report of the Isthmian Canal Commission for the Fiscal Year Ended June 30, 1910,* 313. Figures taken from the March 1910 data. While complete demographic data is not provided in this report, I have extrapolated from the data provided in the table for the gold and silver roles and for the regions of origin for the 15,045 employees enumerated as "laborers" to conclude the demographics in March 1910 closely approximated the demographics in June 1907.

105. Goethals, "Human Element," 724.

106. George W. Goethals, "The Building of the Panama Canal: Labor Problems Connected with the Work," *Scribner's Magazine* 57 (April 1915): 398–401. See also Goethals to Toodles, April 4, 1907. Roosevelt delegated supervision of the ICC to the secretary of war. Throughout the construction period, most executive actions related to the Panama Canal came from the secretary of war's office.

107. Goethals, "Labor Problems," 411.

108. Goethals, "Labor Problems," 412.

109. Goethals to Toodles, May 25, 1907, container 3, Goethals Papers, LC.

110. All quotations in this and the previous paragraph are from Goethals, "Labor Problems," 413. Italics are in the original.

111. This is recounted in Goethals, "Labor Problems," 415–416.

112. *Annual Report of the Isthmian Canal Commission for the Fiscal Year Ended June 30, 1910*, 37. The next year's report notes, "The past year has been the first since the inception of the work that no contract laborers were brought to the Isthmus." See *Annual Report of the Isthmian Canal Commission for the Fiscal Year Ended June 30, 1911*, 62nd Cong., 2nd sess., 1911, H. Doc. 162 (Washington, DC: Government Printing Office, 1911), 42. While the ICC felt that it was necessary to recruit 941 Barbadians later in 1911, it found that it had surplus laborers in mid-1912 and allowed the United Fruit Company to contract 1,339 ICC laborers for work in Guatemala. See *Annual Report of the Isthmian Canal Commission for the Fiscal Year Ended June 30, 1912*, 50. A last round of recruiting took place in December 1912 to reinforce the workforce for the final phase of construction. See *Annual Report of the Isthmian Canal Commission for the Fiscal Year Ended June 30, 1913*, 54.

113. See Parker, *Panama Fever*, 337–338.

114. Once again, Julie Greene has produced the best work on the gold roll and silver roll at the Panama Canal. See especially Greene, *The Canal Builders*. Matthew Parker's treatment is also particularly illuminating in Parker, *Panama Fever*.

115. Parker, *Panama Fever*, 382–383. See also Goethals, "Human Element," 721–722.

116. See Greene, *The Canal Builders*, 62–69, and Parker, *Panama Fever*, 383. Definitive evidence of the racialization of the gold and silver rolls may be found in Executive Secretary to Tom M. Cooke, February 15, 1907, file 02-C-55, box 12, entry 30, RG 185, NARA II. The former states, "In accordance with instructions from the Chief Engineer such colored employees as are now paid on the gold rolls are to be transferred to the silver rolls, paying them the equivalent in silver to what they were drawing in gold."

117. Harry A. Franck, *Zone Policeman 88* (New York: Century, 1913), 29.

118. See, for example, Goethals to Henry A. Hart and John Thomas, March

18, 1910, and Goethals to John Price, March 19, 1910, file 02-C-55, box 12, entry 30, RG 185, NARA II. See also Goethals, "Labor Problems," 395–396.

119. Williamson, manuscript, 42. In the original, the term "prejudices" is spelled "preducies." Williamson's own racial prejudices are apparent throughout the manuscript, especially on pages 29 and 37.

120. Goethals to "Friend Hank," April 28 and May 19, 1877, Goethals Files, USMA. For more on the Whittaker incident, see Donald B. Connelly, *John M. Schofield and the Politics of Generalship* (Chapel Hill: University of North Carolina Press, 2006), 261–268.

121. Goethals to Toodles, April 4, 1907, container 3, Goethals Papers, LC.

122. Goethals, "Labor Problems," 397.

123. Quotation from Goethals to Ada M. Young, May 8, 1922, printed in Patricia W. Romero, ed., *I Too Am America: Documents from 1619 to the Present* (Cornwells Heights, PA: Publisher's Agency, 1978), 190. Writing to Young's widow, Goethals described the events of May–August 1889 in a somewhat detached manner: "I regret to state that I know little of Colonel Young's career at West Point outside of the Section Room in Civil and Military Engineering. He had considerable difficulty with the course and was deficient in it. . . . I was leaving West Point, intending to remain there during the summer; my sympathies were aroused, and I offered to give him a certain amount of time daily in order to assist him in preparation for the examination which he was to take the last of August. This I did and subsequently learned that he successfully passed it." See also the entry on June 8, 1889, in Private Notebook, Secretary of the Academic Board, "Extracts from the Proceedings of the Academic Board Private Sessions," 1880–1908, USMA, and Brian G. Shellum, *Black Cadet in a White Bastion: Charles Young at West Point* (Lincoln, NE: Bison Books, 2006), 116, 123–125.

124. Charles Young was also the last African American to graduate from West Point until Benjamin O. Davis Jr. graduated with the class of 1936. Theodore J. Crackel, *West Point: A Bicentennial History* (Lawrence: University Press of Kansas, 2002), 147–149; Shellum, *Black Cadet in a White Bastion*, 125–128; and "Official Register of the Officers and Cadets of the U.S. Military Academy, West Point, NY, June, 1889," Official Registers of Officers and Cadets, USMA, 11.

125. Charles Young to Delamere Skerrett, July 13, 1915, reprinted in Shellum, *Black Cadet in a White Bastion*, 131–132.

126. Goethals described "Sunday court" in Goethals, "Human Element," 725–728. Some unvarnished records of investigations resulting from Sunday mornings and other encounters with employees can be found in box 1 of the T. B. Miskimon Papers at the Booth Family Center for Special Collections, Georgetown University Library, Washington, DC.

127. Marie Gorgas characterized Goethals's Sunday routine as that of a "Venetian dodge" and "patriarchal despot." See Gorgas and Hendrick, *Wil-*

liam Crawford Gorgas, 218–219. Given the preponderance of assessments that disagree with hers, it is safe to assume that her view was heavily influenced by the personal animosity she felt toward Goethals for what she perceived to be the wrongful treatment of her husband, William C. Gorgas. For the opposite view, see Edwards, "The Boss of the Job." A similarly glowing report can be found in Bishop and Bishop, *Goethals,* 241–249. While I avoid relying too heavily on this source due to its extreme bias that borders on hero worship, it can be given some weight on this issue, as Joseph Bucklin Bishop was a regular observer of "Sunday court" sessions as a member of the ICC.

128. Williamson, manuscript, 42–43.

129. Goethals, "Human Element," 725–726.

130. See Goethals, "Human Element," 724–734. Quotation on page 727.

131. The comparative stability of the two sides of the workforce is well documented in the annual reports of the ICC. See especially *Annual Report of the Isthmian Canal Commission for the Fiscal Year Ended June 30, 1910,* 37; *Annual Report of the Isthmian Canal Commission for the Fiscal Year Ended June 30, 1911,* 42; *Annual Report of the Isthmian Canal Commission for the Fiscal Year Ended June 30, 1912,* 50; and *Annual Report of the Isthmian Canal Commission for the Fiscal Year Ended June 30, 1913,* 54. All of these document show stability in the "silver" force and explicitly characterize the "gold" force as unstable due to high personnel turnover.

132. Edwards, "The Boss of the Job," 395.

133. Quotation from Crowther, "Don't Fear to Attempt a Thing," 92. On excavation, 8,076,327 cubic yards were excavated between 1904 and 1907; 24,792,703 cubic yards of material were excavated between July 1, 1907, and June 30, 1908. See *Annual Report of the Isthmian Canal Commission for the Fiscal Year Ended June 30, 1907,* 39, and *Annual Report of the Isthmian Canal Commission for the Fiscal Year Ended June 30, 1908,* 60th Cong., 2nd sess., 1908, H. Doc. 1054 (Washington, DC: Government Printing Office, 1908), 35.

134. J. B. Aleshire to Goethals, March 1, 1910, container 9, Goethals Papers, LC; W. P. Duvall to Goethals, February 7, 1910, container 9, Goethals Papers, LC; Daniel L. Tate to Goethals, March 19, 1910, container 10, Goethals Papers, LC; J. W. Watson to Goethals, container 10, Goethals Papers, LC; W. W. Wotherspoon to Goethals, April 18, 1910; Nelson A. Miles to Goethals, March 11, 1908, container 7, Goethals Papers, LC.

135. Robert K. Evans, "National Enlistment," *Infantry Journal* 8 (July/August 1911): 4.

136. Lt. Col. Collin H. Hall, "War and Public Opinion," *Infantry Journal* 7 (July 1910): 823–827. Quotations on pages 824 and 826.

5. Crisis

1. All data comes from official War Department statistics compiled in Leonard P. Ayres, *The War with Germany: A Statistical Summary,* 2nd ed.

(Washington, DC: Government Printing Office, 1919), on pages 15, 104, and 105.

2. Daniel R. Beaver emphasizes continuity as well as change in the wake of the Root reforms. See Beaver, *Modernizing the American War Department: Change and Continuity in a Turbulent Era, 1885–1920* (Kent, OH: Kent State University Press, 2006). This theme and an emphasis on change as a somewhat turbulent and incremental process are also readily apparent in J. P. Clark, *Preparing for War: The Emergence of the Modern U.S. Army, 1815–1917* (Cambridge, MA: Harvard University Press, 2017).

3. See Clark, *Preparing for War*, 240–241.

4. James E. Hewes Jr., *From Root to McNamara: Army Organization and Administration, 1900–1963* (Washington, DC: US Army Center of Military History, 1975), 10–50; Otto Nelson, *National Security and the General Staff* (Washington, DC: Infantry Journal Press, 1946), 73–273; Russell F. Weigley, *History of the United States Army* (Bloomington: Indiana University Press, 1984), 326–341; and Clark, *Preparing for War*, 241–244.

5. As a result of this legislation, only nineteen General Staff officers were assigned to the War Department in Washington, DC, in the spring of 1917. Of these nineteen, only eleven were duty positions dedicated to shaping operational plans and coordinating mobilization efforts. By comparison, Germany and England went to war in 1914 with 650 and 232 officers assigned to their general staffs. The National Defense Act of 1916 essentially gutted the General Staff, leaving it drastically undermanned at the beginning of its first major test. See Clark, *Preparing for War*, 253–254; Weigley, *United States Army*, 350–353; Coffman, *The War to End All Wars: The American Military Experience in World War I* (Lexington: University Press of Kentucky, 1998), 23–24.

6. T. A. Bingham, "The Prussian Great General Staff and What It Contains That Is Practical from an American Standpoint," *Journal of the Military Service Institution of the United States* 13, no. 58 (July 1892): 666–676.

7. Henry T. Allen, "Proposed Reorganization for Our Central Staff," *Journal of the Military Service Institution of the United States* 27, no. 106 (July 1900): 26–30; and Henry T. Allen, "The Organization of a Staff Best Adapted to the United States Army," *Journal of the Military Service Institution of the United States* 28, no. 110 (March 1901): 169–183. The popularity of this view can be inferred by the fact that the latter article earned first honorable mention in the journal's essay contest on the need for a general staff. The lack of consensus, however, can be inferred from the fact that the editors considered no entry worthy of first prize, and Allen's first honorable mention was the highest award given.

8. Vaulx 8, "The Evolution of a General Staff," *Journal of the Military Service Institution of the United States* 33, no. 125 (September/October 1903): 200–206. Quotations on pages 206 and 200.

9. John J. Pershing, *My Life before the World War, 1860–1917*, ed. John T.

Greenwood (Lexington: University Press of Kentucky, 2013), 214. Pershing drafted this manuscript in the 1930s. His disdain for his time on the early General Staff is evident in the fact that he devoted only four paragraphs to the subject in a memoir that is 362 pages long.

10. The quotation is from John J. Pershing, *My Experiences in the World War* (New York: Frederick A. Stokes, 1931), 1:17.

11. Goethals's official and personal correspondence from the Canal Zone is compiled in boxes 5–39, Goethals Papers, LC. For evidence of coordination with the General Staff regarding the defense of the Canal Zone, see W. W. Wotherspoon to Goethals, June 23, 1911, and Wotherspoon to Leonard Wood, June 20, 1911, box 13, Goethals Papers, LC. It is worth noting, however, that even on this issue, Goethals was working not with the General Staff per se but with the chief of staff, the president of the War College, and several bureau chiefs.

12. Supply shortages and a lack of logistical planning were most readily apparent when the United States mobilized National Guard units to support the Punitive Expedition. See US Army Center for Military History, *History of Military Mobilization in the United States Army, 1775–1945* (Washington, DC: Government Printing Office, 2006), 196–201; Weigley, *United States Army,* 350–351.

13. Figures drawn from Weigley, *United States Army,* 599 and 350.

14. On political and public attitudes about the war, Michael S. Neiberg's recent work has no peer. See Neiberg, *The Path to War: How the First World War Created Modern America* (New York: Oxford University Press, 2016), chaps. 2–6. For congressional inaction on the army's requests for appropriations, see Clark, *Preparing for War,* 257–258.

15. War Department Special Orders No. 263, November 9, 1916, file 3644-ACP-1880, RG 94, NARA I. Goethals's service as governor of the Canal Zone is covered in Joseph Bucklin Bishop and Farnham Bishop, *Goethals: Genius of the Panama Canal* (New York: Harper & Brothers, 1930), 250–270. Researchers looking into Goethals's service as governor should look first at folders 11–12 in box 3 and folders 1–2 in box 4, Goethals Papers, LC.

16. Clark, *Preparing for War,* 252–253; Weigley, *United States Army,* 342–354; Edward M. Coffman, *The Regulars: The American Army, 1898–1941* (Cambridge, MA: Belknap Harvard, 2004), 140, 195–201. Quotation from Goethals to "Dody" [George R. Goethals], February 25, 1917, box 4, Goethals Papers, LC.

Ultimately, the Preparedness Movement was more of a political tool than an effective means for preparing either the nation or its army for war. It helped persuade Congress to more than double the size of the army through the National Defense Act of 1916. But the increase was to happen in increments spread over five years. The army would be only marginally larger when the United States entered the war in April 1917. In the meantime, both the institutional struggle over the General Staff and the operational deployment in Mexico and along the border consumed the army's attention. For more, see John Patrick Finnegan, *Against the Specter of a Dragon: The Campaign for American Military Preparedness, 1914–1917* (Westport, CT: Greenwood Press, 1974).

17. John Whiteclay Chambers II, *To Raise an Army: The Draft Comes to Modern America* (New York: Free Press, 1987), 6–7, 13–71. See also Clark, *Preparing for War*, 256.

18. Chambers, *To Raise an Army*, 136–141; J. Lee Thompson, *Never Call Retreat: Theodore Roosevelt and the Great War* (New York: Palgrave Macmillan, 2013), 171–185.

19. Goethals mentioned that he and his friend and colleague Harry Hodges gave his son "a good send off to Teddy, but I very much question if the present administration gives him the opportunity should war eventuate." He qualified that doubt, however, by noting that the administration "may have nothing to say about the matter" due to Roosevelt's many friends in Congress. See Goethals to "Dody," February 25, 1917, box 4, Goethals Papers, LC. Later letters, however, reveal that while army officers were more than happy to take advantage of the opportunity presented by a volunteer division under Roosevelt, they did not necessarily agree with the principle of raising such a division. In April, Goethals reported that "the inconsistency of Teddy advocating conscription and then wanting his volunteers has been irritating to a great many." One month later, Goethals wrote, "Sentiment among army men seems divided on the subject of sending Teddy, the majority inclined against him." See Goethals to "Dodie," April 29 and Dody, May 18, 1917, box 4, Goethals Papers, LC.

20. Marshall's role in Roosevelt's volunteer division is revealed in Forrest Pogue's notes of an interview with him on September 28, 1956. See Larry I. Bland and Joellen K. Bland, eds., *George C. Marshall: Interviews and Reminiscences for Forrest C. Pogue*, rev. ed. (Lexington, VA: Marshall Foundation, 1991), 584.

21. See Lloyd E. Ambrosius, "Democracy, Peace, and World Order," in *Reconsidering Woodrow Wilson: Progressivism, Internationalism, War, and Peace*, ed. John Milton Cooper Jr. (Baltimore: Johns Hopkins University Press, 2008), 226; Richard F. Hamilton and Holger H. Herwig, *Decisions for War, 1914–1917* (New York: Cambridge University Press, 2004), 216–222.

22. David F. Trask, *The AEF and Coalition Warmaking, 1917–1918* (Lawrence: University Press of Kansas, 1993), 2.

23. Justus D. Doenecke, *Nothing Less than War: A New History of America's Entry into World War I* (Lexington: University Press of Kentucky, 2011), 248–282.

24. Quoted in *The Papers of Woodrow Wilson*, ed. Arthur S. Link et al. (Princeton, NJ: Princeton University Press, 1983), 41:305n3.

25. Robert Lansing, memorandum of the cabinet meeting, March 20, 1917, in *Papers of Woodrow Wilson*, 41:444.

26. Tasker H. Bliss, memorandum for the chief of staff, March 20, 1917, vol. 210, Bliss Papers, LC.

27. Hugh Scott to Joseph E. Kuhn, March 27, 1917, vol. 210, Bliss Papers, LC.

28. Bliss to J. W. Heard, March 26, 1917, vol. 210, Bliss Papers, LC.

29. For more on Wilson's shortcomings in strategy and communications and their impact on the army in 1917, see Rory M. McGovern, "'We Will All Be Wiser in a Few Days': Woodrow Wilson, Grand Strategy, and the U.S. Army in 1917," *Journal for the Liberal Arts and Sciences* 20, no. 2 (Spring 2016): 6–26. See also Trask, *The AEF & Coalition Warmaking*, 6–7.

30. Statistics for American shipping, industrial production, and logistics operations in support of the war effort is found in Ayres, *War with Germany*, 37–100.

31. William J. Williams, *The Wilson Administration and the Shipbuilding Crisis of 1917* (Lewiston, NY: Edwin Mellen Press, 1992), 1–4.

32. Williams, *Wilson Administration*, 4–11; David M. Kennedy, *Over Here: The First World War and American Society* (New York: Oxford University Press, 2004), 301. On naval modernization, see Peter Karsten, *The Naval Aristocracy: The Golden Age of Annapolis and the Emergence of American Navalism* (New York: Free Press, 1972), chaps. 6–8.

33. Kennedy, *Over Here*, 302–305.

34. Goethals to Dody, June 5, 1916, box 4, Goethals Papers, LC.

35. Goethals to Dody, July 12, 1916; September 13, 1916; October 20, 1916; and January 22, 1917, box 4, Goethals Papers, LC.

36. "General Goethals and the U.S. Shipping Board (as told by General Goethals himself)," box 43, Goethals Papers, LC, 1–2. Although undated and unattributed, this source is a first-person account written less than nine months after the events occurred. According to the secretary who typed it, this document "was written in the first person" and "was dictated to me by General Goethals, at my request, in January, 1918." She insisted that the manuscript was a "transcription of my shorthand notes" that "was seen and O.K.'ed by General Goethals." See Martha Wellington to Farnham Bishop, August 12, 1929, box 43, Goethals Papers, LC. On the Shipping Board's design to use Goethals for public relations purposes, see Williams, *Wilson Administration*, 75–77.

37. Williams, *Wilson Administration*, 53–57, 67. The sole member of the board with true expertise in shipping and shipbuilding was John A. Donald.

38. Goethals to Dody, April 19, 1917, box 4, Goethals Papers, LC.

39. Woodrow Wilson to Goethals, April 11, 1917, box 43, Goethals Papers, LC.

40. "General Goethals and the U.S. Shipping Board," LC, 3.

41. Goethals to "Dodie," April 29, 1917, box 4, Goethals Papers, LC.

42. Goethals to "Dodie," April 19, 1917, box 4, Goethals Papers, LC.

43. "General Goethals and the U.S. Shipping Board," 3–4. See also Williams, *Wilson Administration*, 90–91. Goethals's quotation is from Goethals to "Dodie," April 19, 1917, box 4, Goethals Papers, LC.

44. Goethals to "Dodie," April 29, 1917, box 4, Goethals Papers, LC.

45. "General Goethals and the U.S. Shipping Board," 4–5.

46. Goethals to Dody, May 4, 1917, box 4, Goethals Papers, LC.

47. "General Goethals and the U.S. Shipping Board," 5.

48. Denman's resentment played out largely in his conversations with reporters and his lobbying of Woodrow Wilson for support. It became most apparent in May and June 1917 when he systematically attacked contracts that Goethals had negotiated with steel firms. By charging that Goethals had accepted artificially high prices for steel plates, Denman was attempting to force a final showdown with Goethals through President Wilson by implicitly arguing that Goethals's continued management of shipbuilding would lead to considerable financial waste. See Williams, *Wilson Administration*, chap. 4, especially pages 123–128.

49. Williams, *Wilson Administration*, 96–98, 154–155.

50. Goethals's grandson, the late Thomas Goethals, described the deteriorating state of their marriage in a discussion with the author at Vineyard Haven, Massachusetts, in December 2012. David McCullough has suggested that Goethals may have had at least one affair while in Panama. See David McCullough, *The Path between the Seas: The Creation of the Panama Canal, 1870–1914* (New York: Simon & Schuster, 1977), 571, 650n571. Thomas Goethals vehemently denied this suggestion during our discussion. I have seen no evidence that either confirms or denies Goethals's fidelity to his wife.

Goethals's surviving correspondence is in the Goethals Papers, LC. Boxes 3–4 contain family correspondence and are the most revealing of Goethals's personal life. Many of the other boxes have more to do with Goethals's professional and public life, but scattered throughout are letters to and from a few close friends that also provide interesting windows to Goethals's personal life. Letters to and from Gustav Fiebeger and Clarence Edwards stand out in this regard.

51. Goethals to Dody, May 11, 1917, box 4, Goethals Papers, LC.

52. Goethals's speech is reprinted in "The Goethals Plan for Shipbuilding," *Lumber World Review* 32, no. 11 (June 10, 1917): 41. See also Goethals to "Dodie," May 28, 1917, box 4, Goethals Papers, LC, which demonstrates clearly that Goethals courted not only the press but also influential officials and business leaders in his public advocacy for his shipbuilding program. "General Goethals and the U.S. Shipping Board," 5; Williams, *Wilson Administration*, 108–128, 137–148, 163–173.

53. Woodrow Wilson to Goethals, July 19, 1917, box 43, Goethals Papers, LC. See also Williams, *Wilson Administration*, 170–174.

54. Goethals to Wilson, July 20, 1917, box 43, Goethals Papers, LC.

55. "General Goethals and the U.S. Shipping Board," 6; Williams, *Wilson Administration*, 175–180.

56. Ayres, *War with Germany*, 39–40.

57. Examples include the Council of National Defense, the War Industries Board, the Committee on Public Information, the National War Labor Relations Board, etc. See especially Kennedy, *Over Here*, chaps. 1 and 2. The ill-defined authority of such boards becomes particularly clear in the records of the Council of National Defense. The minutes of a joint meeting of the Council of National Defense and the Advisory Commission on March 31 and April 26, 1917, show that the CND was completely and unknowingly replicating the work of the Shipping Board at that time. Minutes from July 8, 1917, note, "The Commission, being apart from and not a part of the Government is probably not fully advised concerning the progress actually being made in connection with the war program" and that it is unsure whether the ultimate goal was to "raise, equip, and train 500,000 or 1,000,000 soldiers." See Minutes of Special Joint Meeting of the Council of National Defense and the Advisory Commission, March 31, 1917; Minutes of Meeting of the Advisory Commission of the Council of National Defense, April 26, 1917; and Minutes of Meeting of the Advisory Commission of the Council of National Defense, July 8, 1917, in vol. 413, Bernard Baruch Papers, Seeley G. Mudd Manuscript Library, Princeton University.

58. The best, if perhaps overly laudatory, account of the WIB is still Robert D. Cuff, *The War Industries Board: Business-Government Relations during World War I* (Baltimore: Johns Hopkins University Press, 1973). Valuable firsthand accounts may be found in Bernard M. Baruch, *American Industry in the War: A Report of the War Industries Board* (New York: Prentice-Hall, 1941); Bernard M. Baruch, *Baruch: The Public Years* (New York: Holt, Rinehart and Winston, 1960), chaps. 3–4; and Hugh S. Johnson, *The Blue Eagle: From Egg to Earth* (New York: Doubleday, 1935), chap. 10. These accounts are subject to the bias of authors whose personal investment in the WIB and its legacy was considerable. Daniel R. Beaver, "The Problem of American Military Supply, 1890–1920," in *War Business and American Society: Historical Perspectives of the Military-Industrial Complex*, ed. Benjamin Franklin Cooling (Port Washington, NY: Kennikat Press, 1977), 73–92, offers a moderate corrective, that succinctly highlights the problems the WIB and similar agencies experienced throughout 1917 and early 1918.

59. See entries from October 31; November 1, 3, 5, 6, 8, 14; December 5, 11, 12, 17, and 21 in Diary for 1917, vol. 654, Baruch Papers. Baruch was almost obsessively focused on the nitrate issue, noting on November 8, 1917, "When I think how this matter has been handled, I could commit murder."

60. Tasker H. Bliss, memorandum for the chief of staff, March 26, 1917, vol. 211, Bliss Papers, LC.

61. Quotation from Daniel R. Beaver, *Newton D. Baker and the American War Effort, 1917–1919* (Lincoln: University of Nebraska Press, 1966), 62.

62. See Beaver, *Baker,* 50–62; Coffman, *War to End All Wars,* 34–35.

63. Beaver, *Baker,* 1–8. On Garrison's resignation, see Clark, *Preparing for War,* 252–253, and Coffman, *War to End All Wars,* 16–17.

64. Beaver, *Baker,* 8–21.

65. From Baker to Pershing, May 26, 1917, reprinted in Pershing, *My Experiences in the World War,* 1:39.

66. Donald Smythe, *Pershing: General of the Armies* (Bloomington: Indiana University Press, 1986), 13–18.

67. See Smythe, *Pershing,* 16–18. The discrepancy between War Department estimates and Pershing's plans is identified in Coffman, *War to End All Wars,* 128. For statistics on army strength and shipping, see Ayres, *War with Germany,* 15, 37. It must be noted that part of the British reluctance to commit a portion of its surviving shipping to transport American soldiers was due to Pershing's refusal, entirely in keeping with his instructions from Wilson and Baker, to allow his soldiers and small units to be absorbed by British and French armies. But even had Pershing agreed to amalgamation, Britain would have been hard-pressed to commit substantial amounts of shipping to transatlantic troop convoys until at least the fall of 1917.

68. See Beaver, *Baker,* 82–83, and Smythe, *Pershing,* 37–38. Pershing's decision on AEF divisional strength is well covered in David R. Woodward, *The American Army and the First World War* (New York: Cambridge University Press, 2014), 107–112.

69. Edward M. Coffman, *The Hilt of the Sword: Peyton C. March* (Madison: University of Wisconsin Press, 1966), 40–44, 53; Steve R. Waddell, *United States Army Logistics from the American Revolution to 9/11* (Santa Barbara, CA: Praeger, 2010), 198n39.

70. USAWW 2:68; Smythe, *Pershing,* 56–69, 62–63; Coffman, *War to End All Wars,* 168–169.

71. Goethals to "Dody" and Priscilla, July 29, 1917, box 4, Goethals Papers, LC.

72. See Goethals to "Dody" and Priscilla, August 5 and October 29, 1917, box 4, Goethals Papers, LC. The quotation is from the October 29 letter. For Goethals's request to Pershing for command of engineers in France, see Goethals to Pershing (cable), August 3, 1917, and Goethals to Pershing, August 3, 1917, box 40, Goethals Papers, LC. For Pershing's answer, see Pershing to Goethals (cable), August 7, 1917, and Pershing to Goethals, September 11, 1917, box 40, Goethals Papers, LC.

73. The political consequences of the Goethals-Denman controversy are

well documented in Williams, *Wilson Administration*, 144–148, 173–178. For Pershing's crusade against aged and popular generals, see Smythe, *Pershing*, 55.

74. See John Higham, *Strangers in the Land: Patterns of American Nativism, 1860–1925* (New Brunswick, NJ: Rutgers University Press, 2002), chaps. 1–7.

75. Higham, *Strangers in the Land*, chaps. 8–9; Kennedy, *Over Here*, chap. 1. For a brief and recent study of the APL, see Bill Mills, *The League: The True Story of Average Americans on the Hunt for WWI Spies* (New York: Skyhorse, 2013).

76. All correspondence related to this accusation and investigation are located in file 6370-85, box 1901, Military Intelligence Division General Correspondence, 1917–1941, RG 165, NARA II. Many thanks to Tim Nenninger for his assistance in locating this file.

77. See Goethals to Dody, August 19, 1917; Goethals to "Dody" and Priscilla, September 18, 1917; Goethals to Priscilla and Dody, September 23, 1917; Goethals to "Dody" and Priscilla, October 29, 1917; and Goethals to Dody, November 4, 1917, box 4, Goethals Papers, LC.

78. March's remark is in Peyton C. March, *The Nation at War* (Garden City, NY: Doubleday, Doran, 1932), 3. Bullard and Pershing are quoted in Coffman, *War to End All Wars*, 49–50.

79. "Declares America Has Fallen Down in Its War Work," *New York Times*, January 20, 1918, 1.

80. Recently, some scholars have defended the performance of the War Department bureaus in 1917. Daniel R. Beaver offers a limited defense, suggesting that the bureaus did about as well as could be expected reasonably, but that the conditions the bureaus faced were beyond the ability of the federal government to handle with limited preparation. His critique admits that the bureau system itself was ill-suited for the war, but he seems not to find fault with the institution itself for producing such a system. James Charles Fischer takes that argument a step further, arguing that the bureaus turned in an excellent performance in 1917, conducting business exactly as they were designed. According to Fischer, the problem was that the realities of 1917–1918 did not match prewar assumptions, which caused the bureaus to be flooded, through no fault of their own, by unforeseen requirements. See Beaver, *Modernizing*, and James Charles Fischer, "Not Fallen, but Flooded: The War Department Supply Bureaus in 1917" (PhD diss., Ohio State University, 2003).

While it would be unfair to charge the officers manning the bureaus, as Pershing did, with not caring about or putting enormous effort into supporting the AEF, it is similarly unfair to soften the characterization of the bureaus' failure in 1917. Failure due to anachronistic organizing principles and assumptions is still a failure. It is not too harsh to say that the War Department had stumbled or fallen down in 1917. It had. And that makes its recovery in 1918 all the more interesting.

81. Not just while in transit to Europe aboard the *Baltic* but throughout the war, Pershing rarely consulted with the War Department when developing his plans. For a good discussion of Pershing's belief that the AEF was independent from (and perhaps even superior to) the War Department, see Smythe, *Pershing*, 46–49. In another example, Pershing and his planners kept altering their artillery requirements without ever ascertaining what was actually available in quantity in the United States. The only field piece that was manufactured in the United States that the AEF requested in significant quantity was a 4.7-inch field gun that was so new as to still be considered experimental. Further changes to the artillery program made by the AEF staff paralyzed the Ordnance Department, rendering it unable to initiate production until December 1917. See Beaver, *Baker*, 56.

82. The best source for AEF tactical doctrine in 1917 and adaptation in 1918 is Mark Ethan Grotelueschen, The AEF Way of War: The American Army and Combat in World War I (New York: Cambridge University Press, 2007). For very effective and very brief discussions and critique of Pershing's "open warfare doctrine," see Grotelueschen, AEF Way of War, 30–38, and Smythe, Pershing, 72–73.

83. See Woodward, *American Army*, 191–193; Smythe, *Pershing*, 142–151.

84. For the supply crisis of the winter of 1917–1918 and its many consequences, see Woodward, *American Army*, 134–143; Coffman, *War to End All Wars*, 160–161; Kennedy, *Over Here*, 123–126.

85. "Declares America Has Fallen Down in Its War Work," *New York Times*, January 20, 1918, 1.

86. See Beaver, *Baker*, 79–95.

87. Quotations from Pershing to Goethals, December 19, 1917, and Theodore Roosevelt to Goethals, December 19, 1917, box 40, Goethals Papers, LC. See also "Wants Goethals to Supply Army," *New York Times*, December 18, 1917, 1, and "Goethals to Head Army Supplies," *New York Times*, December 19, 1917, 1.

88. Goethals to Dody, December 19, 1917, box 4, Goethals Papers, LC; Goethals to Pershing, December 31, 1917, box 40, Goethals Papers, LC.

89. Goethals to Roosevelt, December 28, 1917, box 40, Goethals Papers, LC.

6. Resolution

1. US War Department, *War Department Annual Reports*, 66th Cong., 2nd sess., 1919, H. Doc. 426 (Washington, DC: Government Printing Office, 1919), 1:714–715.

2. US House of Representatives, *War Expenditures: Hearings before the Select Committee on Expenditures in the War Department*, 66th Cong., 1st–3rd sess., serial 1 (Washington, DC: Government Printing Office, 1921), 522.

3. *War Department Annual Reports*, 1:245–246. See also Phyllis A. Zimmerman, *The Neck of the Bottle: George W. Goethals and the Reorganization of the US Army Supply System, 1917–1918* (College Station: Texas A&M University Press, 1992), 36, 46. Of note, the interpretation this chapter presents is fundamentally at odds with the conclusions presented by Zimmerman. *The Neck of the Bottle* is an excellent factual resource, and I have relied heavily on it for secondary material. However, Zimmerman concludes that Goethals did little more than unnecessarily complicate the bureaucracy of army supply. I believe the evidence shows that Goethals's work in 1918 had a much more significant impact.

4. Steve R. Waddell, *United States Army Logistics from the American Revolution to 9/11* (Santa Barbara, CA: Praeger, 2010), 113–114; Zimmerman, *Neck*, 34–37.

5. *War Expenditures*, 519–520.

6. *War Expenditures*, 522.

7. Quoted in Zimmerman, *Neck*, 48.

8. See *War Expenditures*, 520, and Zimmerman, *Neck*, 46–47. The quotation is from the former.

9. *War Expenditures*, 520.

10. *War Expenditures*, 523.

11. *War Expenditures*, 524.

12. *War Department Annual Reports*, 1:718–721; Zimmerman, *Neck*, 54–55.

13. See *War Expenditures*, 531; *War Department Annual Reports*, 1:720. Goethals found Biddle's successor, Gen. Peyton C. March, to be extremely receptive to his ideas.

14. Zimmerman, *Neck*, 68.

15. *War Expenditures*, 530–531.

16. *War Department Annual Reports*, 1:246–247.

17. *War Expenditures*, 518. See also Zimmerman, *Neck*, 68.

18. *War Expenditures*, 518.

19. Leonard P. Ayres, *The War with Germany: A Statistical Summary* (Washington, DC: Government Printing Office, 1919), 15.

20. The army purchased 96 million pairs of wool socks in 1918 while the country produced 61 million pairs of wool socks in 1914. See Ayres, *War with Germany*, 50.

21. *War Expenditures*, 525–526.

22. *War Expenditures*, 519, 535.

23. Ayres, *War with Germany*, 61. Of course, any given doughboy's ability to receive these supplies depended upon the ability of the AEF Services of Supply to move and distribute supplies effectively, which became a problem in the summer and fall of 1918, as will be discussed later.

24. "The History of the Development of the Purchase, Storage, and Traffic

Division, Its Duties and Functions," pages 13–14, box 1, entry 444, RG 165, NARA II. See also Zimmerman, *Neck*, 68–72.

25. *War Department Annual Reports*, 1:249.

26. The topic dominates minutes of War Industries Board meetings in May 1918. See Minutes, Special Meeting of the War Industries Board, May 1, 1918; Minutes, Meeting of the War Industries Board, May 2, 1918; and Minutes, Meeting of the War Industries Board, May 21, 1918, in vol. 454, Bernard Baruch Papers, Seeley G. Mudd Manuscript Library, Princeton University. See also Zimmerman, *Neck*, 73–75.

27. *War Expenditures*, 532.

28. Goethals went so far as to defend the Shipping Control Committee from what he perceived to be limiting encroachments upon "functions properly belonging to them." See entry for March 1, 1918, Desk Diary No. 1, box 1, Goethals Papers, LC. For a general outline of the relationship between the Storage and Traffic Division and the Shipping Control Committee, see Zimmerman, *Neck*, 70–71.

29. *War Department Annual Reports*, 1:342.

30. *War Department Annual Reports*, 1:249.

31. The problems and problematic nature of the Purchase and Supply Division are well laid out in Zimmerman, *Neck*, 79–81.

32. The War Department's official report stated simply that the Purchase and Supply Division's authority was "supervisory," with "overhead functions with the power to interfere but not remodel." Continuing, it noted, "This organization gave rise to a great deal of duplication and complication." See *War Department Annual Reports*, 1:720.

33. See Charles R. Day, T. N. Perkins, and Hugh S. Johnson, "Report of the Committee Appointed by the Assistant Secretary of War to Plan an Organization for the Office of the Director of Purchase and Supplies," April 1918, box 1, entry 442, RG 165, NARA II. This memorandum is commonly referred to in secondary literature as the final report of the "Committee of Three."

34. *War Expenditures*, 526.

35. On vertical integration, see Alfred D. Chandler Jr., *The Visible Hand: The Managerial Revolution in American Business* (Cambridge, MA: Belknap Press, 1977), chaps. 9 and 11.

36. Fifty years after it was written, the definitive biography of Peyton C. March is still Edward M. Coffman, *The Hilt of the Sword* (Madison: University of Wisconsin Press, 1966). Coffman outlines March's path to chief of staff in chap. 4.

37. See Peyton C. March, *The Nation at War* (New York: Doubleday, Doran, 1932), 187; Coffman, *Hilt of the Sword*, 52–54, 62–63. On their friendship, see especially March to Goethals, September 18, 1919; Goethals to Julius Kahn, September 19, 1919; Goethals to March, March 24, 1923; and March

to Goethals, April 10, 1923, box 40, Goethals Papers, LC. March eventually served as an honorary pallbearer at Goethals's funeral. See "Goethals Buried beside the Hudson," *New York Times*, January 25, 1928, 23.

38. See March, *Nation at War*, 187, and Goethals to "Dody" [George R. Goethals], April 14, 1918, box 4, George W. Goethals Papers, LC, respectively.

39. Goethals to Dody, April 14, 1918; Goethals to S. E. Tillman, April 20, 1918, box 40, Goethals Papers, LC.

40. Goethals to Dody, April 14, 1918; Goethals to Tillman, April 20, 1918.

41. March, *Nation at War*, 188. For the order that created the Purchase, Storage, and Traffic Division, see War Department G.O. 36, April 16, 1918, file 639-204, roll 2, microform M1024, RG 165, NARA II.

42. March, *Nation at War*, 188.

43. "History of the Development of the Purchase, Storage, and Traffic Division," 22–23.

44. Goethals to Henry L. Stimson, May 29, 1918, and Stimson to Goethals, June 28, 1918, box 40, Goethals Papers, LC. See also Zimmerman, *Neck*, 92.

45. Goethals's characterization of the work in the Quartermaster Department is in Goethals to Tillman, April 19, 1918, box 40, Goethals Papers, LC.

46. See Hugh S. Johnson, *The Blue Eagle: From Egg to Earth* (New York: Doubleday, 1935), 88–96. Additionally, Johnson's voluminous official correspondence as director of purchase and supply under Goethals is in entry 445, RG 165, NARA II.

47. Swope was indispensable in matters relating to industry, shipping, and munitions. His extensive notes and correspondence are in entry 443, RG 165, NARA II.

48. Early in his tenure, March did not hide his distaste for the WIB, once declining to invite Baruch to sit down at all during a meeting in the War Department. Later that summer, the two worked out their differences to form a reasonably effective working relationship. See Bernard M. Baruch, *The Public Years: My Own Story* (New York: Holt, Rinehart and Winston, 1960), 57–58.

49. See entries for April 13, and 16, Desk Diary No. 1, and April 18, 1918, Desk Diary No. 2, box 1, Goethals Papers, LC.

50. Goethals to Dody, May 4 and May 10, 1918, Goethals Papers, LC.

51. Charles R. Day, T. N. Perkins, and Hugh S. Johnson, "Report of the Committee Appointed by the Assistant Secretary of War to Plan an Organization for the Office of the Director of Purchase and Supplies," April 1918, box 1, entry 442, RG 165, NARA II.

52. Baruch, *The Public Years*, 57.

53. Johnson, *Blue Eagle*, 93–95; Gerard Swope to Goethals, April 7, 1927, box 40, Goethals Papers, LC. It is worth noting, however, that much of the WIB's considerable efforts were for naught. It succeeded in getting American industry synchronized with the needs of the war effort, but only in mid- and

late 1918. Thus, even when the war ended in November 1918, the AEF still relied almost exclusively on ordnance, munitions, and major end items such as
trucks, tanks, and airplanes produced by Britain and France. Johnson notes
as much on page 92 of his memoir. Historians may have overstated the practical importance of the WIB to the war effort, as the fruits of its work could not
possibly have been apparent until 1919, and even then continuing shipping
shortages would have hampered efforts to transport the massive industrial
output overseas.

54. See Kennedy, *Over Here*, 125–126.

55. *War Expenditures*, 524, 529.

56. "History of the Development of the Purchase, Storage, and Traffic
Division," 23. See also *War Department Annual Reports*, 66th Cong., 2nd sess.,
1919, H. Doc. 426, 1:353.

57. See Goethals, Supply Circular No. 1, April 24, 1918, and Supply Circular No. 2, May 8, 1918, box 208, entry 441, RG 165, NARA II. See also
Zimmerman, *Neck*, 103.

58. Goethals, Supply Circular No. 2, May 8, 1918, box 208, entry 441, RG
165, NARA II.

59. See Supply Circulars 3–14, each issued between May 11 and May 24,
1918, box 208, entry 441, RG 165, NARA II.

60. Goethals, Supply Circular No. 3, May 11, 1918, box 208, entry 441,
RG 165, NARA II.

61. Johnson, *Blue Eagle*, 91.

62. Goethals to Dody, May 31, 1918, box 4, Goethals Papers, LC.

63. *War Department Annual Reports*, 66th Cong., 2nd sess., 1919, H. Doc.
426, 1:373.

64. Goethals to Dody, May 31, 1918.

65. David F. Trask, *The AEF and Coalition Warmaking, 1917–1918* (Lawrence: University Press of Kansas, 1993), 43–89; Hew Strachan, *The First
World War* (New York: Penguin, 2003), 293–299.

66. *War Department Annual Reports*, 1:571–574; USAWW 2:257–259, 261–
262; David R. Woodward, *The American Army and the First World War* (New
York: Cambridge University Press, 2014), 169–171; Donald Smythe, *Pershing:
General of the Armies* (Bloomington: Indiana University Press, 1986), 99–104.

67. Goethals to Dody, May 4, May 10, May 18, and May 31, 1918, box 4,
Goethals Papers, LC. The quotation is from the letter written on May 4.

68. David C. Shanks, *As They Passed through the Port* (Washington: Carey,
1927), 154–155, 181–187; Woodward, *American Army*, 170.

69. March, *Nation at War*, 192–193; Zimmerman, *Neck*, 121–124.

70. Ayres, *War with Germany*, 15, 87. At the time of the armistice, 1,971,000
American soldiers were serving in France.

71. Goethals to Dody, May 31, 1918.

72. Smythe, *Pershing*, 171, 206–208.

73. Pershing's and March's competing interpretations of the relationship between the chief of staff and a field army commander are treated most succinctly and effectively in Smythe, *Pershing*, 88–89. These matters, and the relationship between March and Pershing more generally, receive excellent treatment in Coffman, *Hilt of the Sword*, 104–118; Brian Neumann, "A Question of Authority: Reassessing the March-Pershing Feud in the First World War," *Journal of Military History* 73, no. 4 (October 2009): 1117–1142; and Woodward, *American Army*, 181–185.

74. Smythe, *Pershing*, 27–29, 161–162; Woodward, *American Army*, 185–186; Waddell, *United States Army Logistics*, 120–121

75. Quoted in Smythe, *Pershing*, 162.

76. Goethals to Dody, June 9, 1918, box 4, Goethals Papers, LC; Coffman, *Hilt of the Sword*, 106–107; Neumann, "A Question of Authority," 1131–1132; Smythe, *Pershing*, 162.

77. Quoted in Neumann, "A Question of Authority," 1132.

78. John J. Pershing, *My Experiences in the World War* (New York: Frederick A. Stokes, 1931), 2:179–191; James G. Harbord, *The American Army in France* (Boston: Little, Brown, 1936), 350–355; Woodward, *American Army*, 189–190; Coffman, *Hilt of the Sword*, 108–110; Neumann, "A Question of Authority," 1132–1134; Smythe, *Pershing*, 163–168.

79. Goethals to Dody, June 9, 1918.

80. Goethals to Dody, June 23, 1918, box 4, Goethals Papers, LC; Johnson, *Blue Eagle*, 92.

81. Goethals to Dody, July 14, 1918, box 4, Goethals Papers, LC.

82. Goethals to Dody, July 29 and August 5, 1918, box 4, Goethals Papers, LC.

83. Such sentiment affected even the chief of staff of the army, who wrote in his memoirs, "The decision not to send him abroad was a great blow to Goethals. Like all other Army officers, with one or two marked exceptions, he was eager to serve in France, and I sympathized with that feeling." See March, *Nation at War*, 196.

84. Goethals to Dody, July 29, 1918, box 4, Goethals Papers, LC.

85. Goethals to Dody, July 21, 1918, box 4, Goethals Papers, LC.

86. Goethals, memorandum for the chief of staff, July 18, 1918, box 1, entry 442, RG 165, NARA II. Quotation from page 1.

87. Goethals, memorandum for the chief of staff, July 18, 1918, box 1, entry 442, RG 165, NARA II. Goethals's critique of the existing system is on pages 6–9. The quotations are from page 6.

88. Goethals, memorandum for the chief of staff, July 18, 1918, box 1, entry 442, RG 165, NARA II. Quotations from pages 7, 8, and 9. All underlines are in the original.

89. Goethals, memorandum for the chief of staff, July 18, 1918, box 1, entry 442, RG 165, NARA II. Goethals's detailed proposal for consolidating all

supply processes under the PS&T can be found on pages 10–24. Quotations are from page 10. Emphases are in the original.

90. Goethals to Dody, August 18 and August 25, 1918, box 4, Goethals Papers, LC.

91. March, *Nation at War*, 188.

92. "History of the Development of the Purchase, Storage, and Traffic Division," 23. See also Goethals to Dody, August 11, 1918, box 4, Goethals Papers, LC.

93. Johnson, *Blue Eagle*, 90.

94. Cable P-1342-S, June 19, 1918, *USAWW* 2:476–479 and Cable P-1369-S, June 25, 1918, *USAWW* 2:482–483. See also Smythe, *Pershing*, 146; Zimmerman, *Neck*, 114–115.

95. Scrap Notes re: 100 Division Program and 80 Division Program, box 1, entry 443, RG165, NARA II; Woodward, *American Army*, 193; March, *Nation at War*, 100–101; Zimmerman, *Neck*, 118. Significantly, however, even these estimates were based upon unrealistic expectations of American ship production.

96. *War Department Annual Reports*, 66th Cong., 2nd sess., 1919, H. Doc. 426, 1:240–241; Cable No. 74, July 23, 1918, *USAWW* 2:544.

97. Neumann, "A Question of Authority," 1137–1138; Smythe, *Pershing*, 210.

98. *War Department Annual Reports*, 1:471–472; Goethals to Dody, August 25, 1918.

99. This portion of the order is reprinted in March, *Nation at War*, 49–50.

100. *War Department Annual Reports*, 66th Cong., 2nd sess., 1919, H. Doc. 426, 1:354; Peyton C. March, memorandum, August 26, 1918, box 1, entry 442, RG 165, NARA II.

101. Goethals wrote no letters to his son George between August 25 and September 29, 1918. See box 4, Goethals Papers, LC.

102. Quotation from Goethals to Dody, October 27, 1918, box 4, Goethals Papers, LC. See also Goethals to Dody, November 3 and November 10, 1918, box 4, Goethals Papers, LC.

103. Quotations from "History of the Development of the Purchase, Storage, and Traffic Division," 25. On Goethals's reorganization activities in September and October, see Goethals, memoranda to the chief of staff, September 29 and October 8, 18, and 29, 1918, box 1, entry 442, RG 165, NARA II; and Goethals to Dody, November 3, 1918.

104. See, for example, Charles M. Schwab to Goethals, July 29, 1919, box 40, Goethals Papers, LC; March, *Nation at War*, 196; and Donald Wilhelm, "The Master of Mobilization," *Independent* 95 (September 7, 1918): 316, 333.

105. March to Goethals, April 10, 1923, box 40, Goethals Papers, LC.

106. Erich von Ludendorff, quartermaster general of the German army, wrote that in 1918, the American troop shipment program "weighed heavily

in the balance against us." He described it as an issue "of the greatest importance," before stating categorically that "it was for this reason that America became the deciding factor in the war." See Erich von Ludendorff, *Ludendorff's Own Story, August 1914–November 1918: The Great War from the Siege of Liege to the Signing of the Armistice as Viewed from the Grand Headquarters of the German Army* (New York: Harper & Brothers, 1919), 2:276. It is worth considering, however, that Ludendorf had an interest in pointing to American troop shipments as the decisive factor in Germany's defeat, as that interpretation implicitly places more blame for the defeat on German political failures that drew the United States into the war than on his own military failures that left the German army too weak to withstand pressure from the newly reinforced Allies.

107. See US House of Representatives, *Army Reorganization Hearings before the Committee on Military Affairs*, 66th Cong., 1st sess., 1919 (Washington: Government Printing Office, 1919), 1:493, 765.

108. John D. Milett, *The Army Service Forces: The Organization and Role of the Army Service Forces* (Washington, DC: US Army Center of Military History, 1985), 13–16.

109. J. P. Clark, *Preparing for War: The Emergence of the Modern US Army, 1815–1917* (Cambridge, MA: Harvard University Press, 2017), 269–272.

Epilogue

1. Edward M. Coffman, *The Regulars: The American Army, 1898–1941* (Cambridge, MA: Belknap Press, 2004), 281–289. See also David E. Johnson, *Fast Tanks and Heavy Bombers: Innovation in the U.S. Army, 1917–1945* (Ithaca, NY: Cornell University Press, 1998), 223–224.

2. Carlo D'Este, *Eisenhower: A Soldier's Life* (New York: Holt, 2002), 177–183, 191–192, 228.

3. Johnson, *Fast Tanks and Heavy Bombers*, 63–183, 222–223.

4. Marshall is quoted in Richard Overy, *Why the Allies Won* (New York: W. W. Norton, 1995), 273. For a complete history of the Army Service Forces, see John D. Milett, *The Army Service Forces: The Organization and Role of the Army Service Forces* (Washington, DC: US Army Center of Military History, 1985). That Goethals's Purchase, Storage, and Traffic Division was the antecedent of the Army Service Forces is also shown in James E. Hewes Jr., *From Root to McNamara: Army Organization and Administration, 1900–1963* (Washington, DC: US Army Center of Military History, 1975), 90.

5. "Gen. Goethals Dies after Long Illness," *New York Times*, January 22, 1928, 30; author's interview with Thomas R. Goethals Jr., December 21, 2012, Vineyard Haven, MA. For more on Goethals's postwar work, see J. Joseph Bucklin Bishop and Farnham Bishop, *Goethals: Genius of the Panama Canal* (New York: Harper & Brothers, 1930), 402–441.

6. Goethals to S. M. Reynolds, July 5, 1917, box 40, Goethals Papers, LC;

Donald Wilhelm, "The Master of Mobilization," *Independent* 95 (September 7, 1918): 316.

7. "Gen. Goethals Dies after Long Illness"; Bishop and Bishop, *Goethals,* 442–460.

8. See, for example, "George W. Goethals," *Nation* 126, February 1, 1928, 111; "When Goethals Made the Dirt Fly," *Literary Digest* 96, February 11, 1928, 45–52; and "Gen. Goethals Dies after Long Illness."

9. "Army Men Pay Tribute," *New York Times,* January 22, 1928, 30.

10. Peyton C. March, *The Nation at War* (New York: Doubleday, Doran, 1932), 196.

11. For Goethals's views on training and education in 1922, see Samuel Crowther, "Don't Fear to Attempt a Thing Just Because It Looks Big," *American Magazine,* January 1922, 16. Pershing's tenure as chief of staff is covered well in Donald Smythe, *Pershing: General of the Armies* (Bloomington: Indiana University Press, 1986), 275–280. Although in a more technological context, this type of resistance to change is a major theme in Elting E. Morrison, *Men, Machines, and Modern Times* (Cambridge: MIT Press, 1966). See especially pages 37–44 and 76 for Morrison's best treatment of resistance to change.

Bibliography

Archival Sources

Alabama Department of Archives and History, Montgomery
    Joseph Wheeler Family Papers, 1809–1943
Booth Family Center for Special Collections, Georgetown University,
    Washington, DC
    T. B. Miskimon Papers
City College of New York Archives and Special Collections
    Annual Registers
    George W. Goethals File
    Merit Rolls
    NYCC Office of the Registrar
Manuscript Division, Library of Congress, Washington, DC
    Tasker Bliss Papers
    George W. Goethals Papers
    William T. Sherman Papers
    William H. Taft Papers
National Archives and Records Administration I, Washington, DC
    Record Group 77, Records of the Office of the Chief of Engineers
    Record Group 94, Records of the Office of the Adjutant General
    Record Group 393, Records of United States Army Continental
        Commands, 1821–1920
    Record Group 395, Records of USA Overseas Operations and
        Commands, 1898–1942
National Archives and Records Administration II, College Park, MD
    Record Group 165, Records of the War Department General and
        Special Staffs
    Record Group 185, Records of the Panama Canal
Office of History, US Army Corps of Engineers, Alexandria, VA
    David D. Gaillard Papers

Seeley G. Mudd Manuscript Library, Princeton University
  Bernard Baruch Papers
US Military Academy Special Collections and Archives, West Point, NY
  George W. Goethals Files
  Official Register of Officers and Cadets of the US Military Academy,
    1877–1889
Virginia Military Institute Archives, Lexington
  Sydney B. Williamson Papers

Contemporary Government Documents and Publications

Abbot, Henry L. "Early Days of the Engineer School of Application." *United States Army Engineer School of Application Occasional Papers*, No. 14. Washington, DC: Army Engineer School of Application, 1904.

Ayres, Leonard P. *The War with Germany: A Statistical Summary.* 2nd ed. Washington, DC: Government Printing Office, 1919.

Carter, William H. *Creation of the American General Staff*, 68th Cong., 1st sess., 1924, S. Doc. 119. Washington, DC: Government Printing Office, 1924.

Isthmian Canal Commission. *Annual Report of the Isthmian Canal Commission for the Fiscal Year Ended June 30, 1907*, 60th Cong., 1st sess., 1907, S. Doc. 55. Washington, DC: Government Printing Office, 1907.

——. *Annual Report of the Isthmian Canal Commission for the Fiscal Year Ended June 30, 1909*, 61st Cong., 2nd sess., 1909, H.R. Doc. 263. Washington, DC: Government Printing Office, 1909.

——. *Annual Report of the Isthmian Canal Commission for the Fiscal Year Ended June 30, 1910*, 61st Cong., 3rd sess., 1910, H.R. Doc. 1030. Washington, DC: Government Printing Office, 1910.

——. *Annual Report of the Isthmian Canal Commission for the Fiscal Year Ended June 30, 1911*, 62nd Cong., 2nd sess., 1911, H.R. Doc. 162. Washington, DC: Government Printing Office, 1911.

——. *Annual Report of the Isthmian Canal Commission for the Fiscal Year Ended June 30, 1912*, 62nd Cong., 3rd sess., 1912, H.R. Doc. 967. Washington, DC: Government Printing Office, 1912.

——. *Annual Report of the Isthmian Canal Commission for the Fiscal Year Ended June 30, 1913*, 63rd Cong., 2nd sess., 1913, H.R. Doc. 426. Washington, DC: Government Printing Office, 1913.

US Army Center for Military History. *The United States Army in the World War, 1917–1919.* 17 vols. Washington, DC: Center for Military History, 1988.

US Army Corps of Engineers. *Annual Report of the Chief of Engineers to the Secretary of War for the Year 1881*, 47th Cong., 1st sess., House Executive Document 1, pt. 2, vol. 2. Washington, DC: Government Printing Office, 1881.

US Congress. House of Representatives, *Address of Col. George W. Goethals, United States Army, at the Graduation Exercises of the Class of Nineteen Twelve, United States Military Academy, West Point, N.Y., Wednesday, June 12, 1912,*

62nd Cong., 2nd sess., 1912, H. Doc. 904. Washington, DC: Government Printing Office, 1912.

——. *Army Reorganization Hearings before the Committee on Military Affairs*, 66th Cong., 1st sess., 1919, vol. 1. Washington: Government Printing Office, 1919.

——. *War Expenditures: Hearings before the Select Committee on Expenditures in the War Department*, 66th Cong., 1st–3rd sess., serial 1. Washington, DC: Government Printing Office, 1921.

US Congress. Senate. *Report of the Commission Appointed by the President to Investigate the Conduct of the War Department in the War with Spain*, 56th Cong., 1st sess., S. Doc. 221. 8 vols. Washington, DC: Government Printing Office, 1900.

US Department of War. *Annual Reports of the War Department*, 46th Cong., 2nd sess., 1880, House Executive Document 2, vol. 2, pt. 1. Washington, DC: Government Printing Office, 1880.

——. *Annual Reports of the War Department*, 56th Cong., 1st sess., 1899, House Executive Document 2. Washington, DC: Government Printing Office, 1899.

——. *Annual Reports of the War Department*, 56th Cong., 2nd sess., 1900, House Executive Document 2. Washington, DC: Government Printing Office, 1900.

——. *Annual Reports of the War Department*, 57th Cong., 1st sess., 1901, House Executive Document 2. Washington, DC: Government Printing Office, 1901.

——. *Annual Reports of the War Department*, 57th Cong., 2nd sess., 1902, House Executive Document 2. Washington, DC: Government Printing Office, 1902.

——. *Annual Reports of the War Department*, 58th Cong., 1st sess., 1903, House Executive Document 2. Washington, DC: Government Printing Office, 1903.

——. *Letter from the Secretary of War, Transmitting the Information Required by a Resolution of the House of Representatives of the 16th January Last, in Relation to an Examination of the Muscle Shoals in Tennessee River, with a View to Removing the Obstructions to the Navigation Thereof and the Construction of a Canal around the Same*, 20th Cong., 1st sess., 1828, H. Doc 284. Washington, DC: Gales & Seaton, 1828.

——. *Letter from the Secretary of War, Transmitting Report of the Surveys on the Tennessee River, Made in Compliance with the Act of March 2, 1867*, 40th Cong., 2nd sess., 1868, House Executive Document 271. Washington, DC: Government Printing Office, 1868.

——. *Report of the Secretary of War*, 48th Cong., 1st sess., 1883, House Executive Document 1. Washington, DC: Government Printing Office, 1883.

——. *Report of the Secretary of War*, 49th Cong., 1st sess., 1885, House Executive Document 1. Washington, DC: Government Printing Office, 1885.

——. *Report of the Secretary of War*, 49th Cong., 2nd sess., 1886, House Executive Document 1. Washington, DC: Government Printing Office, 1886.

——. *Report of the Secretary of War*, 51st Cong., 2nd sess., 1890, House Executive Document 1. Washington, DC: Government Printing Office, 1890.

————. *Report of the Secretary of War*, 52nd Cong., 1st sess., 1891, House Executive Document 1. Washington, DC: Government Printing Office, 1891.

————. *Report of the Secretary of War*, 52nd Cong., 2nd sess., 1892, House Executive Document 1. Washington, DC: Government Printing Office, 1892.

————. *Report of the Secretary of War*, 53rd Cong., 2nd sess., 1893, House Executive Document 1. Washington, DC: Government Printing Office, 1893.

————. *Report of the Secretary of War*, 53rd Cong., 3rd sess., 1894, House Executive Document 1. Washington, DC: Government Printing Office, 1894.

————. *Report of the Secretary of War*, 54th Cong., 1st sess., 1895, House Executive Document 2. Washington, DC: Government Printing Office, 1895.

————. *Report of the Secretary of War*, 54th Cong., 2nd sess., 1896, House Executive Document 2. Washington, DC: Government Printing Office, 1896.

————. *War Department Annual Reports*, 66th Congress, 2nd sess., 1919, H.R. Doc. 426, vol. 1. Washington, DC: Government Printing Office, 1919.

Contemporary Newspapers and Periodicals
American Magazine, 1922
Brooklyn Daily Eagle, 1913
Florence Herald, 1889–1894
Harper's Weekly, 1890–1895
Independent, 1918
Infantry Journal, 1910–1911
Journal of the Military Service Institution of the United States, 1892–1903
Lumber World Review, 1917
Nation, 1928
New York Herald Tribune, 1928
New York Times, 1898–1928
Outlook, 1911–1915
Scientific American, 1912
Scribner's Magazine, 1915

Published Contemporary Journal Articles, Papers, and Memoirs
Allen, Henry T. "The Organization of a Staff Best Adapted to the United States Army." *Journal of the Military Service Institution of the United States* 28, no. 110 (March 1901): 169–183.

————. "Proposed Reorganization for Our Central Staff." *Journal of the Military Service Institution of the United States* 27, no. 106 (July 1900): 26–30.

Baruch, Bernard M. *American Industry in the War: A Report of the War Industries Board*. New York: Prentice-Hall, 1941.

————. *Baruch: The Public Years: My Own Story*. New York: Holt, Rinehart, and Winston, 1960.

Bland, Larry I., and Joellen K. Bland, eds. *George C. Marshall: Interviews and*

Reminiscences for Forrest C. Pogue. Rev. ed. Lexington, VA: George C. Marshall Research Foundation, 1991.

Chester, Capt. James. "Military Misconceptions and Absurdities." *Journal of the Military Service Institution of the United States* 14 (July–December 1893): 502–518.

Evans, Robert K. "National Enlistment." *Infantry Journal* 8 (July/August 1911): 4.

Fiebeger, Gustav J. "George Washington Goethals." In *Fifty-Ninth Annual Report of the Association of Graduates of the United States Military Academy at West Point, New York, June 8, 1928*, 126–135. Saginaw, MI: Seeman & Peters, 1929.

Franck, Harry A. *Zone Policeman 88*. New York: Century, 1913.

Goethals, George W. "The Building of the Panama Canal: Success of Government Methods," *Scribner's Magazine* 57, no. 3 (March 1915): 265

———. "The Building of the Panama Canal: Labor Problems Connected with the Work," *Scribner's Magazine* 57 (April 1915): 398–401.

———. "The Building of the Panama Canal: Organization of the Force," *Scribner's Magazine* 57 (May 1915): 533.

———. "The Building of the Panama Canal: The Human Element in Administration," *Scribner's Magazine* 57 (June 1915): 721.

———. "Electricity in Permanent Seacoast Defenses." *Transactions of the American Institute of Electrical Engineers* 19 (October 1902): 665–683.

———. "Electricity in Permanent Seacoast Defenses." *Journal of the United States Artillery* 19 (1903): 47–65.

———. "Fortifications" *Transactions of the American Society of Engineers* 54 (March 1905): 57–76.

———. *Government of the Canal Zone*. Princeton, NJ: Princeton University Press, 1915.

Gorgas, Marie D., and Burton J. Hendrick. *William Crawford Gorgas: His Life and Work*. Garden City, NY: Doubleday, Page, 1924.

Gorgas, William C. *Sanitation in Panama*. New York: D. Appleton, 1915.

Grant, Ulysses S. *Memoirs and Selected Letters*. Edited by Mary Drake McFeely and William S. McFeely. New York: Library of America, 1990.

Hall, Lt. Col. Collin H. "War and Public Opinion." *Infantry Journal* 7 (July 1910): 823–827.

Harbord, James G. *The American Army in France*. Boston: Little, Brown, 1936.

Johnson, Hugh S. *The Blue Eagle: From Egg to Earth*. New York: Doubleday, 1935.

March, Peyton C. *The Nation at War*. Garden City, NY: Doubleday, Doran, 1932.

Pershing, John J. *My Experiences in the World War*. 2 vols. New York: Frederick A. Stokes, 1931.

——. *My Life before the World War, 1860–1917*. Edited by John T. Greenwood. Lexington: University Press of Kentucky, 2013.

Roosevelt, Theodore. *Theodore Roosevelt: An Autobiography*. New York: Charles Scribner's Sons, 1913.

Shanks, David C. *As They Passed through the Port*. Washington: Carey, 1927.

Stevens, John F. *An Engineer's Recollections*. New York: McGraw-Hill, 1936.

Wilson, Woodrow. *The Papers of Woodrow Wilson*. Edited by Arthur S. Link et al. 69 vols. Princeton, NJ: Princeton University Press, 1966–1993.

Wood, Robert E. *Monument for the World*. Chicago: Encyclopaedia Britannica, 1963.

Secondary Sources

Abrahamson, James L. *America Arms for a New Century: The Making of a Great Military Power*. New York: Free Press, 1981.

Allsep, L. Michael, Jr. "New Forms for Dominance: How a Corporate Lawyer Created the American Military Establishment." PhD diss., University of North Carolina, 2008.

Ambrose, Stephen A. *Duty, Honor, Country: A History of West Point*. Baltimore: Johns Hopkins University Press, 1966.

Ambrosius, Lloyd E. "Democracy, Peace, and World Order." In *Reconsidering Woodrow Wilson: Progressivism, Internationalism, War, and Peace*, ed. John Milton Cooper Jr. Baltimore: Johns Hopkins University Press, 2008.

Bacevich, Andrew J. *American Empire: The Realities and Consequences of US Diplomacy*. Cambridge, MA: Harvard University Press, 2002.

Ball, Harry P. *Of Responsible Command: A History of the US Army War College*. Carlisle Barracks, PA: Alumni Association of the US Army War College, 1983.

Barr, Ronald J. *The Progressive Army: US Army Command and Administration, 1870–1914*. New York: St. Martin's Press, 1998.

Beaver, Daniel R. *Modernizing the American War Department: Change and Continuity in a Turbulent Era, 1885–1920*. Kent, OH: Kent State University Press, 2006.

——. *Newton D. Baker and the American War Effort, 1917–1919*. Lincoln: University of Nebraska Press, 1966.

——. "The Problem of American Military Supply, 1890–1920." In *War Business, and American Society: Historical Perspectives of the Military-Industrial Complex*, edited by Benjamin Franklin Cooling, 73–92. Port Washington, NY: Kennikat Press, 1977.

Bensel, Richard F. *The Political Economy of American Industrialization, 1877–1900*. New York: Cambridge University Press, 2000.

——. *Yankee Leviathan: The Origins of Central State Authority in America, 1859–1877*. New York: Cambridge University Press, 1990.

Betros, Lance. *Carved from Granite: West Point since 1902.* College Station: Texas A&M University Press, 2012.

——, ed. *West Point: Two Centuries and Beyond.* Edited by Lance Betros. Abilene, TX: McWhiney Foundation Press, 2004.

Bingham, T. A. "The Prussian Great General Staff and What It Contains That Is Practical from an American Standpoint." *Journal of the Military Service Institution of the United States* 13, no. 58 (July 1892): 666–676.

Bishop, Joseph Bucklin, and Farnham Bishop. *Goethals: Genius of the Panama Canal.* New York: Harper & Brothers, 1930.

Blight, David W. *Race and Reunion: The Civil War in American Memory.* Cambridge, MA: Belknap Press, 2001.

Brereton, T. R. *Educating the US Army: Arthur L. Wagner and Reform, 1875–1905.* Lincoln: University of Nebraska Press, 2000.

Browning, Robert S., III. *Two If by Sea: The Development of American Coastal Defense Policy.* Westport, CT: Greenwood Press, 1983.

Chambers, John Whiteclay, II. *To Raise an Army: The Draft Comes to Modern America.* New York: Free Press, 1987.

——. *The Tyranny of Change: America in the Progressive Era, 1890–1920.* 2nd ed. New Brunswick, NJ: Rutgers University Press, 2000.

Chandler, Alfred D., Jr. "Theodore Roosevelt and the Panama Canal: A Study in Administration." In *The Letters of Theodore Roosevelt,* ed. Elting E. Morison, John M. Blum, and Alfred D. Chandler Jr., 6:1547–1557. Cambridge, MA: Harvard University Press, 1952.

——. *The Visible Hand: The Managerial Revolution in American Business.* Cambridge, MA: Belknap Press, 1977.

Clark, J. P. "The Many Faces of Reform: Military Progressivism in the US Army, 1866–1916." PhD diss., Duke University, 2009.

——. *Preparing for War: The Emergence of the Modern US Army, 1815–1917.* Cambridge, MA: Harvard University Press, 2017.

Clary, David A. *Fortress America: The Corps of Engineers, Hampton Roads, and United States Coastal Defense.* Charlottesville: University of Virginia Press, 1990.

Coffman, Edward M. *The Hilt of the Sword: The Career of Peyton C. March.* Madison: University of Wisconsin Press, 1966.

——. *The Old Army: A Portrait of the American Army in Peacetime, 1784–1898.* New York: Oxford University Press, 1986.

——. *The Regulars: The American Army, 1898–1941.* Cambridge, MA: Belknap Press of Harvard University Press, 2004.

——. *The War to End All Wars: The American Military Experience in World War I.* Lexington: University Press of Kentucky, 1998.

Connelly, Donald B. *John M. Schofield and the Politics of Generalship.* Chapel Hill: University of North Carolina Press, 2006.

Connelly, Donald B. "The Rocky Road to Reform: John M. Schofield at West Point, 1876–1881." In *West Point: Two Centuries and Beyond*, 175–178. Abilene, TX: McWhiney Foundation Press, 2004.

Cooper, John Milton, Jr. *The Warrior and the Priest: Woodrow Wilson and Theodore Roosevelt*. Cambridge, MA: Belknap Press, 1983.

——. *Woodrow Wilson: A Biography*. New York: Vintage, 2009.

Cosmas, Graham A. *An Army for Empire: The United States Army in the Spanish-American War*. College Station: Texas A&M University Press, 1994.

Crackel, Theodore J. *West Point: A Bicentennial History*. Lawrence: University Press of Kansas, 2002.

Cremin, Lawrence. *The Transformation of the School: Progressivism in American Education, 1876–1951*. New York: Alfred A Knopf, 1961.

Crowther, Samuel. "Don't Fear to Attempt a Thing Just Because It Looks Big." *American Magazine*, January 1922, 16.

Cuff, Robert D. *The War Industries Board: Business-Government Relations during World War*. Baltimore: Johns Hopkins University Press, 1973.

Cumings, Bruce. *Dominion from Sea to Sea: Pacific Ascendancy and American Power*. New Haven, CT: Yale University Press, 2009.

Davidson, Donald. *The Tennessee*. Vol. 1, *The Old River: From Frontier to Secession*. Southern Classics Series ed. Nashville: J. S. Sanders, 1991.

——. *The Tennessee*. Vol. 2, *The New River: Civil War to TVA*. Southern Classics series. Nashville: J. S. Sanders, 1992.

D'Este, Carlo. *Eisenhower: A Soldier's Life*. New York: Holt, 2002.

Doenecke, Justus D. *Nothing Less than War: A New History of America's Entry into World War I*. Lexington: University of Kentucky Press, 2011.

Filene, Peter G. "An Obituary for 'The Progressive Movement.'" *American Quarterly* 22 (Spring 1970): 20–34.

Finnegan, John Patrick. *Against the Specter of a Dragon: The Campaign for American Military Preparedness, 1914–1917*. Westport, CT: Greenwood Press, 1974.

Fischer, James Charles. "Not Fallen, but Flooded: The War Department Supply Bureaus in 1917." PhD diss., Ohio State University, 2003.

Fitzpatrick, David J. *Emory Upton: Misunderstood Reformer*. Norman: University of Oklahoma Press, 2017.

Flanagan, Maureen A. *America Reformed: Progressives and Progressivisms, 1890s–1920s*. New York: Oxford University Press, 2007.

Galambos, Louis. "The Emerging Organizational Synthesis in Modern American History." *Business History Review* 44, no. 3 (Autumn 1970): 279–290.

Ganoe, William A. *The History of the United States Army*. New York: Appleton, 1924.

Gibson, John M. *Physician to the World: The Life of General William C. Gorgas*. Durham, NC: Duke University Press, 1950.

Graham, Patricia Albjerg. *Schooling in America: How the Public Schools Meet the Nation's Changing Needs*. New York: Oxford University Press, 2005.

Grandstaff, Mark R. "Preserving the 'Habits and Usages of War': William Tecumseh Sherman, Professional Reform, and the US Army Officer Corps, 1865-1881, Revisited." *Journal of Military History* 62 (July 1998): 521-545.

Greene, Julie. *The Canal Builders: Making America's Empire at the Panama Canal.* New York: Penguin Books, 2009.

——. "Movable Empire: Labor, Migration, and US Global Power." *Journal of the Gilded Age and Progressive Era* 15, no. 1 (January 2016): 4-20.

——. "Spaniards on the Silver Roll: Liminality and Labor Troubles in the Panama Canal Zone, 1904-1914." *International Labor and Working-Class History* 66 (Fall 2004): 78-98.

Griffin, Walter R. "George W. Goethals and the Panama Canal." PhD diss., University of Cincinnati, 1988.

——. "George W. Goethals, Explorer of the Pacific Northwest, 1882-1884." *Pacific Northwest Quarterly* 62, no. 4 (October 1971): 129-141.

Grotelueschen, Mark Ethan. *The AEF Way of War: The American Army and Combat in World War I.* New York: Cambridge University Press, 2007.

Grubb, W. Norton, and Marvin Lazerson. "Education and the Labor Market: Recycling the Youth Problem." In *Work, Youth, and Schooling: Historical Perspectives on Vocationalism in American Education,* edited by Harvey Kantor and David Tyack, 110-141. Stanford, CA: Stanford University Press, 1982.

Gruber, Ira D. *Books and the British Army in the Age of the American Revolution.* Chapel Hill: University of North Carolina Press, 2010.

Hamilton, Richard F., and Holger H. Herwig. *Decisions for War, 1914-1917.* New York: Cambridge University Press, 2004.

Hart, B. H. Liddell. *Strategy.* 2nd rev. ed. New York: Praeger, 1967.

Hewes, James E., Jr. *From Root to McNamara: Army Organization and Administration, 1900-1963.* Washington, DC: US Army Center of Military History, 1975.

Higginbotham, Don. *George Washington and the American Military Tradition.* Athens: University of Georgia Press, 1985.

Higham, John. *Strangers in the Land: Patterns of American Nativism, 1860-1925.* New Brunswick, NJ: Rutgers University Press, 2002.

Hine, Robert V., and John M. Faragher. *The American West: A New Interpretive History.* New Haven, CT: Yale University Press, 2000.

——. *Frontiers: A Short History of the American West.* New Haven, CT: Yale University Press, 2008.

Hobsbawm, Eric. *The Age of Empire: 1875-1914.* New York: Vintage, 1989.

Hofstadter, Richard. *The Age of Reform: From Bryan to F.D.R.* New York: Vintage, 1955.

Hull, Isabel V. *Absolute Destruction: Military Culture and the Practices of War in Imperial Germany.* Ithaca, NY: Cornell University Press, 2005.

Huntington, Samuel P. *The Soldier and the State: The Theory and Politics of Civil-Military Relations.* Cambridge, MA: Belknap Press of Harvard University Press, 1957.

Johnson, David E. *Fast Tanks and Heavy Bombers: Innovation in the US Army, 1917–1945*. Ithaca, NY: Cornell University Press, 1998.

Johnson, Leland R. *The Davis Island Lock and Dam, 1870–1922*. Pittsburgh: US Army Engineer District, 1985.

———. *Engineers on the Twin Rivers: A History of the US Army Engineers Nashville District, 1769-1978*. Nashville: US Army Engineer District, 1978.

———. *The Ohio River Division, US Army Corps of Engineers: The History of a Central Command*. Cincinnati: US Army Corps of Engineers Ohio River Division, 1992.

Karsten, Peter "Armed Progressives: The Military Reorganizes for the American Century." In *Building the Organizational Society: Essays on Associational Activities in Modern America*, edited by Jerry Israel, 197–232. New York: Free Press, 1972.

———. *The Naval Aristocracy: The Golden Age of Annapolis and the Emergence of American Navalism*. New York: Free Press, 1972.

Kennedy, David M. *Over Here: The First World War and American Society*. 25th anniversary ed. New York: Oxford University Press, 2004.

Kramer, Paul A. *The Blood of Government: Race, Empire, the United States, and the Philippines*. Chapel Hill: University of North Carolina Press, 2006.

LaFeber, Walter. *The New Empire: An Interpretation of American Expansion, 1860–1898*. Ithaca, NY: Cornell University Press, 1963.

———. *The Panama Canal: The Crisis in Historical Perspective*. Rev. ed. New York: Oxford University Press, 1989.

Lee, Wayne E. "Mind and Matter: Cultural Analysis in American Military History: A Look at the State of the Field." *Journal of American History* 93 (2007): 1116–1162.

———, ed. *Warfare and Culture in World History*. New York: New York University Press, 2011.

Licht, Walter. *Working for the Railroad: The Organization of Work in the Nineteenth Century* Princeton, NJ: Princeton University Press, 1983.

Limerick, Patricia Nelson. *The Legacy of Conquest: The Unbroken Past of the American West*. New York: W. W. Norton, 1987.

Linn, Brian McAllister. *The Echo of Battle: The Army's Way of War*. Cambridge, MA: Harvard University Press, 2007.

Ludendorff, Erich von. *Ludendorff's Own Story, August 1914–November 1918: The Great War from the Siege of Liege to the Signing of the Armistice as Viewed from the Grand Headquarters of the German Army*. New York: Harper & Brothers, 1919.

Machoian, Ronald G. *William Harding Carter and the American Army: A Soldier's Story*. Norman: University of Oklahoma Press, 2006.

Major, John. *Prize Possession: The United States and the Panama Canal, 1903–1979*. New York: Cambridge University Press, 1993.

Maurer, Noel, and Carlos Yu. *The Big Ditch: How America Took, Built, Ran, and*

Ultimately Gave Away the Panama Canal. Princeton, NJ: Princeton University Press, 2011.

McCullough, David. *The Path between the Seas: The Creation of the Panama Canal, 1870 - 1914.* New York: Simon & Schuster, 1977.

McGerr, Michael. *A Fierce Discontent: The Rise and Fall of the Progressive Movement in America, 1870-1920.* New York: Oxford University Press, 2003.

McGovern, Rory M. "The School of Experience: George W. Goethals and the US Army, 1876-1907." *Journal of Military History* 81, no. 2 (April 2017): 395-424.

——. "'We Will All Be Wiser in a Few Days': Woodrow Wilson, Grand Strategy, and the US Army in 1917." *Journal for the Liberal Arts and Sciences* 20, no. 2 (Spring 2016): 6-26.

McPherson, James M. *War on the Waters: The Union and Confederate Navies, 1861-1865.* Chapel Hill: University of North Carolina Press, 2012.

Milett, John D. *The Army Service Forces: The Organization and Role of the Army Service Forces.* US Army in World War II series. Washington, DC: US Army Center of Military History, 1985.

Millett, Allan R. *The General: Robert L. Bullard and Officership in the United States Army, 1881-1925.* Westport, CT: Greenwood Press, 1975.

Millis, Walter. *Arms and Men: A Study in American Military History.* New Brunswick, NJ: Rutgers University Press, 1986.

Mills, Bill. *The League: The True Story of Average Americans on the Hunt for WWI Spies.* New York: Skyhorse, 2013.

Morrison, Elting E. *Men, Machines, and Modern Times.* Cambridge: MIT Press, 1966.

Murray, Williamson. *Military Adaptation in War, with Fear of Change.* New York: Cambridge University Press, 2011.

Muth, Jörg. *Command Culture: Officer Education in the US Army and the German Armed Forces, 1901-1940, and the Consequences for World War II.* Denton: University of North Texas Press, 2011.

Neiberg, Michael S. *The Path to War: How the First World War Created Modern America.* New York: Oxford University Press, 2016.

Nelson, Otto L. *National Security and the General Staff.* Washington, DC: Infantry Journal Press, 1946.

Nenninger, Timothy K. *The Leavenworth Schools and the Old Army: Education, Professionalism, and the Officer Corps of the United States Army, 1881-1918.* Westport, CT: Greenwood Press, 1978.

Neumann, Brian. "A Question of Authority: Reassessing the March-Pershing Feud in the First World War." *Journal of Military History* 73, no. 4 (October 2009): 1117-1142.

Nugent, Walter. *Habits of Empire: A History of American Expansion.* New York: Vintage Books, 2009.

O'Connell, Robert L. *Fierce Patriot: The Tangled Lives of William Tecumseh Sherman.* New York: Random House, 2014.

Overy, Richard. *Why the Allies Won*. New York: W. W. Norton, 1995.

Pappas, George S. *Prudens Futuri: The US Army War College, 1901–1967*. Carlisle, PA: Alumni Association of the US Army War College, 1967.

Parker, Matthew. *Panama Fever: The Epic Story of the Building of the Panama Canal*. New York: Anchor Books, 2007.

Perrow, Charles. *Organizing America: Wealth, Power, and the Origins of Corporate Capitalism*. Princeton, NJ: Princeton University Press, 2002.

Person, Gustav J. "The Engineer School of Application at Willets Point." *Engineer* 42 (May–August 2012): 49–52.

Pogue, Forrest C. *George C. Marshall*. Vol. 1, *Education of a General, 1880–1939*. New York: Viking Press, 1963.

Rodgers, Daniel T. *Atlantic Crossings: Social Politics in a Progressive Age*. Cambridge, MA: Belknap Press, 2000.

———. "In Search of Progressivism." *Reviews in American History* 10, no. 4 (December 1982): 113–132.

Romero, Patricia W., ed. *I Too Am America: Documents from 1619 to the Present*. Cornwells Heights, PA: Publisher's Agency, 1978.

Rudolph, Frederick. *The American College and University: A History*. 2nd ed. Athens: University of Georgia Press, 1990.

Rudy, S. W. *The College of the City of New York: A History, 1847–1947*. New York: City College Press, 1949.

Schifferle, Peter J. *America's School for War: Fort Leavenworth, Officer Education, and Victory in World War II*. Lawrence: University Press of Kansas, 2010.

Shellum, Brian G. *Black Cadet in a White Bastion: Charles Young at West Point*. Lincoln, NE: Bison Books, 2006.

Skelton, William B. *An American Profession of Arms: The Army Officer Corps, 1784–1861*. Lawrence: University Press of Kansas, 1992.

———. "West Point and Officer Professionalism, 1817–1877." In *West Point: Two Centuries and Beyond*, edited by Lance Betros, 22–37. Abilene, TX: McWhiney Foundation Press, 2004.

Sklar, Martin J. *The Corporate Reconstruction of American Capitalism, 1890–1916*. New York: Cambridge University Press, 1988.

Skowronek, Stephen. *Building a New American State: The Expansion of National Administrative Capacities, 1877–1920*. New York: Cambridge University Press, 1982.

Smythe, Donald. *Pershing: General of the Armies*. Bloomington: Indiana University Press, 1986.

Spector, Ronald. *Professors of War: The Naval War College and the Development of the Naval Profession*. Newport, RI: Naval War College Press, 1977.

Starr, Paul. *The Social Transformation of American Medicine: The Rise of a Sovereign Profession and the Making of a Vast Industry*. New York: Basic Books, 1982.

Strachan, Hew. *The First World War*. New York: Penguin, 2003.

Tate, Michael L. *The Frontier Army and the Settlement of the West*. Norman: University of Oklahoma Press, 1999.

Thelin, John R. *A History of American Higher Education*. 2nd ed. Baltimore: Johns Hopkins University Press, 2004.

Thompson, J. Lee. *Never Call Retreat: Theodore Roosevelt and the Great War*. New York: Palgrave Macmillan, 2013.

Trask, David F. *The AEF and Coalition Warmaking, 1917-1918*. Lawrence: University Press of Kansas, 1993.

Trask, Donald F. *The War with Spain in 1898*. Lincoln, NE: Bison Books, 1981.

Turner, Frederick Jackson. *The Frontier in American History*. New York: Henry Holt, 1920.

Tyack, David B. *Turning Points in American Educational History*. Waltham, MA: Blaisdell, 1967.

US Army Center for Military History. *History of Military Mobilization in the United States Army, 1775-1945*. Washington, DC: Government Printing Office, 2006.

Utley, Robert M. *Frontier Regulars: The United States Army and the Indian, 1866-1891*. Lincoln, NE: Bison Books, 1973.

Utley, Robert M., and Wilcomb E. Washburn. *Indian Wars*. Boston: Mariner Books, 2002.

Vaulx 8. "The Evolution of a General Staff." *Journal of the Military Service Institution of the United States* 33, no. 125 (September/October 1903): 200-206.

Veysey, Laurence. *The Emergence of the American University*. Chicago: University of Chicago Press, 1982.

Waddell, Steve R. *United States Army Logistics from the American Revolution to 9/11*. Santa Barbara, CA: Praeger, 2010.

Wainwright, John D. "Root versus Bliss: The Shaping of the Army War College." *Parameters* 4 (March 1974): 52-65.

Watson, Samuel J. *Jackson's Sword: The Army Officer Corps on the American Frontier, 1810-1821*. Lawrence: University Press of Kansas, 2012.

———. *Peacekeepers and Conquerors: The Army Officer Corps on the American Frontier, 1821-1846*. Lawrence: University Press of Kansas, 2013.

Weigley, Russell F. *History of the United States Army*. Enlarged ed. Bloomington: Indiana University Press, 1984.

White, Richard. *Railroaded: The Transcontinentals and the Making of Modern America*. New York: Norton, 2011.

Wiebe, Robert H. *The Search for Order, 1877-1920*. New York: Hill and Wang, 1967.

Williams, William Appleman. *The Tragedy of American Diplomacy*. Cleveland: World, 1959.

Williams, William J. *The Wilson Administration and the Shipbuilding Crisis of 1917*. Lewiston, NY: Edwin Mellen Press, 1992.

Woodward, David R. *The American Army and the First World War.* New York: Cambridge University Press, 2014.

Wooster, Robert K. *The American Military Frontiers: The United States Army in the West, 1783–1900.* Albuquerque: University of New Mexico Press, 2009.

———. *Nelson A. Miles and the Twilight of the Frontier Army.* Lincoln: University of Nebraska Press, 1993.

Zimmerman, Phyllis A. *The Neck of the Bottle: George W. Goethals and the Reorganization of the US Army Supply System, 1917–1918.* College Station: Texas A&M University Press, 1992.

Index

Numbers in italics refer to pages with illustrations.